D1011716

FOREIGN DIALECTS

FOREIGN DIALECTS

A Manual for
Actors, Directors, and Writers

by

LEWIS HERMAN

and MARGUERITE SHALETT HERMAN

A Theatre Arts Book

Routledge

New York   London

Published in 1997 by

Routledge
29 West 35th Street
New York, NY 10001

Published in Great Britain in 1997 by

Routledge
11 New Fetter Lane
London EC4P 4EE

Copyright © 1997 by Routledge

Printed in the United States of America

All rights reserved. No part of this book may be reprinted or reproduced or utilized in any form or by any electronic, mechanical, or other means, now known or hereafter invented, including photocopying and recording, or in any information storage or retrieval system without permission in writing from the publishers.

Library of Congress Cataloging-in-Publication Data

Herman, Lewis, 1905–
    [Manual of foreign dialects for radio, stage and screen]
    Foreign dialects : a manual for actors, directors, and writers /
Lewis Herman and Marguerite Shalett Herman.
            p.   cm.
    "A Theatre Arts book."
    Originally published: Manual of foreign dialects for radio, stage and screen.
Chicago : Ziff-Davis Pub., 1943.
    ISBN 0-87830-020-1 (pb)
    1. Acting.   2. English language—Pronunciation by foreign speakers   3. English
language—Dialects.   I. Herman, Marguerite Shalett.   II. Title.
PN2071.F6H4   1996
427—dc20   96–30631
                                                                    CIP

Contents

To

STEPHANIE

Our Daughter

How to Use the Manual

FOR THE ACTOR

It is impossible to learn a dialect simply by reading through the chapter, lifting out a few high lights and using them to put over the dialect. Each element—characterization, lilt, etc.—should be attacked by itself. When it has been learned thoroughly, the next element should be studied. When all of the elements have been learned progressively, the result should be a finished and authentic dialect.

PHONETIC SYMBOLS

Before attempting to learn any of the dialects, it is imperative that the student become completely familiar with the chart of phonetic symbols. Only when all of them have been learned, so that the student is completely conversant with them and can recognize and use them immediately, will he be able to go a step farther and learn a dialect.

When the authors first planned this book, they debated the system of phonetics they would use to present the various vowel and consonant changes as closely as possible. They decided to use a simple phonetic system, rather than the alphabet of the International Phonetic Association now in use in many universities. A rough count of the symbols and diacritical markings used in the I.P.A. system revealed that it would be necessary for a dialects student to learn approximately 176 varied signs. In other words, before a student could begin to learn a dialect, he would have to learn the equivalent of almost seven new alphabets!

The system of the International Phonetic Association is excellent for its particular purpose, which is, mainly, to record faithfully the exact speech habits of the world of languages. However, dialects, as used by the acting profession, require only a knowledge of the broader aspects of these habits. And that is what this book deals with: the principal vowel and consonant changes in most of the foreign-American dialects, together with such other material as could be helpful in limning the foreign character more faithfully. Hair-splitting, regarding the superfine pronunciation of a vowel sound, is not necessary to the teaching of dialects because no two residents of the same country, of the same province, of the same city, or even of the same household would speak all their vowel and consonant sounds exactly alike. In fact, this inconsistency is even observed in the speech of a single person.

With the exception of very few symbols—and those only in individual dialects—all the phonetic representations are symbols with which the average person has been long acquainted. The long "a" of "take," for example, is represented phonetically as "AY" (tAYk); the long "o" of "bone" is represented phonetically as "OH" (bOHn), and so on. Anyone can read the simplified phonetic system used in this book after a few hours of orienting himself to it.

The authors were faced with a corollary dilemma. Throughout each chapter, in giving drill words for exercises, it was necessary to use words as, for example, **"A:" .... as in "ask," "draft," "laugh," etc.** The American pronunciation of the "a" in "ask" varies with the state and even with the city in which each dialect student resides. In Boston, for instance, this "a" would be pronounced "AH," as in "AHsk." In the Middle West, however, the same "a" would be flattened out into the "a" of "candy." Even the example word "candy," given in the previous sentence, has its variations in certain localities, and may not coincide with the treatment given it in some locality other than the Middle West.

Because both authors of this book have lived in the Middle West most of their lives, it is natural that theirs be a Middle Western pronunciation and that the example words they use illustrate the sounds they, themselves, as Middle Westerners, give to them. To them "ask" is "A:sk" and not "AHsk." However, these inconsistencies will be few and the local variants will not hamper the dialects student greatly. He should be able to obtain from this book sufficient material to become proficient in any or all of the major foreign dialects.

CHOOSING THE DIALECT

Once the symbols have been learned, the student may choose the dialect he believes is best suited to his needs and talents. He may, of course, be seeking to learn a specific dialect. Or, if he has no particular preference, he may want to choose a dialect that will fit in with his educational or environmental background.

For example, if the student has studied French at school or has parents or friends who speak French fluently, it is obvious that he should first essay the French dialect. Or if the student has a friend or relative who speaks the German dialect, from whom he can learn many important German-American dialect elements first hand, then he should choose the German dialect. In other words, it is necessary to choose the dialect that lends itself best to study.

It may be that the student has no preference or background for any one particular dialect. In that case, he should follow the news. Radio shows, moving-pictures and stage dramas are often topical and their action takes place in those countries that are headlined in the day's news with characters who will be called upon to speak the dialects of those countries.

It was impossible to treat all the dialects in equal detail. However, the foreign dialects most called for in the acting profession have been thoroughly discussed, while a number of dialects, such as the Czech, Hungarian, and Lithuanian have not been treated as comprehensively as the rest.

Generally speaking, though, the order of importance of foreign dialects, insofar as the number of professional calls for them is concerned, is as follows: British, German, French, Cockney, Irish, Yiddish, Italian, Spanish, Japanese, Scotch, Russian, Swedish, Chinese, Greek and Polish. Although this is an arbitrary listing, it is based on the authors' experience and research.

LILT

In this book, examples of the dialect lilts have been given both in musical form, for those who can read music, and in a simple, stepladder form for those who cannot. Try the musical graphs on a piano or violin and then imitate the notes with your voice. Or read the stepladder form using higher notes when the syllables go up and lower notes when they go down and gliding on the syllables that are followed with rising or falling dots. Do this before going into a detailed study of the vowel and consonant changes.

If there are any unusual symbols in the lilt, look them up in the chapter itself. For example, a lilt is given in the Cockney chapter for the question, "Are you going home?" In the phonetic symbols this reads, "AW yuh gAOWin' 'AOWm?" This unusual symbol is the "AOW" substitute for the American long "o" (OH). Such unusual symbols are not listed in the chart at the front of this book since they apply only to certain individual chapters. But in the chapters in question you will find a detailed explanation of them. Turn to the vowel section in the chapter on the Cockney dialect and look up the vowel sound "OH" as in "bone." A detailed explanation of this "AOW" symbol and sound will be found. If, on the other hand, the Spanish dialect is being studied, it will be noticed that, in the lilt example, the word "have" is written phonetically as "'AHbv." A reference to the consonant "V" under consonant changes should reveal the reason for the spelling of "v" as "bv" and should explain the method of achieving the combination sound. It would be well to remember that the example lilts given are only generalizations of the native lilt of the dialect and should be used as guideposts only. The change in meaning, effected by shifting the emphasis from one word to another, and from one syllable to another, can change the lilt. But, generally speaking, the lilt will fall into the patterns of the examples given.

UNUSUAL DIALECT ELEMENTS

After your first study of the lilt, it is best to go into the treatment of whatever unusual element there may be in the dialect you are studying. In the Russian dialect, for example, it would be necessary first to study the section on "The Added Consonantal 'Y'"; in the French, it is suggested that the "French Nasal" be learned; while, in the Cockney, the subject of the "Cockney Glide" would be consulted.

Here, again, if an unusual vowel or consonant change is encountered, reference should be made immediately to the sections of the chapter which explain their proper use.

VOWEL CHANGES

Now the student will be getting into the meat of the dialect. The detailed explanation should be first studied and absorbed. Then the word examples should be spoken aloud. Next, reference should be made to the section under "Emphasis" for suggestions in placing the proper syllabic emphasis on the words. If an unusual consonant symbol is encountered, reference should be made to the consonant section for identification and the proper pronunciation of the consonant sound. Then the example word should be pronounced with the newly learned consonant sound. This should be done for all the example words listed under all the vowel sounds. The words should be pronounced very slowly at first. Then they should be read at a faster tempo until you are able to read them at their natural speed.

The vowel changes should not be forced. Instead, they should be sounded naturally, as though they are part of the natural pronunciation. An effort should be made to get the pronunciation as close to the American pronunciation as possible. That is to say, the American pronunciation should not be achieved but should simply be approximated. The effect should be as though the new dialect were being fashioned around the form of normal American speech.

This is especially important when learning the Japanese and Chinese dialects. The aspirate "uh" used in these dialects can clothe the interpretation with credibility or swathe it beyond recognition. The same principle applies to the radical vowel and consonant changes. In acquiring this aspirate "uh," by the way, it is suggested that the concluding consonant sound be pronounced heavily. Thus, in the American word "take" (tAYk), spelled phonetically in the Japanese dialect as "tEHkuh," a very heavily pronounced "k" sound will produce this aspirate "uh" quite naturally. The same method can be used in prononouncing the aspirate "uh" that follows Italian dialect consonants.

Use the "Word Exercise" list following the "vowel" sections to test your knowledge of the vowel changes.

CONSONANT CHANGES

This step should prove much easier than the preceding ones. The vowel changes have already been learned and a great many of the consonant changes have been referred to and learned. Throughout this consonant change section—and the vowel changes section, as well—it will be observed that variations of changes are given. The Irish "s," for example, may be pronounced either as "s" or as "sh." In some cases, the reasons for these variances have been given and the dialect characterization should follow the suggestions. In other cases preferred variations are noted. These, too, should be followed unless a specific characterization is desired.

The change of the Italian medial "t" to either "d" or "r," for example, depends on what interpretation is intended for the dialect character.

Again, when practicing on the example words, care should be taken to pronounce them very slowly at first and build up the tempo until the exact speed is acquired. At the same time, reference should be made to the section under "Emphasis" for the proper treatment of the syllabic emphasis.

Use the "Word Exercise" list following the "Consonant" sections to test your knowledge of the consonant changes.

GRAMMAR CHANGES

Although this section is not as vital to the actor as it is to the writer, the former should study it for a more complete understanding of the dialect. Many scripts are written in straight dialog so that the actor finds it difficult to superimpose his dialect changes on American grammatical forms. He can learn from this section what grammatical changes are most characteristic of the dialect and, when necessary, can make the adjustments in his script lines.

In addition, this section can be used by the actor as a source of practice material. All the example sentences are written out phonetically, as is the concluding monolog. Reference should be made to the "Lilt" and "Emphasis" sections. At this time, special notice should be paid in the "Emphasis" section to the material dealing with word emphasis in the sentence. Then, using the suggestions given, the example sentences should be read aloud—slowly, first, and then with increasing tempo until the natural speed has been approximated. At the same time, the suggestions given under "Lilt" should be applied until the correct lilt and emphasis have been achieved.

At this time, the common foreign expressions and interjections may be learned. Here, again, it is really within the province of the writer to insert them into the script. But, when they have not been used, the actor may put them in with the director's approval—but only sparingly.

Use the "Sentence Exercise" list following the "Grammar" sections to test your knowledge of the grammar changes, foreign expressions and interjections.

"WEAK" AND "STRONG" FORMS

The majority of foreigners rarely use American contractions if the language is still fairly new to them. Many of them retain "is not" and "have not" rather than "isn't" and "haven't" even after they are proficient in the American language. The American tourist on the Continent makes the same errors as the Continental tourist or immigrant makes in America. He tries to be exact in his pronunciation of the adopted language, while the natives of the country are usually indifferent to the formal rules of grammar. Few Americans would ever say, "I do not care." But they would say, "I don't care."

This desire to speak correctly causes the foreigner to err in selecting the strong or weak forms of an American word. The American language is not a phonetic language. It is not pronounced exactly as it is spelled. For example the words "to" and "from" are both spelled with an "o" yet in each word the "o" receives a different sound. The strong form of the word "to" is "tOO," and it is the strong form the foreigner invariably uses. In the sentence, "go to the store" the American would use the weak form of "to" and say,

"gOH tuh THuh stAWr"

It will be noticed that the American also used the weak form of "the" rather than the strong form which is "THEE."

This slurring of vowel sounds is difficult for many foreigners to acquire. One reason may be that they are concentrating all their efforts on learning the new and often strange sounds of the American language. It may seem sacrilegious to them to dispense with the new sound once it has been learned. When they begin to mingle with the American people and make friends, then they will begin to use the weak forms occasionally if their friends point their mistakes out to them. For the most part foreigners are completely unconscious that they speak in a dialect. They speak and are understood; they listen and understand. That is their goal and it is achieved.

Because the use of the strong or weak forms depends entirely on the individual dialect-speaking person, they are only rarely designated in this manual. This is a matter between actor and director. If the foreigner has recently arrived, he will most probably use the strong forms. Young people will include some weak forms, since youngsters are more adaptable than their elders. If the person has been in this country any length of time, he will use a number of weak forms. But of course, this depends on his temperament, his love for his own country, his ability to make friends, his economic standing and so forth.

Ordinarily, in this manual, the suggested substitutions for vowel changes are carried throughout the chapter. But, occasionally, when the strong form was not advisable, the weak form was used. So the student should not be confused when confronted with these puzzling, seemingly erroneous, variations.

POLISHING UP

When the complete dialect has been studied, the student should begin to practice what he has learned by reading first from a child's primer. Wherever possible, the necessary grammatical changes should be made. Occasionally language carry-overs and interjections should be inserted. The suggestions on syllabic emphasis and word emphasis should be followed. The proper lilt should be sung. And, after each sentence, reference should be made to the Manual to check on incorrect deviations. The sentence should then be read over again with the proper corrections made.

Only after a perfect dialect has been achieved, by this method, should the next and final step be attempted. At this time the student should discard the primer and try to use the dialect ad lib—that is, extemporaneously, without benefit of script.

Again, after each sentence, reference should be made to the Manual to check the dialect. When the errors have been noted, the sentence should be repeated, again ad lib, with the correction made. Then another sentence should be tried.

This is the supreme test of a dialect. If it can be spoken by the student as correctly as though he were using his own American language, he can then be said to be the complete master of the dialect—he can then feel certain that he has all its elements in complete control and ready for use.

MOUTH AND TONGUE EXERCISES

Speaking in a dialect is not only a matter of vowel and consonant changes. To be believable, these changes must be made with ease and confidence. The sounds peculiar to the dialect should not be exaggerated. They must be spoken with the same facility the actor uses in his American speech. They must sound as though they are habitual to the actor.

If an actor, or student, has studied one or more foreign languages, he will find that many changes will be fairly simple. This will often be true even if the dialect he is learning is not based on a language he knows. But, whether the actor has a background in languages or not, certain exercises for limbering the mouth and tongue should prove helpful in acquiring the dialect changes.

Throughout the exercises,

> A.   breathe with your diaphragm, not your chest and
> B.   keep your body relaxed.

These exercises may be practiced either sitting in a chair or standing.

THROAT RELAXATION

1.   Lower your head forward, slowly. Roll it slowly in a circle so that your right cheek almost touches your right shoulder; then let it fall backward of its own weight and continue moving it slowly toward your left shoulder. Again, let it fall forward of its own weight and continue this slow circling process five times to the right and five times to the left.

JAW RELAXATION

2.   Let your jaw drop. Move it back and forth and up and down with your hand. Try to keep your jaw relaxed so that your hand can actually direct it.

3.   Say the word "blah" fifteen times, keeping the jaw and throat muscles relaxed.

THROAT AND JAW RELAXATION

4. If you have not felt the desire to yawn up to this point, do so now. A great, big yawn. Try to yawn again. Don't stifle it. Let it be a wide yawn. Throughout these exercises, yawn as often as possible.

RESONANCE

5.   Place the lips together lightly and hum. Try the hum on one note first. Be sure there is a tingling sensation in the lips. The lips must be relaxed. When the tingling sensation has been achieved, hum a tune. It is preferable to choose a tune with a fairly wide range of notes. This exercise will also be helpful if it is used just before an audition or performance. It gives resonance to the voice and clears the head and throat.

MOUTH FLEXIBILITY

6.   Say "mmmmm-EEEEEE-AH:-OH:-OO" (meow). Hum on the "m," draw the lips back sharply for the "EE" sound, open the mouth and throat wide for the sustained "AH." Blend the "AH," "OH," and "OO" together for a final pursing of the lips.

THROAT FLEXIBILITY

7.   Open your mouth. Place one hand at your throat. Draw your tongue back toward your throat so that you feel your Adams-apple move down and then up.

TONGUE FLEXIBILITY

8.   Say a series of "la's" as rapidly as possible: lalalalalalalalalalalalalalalala. Sing a song, using "la" in place of the words.

9.   Trill the tip of your tongue while expelling a full breath of air. If you have difficulty with the trill (which is used in many dialects for the sound of "r"), point the tip of your tongue toward the hard palate just behind the upper front teeth. The tongue should not touch the hard palate but it should be very close. Exhale a full breath of air. As you exhale, bring the tongue up sharply so that it is vibrated by the exhalation. The position of the tongue must not be farther back than the gum just behind the upper front teeth.

UVULA FLEXIBILITY

10.   Hold a few drops of water at the back of your mouth and gargle them. Then, try to produce a gargling sound without the water. Practice saying the following syllables using the gargled "r" sound:

rrrrrrrrrrrrrrOHrrrrrrrrrrrrrr

rrrrrrrrrrrrrrAHrrrrrrrrrrrrrr

rrrrrrrrrrrrrrEErrrrrrrrrrrrrr

rrrrrrrrrrrrrrEHrrrrrrrrrrrrrr

LIP FLEXIBILITY

11.   Bring your lips lightly together and exhale a full breath of air through them, so that the lips vibrate visibly.

GLOTTAL STOP

12.   Whisper the sentence "I am at Ann's apartment." A loud, forcible whisper should be used, and each word should be spaced. It will be noticed that there is a slight catch in the throat before each initial vowel. This "catch" is similar to the glottal stop used in Scotch, Cockney and German.

ASPIRATE "UH"

13.   Pronounce the following words slowly. Draw out the vowels and sound the final consonant hard and sharp.

take   (tAY:k)   late   (lAY:t)   reap   (rEE:p)

It will be noticed that without undo force, the final consonant has an aspirate "uh" following. This very slight breath of air is used in many of the dialects and it must be as short and unobtrusive as it is in the above American words.

When you are practicing the above exercises, as well as the dialect changes given throughout the Manual, it is wise to go slowly at first. Be sure of every change before you attempt to use it in a word.

The actor must be master of a dialect. He must be so sure of every change that there will be no need to pause and think back. He must be in complete control, not only of his dialect, but of his mouth and tongue. There must be no fear that in trying to produce a dialect sound, he will be tripped up by his familiar American pronunciation of that sound. A dialect can be an invaluable and loyal servant to the actor who is completely and confidently its master.

FOR THE PRODUCER

Usually, it is to the producer or director that the actor turns for suggestions and aid in his dialect interpretation. It is the producer who determines the degree of dialect that is to be used, that is, the amount of dialect which will make for a happy combination of character presentation and understandability.

That is why it is essential that he possess, together with his knowledge of pacing, timing, interpretation and sundry other technical details, a complete knowledge of dialects. It is not necessary that he be able to use the dialects himself, although it is preferable. But if he knows the various elements that contribute to the dialects, he has fortified himself so that his actors' dialect interpretations will not spoil the effect of what is an otherwise perfect show.

The actor needs to know only one of the several varieties of vowel or consonant changes in order to be able to give a credible dialect performance. But the director must know about all of these changes so that he can suggest the correct variance if the form the actor is using does not jibe with the requirements of the character being portrayed.

The director should also make himself conversant with the grammatical changes. The job of cutting, of adding, of reversing lines is directly incumbent on him. And if the lines, as written by the author, do not aid the actor in delineating the role of the character in the script, the producer should be able to adjust them according to his knowledge of the dialect's grammatical changes.

FOR THE WRITER

The writer can assure himself of a proper reading of his dialect lines if he is able to write in the dialect changes himself. It is not enough to depend on the ability of the actor to make these changes. It is best if the actor can devote all his time to determining and working out the proper dramatic interpretation without having to waste precious minutes rewriting dialect lines that have been written in straightforward American speech.

The writer should first go through the vowel and consonant changes and note particularly the elisions that have been suggested. In the Cockney, for example, the proper use of the elided "h" should make for a better dialect interpretation of the Cockney dialect. Dropped consonants, especially the "g" in words with an "ing" ending and words that end with two consonants, should be noted in the script. Occasional consonant changes can also be suggested, as in the Russian where the "v" is changed to a sound approximating a combination of "v" and "w."

Then, again, the writer can make excellent use of the various sections on "Contractions," "Original Language Carry-overs," and "Typical Interjections." A number of these judiciously sprinkled through a script can do wonders toward making an authentic dialect presentation.

But of greatest use to the writer are the sections on "Grammatical Changes." Here will be found listed many of the errors in grammar made by the foreigner. The lilt of dialect speech, in many cases, results from these grammatical changes. In the Irish dialect, for example, it would be possible to suggest the Irish character simply by using the Irish syntax peculiarities, while it would be very difficult to write dialog for an Irish character without using these Irish methods of word-placement. The Russian habit of dropping articles, the Japanese insistence on using the adverb instead of the adjective, the German phrase inversion—all of these are necessary to the authentic foreigner's dialog.

A reference to the many monologs concluding the major dialects should give the writer an opportunity to see these grammatical changes in action. All have been written so that most of the grammatical changes are exemplified. A thorough study of these monologs, together with a study of the vowel and consonant changes and the grammatical changes, should equip the writer with sufficient knowledge to be able to write such convincing and authentic foreign dialog that even the most inept dialect actor could present a true-to-life dialect characterization equal in quality to the worth of the script.

PHONETIC SYMBOLS USED IN THIS BOOK

These symbols represent only the *sounds* of the vowels and consonants used in American speech (they do not represent spelling). Symbols for sounds peculiar to each of the foreign dialects will be found in the chapter devoted to that particular dialect. Corresponding I.P.A. (International Phonetic Association) symbols have been listed in this chart for the benefit of those who are acquainted with them. For clarity, symbols are shown in **BOLD-FACE** type in this chart. However, in the actual text of the book, this heavier type is used only to denote emphasis. *Italic* letters will be used throughout the text to indicate the changes made from the American word to the dialect word.

VOWEL	WORD	SYMBOL	I.P.A.	VOWEL	WORD	SYMBOL	I.P.A.
"a"	"take"	"**AY**"	[ei]	"o"	"on"	"**O**"	[ɒ]
"a"	"alone"	"**UH**"	[ə]	"o"	"bone"	"**OH**"	[ou]
"a"	"palm"	"**AH**"	[ɒ]	"o"	"off"	"**AW**"	[ɔ]
"a"	"ask"	"**A:**"	[a:]	"oo"	"food"	"**OO**"	[u]
"a"	"bad"	"**A**"	[a]	"oo"	"good"	"**oo**"	[U]
"a"	"ball"	"**AW**"	[ɔ]	"u"	"unit"	"**yOO**"	[ju]
"e"	"he"	"**EE**"	[i]	"u"	"up"	"**U**"	[ʌ]
"e"	"get"	"**EH**"	[ɛ]	"u"	"curb"	"**ER**"	[ə:r]
"i"	"ice"	"**I**"	[ɒi]	"ou"	"out"	"**OW**"	[ɒu]
"i"	"sit"	"**i**"	[I]	"oi"	"oil"	"**OI**"	[ɔi]

CONSONANT SYMBOLS

CONSONANT	WORD	SYMBOL	I.P.A	CONSONANT	WORD	SYMBOL	I.P.A
"c"	"cat"	"**k**"	[k]	"ch"	"loch"	"**kh**"	[X]
"g"	"go"	"**g**"	[g]	"ch"	"church"	"**tch**"	[tʔ]
"g"	"George"	"**j**"	[dʒ]	"sh"	"she"	"**sh**"	[ʔ]
"q"	"quick"	"**kw**"	[kw]	"th"	"the"	"**TH**"	[ð]
"x"	"tax"	"**ks**"	[ks]	"th"	"thin"	"**th**"	[θ]
	"exert"	"**gz**"	[gz]	"z"	"azure"	"**zh**"	[ʒ]
	"luxury"	"**ksh**"	[kʔ]				
	"xenon"	"**z**"	[z]				

VOWEL SYMBOLS

The other consonant sounds are the same as those in the American language.

(')	dropped letter or syllable
(/)	glottal stop
(:)	vowel elongation
(-)	a hyphen used between letters does not indicate a pause but is inserted only for the sake of phonetic clarity.

CHAPTER ONE

Dialect Characterization

And the Gileadites took the fords of the Jordan against the Ephraimites. And it was so, that, when any of the fugitives of Ephraim said, Let me go over, the men of Gilead said unto him, Art thou an Ephraimite? If he said, Nay; then said they unto him, Say now Shibboleth; and he said Sibboleth; for he could not frame to pronounce it right: then they laid hold on him, and slew him at the fords of the Jordan. And there fell at that time of Ephraim forty and two thousand.

—Judges XII

Had the Ephraimites studied the dialect of the Gileadites they might have saved their lives. So far as is known, no such drastic punishment has ever been applied to actors whose dialects lack authenticity. But it would be well for them to bear in mind the biblical precept.

Few actors can simulate an acceptable and convincing dialect. Since they have had no authentic source book to turn to, many have attempted to imitate the imitators. The resulting dialect is usually completely out of focus. There are certain "musts" in every dialect. For example, the foreigner may, in time, acquire much of the lilt of his adopted country but it is very unlikely that he will ever assume the lilt of another foreigner or foreign group. This was well illustrated in a certain radio program from Hollywood. A Russian actor had been given the part of a German officer. Though he tried sincerely to mask his genuine dialect in favor of a superimposed German dialect, it was obviously too great a step. The result was ludicrous.

To be effective, the dialect must be spoken as though it is authentically foreign. There must be no slip-backs into the natural speech or speech pattern. The dialect must be subtle, compelling and convincing.

The art of the dialect is a difficult one. Though some with a rare talent for mimicry are aided by a natural aptitude, it usually requires long and sincere service. It demands hard work and keen curiosity. It calls for constant practice. The singer, the violinist, the pianist—all who perform—must practice assiduously to keep in creative fettle. A dialect, like any other skill, must be kept in constant use if it is to continue to be valuable.

The technique of dialects is, in many respects, similar to the technique of painting. Before the student can master the art of using only essential brush strokes, he must learn all the details regarding the structure of the article beneath the mere surface he is to paint. After all, an artist paints what is only the skin of a subject. But, before he can do that correctly, he must know the intimate anatomy of the body beneath the skin. With this knowledge tucked away in his mind, he can forget what he knows about body structure and, with a few deft strokes, suggest the effect of the structure on the surface he is painting. The same applies to dialects. It is necessary to know *all* the vowel and consonant changes so that, when it becomes necessary to drop those that may tend to clutter up the dialect, the actor can do so with the sure knowledge that what he is dropping can be dropped and what he is using is essential.

The study of dialects should be approached with the same respect as the study of a foreign language. There should be no attempt to skim through a chapter with the expectation of absorbing the dialect by osmosis or by some magical formula. Care should be taken to learn all the elements correctly. A great help is to speak in the dialect as often as possible. Practice on friends or relatives who may be more understanding and cooperative than others. A simple, child's primer should be read and re-read, in dialect, until it runs smoothly. One of the best tests of a dialect is: Is it believable in spontaneous conversation? If the actor can ad lib authentically, he may be sure that his dialect is credible.

Some script writers are unable to write a dialect which sounds authentic. They may not invert their phrases properly. Their sentences may not sing in the rhythm of the native language. The actor must watch the script for such obvious faults and make the required revisions. The studies of the real foreign dialects in this book will aid the actor in making these necessary changes.

Once he has mastered the rules and suggestions given in this book, the serious dialect student should go further. He should observe and study the people who speak the dialect he is trying to learn. From them he should acquire vocal pitch, rhythm, lilt and emphasis. These points can be treated only superficially in this book. They must be heard from the lips of speakers of the genuine dialect to be learned correctly.

The most accessible source of genuine dialects is the radio. Every large city has a radio station that broadcasts foreign language programs. Often the announcers of these particular programs speak with a dialect. In addition, the foreign language is used from which one can learn, to a certain extent, the rhythm, lilt, pitch, accent, and emphasis. Apart from the foreign language programs, radio provides other collateral aids to the student.

From time to time, personal interviews are made via radio, often with foreign officials. Unfortunately, these officials tend to have little or no dialect, and what they have is often colored with a British dialect. But, certain peculiarities of the dialect will still be evident. Foreigners, other than diplomats, will be found to be more instructive.

Foreign language films can serve the same purpose as foreign language radio programs. What is gathered from these primary sources will complement what has been learned in this book.

The lilts of the major dialects have been given in many of the following chapters. For those who are unable to read music, a visual device of step laddering the rise and fall of the individual syllables has been used. The student can determine from these illustrations, the rise and fall of the syllables, the gradual rising and falling vowel or consonant glides and the abrupt, glideless risings and fallings.

But for the student who can read music, there has been included, in addition to the step-ladder device, a regular musical staff on which the notes of the lilt have been transcribed by an eminent musician—Professor Robert Dolejší.

In these tonal settings—which are only approximations of the human voice in the various speech dialects—one of the most striking revelations is the extraordinary scope or range that is evident in even a brief phrase of two or three syllables. It will be observed that the examples emphasize also the rhythmic meter of each phonetic illustration. This will enable the student to determine, not only the voice pitch and range, but also the actual rhythm of each example, which is of paramount importance.

Each notation has been purposely retained in one clef—although some unusually extended intervals occur which ordinarily would demand the use of two clefs—in order to give a more impressive visual portrait of tonal skips and glides. The fact must be explained, though, that there are, at times, certain inflections in the speaking voice that fall into a tonal category that defies actual notation. They are an almost imperceptible degree above or below the note indicated but do not demand the next full semi-tone above or below to serve as an illustration. It is, in fact, this characteristic of tonal variation that distinguishes speech from actual song. In addition, there will be present a degree of variance in different individuals. But the tonal illustrations, as given in the following chapters, under the "Lilt" sections, are as near to actual tones spoken in the various phrases as the notation of musical science permits.

The art of the dialect is the twin art of being consistent with the fundamental and radical changes and of being consistently inconsistent with the less-important changes. For instance, a Parisian would consistently use the guttural "r." But he might use "d" for "TH" one time, as in "dEE" (the), and be apt to say "THEE" (the) the next time. This must naturally depend on several factors: How long he has been in America, his general aptitude and his educational background.

If the dialect is to be very light, the radical changes may also become inconsistent. But if this point is reached, the character will be speaking an almost perfect American speech.

In a light dialect, the lilt need not be pronounced but it must be suggested. And when the character is under emotional stress, the lilt must be accentuated.

Being inconsistent, or lightening the dialect, does not mean that American may be spoken every sentence or so. No matter how light the dialect, no matter how inconsistent the pronunciation, the flavor of the dialect must be retained. The word attack, the emphasis, the manner of shortening or elongating vowels, the manner of pronouncing consonants—all these must be used consistently.

A favorite trick of radio actors who are called upon to double and sometimes to shift from one dialect into another, may be useful to the dialect student as an aid in falling into the dialect he intends to use. Because a dialect is, after all, a sort of second language that has been superimposed on the natural American language of the actor, a psychological block often prevents him from getting started with the dialect. The trick he uses is to memorize a phrase or sentence in the dialect—one that he can do perfectly. Then, when he finds it necessary to fall into the dialect, he simply repeats the memorized line over to himself, thus priming his dialect into action. For example, a phrase for the German dialect might be: "dis is dUH grAY:dt OH:sh'n" (this is the great ocean); or, in Swedish such a phrase might be: "ØH: mI: gʊ'nAs" (Oh! my goodness), the exact words depending upon the individual preference of the actor.

One fact must be remembered at all times: It is the actor's job to *communicate*. If his speech is incomprehensible to his audience, his artistry is wasted. Clarity and distinctness must characterize the speech in dialect as well as in a straight part—even more so because dialect speech is foreign to the ears of an audience. This demands that the actor know *all* the elements of the dialect changes so that he will be able to discard those that make for a thick, soupy dialect and highlight those that contribute to a subtle dialect characterization.

A satisfactory, authentic dialect cannot be learned overnight, just as a foreign language cannot be learned in such a short period. A dialect *is* another language. That must be kept in mind continually. It is studied practice that results in the studied naturalness for which the actor continually strives. In the same way, his foreign dialect must have this attribute of naturalness, of easy familiarity. It is only by practicing hard and long that an actor can present a dialect that is, at once, authentic, colorful, natural, understandable—a perfect speech projection of the foreign character he is portraying.

CHAPTER TWO

The Cockney Dialect

THE COCKNEY LILT

Since most of the Cockney vowels are elongated into diphthongs and triph-thongs, the resulting rhythm tends to be choppy. This effect is heightened also by both the glottal stops, with which the dialect abounds, and by the weak attack on those consonants that are sounded. The slow tempo of the Cock-ney dialect has a leavening effect on the erratic rhythm.

Generally speaking, Cockney is delivered in a high-pitched voice. The vowel elongation brings with it a nasal whine that is further typical. These two traits are the result of the Cockney's habit of speaking with his mouth constantly half-open (he is adenoidal, remember) and with a slack movement of his jaws.

There is a great deal of inflection in the Cockney dialect, especially with cer-tain vowels. The long "o" for example becomes "AOW" (this is discussed fully in the section on "Vowel Changes") and often this triphthong takes several notes.

One of the most widely used patterns in question sentences is:

(Are you going home?)

The first word "AW" (are) would be spoken higher than in American. The next two words, "yuh" (you) and "gAOWin'" (going) would then be given declining notes. The lowest note would be reached with "A," the first letter of the triphthong "AOW." The last part of the triphthong would be infected upward on a glide until the highest note is reached with "m."

In a simple declarative sentence, the tonal pattern would be as follows:

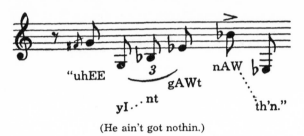

"uhEE   **3**   gAWt   nAW
         yI·· nt   th'n."

(He ain't got nothin.)

EMPHASIS

Stress, in Cockney, is laid mostly on the drawn-out, diphthongized vowels, of which there are many. In the sentence, "tI:k THuh bliOOmi nAW sAOWm." (take the blooming horse home), the emphasis is placed on the boldface syllables. The "I" in "tI:k" is pronounced "**AH-EE**" and is further discussed in "Vowel Changes." Sentence emphasis is similar to American, but vowels within words should be emphasized according to their length; that is, triphthongs first, diphthongs next, and monothongs last.

VOWEL CHANGES

"AY" .... as in "take," "break," "they," etc.

The Cockney changes this long "a" (AY) to long "i" (I:). The sound of this "I:" is "**AH-EE**" with the stress on the initial "AH" sound. The word "take" would be pronounced "tAH-EEk" but for the sake of simplicity the symbol "I:" will be used, as in "tI:k." The colon (:) after "I" signifies elongation.

DRILL WORDS

brI:k	(break)	vI:kI:t	(vacate)	bI:k	(bake)
THI:	(they)	EHdookI:t	(educate)	tI:sti	(tasty)
lI:k	(lake)	strI:t	(straight)	mI:bi	(maybe)

"UH" .... as in "alone," "sofa," "final," etc.

This "UH" sound of "a" in American is written "ER" in Cockney and is pronounced like the "ur" of "curb" with the "r" silent. In a great many books and plays, a Cockney character is written as saying "erlong" or "erbout" although the "r" is used only for flavoring and should not be sounded.

DRILL WORDS

ERlAOWn	(alone)	ERbAWd	(aboard)
sAOWfER	(sofa)	ERbAHv	(above)
ERbOI:d	(abide)	ERbrAHpt	(abrupt)

mERlishUHs	(malicious)
ERbiliti	(ability)
ERbrI:siv	(abrasive)

"AH" . . . . as in "father," "arm," "park," etc.

The sound of "AW:" is always given to this "AH," as in the word "fAWTHER" (father). The Cockney "AW:" is deeper and richer than the American sound which comes from the middle of the mouth. The Cockney "AW" comes from far back (or down) in the throat and the lips are pursed instead of being slightly opened and rounded. This is an important variance and should be practiced for perfection.

DRILL WORDS

kAW:v	(carve)	dAW:lin'	(darling)
AW:m	(arm)	tAW:t	(tart)
pAW:k	(park)	rigAW:dz	(regards)

'AW:mlUHs	(harmless)
AW:mi	(army)
bAW:kER	(barker)

"A:" . . . . as in "ask," "draft," "laugh," etc.

In general, the Cockney pronounces this "A:" as "AW," as in "AW:sk" (ask). But because of the infiltration of the British dialect into Cockney, this "A:" is also given an "AH" sound, as in "AHsk" (ask). The latter form is suggested. The former may be used when a varying character delineation is necessary.

DRILL WORDS

drAHft	(draft)	bAHskUHt	(basket)
lAHf	(laugh)	mAHstER	(master)
stAHf	(staff)	tAHsk	(task)

fAHst	(fast)
pAHsTCHER	(pasture)
klAHs	(class)

The beginner in dialect study may be somewhat confused by the difference in pronunciation of words like "ask" (AHsk) and "bad" (bEHd). There is no hard and fast rule which can be given for this puzzling variance. Aside from individual preference, there is also a sectional preference. It will be remembered in *Pygmalion* that Shaw brought this point up quite sharply. Certain sections adhere to certain pronunciations. The following general rules are given to help clear up most of the doubt.

> 1. *IN COCKNEY, WHEN SHORT "a" IS FOLLOWED BY "f," "ft," "nch," "nce," "nt," "sk," "sp," "ss," "st," AND "th" IT SHOULD BE PRONOUNCED AS "AH."*

However, when "th" is followed by a vowel, the preceding short "a" usually becomes "EH," as in: "pEHthAWlUHji" (pathology). But, when "th" is final, or followed by a consonant, the short "a" follows the rule and becomes "AH," as in "pAHth" (path), "pAHthwI:" (pathway).

A few other examples of Rule 1 are: "dAHns" (dance), "fAHst" (fast), "brAHntch" (branch), and "grAHsp" (grasp).

2. ALL THREE-LETTER WORDS USING SHORT "a" SUBSTITUTE "EH."

The exceptions to this rule are the words: "AHft" (aft), "AHsk" (ask), "AHsp" (asp), and "AHs" (ass).

3. MOST WORDS USING SHORT "a" BEFORE A SINGLE FINAL CONSONANT, OR A SINGLE CONSONANT SOUND FOLLOWED BY A VOWEL, SUBSTITUTE "EH."

Examples of this rule are found in the words: "kEHb" (cab), "pEHkuht" (packet), "mEHth'mEHtiks" (mathematics), and "'EHm" (ham).

4. IN GENERAL, WORDS IN WHICH SHORT "a" IS FOLLOWED BY THREE DIFFERENT CONSONANT SOUNDS SUBSTITUTE "EH."

This rule is illustrated in words like "pEHntri" (pantry), "bEHnkrAHpt" (bankrupt), and "frEHnkli" (frankly).

"A" .... as in "bad," "am," "narrow," etc.

Certain words which take short "a" in American are given an "EH" sound in Cockney. General rules for these have been given above.

DRILL WORDS

bEHd	(bad)	lEHtUHs	(lattice)
EHm	(am)	dEHndi	(dandy)
nEHrER	(narrow)	mEHnER	(manner)
	fEHsinI:t	(fascinate)	
	grEHjiOOI:t	(graduate)	
	fEHshUHn	(fashion)	

"AW" .... as in "ball," "falter," "enthrall," etc.

When the vowel sound "AW" is followed by an "l" the Cockney usually adds a slight "OO" (as in "food"), making "ball" as "bAW-OOl." The main emphasis should be on the initial "AW" sound while the "OO" is thrown off. See under "L" in "Consonant Changes" for additional material.

DRILL WORDS

fAW-OOltER	(falter)	stAW-OOl	(stall)
EHnthrAW-OOl	(enthrall)	'AW-OOl	(hall)
kAW-OOl	(call)	AW-OOl	(all)
	skwAW-OOl	(squall)	
	pAW-OOltri	(paltry)	
	ERpAW-OOl	(appal)	

"AW" .... as in "caught," "thought," "taught," etc.

Three alternatives confront the student in pronouncing this "AW" sound. In most cases, the Cockney retains this "AW" as in "kAWt" (caught). Sometimes, however, a voiced "r" is added making its pronunciation "kAWrt" (caught). Then again, there are a great many Cockneys who give it the "AW-OO" of "bAW-OOl" (ball), making the word "kAW-OOt" (caught). Of the three, the best is the simple "AW." The other two, particularly the "AWr" sound, can be used for changing a characterization. But it should be remembered that this "AW" differs from the American "AW" in that it is richer and darker. (See "AH" as in "father.")

"EE" .... as in "he," "treat," "people," etc.

In Cockney, the long "e" sound (EE) is changed to "uhEE." The aspirate "uh" is only slightly suggested, but the suggestion must be retained for the authentic pronunciation. It must be remembered that the preliminary sound before "EE" is *not* "AH" or "OO" but simply the aspirate "uh." Although Shaw represents this "uh" sound as the "er" of "after," it should be noted that "er" endings drop the "r," in Cockney and become simply "uh." The authors of this book have found, in conducting classes, that the correct pronunciation of this sound is one of the most difficult in the entire Cockney dialect. And, since this long "e" sound is one of the commonest in the English language, it is essential that the proper pronunciation be mastered. Remember to keep the "uh" of "uhEE" very short.

NOTE: Exceptions to this rule are "been" which is always "bin," and long "EE" words which end in "r" and take "iyER" as in "flyER" (fear), "iyER" (here), and "kliyER" (clear).

DRILL WORDS

'uhEE	(he)		wuhEE	(we)
truhEEt	(treat)		thruhEE	(three)
puhEEpOOl	(people)		suhEEm	(seem)
	ruhEEluhEEs	(release)		
	fuhEEmI:OOl	(female)		
	duhEEpEHnd	(depend)		

"EE" .... as in "country," "army," "navy," etc.

The long "e" sound given to the concluding "y" in American is changed to a short "i" in Cockney.

DRILL WORDS

kAHntri	(country)		kAWkni	(Cockney)
AWmi	(army)		lI:di	(lady)
nI:vi	(navy)		siti	(city)
	rEHdi	(ready)		
	'AWti	(haughty)		
	biyiOOti	(beauty)		

"EH" .... as in "bet," "said," "friend," etc.

Usually, there is no change in the Cockney's pronunciation of this short "e."

Sometimes, however, a short "i" is substituted, as in "stidi" (steady), "git" (get), and "jint" (gent). See "L," under "Consonant Changes," for further material.

"I" . . . . as in "ice," "aisle," "guile," etc.

Much of the Cockney flavor is derived from this sound in the dialect. The long "I," broken down, becomes "AH-EE" in American. The Cockney makes this "AW-EE" as in the word "AW-EEs" (ice), which is represented by the symbol "OI," because of the American familiarity with this "OI" as shown in the American words "noise" and "oil." Thus, the word "ice" will be written as "OIs." Some Cockneys prefer to give long "I" a simple "AH" sound, as "AHs" (ice), "nAHs" (nice), and "nAHt" (night).

Cockneys who have lifted themselves out of the lower classes attempt to ape the British speech and erroneously distort this long "I" to "AY" as in "tAYm" (time), "nAYt" (night), and "frAY" (fry). If the Cockney part calls for a *nouveau riche* of this type, it would be well to use this long "a" (AY) treatment. The preferred treatment is "OI."

DRILL WORDS

OI	(I)	strOIk	(strike)
rOIt	(right)	dOInER	(diner)
spOIn	(spine)	sOIfER	(cipher)

bOIsikOOl   (bicycle)
stOI-OOl   (style)
snOIpER   (sniper)

"i" . . . . as in "it," "women," "busy," etc.

Short "i" is given the same pronunciation in Cockney as it is in American. However, some Cockneys substitute "EE" for it, as in "pAOWzEEshUHn" (position) and "ER dEEshUHn" (edition).

"O" . . . . as in "on," "bond," "Johnny," etc.

The Cockney version of this "O" is "AW" and the sound is brought up from the throat, which gives it a richer quality than the American "AW" sound. This effect is also aided by pursing the lips.

DRILL WORDS

AWn	(on)	'AWt	(hot)
bAWnd	(bond)	bAWdi	(body)
jAWni	(Johnny)	blAWnd	(blond)

hAWnEHs'   (honest)
blAWsUHm   (blossom)
kAWdfish   (codfish)

"OH" . . . . as in "bone," "sew," "dough," etc.

The Cockney's habit of drawing out his vowels, sometimes interminably, is best illustrated in his version of "OH." It is one of the dialect's most identifying characteristics. For, in Cockney, this sound is triphthongized into "AOW," as in "bAOWn" (bone), "sAOW," (sew), and "dAOW" (dough). Broken down into its three parts, this triphthong would read "A-OH-OO" ("A" as in "bad," "OH" as in "go," and "OO" as in "food").

DRILL WORDS

rAOWd	(road)		ERlAOWn	(alone)
tAOWld	(told)		mAOWtER	(motor)
grAOW	(grow)		klAOWz	(clothes)

gAOWld   (gold)
sAOWdER   (soda)
flAOWt   (float)

"AW" .... as in "off," "cough," "water," etc.

This vowel sound retains its American pronunciation. But it is held longer in duration by the Cockney and is brought up from deeper in the throat. A variation which may be used to change the characterization adds a voiced "r" to the "AW" making it "AWr," as in "AWrf" (off) and "kAWrf" (cough).

"OO" .... as in "food," "do," "blue," etc.

Because of his addiction to diphthongs, the Cockney changes this double "o," (OO) to "i-OO" as in "fi-OOd" (food) with the emphasis on the "OO" and the short "i" merely suggested. Be sure that this short "i" is not pronounced as the consonantal "y," as in "fyOOd" (food)—it must retain its own sound, however slight. Exception: "pAW'" for "poor," as in "pAW' fEHlER" (poor fellow).

DRILL WORDS

diOO	(do)		siOOnER	(sooner)
bliOO	(blue)		siOOp	(soup)
miOOd	(mood)		miOOn	(moon)

fiOOl   (fool)
diOOm   (doom)
stiOOp   (stoop)

"oo" .... as in "good," "wolf," "full," etc.

Ordinarily, the Cockney pronunciation of this sound is the same as in American. A variation, however, gives this double "o," (oo), the double "o" of "food," (OO). This is an infiltration from the Scotch and has been variously spelled as "guid" and "gude."

"yOO" .... as in "unit," "cube," "beauty," etc.

The American "yOO" sound becomes "iyiOO." This sound looks more complicated than it actually is. A short "i" sound precedes the "y," and the "OO" retains its customary initial short "i." Thus, the "yOO" sound becomes "iyiOO."

DRILL WORDS

diyiOO	(due)		biyiOOti	(beauty)
iyiOOnit	(unit)		miyiOOzik	(music)
kiyiOOb	(cube)		kiyiOOt	(cute)

iyiOOnifAWm   (uniform)
iyiOOnOIt   (unite)
fyiOOtOIl   (futile)

"U".... as in "up," "love," "does," etc.

The "AH" sound of the American word "alms" is given to this short "u." It use abounds in Cockney speech and, for that reason, its correct dialect interpretation should always be consistent. The use of this "AH" is an important change and a complete mastery of it must be achieved to make for an authentic dialect.

DRILL WORDS

AHp	(up)		blAHnt	(blunt)
lAHv	(love)		fAHn	(fun)
dAHz	(does)		AHndAHn	(undone)

bAHntch   (bunch)
lAHgij   (luggage)
lAHvli   (lovely)

"ER".... as in "curb," "earn," "fern," etc.

The Cockney vowel sound in this "ER" combination is exactly the same as the American. The change occurs with the "r" which is never sounded. Like the other combinations of "ur," "er," "ir," "or," and "yr," the phonetic representation is "ER" with the "r" crossed out to indicate that it is silent. The preceding vowel sound remains the same.

DRILL WORDS

kER b	(curb)		wER th	(worth)
ER n	(earn)		stER	(stir)
fER n	(fern)		flER t	(flirt)

sER t'n   (certain)
lER nin'   (learning)
distER b   (disturb)

"OW".... as in "out," "cow," "house," etc.

Many Cockneys change this "OW" to an elongated "AH:." Some use "A-OO," as in: "A-OOt" (out), "nA-OO" (now), and "'A-OO" (how). Others treat the sound as "AH-UH" with the first syllable receiving greater emphasis, as in "**AH-UHt**" (out). The preferred change is "AH:."

DRILL WORDS

AH:t	(out)		kAH:nt	(count)
kAH:	(cow)		mAH:th	(mouth)
'AH:s	(house)		stAH:t	(stout)

mAH:ntUHn   (mountain)
dAH:ntAH:n (downtown)
ER bAH:t   (about)

"OI".... as in "oil," "boy," "noise," etc.

The Cockney gives this the same sound as the American, but he emphasizes the initial part of the diphthong more heavily. When broken down, "OI" becomes "AW-EE" and it is the "AW" that receives the emphasis, as in "b**AW**-EE" (boy). Because of its similarity to American, this sound is written "OI" in this chapter.

WORD EXERCISES

Pronounce the following words in the Cockney dialect using the material learned in the preceding Vowel Changes:

1.	notice	11.	royalty
2.	baby	12.	taskmaster
3.	fountain	13.	perambulator
4.	hospitalization	14.	aspirin
5.	blooming	15.	foolhardy
6.	dutiful	16.	farmhand
7.	been	17.	fan
8.	deceitful	18.	vacation
9.	beautiful	19.	sightseeing
10.	photophone	20.	shortcoming

When all the above words have been pronounced, refer to the correct pronunciation given below and check the vowel sounds that were incorrectly sounded. Repeat them over correctly a number of times until they have been committed to memory.

1.	nAOWtuhs	11.	rOIoo'ti
2.	bI:bi	12.	tAHs'mAHstER
3.	fAH:ntuhn	13.	prEHm
4.	'AWrspi/uhluhzI:shuhn	14.	AHsp'rin
5.	bliOOmin'	15.	fiOOl'AW:di
6.	jiOOtifoo'	16.	fAW:m'EHnd
7.	bin	17.	fEHn
8.	disuhEE/foo'	18.	vI:kI:sh'n
9.	biyiOO/ifoo'	19.	sOI/suhEEuhn'
10.	fAOWtAOWfAOWn	20.	shAW/kAHmin'

CONSONANT CHANGES

B—The same as in American.

C—See "K" and "S."

D—When "d" is followed by either a "y" or "i" sound, the "d" gets a "j" treatment, as in: "di*j*UH" (di*d y*ou), "imuhEE*j*it" (imme*di*ate), and "'i*j*UHs" (hi*de*ous). Final "d" is often omitted, especially after "n" and "l," as in: "fOIn'" (fin*d*), and "fAOWl'" (fol*d*).

F—The same as in American.

G—Hard "g" is the same as in American. Soft "g" is pronounced as the American "j." Words with the participial ending of "ing" always drop the final "g," as in "diOOin'" (doing), "gAOWin'" (going), and "spuhEEkin'" (speaking). When the "ing" is part of the word, the concluding "g" is sometimes changed to a "k" as in, "nAHthin*k*" (nothing), "sAHmthin*k*" (something), and "thin*k*" (thing).

H—The most identifying consonant change in the Cockney dialect comes with the addition or omission of the letter "h" at the beginning or middle of a word. The beginner, with no knowledge or training in correct Cockney, scatters extra "h's." The rule for dropping the "h," which must be strictly adhered to, is:

> 5. *ALWAYS DROP THE "H" WHEN IT IS THE FIRST LETTER OF A WORD OR WHEN IT IS IN THE MIDDLE OF A WORD AND IS PRECEDED BY A CONSONANT AND FOLLOWED BY A VOWEL.*

A good example of this is the sentence, "its THUH kAWnstUHn tEHmER rEHmER rEHmER rUH THuhEE yAWsi zoof zAWn THuhEE yAW dOIwI:." (It's the constant *h*ammer, *h*ammer, *h*ammer of the *h*orses' *h*oofs on the *h*ard *h*ighway.) Turn to the "Glide Rule" section of this chapter for an explanation of the phonetic rendering of the above sentence to see how the "h's" are affected by this rule.

Another sentence showing the dropped "h" is "mEHni kOIn zUH puhEEpOO linEHbit THuhEE yAHsAOWl." (Many kinds of people inhabit the household.)

Most authorities agree that the Cockney rarely, if ever, adds the "h" to his words despite the predilection of so many amateur dialecticians to do so. Usually it is the newly rich who fear that their lower origin will be exposed by their dropping of "h's" and who, in their anxiety to sound all their "h's" meticulously, add them to words which actually do not require them. It is therefore suggested that this treatment be reserved for that type of character only and that no added "h's" should be included in the ordinary Cockney dialect. If they are to be used, here is a rule governing their usage.

> 6. *ADD AN "H" TO THE FIRST WORD OF A SENTENCE IF IT BEGINS WITH A VOWEL OR TO A WORD THAT BEGINS WITH A VOWEL AND IS PRECEDED BY A WORD THAT ENDS EITHER WITH A VOWEL, A "Y" OR A WEAKLY STRESSED CONSONANT.*

An example is "*h*EHpOOlz AW *h*AW-OOlwI:z fAHn din *h*AWtchUHdz." (Apples are always found in orchards.)

J—The same as in American.

K—The letter "k" is nearly always replaced by the glottal stop. See "Glottal Stop" section for a more detailed explanation of this point. The glottal stop is a definite characteristic of the Cockney dialect and should be mastered. Used consistently, this glottal stop would make the dialect too thick for general understanding. But an occasional use of the glottal stop (/) for "k" is absolutely necessary for a credible dialect. This substitution of glottal stop for "k" should be used only when "k" is final, as in "too/" (took) and "brAOW/" (broke).

However, final "k" must be sounded as "k" when the next word begins with a vowel, as "too kit" (took it). Further discussion of this point will be found in "The Cockney Glide."

L—The "l" receives two different treatments in the Cockney dialect and both should be used depending upon their position in a word. The first "l" is pronounced exactly as it is in American and should so be used.

7. WHEN "l" IS PRECEDED BY A CONSONANT OR PRECEDED AND FOLLOWED BY VOWEL SOUNDS, THE AMERICAN "l" SHOULD BE USED.

For example, take the word "flEHtER" (flatter). The consonant "f" precedes "l"; therefore "l" is retained. The words "kluhEEn" (clean) and "plI: t" (plate) also retain the American sound of "l."

Examples of words in which "l" is between two vowels and thus remains "l" are: "sAOWlAOW" (solo), "bili" (Billy), "wilin'" (willing), and "fEHlER" (fellow). The second treatment of the "l" is the prefixing of the "OO" sound (the "OO" as in "food"). Thus, "l" is pronounced as "EHl" in American and "EH-OOl" in Cockney.

The rule for this "l" is:

8. WHEN "l" IS PRECEDED BY A VOWEL AND FOLLOWED BY A CONSONANT, IT RECEIVES AN "OO" SOUND BEFORE IT.

Some examples of this treatment will be found in "fiOOltER" (filter), "bEH-OOlkAWni" (balcony), and "fAW-OOl" (fall).

This change may also be carried over to words which have a weak vowel before "l" or which end with "le," as in "nAW'mOOl" (normal), "fAW'mOOl" (formal), "bAHndOOl" (bundle), and "bEHtOOl" (battle). However, final "l" is often dropped. (See "The Cockney Glide.") If the "l" is dropped, the preceding "OO" sound will remain, as "fAW'mOO/" (formal), "nAW'mOO/" (normal), "bE-HtOO/" (battle).

9. WHEN "l" IS FINAL IN A WORD IT MAY BE REPLACED BY A GLOTTAL STOP (/) UNLESS THE NEXT WORD BEGINS WITH A VOWEL.

Thus, the Cockney would say "fAWmOO/dAHns" (formal dance), but "fAW-mOO lEREH:'" (formal affair). The final "l" must be carried over as a glide if the next word begins with a vowel.

10. WHEN "l" IS FOLLOWED BY A CONSONANT AND PRECEDED BY A VOWEL, THE "l" MAY BE DROPPED BUT ITS VOWEL SOUND, "OO," MUST REMAIN.

Examples of this rule will be found in such words as "fEHOO't" (felt), "biOO'd" (build), "fiOO'tER" (filter), "stiOO't" (stilt), and "siOO'vER" (silver).

Words in which a long "OH" or, in Cockney, "AOW," precedes the "l" followed by a consonant, will drop the "OO" before "l." This "OO" is not needed as its sound is incorporated in the triphthong "AOW" and is expressed by the "W." This will be easily seen in the word "tAOW'd" (told), or "tAOWld" (told).

M—The same as in American.

N—The same as in American. It may sometimes change to "m" as in, "miOO'yAHms" (millions) and "'lEH'uhm" (eleven).

P and **Q**—The same as in American.

R—An absolute rule which must be adhered to at all times, to make the Cockney dialect truly authentic, is this:

11. THE LETTER "r" IS SOUNDED ONLY WHEN IT IS FOLLOWED BY A VOICED VOWEL.

For example, in the words "sirAHp" (syrup) and "fAWrEHs'" (forest), the "r" must, of necessity, be pronounced. But the "r" is never pronounced in words like "tER nip" (turnip), "bER n" (burn) or "tAW" (tar). The crossed "r" (R) sign, indicating that the "r" is silent, is used only in words which retain the "r" flavor. For example, "flER t" (flirt), retains the same vowel sound as in American, but the "r" is silent. Whereas the word "kAW" (car), changes the vowel sound. Review the "AH" of "father" and the "ER" of "curb" in the section on "Vowel Changes." For the pronunciation of "r" between vowels, refer to "R" in the British Chapter.

For the use of final "r," see the "Glide Rule" section.

Sometimes an extra "r" is added to certain words, as in "jAWrin'" (jawing), "OIdiyUHr" (idea), "fEHlER" (fellow). At other times, the "r" is transposed so that the words become "pERdiyiOOs" (produce), "tchiOOdERn" (children), " 'AHnERd" (hundred), and "pERmiskis" (promiscuous). It will be noticed that to avoid pronouncing it the Cockney juggles the "r" so that it will come after a vowel sound, rather than after a consonant.

S—The same as in American.

T—This letter is often replaced by a glottal stop. See section titled "Glottal Stop" for a more detailed explanation of this point. The glottal stop is a definite characteristic of the Cockney dialect and should be used often—and correctly. Its use, however, should not be overdone so that the dialect becomes too thick. The glottal substitute for "t" should be used only when "t" is final or followed by "le," as in "lAW/" (lot), "bi/" (bit), and "li/OO'" (little). When the "t" precedes an unvoiced vowel followed by an "l," the glottal may also be used, as in " 'AWspi/OO/" (hospital). "t" is sometimes added after "s," as "sinst" (since) and "wAHnst" (once). Final "t" is usually dropped after "s," "p," "k" as in "pAHs'" (past), "krEHp'" (crept), and "strik" (strict). See the "Glide Rule" section to learn when a word which ends in "t" must retain the "t."

V—The same as in American.

W—When the "w" sound gets little or no accent in a word, it is dropped completely, as in, "AWl'UHz" (always), "bEHk'ER dz" (backwards), and "AWkER d" (awkward). The "w" must follow a consonant and precede a vowel if it is to be dropped.

X—The same as in American.

Z—The same as in American. Some Cockneys occasionally add a "z" sound to words like "nAOW'EHz" (nowheres) and "sAHm'EHz" (somewheres).

WORD EXERCISES

Pronounce the following words in the Cockney dialect using the material learned from the preceding Consonant Changes:

1.	broke it	11.	fire fighter
2.	fine house	12.	hobbyhorse
3.	immediately	13.	falter
4.	call	14.	motorcar
5.	children	15.	building
6.	backwards	16.	strictly
7.	formal occasion	17.	thirty-four
8.	broker	18.	broke them
9.	brother	19.	always
10.	something	20.	production

After the above words have been pronounced, refer to the list given below for the correct pronunciation of the words. Check the consonant sounds that were incorrectly pronounced. Repeat them correctly a number of times until they have been perfectly memorized.

1.	brAOWki/	11.	fOIyERfOItER
2.	fOInAH:s	12.	'AWbiy'AWs
3.	imuhEEjER/li	13.	fAW-OO/tER
4.	kAW-OO'	14.	mAOWtER kAW:
5.	tchiOO/dER n	15.	biOO'din'
6.	bEHk'ER dz	16.	strik'li
7.	fAWmOO luhkI:zhuhn	17.	fER /ifAW:
8.	brAOWkER	18.	brAOW kuhm
9.	brAHvER	19.	AWl'UHz
10.	sAHmfink	20.	pER dAHksh'n

VOWEL AND CONSONANT COMBINATIONS

EN, IN, etc.

Although the Cockney shortens "ing" to "in," he lengthens "in" or "en" to "ing" or "eng." Thus, "gAWdUHnin" (gardening), but "gAWding" (garden). A few other examples are "pAWding" (pardon), "sAHding" (sudden), and "kEHpting" (captain). Used consistently, this change would make the Cockney too unintelligible, but a judicious sprinkling will color the dialect characterization considerably.

TH, th

A great many Cockneys substitute a "v" for the "TH" of "the" as in "mAH*v*ER" (mo*th*er), "brAH*v*ER" (bro*th*er), "*v*is" (this), and even "*v*ER" (the). Also, like many Americans, and many other foreigners, some Cockneys use "d" for voiced "TH," as in "*d*is" (*th*is), "*d*EHm" (*th*em), and "*d*AOWz" (*th*ose).

For the unvoiced "th" of "thank," they substitute "f," as in "*f*ruhEE" (*th*ree), "*f*ERs'" (thirst), and "*f*ing" (thing).

The above changes are not used consistently by the Cockney and should not be used consistently by the actor. A normal "TH" or "th" should be used in most cases.

OW

When "ow" is final in a word, it often becomes "ER," as in "fEHlER" (fellow), "yEHlER" (yellow), and "bAWrER" (borrow). When used before a vowel-beginning word, the "r" sound must be added to the above examples, as in "yEHlER rEHg" (yellow egg). See "The Cockney Glide."

UNACCENTED SYLLABLES

Because he is sparing with the use of his mouth and jaws, the Cockney drops entire syllables as well as vowels and consonants. This slackness accounts for the dropping of the unaccented syllables in such words as "'stEHd" (*in*stead), "'sEHp'" (*ex*cept), and "'kAWz" (*be*cause). He drops not only the initial unaccented syllable but also the medial unaccented syllable as in "b'luhEEv" (b*e*lieve), "fEHm'li" (fam*i*ly), and "s'pAOWz" (s*u*ppose).

THE GLIDE VOWEL

In connection with the Cockney word glide, there is also an introduction of glide vowels where they actually do not belong, as in "EHn**UH**ri" (Henry), "AHm-b**UH**rEHlER" (umbrella), and "mistchuhEEv**uhEE**UHs" (mischievous).

THE COCKNEY GLIDE

The internal vowel glide, discussed above, is a suggestion of a habit which typifies the Cockney dialect. This habit is extended to the glide which connects words as well as syllables. The key to an authentic Cockney dialect is the mastery of this simple speech habit. With the use of a few of the more important vowel and consonant changes, the omission of the "h," a fairly accurate reproduction of the Cockney's musical lilt and the accurate handling of this glide a credible Cockney dialect can be achieved.

THE GLIDE RULE

12. WHEN A WORD BEGINS WITH A VOWEL, IT CARRIES OVER FROM THE PRECEDING WORD THE CONCLUDING CONSONANT SOUND, WHETHER THIS IS A CONSONANT OR A VOWEL ENDING WITH AN UNVOICED CONSONANT SOUND.

Now, let us see how this rule operates. The phrase "an orange" would be pronounced "EH *n*AWrUHnj." Observe that the word "orange," beginning with the vowel "o," carries over the concluding consonant (n) of the word "an."

Another example phrase is "THuhEE yEHnsUHm mEHn" (the handsome man). The initial word (the) actually ends with a vowel. However, when pronouncing "EE," the mouth is in position for the sound of the consonant "y." And it is this unvoiced "y" sound which is vocalized and carried to the next word, if it begins with a vowel. Since the "h" is dropped in Cockney, "handsome" does begin with a vowel and the "y" is sounded.

NOTE: Although a word ending in long "e" (EE) will use the unvoiced consonant "y" as a glide, the "y" is not used for all vowel glides, because not all vowels carry the same unvoiced consonant sound. This will be seen clearly in the phrases "uhEE yEH dit" (he had it), "gAOW wAWn" (go on) and "sAOWfER riz" (sofa is). The "he," "go" and "sofa" words take "y," "w" and "r" respectively for their glides. This will be true of all final "EE," "AOW" and "ER" vowels.

A list of the unvoiced consonant sounds of the final glide vowels is given below to serve as an accurate guide.

> "I:" takes "y"—"THI: *y*EHv" (they have)
> "EE" takes "y"—"suhEE *y*it" (see it)
> "i" takes "y"—"lI:di *y*iz" (lady is)
> "OI" takes "y"—"frOI *y*it" (fry it)
> "ER" takes "r"—"sAOWfER *r*iz" (sofa is)
> "AW" takes "r"—"sAW *r*it" (saw it)
> "AH" takes "w"—"kAH: wiz" (cow is)
> "OO" takes "w"—"bliOO *w*OIz (blue eyes)
> "AOW" takes "w"—"grAOW *w*AHp" (grow up)

Two different pronunciations of the word "the" are used by Cockneys, as they are by Americans. "THuh" is used when the next word begins with a consonant, "THuh dAWg" (the dog). "THuhEE" is used when the next word begins with a vowel, "THuhEE *y*AHs" (the house). Although "house" begins with a consonant (h), when pronounced in Cockney, the "h" is dropped making "house" an initial vowel word.

Now let us observe the glide rule in a sentence.

"He took an answer to him all right."

Written phonetically, as it would be pronounced with the use of the glide rule, the sentence would read:

"uhEE too *k*UH *n*AHnsER tiOO *w*i *m*AWOO' rOIt."

Here, it will be seen that the concluding "k" of "took" is retained and glided over to begin the next word "an," because "an" begins with a vowel. And the "n" of "an" is glided over to begin the word "answer," which also begins with a vowel. The word "tiOO" (too) ends with a vowel and the next word "im" (him) begins with a vowel. But, according to the chart, final "OO" vowels take the consonant "w" for their glide. The "h" is dropped in Cockney, so "him" is an initial vowel word. Thus "him" would take the "w." The following word (all) begins with a vowel and the final consonant "m" is glided over from "him" to begin "all." The final consonant sounds of "he," "answer," and "all" are not glided because the next words begin with consonants, thus the "l" of "all" is dropped.

It must be remembered, in using the word glide, that the original word spelling cannot be considered in determining whether the words are to be connected with glides. The only consideration is the *pronunciation* of the words in *Cockney*.

The fact must also be remembered that the concluding consonant which is glided over to the initial vowel of the next word is not *always* the concluding consonant of a word, as it is written. It can also be the concluding, unvoiced consonant sound, as it is *pronounced* in Cockney. For example, ordinarily the final "g" is dropped by the Cockney in words like "wAWkin'" (walking), "stEHndin'" (standing), and "flOIin'" (flying). The concluding consonant in these words, then, as they would be pronounced, is "n" and not "g." It is this "n" that is glided to the next word if this word begins with a vowel. The following sentence illustrates this:

"Running and walking are builder-uppers."

Phonetically, it would read:

"rAHni *n*UHn' wAWki *n*AW' bildER rAHpER z."

It can be seen that "g" was dropped completely, and in the two verbs, "running" and "walking," the "n" was used as the glide consonant.

The letter "d" was dropped from "and," not because of the glide but because it is usually dropped after "n." And the "r" was dropped from the word "are," because "r" is never sounded unless followed by a vowel. However the unvoiced "r" of "bildER" (builder) was retained and glided over to the next word which began with a vowel, "AHpERz" (uppers).

Another important point to remember in applying the glide is that words which begin with "h," drop the "h" and thus begin with a vowel. (See under the consonant "H.") The final consonant or the consonant sound of the preceding word must be carried over to begin the "h"-dropped word, as "uhEE yi zEHpi" (he is happy), and "THI: *y*EHv" (they have).

An exception to the initial dropped "h" words is "hAWnEHs'" (honest). Although this word is normally pronounced without the "h," the Cockney perversely retains it.

Additional glide rule advice and examples will be found in the sections on "Grammar," "Contractions" and "Elisions and Glottal Stops."

GLIDE RULE EXERCISES

Pronounce the following sentences in the Cockney dialect using the material learned from the Cockney Glide:

1. They have to go home.
2. Try a hat on now, dearie.
3. I saw it happen alone.
4. How is the old lady standing up under it?
5. Did he know who narked on him?
6. The car is still running on petrol.
7. Will he go up to his roof now?
8. He's balmy and a bit on the howling side if you ask me.
9. Take a walk and hop it, now.
10. An honest man is hard to find nowadays.

Pronounce each sentence and then refer to the following list of correct pronunciations. Correct whatever mistakes were made and repeat the correct treatment a number of times until it is familiar. Do this with every sentence.

1. THi yEHv tuh gAOW wAOWm.
2. trOI yUH nEH tAW nAH: di:ri.
3. hOI sAW ri tEHpuh nER lAOWn.
4. 'AH zuhEE yAOW lI:di stEHndi nAH pAHndER rit?
5. di duhEE nAOW wiOO nAW:k dAW nim?
6. THuh kAW: riz stiOO' rAHni nAWn pEHtr'l.
7. wiOO luhEE gAOW wAHp tiOO wiz riOOf nAH:?
8. 'uhEEz bAWmi yUH nUH bi tAWn THUH yAH:lin sOI dif yUH wAWsks muhEE.
9. tI: kUH wAW kUH nAW pi/ nAH:.
10. UH hAWnuhs mEH ni zAW: tUH fOI nAH:ruhdI:z.

ELISIONS AND GLOTTAL STOPS

Cockney is replete with elisions and glottal stops. Technically, a glottal stop is that sound produced at the back of the mouth when the glottis is suddenly closed and then opened. It results when a consonant is not sounded but is substituted by the glottal stop. Say the word "took" and cut it off just before the "k" is sounded. The glottis will then be in a closed position. Open it quickly and the glottal stop will be completed. Using this system practice words like "took," "book," "tuck," and "cook" until the glottal stop is mastered. The glottal stop will be represented by (/).

***13. THE GLOTTAL STOP IS USED WITH FINAL "T" AND FINAL "K"
OR WHEN EITHER OF THESE CONSONANT SOUNDS IS
FOLLOWED BY THE "L" (EH-OOL) SOUND.***

Here is an example sentence making use of the entire rule: "tI:/ THuh lAW/ uh pi/OOlz tuh THuh AWspi/OOl," (Take the lot of pickles to the hospital.) In this sentence the "k" of "take" is glottalized and dropped. The "t" of "lot" is also dropped because of the glottal stop, despite the fact that the next word (of) begins with a vowel. Usually, the "t" would glide over the begin "of," but when the glottal stop is used, the glide rule is not used. In the word "pickles," the "k" sound is followed by the "el" (EH-OOl) sound and receives the glottal stop. The "t" of "hospital" also precedes the "el" (EH-OOl) sound and is replaced by the glottal stop.

There is a tendency to glottalize "p," although this is not as widely used as the "t" and "k" glottal stops. Unless a very thick dialect is desired, the glottal for "p" should not be used.

The glottal stop should not be used too often—although many Cockneys use it consistently—because it can make a dialect unintelligible. For this reason, it has been indicated in this chapter only rarely.

Since the Cockney dialect is spoken with haphazard pronunciation, it is full of elisions. Cockneys seem to feel that half a word is better than the complete word. Whenever possible they pronounce the first half and then talk right along forgetting the second half of the word completely. If used too often, this habit of eliding words will keep the audience anxiously waiting for the other shoe to drop. It will also make the dialect too thick. Much of the Cockney's unintelligibility is due to this negligent manner of speaking.

In the word "myself," for example, the "y" is dropped and replaced by the aspirate "uh," making the word "muhsEH-OO'f." This aspirate "uh" sound should never be pronounced as "AH" or "AW" or "oo," but simply as "uh." The aspirate "uh" must be very short.

Although the word "to" should be pronounced as "tiOO," the pro nunciation is usually just simply "tuh" using the aspirate "uh" rather than "iOO." In the sentence, "gi vi/tuh wim tuh print," (give it to him to print), the "to" before "him" retains the use of the final consonant "w" for a glide. This "tuh" pronunciation of "to" is the weak form. The strong form, "tiOO" is used only for emphasis, as in "gAOW **tiOO** wi/ nAW/ ERwI: fruh mi/." (Go **to** it, not away from it.) In this example sentence, the word "from" also takes the weak form, so that it is pronounced as "fruhm" rather than "frAWm." Strong and weak forms are used in Cockney as they are in familiar American speech.

The word "of" is usually changed to "uh" in Cockney, except when it precedes an initial-vowel word, "spuhEEki nuh vit" (speaking of it). Although "of" is reduced to the simple "uh" sound, the "v" is still used as a glide. When "of" precedes a consonant-beginning word, the "v" is naturally dropped, as in "plEHnti yuh brEHd" (plenty of bread).

The word "for" is also elided and becomes "fuh" before a consonant-beginning word as, "fuh nAHthin" (for nothing). When "for" precedes an initial-vowel word, the unvoiced "r" is sounded for the glide, as in, "fuh r it" (for it).

This habit of elision changes the word "your" to "yuh." Followed by a word beginning with a consonant, it does not carry over its unvoiced "r" sound, as in, "yuh lOIf" (your life). Many books and plays using the Cockney dialect incorrectly write this word as "yer," when before a consonant it is actually "yuh." However, before a vowel it transfers its unvoiced "r" to that vowel, as in: "yuh *r*EHpinuhs" (your happiness).

The commonly used word "you" (yiOO) also receives the aspirate "uh" and becomes "yuh." Before a consonant word it would be, "yuh kAHnt" (you can't). But when it precedes a word beginning with a vowel, it transfers its unvoiced "w" sound to that word, as in: "yuh *w*EHv" (you have).

The word "my," which would normally be "mOI" in the Cockney dialect, becomes "muh" with the use of the elision. Followed by a consonant-beginning word, it is simply "muh" as in: "muh nI:m zERbERt" (my name's Herbert). But, before an initial-vowel word, it retains the unvoiced "y" of its "mOI" pronunciation and glides the "y" to the next word, as in: "muh *y*AOWm zin lAHn'uhn" (my home's in London.)

Some Cockneys change the word "my" to "me" and say, "muhEE yAOWm zin lAHn'uhn" (me home's in London).

Ordinarily, following the common pronunciation of the long "I" vowel sound, as in "nice" (nOIs), this word should be given an "OI" treatment. Many Cockneys do so. But, on the other hand, a great many also give it an "AH" sound, as do the American southerners. Still others use the aspirate "uh" and pronouce "I" as "uh." The most commonly used, and therefore the one suggested for use here, is "OI." When broken down, this sound is "AW-EE," like the vowel sound in the American word "boy." When used before a vowel, it glides its unvoiced consonant "y" to the next word, as in: "OI *y*I:nt gAOWin'" (I ain't going).

GRAMMAR

The errors in a Cockney's speech make for a grammatical word-color that is distinctly Cockney. They are important adjuncts to the dialect's correct presentation. Naturally, because of the similarity of racial roots and cultures, the Cockney's errors in grammar approximate those of his American cousin. But some of them are peculiar only to the Cockney.

The double negative is one of the most frequent errors that the Cockney makes. Some example usages are:

"OI duh nAOW nAHfin kuhbAH/ THEHt."
(I *don't* know *nothing* about that.)
(I *don't* know *anything* about that.)

"OI yI:nt nEHvER suhEE nim nAOWwEHz, nAOWwAH."
(I *ain't never* seen him *nowheres, nohow.*)
(I've *never* seen him anywhere.)

"EHz nAOWbAWdi suhEEn nAHfin kuh nEHvER ruh jAWb?"
(Has *nobody* seen *nothing* of *never* a job?)
(Has anybody heard of a job?)

It can readily be seen that the logic involved is unimportant—especially in the last sentence. Double negatives negate themselves and become even triple negatives.

The substitution of an adjective modifier for a proper adverb modifier is a common error with Americans. But the Cockney uses it almost to distraction. He will say:

"uhEE wAW zAOWm ruhEEOOl kwik."
(He was home *real quick.*)
(He was home *very quickly.*)

"THuh blAOWk wood'n fOIt fEH."
(The bloke wouldn't fight *fair.*)
(The fellow wouldn't fight *fairly.*)

"THuh jAWb wAWz dAHn prAWpER lOIk."
(The job was done *proper like.*)
(The job was done *properly.*)

For the reflexive pronoun, the Cockney substitutes such distortions as:

"uhEE yI:nt dAH nisEHOO'f nAOW wAWm."
(He ain't done *hisself* no harm.)
(He hasn't done *himself* any harm.)

"THEH mEHz wAWnts THEHsEHOO'vz took, sI: sAOW."
(Them as wants *theirselves* took, say so.)
(Those who want *themselves* taken, say so.)

The western-American habit of attaching a "here" to the word "this" and "there" to the words "that," "those" and "them" is also prevalent in Cockney where it will read:

"tI:k THEHt THEH ruhwI: nAH."
(Take that *there* away now.)
(Take that away now.)

"THi siyuh blAOW kiz fEH bAWmi."
(This *here* bloke is fair balmy.)
(This fellow is absolutely crazy.)

"THEHm THEH flAH zi zAOWpuhn."
(Them *there* flowers is open.)
(Those flowers are open.)

The Cockney is also fond of superlatives and comparatives, as demonstrated in the following phrases: "mAOW sAWfli rAWtuhn" (most awfully rotten) or, strangely, "vEHri tEHribli swEHOOl" (very terribly swell). Things are "litluhs'" (littlest) or "wER suhs'" (worstest) or "mAW bigERuh" (more biggerer) or "wER sER" (worster) or "uh blAHdi sOIt mAW rAWfluh" (a bloody sight more awfuller). The expletives, "blAHdi" (bloody), "bliOOmin" (blooming) and "blinkin'" (blinking), together with many others, are constantly in use at times when expletives are not even necessary. The expletive "bloody" is regarded as one of the most objectionable and vulgar in the language, and should be used with discretion.

The Cockney often substitutes a singular verb for a plural one and vice versa, as in:

"THI:wAWz rAHni nERbAHt."
(They *was* running about.)
(They *were* running about.)

"uhEE wER ruh bliOOmin tAWf."
(He *were* a blooming toff.)
(He *was* a real gentleman.)

"it wER ruh shI: m."
(It *were* a shame.)
(It *was* a shame.)

A common Cockney substitution replaces "who," "which," and "that" with "as" and "what," as in:

"uhEE zuh blAOWk wAW/ nAOWz."
(He's a bloke *what* knows.)
(He's a fellow *who* knows.)

"OI spuhEEk sEHz wAH nEH zEH zER rOIts."
(I speaks as one *as* has her rights.)
(I speak as one *who* has her rights.)

"im wAWt wERks, uhEE yuhEEts."
(Him *what* works, he eats.)
(He *who* works, eats.)

Normal pronoun usage is entirely disregarded. The Cockney cheerfully says:

"THuh struhEEt zAH: nuh ni mAW rER wAWt sEH zits THEH: nEHz gAW tuh shAOW wi tzi zuh nAW rERn."
(The street's *our'n* and him or her what says it's *their'n* has got to show it's *his'n* or *her'n.*)
(The street's *ours* and he or she who says it's *his* or *hers* will have to show it's *his* or *her's.*)

Like many Americans, the Cockney often adds an "s" to the present indicative singular, as in:

"OI gi zi muh wAWluh puh nuh-EE yAHp zuhn giz muhEE wAHn bEHk."
(I *gives* him a wallop and he ups and *gives* me one back.)
(I *gave* him a wallop and he up and *gave* me one back.)

"OI suhEE zi mOI gAOW zAHp tuh wi muh nOI sEHz yiOO wI: ts muhEE!"
(I *sees* him, I *goes* up to him and I *says*, you *hates* me!)
(I *saw* him, I *went* up to him and I *said*, you *hate* me!)

A number of Cockneys use the present form of the verb, instead of the past. Then they add "d" or "ed" to the present form and that makes a very satisfying past tense for them.

"OI suhEE duh-EE wAW zuh ruhEEOOl fEHlER."
(I *seed* he was a real fellow.)
(I *saw* that he was a real fellow.)

"yiOO giv dim wAWt fAW rAW-OOl rOIt."
(You *gived* him what for all right.)
(You *gave* him what for all right.)

"wuhEE nAOWd wAW tuhEE wAWz lOIk."
(We *knowed* what he was like.)
(We *knew* what he was like.)

CONTRACTIONS

To present a good copy of the Cockney dialect, it is essential that the student be prepared with a knowledge of those contractions that are most typical. Practically always, "have not," "is not," "are not," and "has not" are supplanted with the all-embracing, social pariah word, "ain't," as in:

"OI yI: nt gAWt nAOW rOIt."
(I *ain't* got no right.)
(I *have* no right.)

"uhEE yI: nt wER kt nAHn."
(He *ain't* worked none.)
(He *hasn't* worked at all.)

"shuhEE yI: nt nAOW biyiOOti."
(She *ain't* no beauty.)
(She *isn't* a beauty.)

When the original forms are used, the two words are contracted as in American, "'EHzuhnt" (hasn't), "'EHduhnt" (hadn't), and "'EHvuhnt" (haven't). It must be remembered that the "h" is dropped, so that the preceding consonant sound must be glided over to begin these words. If they begin the sentence, then, of course, they take no glide and stand alone.

"'EHzuhn tuhEF gAW tuh nERv?"
(Hasn't he got a nerve?)

"OI yEHvuhnt gAWt mAHtch tOIm."
(I haven't got much time.)

"wuhEE yEHvuhnt mEHni yAHz."
(We haven't many hours.)

"THI: yEHzuhn tuh tchAHns."
(They *hasn't* a chance.)
(They *haven't* a chance.)

Only when the Cockney finds it necessary to emphasize a fact very strongly does he separate the two words, as in "OI yEHv **nAWt** gAW tit!" (I have *not* got it!)

Contractions should be used wherever possible. Instead of the complete phrase, "OI dAOWn nAOW" (I don't know), the Cockney would say, "OI duh-nAOW" (I dunno), which is a contraction within a contraction.

The Cockney, like most Britishers, uses a considerable amount of noun contractions. For instance, the Cockney will call a "victrola" a "vic" (vik), or a "picture" a "pic" (pik). This is quite evident in the popular expression, "AW fuh mAOW" ('alf a mo'), which is actually "half a moment." "mAOW" is a contraction of "moment." Other such word contractions are:

sec	"sEHk"	second (of time)
pram	"prEHm"	perambulator
frij	"frij"	Frigidaire
bike	"bOIk"	bicycle
ap	"EHp"	apple

Ordinarily, if the trade name of any household or business device exceeds two syllables it is cut down to its first syllable.

COCKNEY SLANG EXPRESSIONS

Because Cockney is a branch of the English language it has, like American, its own peculiar slang expressions. Foreigners must adopt the slang of their new country if the languages are completely different. Thus a Frenchman must drop his own colorful slang expressions if he wants to be understood by Americans. But the Cockney may keep a great deal of his, since his language is very similar to American.

Only a few of the Cockney's slang expressions are given, and these should be used sparingly so as not to thicken the dialect speech.

A retort to an insult:

"THuh sI: m t' yiOO wi' nAWb zAWn."
(The same to you with knobs on.)

A greeting like the American, "How's tricks?":

"'AHz y' pAW rAOWl' fuh-EEt?"
(How's your poor old feet?)

To an unwelcome newcomer, as in the American, "Here comes nothing.":

"AHftUH TH' lAWd mI:yER kAHmz TH' dAHmkAWt."
(After the Lord Mayor comes the dump-cart.)

To a rude starer, as in the American, "See anything green?":

"suhEE yEHni gruhEE nin mOI yOI?"
(See any green in my eye?)

Also for the same purpose as above:

"gAWt y' rOI fool?"
(Got your eye full?)

To a naive person, as in the American, "Take the hayseed out of your hair.":

"git y' rEH: kAHt."
(Get your hair cut.)

To calm an angry person, as in the American, "Keep your shirt on.":

"kuh-EEp y' rEH: rAWn."
(Keep your hair on.)

A hint to repay a loan:

"its gAW tuh bEHk tiOO wit."
(It's got a back to it.)

To speed a parting, as in the American, "Get going, now.":

"bAWbz y' rAHnkOOl."
(Bob's your uncle.)

To hurry a welcome departure, as in the American, "Scram!":

"'AW pit, nAH!"
(Hop it, now!)

To retort to the above, as in the American, "O.K! O.K!":

"'AH fuh mAOW!"
(Half a moment!)

To ask someone to "step aside," as in the American, "Get out of my way!":

"wAWz y' fAWTHuh rUH glI:zER?"
(Was your father a glazier?)

A contemptuous reply when asked "What?"—an example of Cockney rhyming slang—as in the American, "I don't chew my cabbage twice.":

"kEHts tI:l zAWt!"
(Cat's tails, hot!)

COCKNEY SLANG WORDS

COCKNEY SLANG	PHONETICS	DEFINITION	AMERICAN EQUIVALENT
acid	"EHsid"	impudence	guts or gall
beeno	"buhEEnAOW"	happiness	slaphappy
brass	"brAHs"	money	dough
carve up	"kAW vAHp"	divide	split
clean	"kluhEEn"	scolding abuse	bawl out
cole	"kAOWl"	money	dough
cop a packet	"kAW pUH pEHkuht"	get hurt	socked
packet	"pEHkuht"	a blow	a sock
cosh	"kAWsh"	a blow	a wallop
cully	"kAHli"	a friend	a pal
dekko	"dEHkAOW"	a glance	a gander
dutch	"dAHtch"	treat	dutch treat
'erb	"ERb"	a funny man	a clown
faggot	"fEHguht"	a fool	a sap
freemans	"fruhmEHnz"	for nothing	for nix
go to pot	"gAOW t' pAWt"	ruined	on the skids
gorblimey	"gAWblOImuhEE"	an expletive a rakish cap	dammit
guiver	"guhEEvER"	blarney	the bunk
hank	"'EHnk"	nonsense	the baloney
hog	"'AWg"	a shilling	two bits
josser	"jAWsER"	a fellow	a guy
lay on to be	"lI: yAWn t' buhEE"	pretend	playing 'possum
lovely drippings	"lAHvER luhEE dripinz"	fine	swell stuff
in the lum	"in TH' lAHm"	hard up	badly bent
mivvy	"mivi"	a marvel	hot stuff
mouldies	"mAOWlduhEEz"	pence	chicken feed
nark it	"nAW kit"	stop talking	shuddup
napper	"nEHpER"	head	beezer
old china	"AOWl' tchOInER"	old dear	old boy

peeper	"puhEEpER"	an eye	lamp
peck	"pEHk"	food	grub
perisher	"pEHrishER"	unpleasant person	dope
plosh	"plAWsh"	money	dough
rhino	"rOInAOW"	money	dough
ruck on	"rAH kAWn"	betray	squeal
snitch	"snitch"	nose	shnozzle
swiz	"swiz"	swindle	con
tea leaf	"tuhEE luhEEf"	effeminate	queer
the ready	"TH' rEHdi"	money	dough
trotters	"trAWtERz"	feet	dogs
wallop	"wAWluhp"	beer	suds

NOTE: Too much slang, like too much dialect, can make a dialect too thick and incomprehensible. Slang must be used very sparingly. The average American does not understand its meaning unless its relation to the context is obvious.

AN ORIGINAL MONOLOG

(Alf 'iggins has just jumped up on a soap-box in Hyde Park and is giving the crowd what for.)

I ain't one of them there fellows what hollers for things to be done but what waits for Henry to do it. I'm just one of England's millions. I works hard all day, I have fish and chips for supper and a pint of half-and-half at the Georges afterwards. Then I goes home to my old lady and the kids. I listens to the wireless for the football scores because I gets a flutter or two playing the pools. Then I has a bit of jawing with the old lady after the kids has been put to bed. And then I goes to bed myself. That's me!

Like I said, I'm one of England's millions. And I minds me own business, I does. But when someone comes up and he tries to tell me what's what and how I should do this and that and the other thing—well, that's a horse of another color, like they say—and I ain't going to take it—no, sir! you bloody well know I ain't. I got me rights, I have. And strike me pink if I don't stand up for them. And, what's more I'll fight any man what says I can't. Me old Dad, and his Dad before him, they was quite peaceful too. They was told they was only dirt, too. But they ups and fights and there was a lot of blood losted by them. But they winned their fights for me. And I'm going to fight just as hard to keep them there rights, I am. Perhaps I'll go down fighting—who knows? But if I does, me kids'll know that. And when the time comes for them to fight for their own rights, why, they'll just up and fight for theirselves, too, and no mistake!

PHONETIC PRESENTATION

(Syllables in bold-face type are to be accented.)

"OI   yI:nt   wAH   nuh   **THEHm THEH:'** fEH: .EHlERz"

wAW **tAHlERz** fuh' thinks tuh buhEE **dAHn** bAHt wAWt **wI:ts** fuh rEHnERuhEE tuh diOO wit. OIm jAHs' wAH nAW **vin**gluhnz **mil**yuhmz. OI wERk **zAW** dAW-OOl **dI:,** yOI yEHv **fi** shuhn **tch**ips fuh **sAHpER** ruh nuh pOIn tuh **vAW** fuh **nAW** fuht THuh **jAW**ji **zAW**ftuhwuhz. THEH nOI gAOW zAOWm tuh muhEE yAOW **lI:**di yuhn' THuh kidz. OI lisuhnz tuh THuh **wOI**yERluhs fuh THuh **foo**/bAWOOl skAWz kAW zOI git zuh **flAH**tER rEHt THuh **piOO**lz. THEH nOI yEH zuh bi tuh **jAW**rin' wi THuh yAOW **lI:**di yAHtER THuh kid zEHz bin poo tuh bEHd. EHn THEH nOI gAOWz tuh bEHd muh**sEH-**OOf. **THEH**ts **muhEE!** lOI kOI **sEH** dOIm **wAH** nuh **vin**gluhnz **mil**yuhmz. EH nOI **mOI**nz muhEE **yAOW**n **biz**nuh sOI dAHz. bAHt wEHn **sAH**mwAHn kAHm **zAH** pEH nuhEE **trOI**z tuh tEH-OOl **muhEE wAW**ts **wAW** tuh **nAH** wOI shoo diOO **THi** suhn **THEH** tuhn THuhEE **yAH**THER think—**wEH-**OO', **THEH** tsUH nAW suh vuhn**AH**THER **kAH**lER, lOIk THI: sI:—EH nOI **yI:**nt **gAOW**in' tuh **tI:** kit—**nAOW sER!** yuh **blAH**di wEH-OO **nAOW** wOI yI:nt. OI gAWt muh rOI tsOI yEHv. EHn **strOIK muhEE pin** ki fOI dAOWn stEHn dAHp fuh THEHm. EHn, **wAW**ts **mAW** rOI-OOl fOI **tEH**ni **mEH**n wAWt sEH zOI **kAH**nt. muhEE yAOWl **dEH** duh **niz** dEH duh**fAW** rim, **THI:** wAWz kwOIt puhEEsfOO' **tiOO. THI:** wAWz tAOWl' **THI:** wAW zAOwn'i dER **tiOO.** bAHt THI: **yAHp** zuhn **fOI** tsEHn THEH wAW zuh **lAW** tuhv **blAHD** lAWstid bOI THEHm. bAHt THI: **wind** THEH **rOI**ts fuh **muhEE.** EH **nOIm** gAOWin' tuh fOIt **jAH** stEH **zAW**d tuh **kuhEE**p THEHm THEH rOI tsOI yEHm. prEHp zOI-OO' gAOW **dAHn fOI**tin'—iOO nAOWz? bAH ti fOI **dOIz** muhEE kidz'l **nAOW** THEHt. EHn wEHn THuh tOIm kAHmz fuh **THEHm** tuh fOIt fuh THEH **rAOWn** rOIts, wOI, THI:OOl jAHs **tAH** pEHn **fOIt** fuh **THEH's**EH-OO'vz **tiOO,** EHn' **nAOW** mistI:k!

CHAPTER THREE

The British Dialect

THE LILT

The British tonal pitch is much higher than the American. Because of this he begins his sentences almost a full octave higher than we ordinarily do. Then, instead of adhering regularly to a limited range around the keynote, as in American, he ranges considerably. Sometimes he reaches what, to us, might be a falsetto and then, almost in the next note, he drops a full octave. It is this wide range that also differentiates the British speech from the American.

In the sentence, "AH' yi-OO gEHOOing hEH-OOm?" (Are you going home?), the Britisher would begin about a full octave higher than the American keynote and say:

There are three definite beats in this sentence. The first is "AH'" (are), the second, "gEH-OO" (go) and the last beat is on the first part of "home" (hEH). This last word (home) by changing pitch takes the word from the lowest note in the sentence to the highest.

Naturally, not all British sentences turn upward at the end. There is, however, a definite rising and falling throughout their speech. For example, take the sentence, "I've got the feeling you don't like me." It would be spoken:

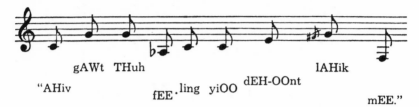

gAWt THuh   lAHik
"AHiv   fEE·ling yiOO dEH-OOnt
                                                    mEE."

The dialect attack of Roland Young, in particular, with his careful, almost inarticulate groping for words, might be explained by the fact that a great many Englishmen suffer from stammering. King George is an example. Arnold Bennett is still another, and Somerset Maugham is similarly afflicted. The most effective method of overcoming this speech impediment is to teach the sufferer to speak slowly and carefully, making certain that he knows exactly what he is going to say before he says it. Perhaps such training is the reason that so many Englishmen speak with such hesitancy. True or not, they do speak deliberately, and it is this word groping that affects the rhythm and emphasis.

Of course, not all Britishers stammer or grope for words. Their attack is usually calm and deliberate and their emphasis is energetic, positive and intense.

EMPHASIS

Generally, the British stress the first syllable of the word as "vEHdi" (very), "sEHkruht'ri" (secretary), and "AWd'n'ri" (ordinary). There is no hard and fast rule which can be given, but words of four syllables or less which end in "y" (pronounced "i") get the first syllable accent.

In the word "ikstrAWd'n'ri" (extraordinary), the stress is on the "AW" (or) of "ordinary." Although this word is actually six syllables, it is made up of two words, "extra" and "ordinary" and as the second word is of more importance, it carries the stress.

In sentence-stress, the word which usually receives the highest or the lowest note is emphasized. This may suggest that the emphasis is tonal, rather than a breathed stress, but actually this is not so. It is only because the word-stress coincides with the tonal emphasis.

VOWEL CHANGES

"AY" .... as in "take," "break," "they," etc.

This long "a" sound becomes "EH-EE" in British. The "EH" receives slightly more stress than the "EE" which should not be pronounced fully. When the long "a" sound is final, as in "mAHndi" (Monday), it changes to short "i."

DRILL WORDS

tEH-EEk	(take)	stEH-EEt	(state)
brEH-EEk	(break)	fEH-EEt	(fate)
THEH-EE	(they)	mEH-EEd	(made)

stEH-EE	(stay)
dEH-EE	(day)
sAHndi	(Sunday)

NOTE: The (-) should not be interpreted as a pause. It is merely added to break up the vowels for simplification.

"UH" .... as in "alone," "sofa," "finally," etc.

This "a" always occurs in unaccented syllables, and when pronounced, the Britisher makes it "uh." This "uh" sound is extremely short and is often dropped when initial or between two consonants. Although vowel changes have been written in capitals to make them more outstanding, this sound will be shown in lower case letters to indicate its brevity.

DRILL WORDS

uhlEH-OOn	(alone)	uhbiliti	(ability)
sEH-OOfuh	(sofa)	uhbAHv	(above)
fAHin'li	(finally)	b'nAHnuh	(banana)

uhbAWd	(aboard)
mEHd'm	(madam)
muhlishuhs	(malicious)

"AH" .... as in "father," "arm," "park," etc.

In the British dialect, the pronunciation of this "AH" is closer to the "o" in the American word "rod." This sound will be represented as "AH:" with the colon (:) indicating elongation. It will be noticed that the greatest change in the following drill words is the deletion of the "r" sound.

DRILL WORDS

fAH:THER	(father)	dAH:'ling	(darling)
AH:'m	(arm)	kAH:'v	(carve)
pAH:'k	(park)	rigAH:'d	(regard)

hAH:'mluhs	(harmless)
AH:'mi	(army)
stAH:'t	(start)

"A:" .... as in "ask," "draft," "laugh," etc.

The usual pronunciation of this "a," for Britishers as well as for some Americans, is "AH:" This "AH:" is used before "f," "ff," "ft," "nce," "nch," "nt," "sk," "sp," "ss," "st," "th," and "TH." The word "laugh" is spelled with a "gh" but it is pronounced as "f" so that the word would be pronounced "lAH:f" (laugh). When "nd" occurs in a word of two syllables or more and is medial or final in that word, the preceding "a" is pronounced "AH:," as in "kuhmAH:nd" (command). The word "and" is pronounced either as "EHnd" or "And."

The combination "nce" in the above list refers to words like "dAH:ns" (dance), "tchAH:ns" (chance) and "glAH:ns" (glance), and not to words ending in "ncy" like "fEHnsi" (fancy) which may also be pronounced "fAnsi," as in American, but never "fAH:nsi" (fancy).

DRILL WORDS

AH:sk	(ask)	bAH:skuht	(basket)
drAH:ft	(draft)	mAH:stER	(master)
stAH:f	(staff)	kAH:nt	(can't)

rAH:THER	(rather)
pAH:styER	(pasture)
pAH:th	(path)

"A" .... as in "bad," "am," "sand," etc.

In the preceding discussion on the "A:" as in "ask," certain consonants were given which govern the pronunciation of the preceding "**a**" and make it "AH:." Consonants other than those mentioned cause the preceding "a" to be pronounced "EH." Although "nd" was included in words of two or more syllables to take "AH:," when "nd" is used in a one syllable word, it makes the preceding "**a**" sound as "EH," as in "EHnd" (and). The "ncy" combination also is preceded by "EH."

If a lighter dialect is required, or if the Britisher has lived in America a considerable length of time and has adopted certain American sounds of speech, the normal short "a" (A) may be used for these words. As a matter of fact, a number of Englishmen prefer it before "f," "n," "s," "ss," "st," "sk," "sp," and "ncy," although in other short "a" words they will use "EH."

The vowel changes to be used must be decided by the actor and based on the character to be portrayed. To avoid confusion "EH" will be used for the short "a" throughout.

DRILL WORDS

pEHtsh	(patch)	bEHd	(bad)
pEHshuhn	(passion)	EHm	(am)
nEHdEH-OO	(narrow)	sEHnd	(sand)

mEHnER	(manner)
grEHjiOOEH-EEt	(graduate)
sEHpling	(sapling)

"AW" .... as in "ball," "falter," "shawl," etc.

This sound may receive the same treatment in the British dialect as in the American. However, if used, it must be a narrower sound than the American "AW." It is suggested that words like "caught," "water," and "taught" be used for practice. The "l" after this "AW" sound, as in "ball," tends to color it and may give the wrong impression as to its actual sound. The "O" sound of "rod" may also be used, as in "skwOsh" (squash), "kwOliti" (quality), and "dOg" (dog).

The following general rules should be observed for the use of the "AW" sound. The "AW" sound of "a" is pronounced as "AW" when it is:

1. followed by "u" or "w" or,
2. followed by final "l" or,
3. followed by "l" and a consonant or,
4. preceded by "w" and followed by "r" plus a consonant.

Examples of these rules are:

AWt'm	(Autumn)	bAWld	(bald)
lAW	(law)	wAW'm	(warm)
uhpAWl	(appal)	fAWl	(fall)

When "a" follows "w" and is, in turn, followed by any consonant (except "g," "k," or "ing") it is usually pronounced as "O" (this is the "o" of "rod"), although the lips are in position for "AW," as in "kwAWliti (quality), "skwAWsh" (squash), and "wAWt" (what).

This tense "AW" sound is made with the mouth almost in position for "OH" but "AW" is sounded. The variant "O" sound of "rod" will also be written as "AW" since the mouth is in position for "AW" while "O" is sounded.

For the "AW" sound of "o" see under "AW" as in "off."

"EE" . . . . as in "he," "treat," "people," etc.

In short words, medially and finally, this long "EE" sound remains the same. That is, as in "trEEt" (treat), "pEEp'l" (people), "hEE" (he), and "shEE" (she). An exception is "nAHiTHER" (neither), although some Britishers do pronounce it as "nEETHER."

"EE" . . . . as in "remain," "return," "refuse," etc.

In a prefix, the long "EE" sound changes to short "i," as in "r*i*mEH-EEn" (remain), "r*i*tERn" (return), and "r*i*fyiOOz" (refuse).

"EE" . . . . as in "evoke," "elect," "emerge," etc.

When used initially, before a consonant, "e" becomes short "i," as in "ivEH-OOk" (evoke), "ilEHkt" (elect), and "imERj" (emerge).

"EE" . . . . as in "east," "each," "eager," etc.

When initial "ea" is normally pronounced "EE" and is not followed by "r" it retains the long "e" (EE) pronunciation, as in "EEst" (east), "EEtch" (each), and "EEgER" (eager).

"EE" . . . . as in "ear," "leer," "hear," etc.

When the long "e" (EE) sound precedes "r," it is changed to short "i." If the "r" is final, it is dropped and replaced by the "ER" sound. (This is discussed under "R" in "Consonant Changes.") Thus, "iER" (ear), "liER" (leer), and "hiER" (here). The "r" is retained, however, if it is followed by another vowel sound, but the preceding "i" for "EE" remains the same, as "*i*dEH-EEk" (ear-ache).

"EE" . . . . as in "silly," "bevy," "money," etc.

When "y" is used finally to replace the "EE" sound, it takes short "i," as in "sil*i*" (silly), "bEHv*i*" (bevy) and "mAHn*i*" (money).

"EH".... as in "bet," "said," "friend," etc.

This short "e" receives its usual "EH" sound. In the words "again" or "against" it may receive the long "a" (AY) treatment as, "uhgAYn" or "uhgAYnst." If short "e" is used in a prefix which is unstressed it becomes "i," as in "iksplEHEEn" (explain) but "EHkspluhnEHEEsh'n" (explanation).

"I".... as in "ice," "aisle," "guile," etc.

If the character to be portrayed is a snob with little or no cultural background, who is trying to affect the speech of his social superiors, change the long "I" to "EH-EE" in words which use "i" to represent the long "I" sound. that is, "I," "ice," and "nice," as spoken by such a person, would become "EH-EE," "EH-EEs," and "nEH-EEs." But other long "I" words which use various other spellings as "aisle" (AHil) and "guile" (gAHil), should take the regular British pronunciation "AHi." Most Britishers, except the type mentioned above, use the "AHi" for all long "I" sounds, no matter what the spelling.

Do not make this sound "AHyi" as that will give it the Cockney flavor, but neither the British nor the Cockney pronunciation. It is simply the "AH" sound of the American word "father" with the short "i" of "sit" which should not be stressed but merely suggested.

When a word ends in "r" preceded by long "i" (AHi), only the "AH" need be used which is elongated to make up for the dropped "r" and becomes "AH:." However, it is also correct to use "AHi," as in "FAHiER" or "FAH:" (fire).

DRILL WORDS

AHis	(ice)	nAHit	(night)
AHil	(aisle)	tAHidi	(tidy)
gAHil	(guile)	kwAHit	(quite)
kwAHiEHt	(quiet)		
rAHitchuhs	(righteous)		
kwAH:	(choir)		

"i".... as in "it," "women," "busy," etc.

This short "i" is the same as it is in American. It is very short in duration when used medially.

"O".... as in "on," "bond," "John," etc.

The Britisher often gives this an "AW" sound which must be narrow and brisk in treatment. In an unaccented syllable it is dropped, as in "kAH:b'n" (carbon). This sound must not be confused with the "AW" of "ball." In the "AW" of "ball" the lips are pursed as for the American "OH" sound, but "AW" is pronounced. In words using short "o," the mouth is shaped for "AW" but "O" is sounded.

DRILL WORDS

AWn	(on)	tAWnik	(tonic)
bAWnd	(bond)	rAWb	(rob)
jAWn	(John)	tAWp	(top)

> shAWt . (shot)
>
> lAWt   (lot)
>
> k'nkliOOd   (conclude)

"OH" .... as in "bone," "sew," "dough," etc.

When broken down, this "OH" sound is actually "OH-OO." The Britisher prefixes an "EH" sound, drops the "OH" and retains "OO," making the sound "EH-OO," as in "sEH-OO" (so). Many Britishers retain the American "OH-OO" but "EH-OO" is preferred.

DRILL WORDS

bEH-OOn	(bone)	rEH-OOd	(road)
sEH-OO	(sew)	tEH-OOld	(told)
dEH-OO	(dough)	uhlEH-OOn	(alone)

grEH-OOn	(grown)
stEH-OOn	(stone)
hEG-OOm	(home)

"AW" .... as in "off," "cough," "water," etc.

This "AW" sound remains the same, but it should be narrower and shorter in duration than the American "AW."

See the pronounciation of "O" as in "on." This sound is generally given to all short "o's," as in "gAWn" (gone), "klAWth" (cloth), and "AWn" (on). Remember, in this sound the mouth is shaped for "AW" but "O" is sounded. The normal American "AW" sound may also be used.

The Britisher often makes this "AW" sound with his lips pursed as for "OH." He often uses this variation when:

1. "o" is followed by final "r" or,
2. "o" is followed by "r" and a consonant or,
3. "o" is followed by "f," "s," or "th."

"OO" .... as in "food," "do," "blue," etc.

In British, a short "i" is prefixed to the long double "OO" making the combination "iOO" as in "fiOOd" (food). Although the same representation is given for this sound in the Cockney, there the "i" of "iOO" has greater stress. But, in British, the "i" is very short and the "OO" is stressed.

DRILL WORDS

fiOOd	(food)	fiOOlish	(foolish)
diOO	(do)	tchiOOz	(choose)
bliOO	(blue)	stiOOp	(stoop)

griOOp	(group)
giOOs	(goose)
miOOn	(moon)

Note: There are certain general rules which may be applied to the Britisher's use of the "y" glide before the "OO" sound, as in "dyiOOti" (duty). In American, this word would usually be pronounced as "dOOtEE." In the British dialect, the following rules for adding the consonantal "y" glide are to be observed:

1. *ALL WORDS SPELLED WITH "u," "ui," "ue," "eu" OR "ew," WHICH TAKE THE LONG DOUBLE "o" (OO) SOUND, ARE AFFECTED BY THE CONSONANTAL "y" GLIDE, EXCEPT WHEN FOLLOWING "r," "w," AND THE CONSONANT SOUNDS "j" AND "tch."*

Following this rule then, words like "food," "doom," or "loot" are not affected by the consonantal "y" glide because, although they are pronounced as long "OO," they are not spelled with "u," "ui," "ue," "eu" or "ew."

Again, words like "prude," "quick," "June," or "chew" do not take the "y" glide and are pronounced as "priOOd," "kwik," "jiOOn," and "tchiOO." The "y" is not used in these words because the consonants preceding the "OO" sounds do not take it, as was stated in Rule 1.

Thus it can be seen why certain long "OO" words in American add the consonantal "y" sound in British, as in "tyiOOn" (tune), "dyiOO" (due), "nyiOO" (new), "nyiOOd" (nude) or "styiOOpid" (stupid).

2. *WHEN "l" IS PRECEDED BY A STRESSED VOWEL AND IS FOLLOWED BY "u," "ui," "ue," "eu" OR "ew," IT IS AFFECTED BY THE CONSONANTAL "y."*

This rule is observed in words like "vEHlyiOO" (value) and "vAWlyiOOm" (volume). However, when "l" is preceded by a consonant, it is not affected by the "y," as in "gliOO" (glue) and "bliOO" (blew).

Initial "l" and "s," "z," and "th" may or may not add this "y." Either form is correct.

"oo" . . . . as in "good," "wolf," "full," etc.

This sound is the same as in American, but it must be projected forward in the mouth. This tends to give it the flavor of the "OO" in the American word "food." Pronouncing "good" as "gOOd" would give it all flavor and no substance. Therefore, this "oo" must be the same as in American: it must be projected and it must not be "OO."

"yOO" . . . . as in "unit," "cube," "beauty," etc.

The "OO" of "yOO" is the same sound as in "food" which in American is "fOOd." The "OO" of "food" becomes "iOO" in British and this applies also to the "OO" of "yOO" which becomes "yiOO." Refer to the note under "OO" as in "food."

DRILL WORDS

yiOOnit	(unit)	myiOOt	(mute)
kyiOOb	(cube)	vyiOO	(view)
byiOOti	(beauty)	fyiOOtAHil	(futile)

tyiOOn   (tune)
yiOOz   (use)
dyiOOti (duty)

"U" .... as in "up," "love," "does," etc.

The American short "u" (U) sound becomes "AH" in British. No matter what the actual spelling of the word, if the vowel sound is short "u," then "AH" is substituted. A variant retains the American sound of "U," as in "hUri" (hurry), "lUnd'n" (London), and "mUndi" (Monday).

DRILL WORDS

AHp	(up)	lAHvli	(lovely)
lAHv	(love)	lAHgij	(luggage)
dAHz	(does)	dAHst	(dust)

kAHntri   (country)
AHnstEHdi (unsteady)
blAHnt   (blunt)

"ER" .... as in "curb," "earn," "fern," etc.

This "ER" sound, no matter what the spelling, remains the same. The "r" following this sound is sometimes dropped, sometimes pronounced as "d," and sometimes spoken as in American, but this in no way changes the vowel sound of "ER." (The "r" is fully discussed under "Consonant Changes.") This sound will be written as "ER" to show that the "r" is dropped, as in "kERb" (curb). If the "r" should be sounded, as in the word "courage," the representation will be "ERd" and the word will be written "kERdij."

DRILL WORDS

ERn	(earn)	wERth	(worth)
fERn	(fern)	bERth	(birth)
ERb	(herb)	distERb	(disturb)

pERpuhl   (purple)
kERt   (curt)
stERding (stirring)

"OW" .... as in "out," "cow," "house," etc.

There are two possible pronunciations of this "OW" sound. One pronunciation is "EH-OO," as in "EH-OOt" (out), "kEH-OO" (cow) and "hEH-OOs" (house). This is the same sound that is given to the long "OH" of "bone" in the British dialect. The other pronunciation, the preferred one, is "AH:." The colon (:) indicates elongation.

DRILL WORDS

AH:t	(out)	kAH:nt	(count)
kAH:	(cow)	stAH:t	(stout)
hAH:s	(house)	dAH:n	(down)

flAH:ERz   (flowers)
AH:ER   (our)
hAH:EHvER   (however)

"OI" .... as in "oil," "boy," "noise," etc.

When broken down, the "OI" representation becomes "AW-EE" in American. The Britisher retains the "AW" and changes "EE" to a very short "i," making the combination "AWi." The "i" must not be sounded alone, but must be blended as part of the "AW."

DRILL WORDS

AWil   (oil)   pAWiz   (poise)
bAWi   (boy)   tchAWis   (choice)
nAWiz   (noise)   injAWi   (enjoy)

fAWil   (foil)
brAWil   (broil)
rikAWil   (recoil)

WORD EXERCISES

Pronounce the following words in the British dialect using the material learned from the preceding Vowel Changes:

1.	martyr	11.	bondholder
2.	photogenic	12.	stonemason
3.	yearbook	13.	procrastinate
4.	taskmaster	14.	market basket
5.	tuneful	15.	daybreak
6.	flabbergasted	16.	fancy
7.	clergyman	17.	moonlight
8.	downtown	18.	unlovely
9.	embroidered	19.	gas burner
10.	quietly	20.	firearm

When you have tried to pronounce all the above words, refer to the list given below for the correct pronunciation. Check the vowel sounds that were incorrectly sounded. Then repeat the corrected version a number of times until it has been completely memorized.

1.	mAH:tER	11.	bAWndhEH-OOldER
2.	fEH-OOtEH-OOjEHnik	12.	stEH-OOnmEH-EEsuhn
3.	yi:book	13.	prEH-OOkrAH:stinEH-EEt
4.	tAH:skmAH:stER	14.	mAH:kuhtbAH:skuht
5.	tyiOOnfool	15.	dEH-EEbrEH-EEk
6.	flEHbERgAH:stuhd	16.	fAnsi or fEHnsi
7.	klERjimuhn	17.	miOOnlAHit
8.	dAH:ntAH:n	18.	AHnlAHvli
9.	imbrAWidERd	19.	gEHsbERnER
10.	kwAH:tli	20.	fAH:rAH:m

CONSONANT CHANGES

B and **C**—The same as in American.

D—The same as in American when used initially, or finally. Medially, the "d" is often dropped after "n" as, "kAHin'li" (kindly), "fAWn'uhs" (fondness), "frEHn'li" (friendly). However, if the "d" is preceded by "n" and followed by a voiced vowel, or if medial "d" is between two vowels, it is pronounced, as "kEHn-dE*R*" (candor) and "mAWdE*R*n" (modern). Occasionally, a Britisher gives it the sound of "j" as in "jiOOk" (duke), "trimEHnjAHs" (tremendous) and grE-HjiOOuhl" (gradual).

F—When medial "f" is spelled with a "ph" and sounded as "f" in American, it becomes "v" in British, as "nEHvyiOO" (nephew) and "nEHvthah" (naphtha).

G—The same as in American.

H—The same as in American. In a "wh" combination, however, speakers in southern England drop the "h," as in "witch" (which), while those in northern England sound the "h" before the "w," as in "h-witch" (which).

J and **K**—The same as in American.

L—The same as in American. Sometimes, when "l" is in an unaccented position and is preceded by a vowel and followed by a consonant, it is dropped, as "foo'fil" (fulfill).

M, N, P, and **Q**—The same as in American.

R—The most distinctive consonant in the British dialect is "r." It is sometimes voiced, as in American, with the tip of the tongue pointed toward the upper teeth, but not touching them; it is occasionally slightly trilled or flapped so that the sound approximates "d"; in other cases it is dropped. The rules governing the changes of this consonant are:

> *1. DROP "R" WHEN IT IS PRECEDED BY A VOWEL AND FOL-LOWED BY A CONSONANT OR WHEN IT IS THE FINAL SOUND IN A WORD.*

Examples of this rule are: "pAH:'k" (park), "AH:'" (are), "bAW:'" (bore), "hE*R*t" (hurt), "fAH:'" (fire) and "kwAH:'" (choir).

> *2. GIVE "R" A SLIGHT TRILL WHICH APPROXIMATES THE SOUND OF "D" WHEN IT IS BETWEEN TWO VOWELS.*

Actually "d" is not substituted for "r," but the sound is so similar that "d" has been used to represent this slightly trilled "r" so as to differentiate it from the normally voiced "r." Hard "d" should never be sounded. Nor should the "r" be strongly trilled. There is more of a short flap to the "r" than an actual trill. Pronounce it just behind the upper teeth. Examples of this rule are "vEHdi" (very), "tEHdib'l" (terrible) and "kEHdi" (carry).

3. INITIAL "R," OR "R" PRECEDED BY A CONSONANT AND FOL-LOWED BY A VOWEL, RECEIVES THE NORMALLY VOICED "R" AS USED BY AMERICANS.

Some examples of this rule are: "rEEd" (read), "trip" (trip), "rEH-OOz" (rose), "pAWltri" (paltry), and "jEHntri" (gentry).

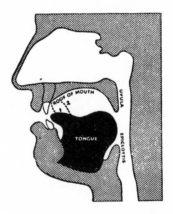

At the start of sounding the British flapped "r," the tongue is in the position of the black area. The sound is formed by the tongue's moving rapidly to the position of the dotted line. This movement is flapped but *once*, in contrast to the trilled "r" of the Scottish dialect.

4. FINAL "R" MUST BE SOUNDED IF THE FOLLOWING WORD BEGINS WITH A VOWEL.

Under Rule 1, above, it will be noticed that "fire" is pronounced "fAH:." But if "fire" is followed by an initial-vowel word, it will be pronounced "fAH:r," as in "fAH:*r* iz AH:t" (fire is out).

S—The same as in American words which receive the hard "s" sound. See "SH" for words which are spelled with an "s" and pronounced "sh."

T—The same as in American when used initially, finally, or between two vowels. However, if "t" is used before a "yOO" sound (yiOO in British), it may remain a clear "t" sound or become "tch" as it often does in American. This combination also changes the following vowel sound from "yiOO" to "yER." Example words are "nEH-EEtyER" (nature), "pAHstyER" (pasture), "lit'ruhtyER" (literature).

Only if the "yiOO" vowel sound is final in the word does it remain the same, as "vERtyiOO" (virtue).

V, W, X, Y, and **Z**—The same as in American.

SH—When spelled "sh" this sound remains the same. However, words which are spelled with "c," "s," or "ss" and pronounced as "sh" in American, sometimes take a clear, hissed "s" sound in British. Examples are "tisyiOO" (tissue), "sEHn-syiOO-uhl" (sensual), "pinsERz" (pincers).

SYLLABLE OMISSIONS AND CHANGES

The British dialect is noted for its elision of syllables which receive secondary stress, as in "lAHibr'i" (library), "bAH:ndr'i" (boundary), "sEHkruhtr'i" (secretary) and "fAHin'li" (finally).

Because of this habit of slurring unimportant vowel sounds, the suffix "age" often becomes "ij," as "mEHdij" (marriage), "kEHdij" (carriage) and "frAHntij" (frontage).

The suffix "ion" is either "uhn" or "'n" as in "pAW'sh'n" (portion) and "lEH-OOshuhn" (lotion).

When the "ate" ending is unstressed, as it is in many nouns and adjectives, it is pronounced as "it," as in "intimit" (intimate). However, when the "ate" ending is used with a verb, it is pronounced as "EH-EEt," as in "intimEH-EEt" (intimate).

WORD EXERCISES

Pronounce the following words in the British dialect using the material learned from the preceding Consonant Changes and Syllable Omissions:

1.	burglarized	11.	roarer
2.	friendliness	12.	fireplug
3.	pasteurize	13.	when
4.	intimate	14.	tissue paper
5.	nephrew	15.	secretary
6.	American	16.	glamorous
7.	ageless	17.	pincers
8.	marriage	18.	wire arm
9.	choir-chair	19.	fascinate
10.	fulfillment	20.	passionate

When you have tried to pronounce all the preceding words, refer to the list given below for the correct pronunciation. Check the consonant sounds that were incorrectly pronounced. Then repeat the corrected version until it has been memorized.

1.	bERglER-AHizd	11.	rAWrER
2.	frEHn'linEHs	12.	fAH: plAHg
3.	pAH:styER-AHiz	13.	wEHn or h-wEHn
4.	intimit or intimEH-EEt	14.	tisyiOOpEH-EEpER
5.	nEHvyiOO	15.	sEHkruht'ri
6.	uhmEHdikuhn	16.	glEHm'ruhs
7.	EH-EEjluhs	17.	pinsERz
8.	mEHdij	18.	wAH:r AH:m
9.	kwAH:tchEH:	19.	fEHsinEH-EEt
10.	foo'film'nt	20.	pEHshuhnuht

GRAMMAR CHANGES

The educated Britisher is usually very careful about his grammar. Therefore, it is difficult to find solecisms that could be used to identify the dialect. However, this precise handling of the grammar makes for a sort of dialect distinction. For example, the Britisher is most sedulous about the correct use of "shall" and "will" and he rarely allows himself to err in their use.

He is consistent in the use of the pronoun "one," almost to the point of absurdity. When this pronoun has been used in a sentence, he will carry it throughout the entire sentence, rather than change it to "he" or "she." An example of this is the sentence, "bAHt if wAHn wER tiOO trAHi it, wAHn wood fAHind THEHt wAHn kood nAWt uhsyiOOm wAHnz rispAWnsibilitiz wiTHAH:t uhsyiOOming wAHnz trAHblz EHz wEHl, kood wAHn?" (But if one were to try it, one would find that one could not assume one's responsibilities without assuming one's troubles as well, could one?)

The word "kwAHit" (quite) is often used in place of "very," "entirely," "positively," "wholly," "absolutely," or "completely" something-or-other, as in "shEE iz kwAHit tchAH:'ming" (she is quite charming). This substitution of "quite" for other more explicit words is gradually being adopted by some Americans. But the Britisher still leads in its use and abuse.

There is a mistaken belief that the Britisher is addicted to the use of the word "gotten," as "wEE'v jAHst gAWt'n bEHk" (We've just gotten back). As a matter of fact, he is very careful to say "wEE'v jAHst gAWt bEHk" (We've just got back). The British dialect student should remember that the use of "gotten" is very rare.

In England, a person's attention is attracted by shouting "AHi sEH-EE" (I say), rather than the American "Hey!" or "Hey, you!" And a leave-taking is not accompanied by "goodbye," but by "good AH:ftERniOOn" (good afternoon) or "good dEH-EE" (good day).

One of the most noticeable differences between American and British speech lies in the choice of words. Following is a list of word variances which should be used. American expressions have a peculiar way of falsifying and negating whatever other good qualities a British dialect may have. Naturally, if the Britisher has been in America a considerable length of time, the British words will slowly give way to their American counterparts.

AMERICAN	BRITISH	PHONETIC REPRESENTATION
alcohol	spirits	spidits
apartment	flat	flEHt
automobile	motor car	mEH-OOtER kAH:
baby carriage	pram	prEHm
baggage	luggage	lAHgij
bathtub	bath	bAH:th
beach	seaside	sEEsAHid
bill (money)	banknote	bEHnknEH-OOt
billboard	hoarding	hAWding
biscuit	scone	skEH-OOn
broiled	grilled	grild
candy	sweets	swEEts
clerk	clark	klAH:k
cookie	biscuit	biskuht
derby	bowler	bEH-OOlER
drugstore	chemist's	kEHmists
elevator	lift	lift
first floor	first storey	fERs' stAWdi
fruit store	fruiterer	friOOtERER
gasoline	petrol	pEHtr'l
grade school	standard	stEHnduhd
guy	fellow	fEHlEH-OO
highball	whiskey and soda	hwiski 'n sEH-OOduh
intermission	interval	intERv'l
janitor	caretaker	kEH:tEH-EEkER
lawyer	solicitor	suhlisitER
lieutenant	lieutenant (navy)	liOOtEHnuhnt
lieutenant	leftenant (army)	leHftEHnuhnt
lunchroom	snack-bar	snEHk-bAH:'
mail	post	pEH-OOst
mailman	postman	pEH-OOstm'n
minister	clergyman	klERjimuhn
movie	cinema	sinuhmuh
necktie	tie	tAHi
package	parcel	pAH:s'l
perfume	scent	sEHnt
pitcher	jug	jAHg
policeman	bobby	bAWbi
race track	race course	rEH-EEs kAWs
radio	wireless	wAH:'luhs
raincoat	waterproof	wAWtERpriOOf
roadster	two-seater	tiOO-sEEtER
roomer	lodger	lAWjER
saloon	pub	pAHb
shoe	boot	biOOt
sidewalk	pavement	pEH-EEvmuhnt

AMERICAN	BRITISH	PHONETIC REPRESENTATION
streetcar	tram	trEHm
suspenders	braces	brEH-EEsuhz
swim	bath	bAH:th
vacation	holiday	hAWlidi
vaudeville	variety	v'rAHiEHti
vaudeville house	music hall	myiOOzik hAWl
window shade	blind	blAHind

The word "jAWli" (jolly) is used often, as in "THEHts jAWli good!" (That's jolly good!), "hEEz jAWli wEHl rAHit!" (He's jolly well right!), and "wEE hEHd uh jAWli good tAHim!" (We had a jolly good time!). "jAWli" may also be pronounced as "jOli" using the "O" sound of the American word "rod." See "O" as in "on."

SENTENCE EXERCISES

Pronounce the following sentences in the British dialect and substitute the correct British word for the American misused words:

1. I saw the mailman at a movie.
2. After her swim the roomer used some perfume.
3. I had no gas so I took a trolley.
4. The minister had his necktie in a package.
5. He took off his raincoat and went into the saloon.
6. The policeman trod the sidewalk at the beach.
7. The janitor fixed the shade on the first floor.
8. I heard the vaudeville actor on the radio.
9. Stop in at the lunchroom for a cookie.
10. I bought shoes and suspenders and mailed them.

When you have made the substitutions, consult the following list of correct British usage. Check the mistakes, correct them and repeat the corrected forms until they are learned thoroughly.

1. AHi sAW THUH pEH-OOstmuhn EHt THuh sinuhmuh.
2. AHftER hER bAH:th, THUH lAWjER yiOOzd sAHm sEHnt.
3. AHi hEHd nEH-OO pEHtr'l sEH-OO AHi took UH trEHm.
4. THUH klERjimuhn hEHd hiz tAHi in UH pAH:s'l.
5. hEE took AWf hiz wAWtERpriOOf EHnd EHntERd THUH pAHb.
6. THUH bAWbi trAWd THUH pEH-EEvmuhnt EHt THUH sEEsAHid.
7. THUH kEH:tEH-EEkER uhjAHstuhd THUH blAHind in THUH fERst stAWdi.
8. AHi hERd THUH v'rAHiEHti stAH:r AWn THUH wAH:luhs.
9. stAWp in EHt THUH snEHkbAH: fAWr UH biskuht.
10. AHi pERtchuhst biOOts EHnd brEH-EEsuhz EHnd pEHOOstuhd THUHm.

BRITISH MONOLOG

"LONDON"

(Adapted from the authors' NBC serial "Woman Of The Shadows")

London is not a place. It's not a city. It's nothing one can lay one's hands on to touch. No! London is something that is...well... it's a feeling. It's an emotion, if you know what I mean. It's an extraordinary experience that takes hold of one's imagination. It's the sort of feeling one experiences when one goes through the accumulated rubbish in one's loft—the antimacassars of one's maiden Aunt Lisbeth, the smoky photographs of one's grandfather's Eton days, the battered tropical helmet of one's choleric, pukka sahib Uncle Gerald—these and the hundreds of other relics and mementos of the dear dead past. Well—that is what London is to me—a vast, dusty treasure trove of faded memories—memories of Shakespeare drinking sack in the Mermaid Tavern on the Cheapside, memories of Doctor Johnson orating pompously to sly Bozzy over a Cheshire Cheese tidbit, memories of Robin Hood, of good King John, of Queen Bess, of Sir Walter Raleigh, of Dickens nosing through the slums, of Wren's architecture, of . . . oh! of the countless wispy ghosts who people the city yet and who make London the storehouse of the dead who will not die, of the past that will not remain in the past. That is what London is to me—a feeling, an emotion—a living experience.

PHONETIC REPRESENTATION

(Syllables in bold-face type are to be accented.)

"lAHnduhn iz nAWt uh pl·· EH EEs. its nAWt uh si. ti.

its **nAH**thing wAHn kEHn lEH-EE wAHnz **hEH**ndz AWn tiOO **tAH**tch. **nEH-OO!** lAHnduhn iz sAHmthing THEHt ... wEHl ... its uh **fEE**ling. its EHn imEH-**OO**sh'n, if yiOO nEH-OO wAWt AHi mEEn. its EHn ikst**rA**Wd'nri ik-sp**id**EE-EHns THEHt tEH-EEks **hEH**-OOld'v wAHnz imEHjin**EH-EE**sh'n. its THuh **sAW**t'v fEEling wAHn EHksp**id**EE-EHnsuhz hwEHn wAHn gEH-OOz thriOO THEE uhk**yiOO**myiOOlEH-EEt'd **rAH**bish in wAHnz **lAW**ft—THEE AH:ntimuh**kEH**sEℛz AHv wAHnz mEH-EEd'n AHnt **liz**buhth, THuh **smEH**-OOki **fEH**-OOtuh-uhgrAH:fs AHv wAHnz **grEH**nfAHTHEℛz EEtuhn dEH-EEz, THuh **bEH**tEℛd **trAW**pik'l **hEH**lmuht AHv wAHnz kAW**lEH**dik **pOO**kuh

sAH-EEb AHnk'l jEHduhld—THEEz EHnd THuh hAHndrEHdz'v AHTHER
rEHliks EHnd mimEHntEH-OOz AHv THuh diER dEHd pAH:st. wEHl—
THEHT iz hwAHt lAHnduhn iz tiOO mEE—uh vAH:st, dAHsti trEHzhER
trEH-OOv AHv fEH-EEd'd mEHm'rEEz— mEHm'rEEz AHv shEH-EEkspiERz
drinking sEHk in THuh mERmEH-EEd tEHvERn AWn tchEEpsAHid, AHv
dAWktER jAWnsuhn AWdEH-EEting pAWmpuhsli tiOO slAHi bAWzi EH-
OOvER uh tchEHshER tchEEz tidbit, mEHm'rEEz AHv rAWbin hood, AHv
good king jAWn, AHv kwEEn bEHs, AHv sER wAWltER rAWli, AHv dikuhnz
nEH-OOzing thriOO THuh slAHmz, AHv rEHnz AHkitEHktyER, AHv . . . EH-
OO! AHv THuh kAH:ntluhs wispi gEH-OOsts hiOO pEEp'l THuh siti yEHt
EHnd hiOO mEH-EEk lAHnduhn THuh stAW'hAH:s AHv THuh dEHd hiOO
wil nAWt dAHi, AHv THuh pAH:st THEHt wil nAWt rimEH-EEn in THuh
pAH:st. THEHt iz hwAHt lAHnduhn iz tiOO mEE—uh fEEling, EHn imEH-
OOsh'n—EH-EE living ikspidEE-EHns!

AUSTRALIAN SLANG

Because the Australian dialect is either British with a Cockney flavor, or Cockney with a British flavor, the sections on British and Cockney must be studied before an Australian dialect can be determined. These are two entirely different dialects. Either of the two versions may be used with confidence. However, the Australian slang is peculiar to Australia and should be used intelligently throughout.

AUSTRALIAN SLANG	AMERICAN COUNTERPART
"bloody cow!" *An expletive.*	"holy cow!"
"bonzer!" *A superlative.*	"the nuts!"
"bowser"	gasoline pump
"clobber"	clothes
"cobber"	pal
"COO. .**EEEE!**" *A traditional greeting.*	"Hey!"
"cupper"	cup of tea
"dead marine"	empty bottle
"fair dinkum"	"honest injun"
"fillet"	a chunk of steak
"flat out"	up to your ears in work
"g'day dig"	"hi fella"
"good job"	"attaboy"
"good-oh"	"O.K."
"Ham and Beef"	delicatessen
"I'll shout you a drink!"	"I'll buy you a drink!"
"larrikin"	roughneck
"lounge"	living room
"mingy"	stingy
"nark"	disagreeable person
"no fear"	"you bet"
"not a skerek left"	no more to eat
"over the road"	across the street
"pub"	hotel
"quarter to eight"	quarter of eight
"screw"	salary
"Small Goods"	delicatessen

"Smith here" *Used in answering the phone.*	"Smith speaking."
"station"	ranch
"ta"	thanks
"throttle box"	throat
"tinned goods"	canned food
"too right!"	"righto!"
"whacko!"	"terrific!"
"work back"	to return to work
"yakka"	hard work

THE BERMUDA DIALECT

The island of Bermuda in the West Indies is a Crown Colony of the British Empire. Although most of its people are of African ancestry it is governed by Britishers. The result among the native population, as in some of the other islands of the West Indies, as far as the dialect is concerned, is a curious mixture of the broad African American accent, somewhat like the African American and the clipped British accent.

VOWEL CHANGES

SOUND	WORD	CHANGE	DIALECT
AY	take	EH:	tEH:k
UH	sofa	AH	sERfAH
AH	father	O	fOdUHr
A:	ask	AH-EH	AHEHsk
A	bat	EH	bEHt
AW	ball	O	bOl
EE	he	EE	hEE
EH	get	A	gAt
I	nice	UHi	nUHis
i	sit	UH	sUHt
O	on	O	On
OH	bone	ER	bERn
AW	off	O	Of
OO	food	yOO	fyOOd
oo	good	yoo	gyood
yOO	unit	yOO	yOOnUHt
U	up	AH	AHp
ER	curb	UHr	kUHrb
OW	out	A-OO	AOOt
OI	oil	AWi	AWil

NOTE: For the pronunciation of the "ER" sound refer to "ER as in curb" in the British chapter.

CONSONANT CHANGES

These are the important consonant changes:

G—dropped in "ing" participial endings, as in "gE*R*uhn'" (going).

R—rolled considerably.

V—changed to "w," as in "*w*UHis" (vice).

W—changed to "v," as in "*v*UHrld" (world).

Z—changed to "s," as in "hEHs" (has).

TH—changed to "d," as in "dE*R*s" (those).

th—changed to "t," as in "tUHnk" (think).

THE DIALECT OF INDIA

The dialects of the natives of India are replete with British pronunciation because of the presence of so many Englishmen in India and also because of the many Indian people who, when educated, travel to England for their advanced schooling. The number of dialects in India makes it impossible to discuss all of their corresponding American dialects. The following suggestions are made only for the upper class, educated Indian.

VOWEL CHANGES

SOUND	WORD	CHANGE	DIALECT
AY	take	EH	tEHk
UH	alone	AY	AYlAWn
	cotton	AH	kAWtAHn
AH	father	AH	fAHd'r
A:	ask	AH	AHss'
A	bad	EH	bEHd
	animate	AH	AHnEEmEHt
AW	ball	AH	bAHl
EE	he	i	hi
	creed	EE	krEEd
EH	get	EH	gEHt
	democracy	EE	dEEmAWkrAHsi
I	nice	I	nIss
i	sit	EE	ssEEt
O	on	AW	AWn
	bond	OH	bOHnd
OH	bone	AW	bAWn
AW	off	AH	AHf
OO	food	oo	food

oo	good	oo	good
yOO	unit	yoo	yoonEEt
U	up	AH	AHb
ER	curb	UH	kUHb
	fir	AH	fAHr
	fern	EH	fEHrn
	words	oo	woo'ds
	order	'r	AHrd'r
OW	out	OHoo	OHoot
out	AW	AWt	
OI	oil	AHEE	AHEEl
le	ample	ool	AHmpool
el	label	ool	lEHbool
al	animal	AHl	AHnEEmAHl

CONSONANT CHANGES

G—dropped in "ing" endings, as in "ssEEnkEEn'" (sinkin*g*).

J—changed to "tch," as in "EH*tch*" (*age*); changed also to "dy," as in "ssAWl*dy*EHss" (sol*di*ers).

P—pronounced as "b" when final, as in "kEH*b*" (ca*p*).

Q—changed to "k," as in "*k*AWt" (*q*uote).

R—rolled but sometimes unsounded after a vowel as in "pAH'k" (pa*r*k).

S—very sibilant when final. Changed also to "z" between vowels, as in "kroo*z*EHt" (cru*s*ade).

V—pronounced as "vw," as in "*vw*EEm" (*v*im) (see Russian "W"); changed also to "f," as in "fI*f*" (fi*ve*).

W—pronounced as "vw," as in "*vw*EHss'" (*w*est).

Z—changed to "s," as in "hAH*ss*" (ha*s*) and "rEE*s*EHn'" (re*s*ent).

TH—voiced "th" changed to "d" as in "*d*i" (*th*e); changed also to "ss," as in "*ss*AW*ss*" (*th*ose).

th—unvoiced "th" changed to "t," as in "*t*EEnk" (*th*ink); changed also to "ss," as in "ssAHm*ss*EEn'" (some*th*ing).

ZH—changed to "sh," as in "vwEE*sh*'n" (vi*si*on).

There seems to be great uncertainty among the Indians concerning "TH" and "th." A single speaker often uses "d," "ss" and "TH" for "TH" along with "t," "ss" and "th" for "th."

CHAPTER FOUR

The Irish Dialect

THE IRISH LILT

"The lilt of Irish laughter," in the song, can apply to the Irish dialect as well. Much of the quality of the Irish dialect can be attributed to the infectious lilt. This is the direct result of a tendency in the Irish speech to fluctuate—in tone, in stress, and in timbre.

Although the keynote in Irish may be about four notes above that of American, the level is not kept at that note but it takes vowel glides up and down and it sometimes even takes a sharp rise or fall without resorting to a glide vowel.

The glibness of the Irish character, the ability to articulate his thoughts—his gift of gab, in others words—do not make for sharp pauses. Rather, there is a swinging, smoothly-flowing speech-song that dips with a musical glide at one time and then swings sharply upward immediately afterward. The pace is a bit faster than American but this is because of the Irishman's ability to voice his thoughts quickly and easily and also because of his habit of falling back on verbal clichés and other hackneyed expressions.

The fluctuation in tonal range is noticed particularly in the speech-pattern of their question sentences, as in:

> "UHz THAH:t AH:lf bUHrg'n?"
> (Is that Alf Bergen?)

The pattern would start off with the keynote of the opening word, "UHz," about four notes above its American treatment.

Here, it can be seen that the rising and falling notes are carried by the glide vowels. In the following sentence, an abrupt drop, instead of a glide, can be heard.

"dUHd uhEE kUHl UHm, sEHzuhEE"
("Did I kill him?" says I.)

In an ordinary statement of fact, the Irishman would become righteously indignant and his ire would evidence itself in his speech pattern as follows:

"AH:n' hi: AH:ftTH'r tTHEHl'n yuh nAWoo!"
(and he after telling you no)
(and after telling you no)

In the preceding sentence, it will be seen that two vowels served as glides, "e" in "he" and "o" in "no." But in the last word, it can be seen that the glide was carried on the consonant "n." Both "n" and "l" are considerably elongated in the Irish and are used like vowels for rising or falling glides.

Much of the Irish lilt is achieved by the tendency to shuttle the sound chamber from the front of the mouth, where they usually speak, to the throat, to which they shift down occasionally. This results in a change of timbre, almost in the same breath, from the flattened timbre of the front-of-the-mouth resonance to the deeper, richer, throaty resonance.

The way to achieve this effect is to use what is known as the inverted vowel sound. This may be accomplished by holding the shaft of the tongue in its normal position when pronouncing a vowel sound; but instead of extending the tip of the tongue forward, it should be curled upward. The result will give the typical, hollow Irish timbre.

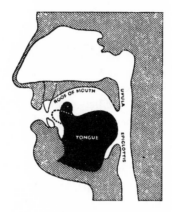

The dotted line indicates the normal position of the tongue tip for pronouncing an American vowel sound. The black area shows the Irish method of inverting the tongue tip by curling it upward instead of extending it forward.

It is with the front-of-the-mouth resonance that the dialect becomes characteristically Irish. The people prefer to keep the jaws almost tightly shut when they speak and use pursed lips only for shaping the sounds. This can be readily observed in motion pictures with the Abbey star, Barry Fitzgerald. Much of his dialect can be attributed to the fact that he seldom moves his jaws and uses only half of his mouth, speaking, as it were, from one side. The effect is as though the words were being ground out of a sausage grinder.

EMPHASIS

The Irish utilize an emphasis both tonal (change of musical note) and stress (increased expulsion of breath) in their syllabic and word emphasis.

At the same time, their innate love of lyrical music results in a coloring of the stressed syllables with tonal emphasis so that the effect is that of an emphatic, energetic attack. The syllable emphasis pattern generally follows that of the British and the American although there is a tendency in the Irish to emphasize concluding syllables, as in: "sAH:krUH**fuhEE**s" (sacrifice). The American would, of course, emphasize the first syllable.

In word-emphasis, it will be seen that the words receive the stress emphasis when they are given tonal emphasis so that the high note and the low note reached in a sentence tonal pattern would also receive the stress emphasis.

It has been mentioned before, though, and it cannot be overstated, that such subjects as lilt and emphasis are too ephemeral to be pinned down with words. They are imbued too much with the stuff of life to be put into cold type. To perfect them, the student must go to the source itself. With them and with the vowel and consonant changes and other material following, a satisfactory Irish dialect can be learned.

EXPLANATION OF PHONETIC SYMBOLS

In this chapter the aspirate "uh" and the mute "a" sound of "UH" will be written either in lower case letters or in caps. This will be done to facilitate legibility. For, usually, a capital "UH" will be used between two lower case consonants, as in: "lUHpEHl" (lapel) while the lower case "uh" will sometimes be written after a capital letter consonant sound, as in: "THuhs" (this). But no matter how it is written this "uh" should be of only short duration.

The (') sign used between consonants indicates that a letter or syllable has been dropped. But there should be no pause made in the sound. It should flow evenly as though the elision had never been in the original word, as in: "wAH:nt-TH'n'" (wanting) where the first (') sign replaces the dropped "i" and the last (') sign indicates the dropped "g." Actually, there is a very slight aspirate "uh" between the two final consonant sounds but, the sounding of both consonants will put the "uh" in naturally without any necessity to write it in.

VOWEL CHANGES

"AY" .... as in "take," "break," "they," etc.

The Irish substitute "EH" for long "a." This may seem to be an exception to the Irish habit of lengthening their vowel sounds, but actually, the Irish lengthen this "EH" sound of long "a" so that it would appear as "EHHHHH." For our purposes, though, the vowel sound will be designated as "EH:," the (:) mark indicating the elongation.

DRILL WORDS

lEH:k	(lake)	tTHEH:stTHi	(tasty)
sEH:	(say)	mEH:bi	(maybe)
dEH:l	(dale)	fEH:th	(faith)
vEH:kEH:t	(vacate)		
EHdiyookEH:t	(educate)		
stTHrEH:t	(straight)		

"UH" .... as in "alone," "final," "sofa," etc.

The Irish retain the American pronunciation of this mute "a."

"AH" .... as in "father," "arm," "park," etc.

The Irish change the "AH" to the "A:" of "ask" and they elongate it to almost twice its normal duration, as in: "A:ruhm" (arm). This "A:" is richer than its

American counterpart although it has been designated phonetically as "A:." It must be remembered, however, that the Irish do not give it an exact "A:" treatment. Instead, the correct sound is one that lies between the "A" of "bad" and the "AH" of "father."

A variation substitutes "AH:," as in: "fAH:TH'r" (father) but the former substitution is preferred.

DRILL WORDS

A:mz	(alms)	dA:ruhluhn'	(darling)
kA:rve	(carve)	hA:ruhmluhs	(harmless)
pA:mz	(palms)	spA:ruhk'l	(sparkle)

A:ruhmi:	(army)
dibA:ruhk	(debark)
rigA:rd	(regard)

"A:" .... as in "ask," "draft," "laugh," etc.

The Irish substitute "AH" for this lengthened "A" but they also elongate it, as in: "AH:s'" (ask), the (:) sign indicating the elongation.

DRILL WORDS

pAH:s	(pass)	tTHAH:s'	(task)
lAH:s	(lass)	mAH:stTH'r	(master)
gAH:f	(gaff)	bAH:sk't	(basket)

pAH:spAHrt	(passport)
pAH:sUHj	(passage)
lAH:ftTH'r	(laughter)

"A" .... as in "bad," "am," "narrow," etc.

This shortened short "a" also receives the "AH:" treatment, as in "bAH:d" (bad), the (:) sign indicating the elongation.

DRILL WORDS

sAH:d	(sad)	pAH:t	(Pat)
mAH:p	(map)	nAH:rUH	(narrow)
AH:m	(am)	sAH:d'l	(saddle)

hAH:nshEH:k	(handshake)
flAH:tTH'r	(flatter)
grAH:diyooEHt	(graduate)

"AW" .... as in "ball," "falter," "shawl," etc.

The preferred substitution for this broad "a" is the elongated "AH:," as in: "bAH:l" (ball). Another variation changes it to "AW-oo," as in "bAW-ool" (ball), but the former is preferred.

DRILL WORDS

kAH:l	(call)	wAH:tTH'r	(water)
shAH:l	(shawl)	skwAH:l	(squall)
brAH:l	(brawl)	fAH:ltTH'r	(falter)

sUHtTHihAH:l   (city hall)
inthrAH:l   (enthrall)
rikAH:l   (recall)

"EE" .... as in "he," "treat," "people," etc.

It is with the pronunciation of long "e" that most actors err in the simulation of the Irish dialect. Contrary to custom, the long "e" vowel sound does not *always* become long "a," as in: "rAYsAYv" (receive). The following rules must be observed for making the proper substitutions:

1. *WHEN "e" IS FOLLOWED BY EITHER "i," "a," OR "re," IT IS CHANGED TO LONG (ELONGATED) "a" (AY:).*

DRILL WORDS

tTHAY:	(tea)	sfAY:uhr	(sphere)
bAY:t	(beat)	rivAY:uhr	(revere)
bAY:n	(bean)	hAY:uhr	(here)
	disAY:t	(deceit)	
	kAHnsAY:v	(conceive)	
	wAY:uhrd	(weird)	

2. *WHEN LONG "e" IS USED IN A PREFIX OR IN A WEAKLY-AC-CENTED SYLLABLE, IT IS ALWAYS CHANGED TO SHORT "i," NOT ELONGATED.*

DRILL WORDS

dipind	(depend)	ritTHUHr'n	(return)
risAY:v	(receive)	bili:v	(believe)
sUHtTHi	(city)	prUHtHi	(pretty)
	silEHk'	(select)	
	disAY:t	(deceit)	
	jEHli	(jelly)	

3. *WHEN LONG "e" IS USED NEITHER IN A PREFIX NOR A WEAKLY-STRESSED SYLLABLE NOR IS FOLLOWED BY "a," "i," OR "re," IT IS CHANGED TO AN ELONGATED SHORT "i" (i:).*

DRILL WORDS

bili:v	(believe)	UHksi:d	(accede)
stTHri:t	(street)	ni:dlUHs	(needless)
spi:d	(speed)	gri:di	(greedy)
	ni:d	(need)	
	fli:	(flee)	
	hi:	(he)	

"EH" .... as in "bet," "said," "friend," etc.

This short "e" is another stumbling block to most who try to simulate the Irish dialect.

Ordinarily, short "e" (EH) is pronounced as it is in American, but under certain conditions, the following rule is to be used:

4. ***WHEN SHORT "e" (EH) IS FOLLOWED BY "m," "n," OR "v," IT IS CHANGED TO SHORT "i" (i).***

DRILL WORDS

tTHint	(tent)	div'l	(devil)
bind	(bend)	siv'n	(seven)
frind	(friend)	niv'r	(never)

imblim	(emblem)
rizimb'l	(resemble)
UHsimb'l	(assemble)

"I" .... as in "ice," "aisle," "guile," etc.

Perhaps the most identifying of all the vowel substitutions in the Irish dialect is the one made for this long "i" (I). It is almost universally changed to "OI," ("AW-EE") as in "nOIs." But, actually, the substitution is not "AW-EE" so much as "uhEE" in which the initial "uh" is only barely sounded while the long "e" final sound is elongated slightly. Naturally, there are a great many Irish people who may broaden the "uhEE" into "AW-EE" (OI), particularly in the lower classes; but, as a rule, the "uhEE" substitute should be used, as in "fuhEEn" (fine). The personal pronoun, "I," should be pronounced "**uhEE**."

DRILL WORDS

muhEE	(my)	luhEEn'r	(liner)
uhEEs	(ice)	suhEEf'r	(cipher)
kruhEE	(cry)	muhEEt	(might)

uhEElUHn'	(island)
stTHuhEEl	(style)
snuhEEp'r	(sniper)

"i" .... as in "it," "women," "busy," etc.

This short "i" vowel sound is broadened in the Irish dialect into an "UH," as in "sUHt" (sit).

DRILL WORDS

UHt	(it)	mUHd'l	(middle)
sUHt	(sit)	lUHtTH'l	(little)
bUHl	(bill)	wUHm'n	(women)

sUHvUHly'n	(civilian)
stTHUHmiyoolEH: t	(stimulate
sUHnsAY:uhr	(sincere)

"O" .... as in "on," "bond," "John," etc.

In lengthening this vowel sound, the Irish broaden it to "AH:," as in "AH:n" (on), the (:) sign indicating the elongation.

DRILL WORDS

hAH:d	(hod)	bAH:TH'r	(bother)
bAH:b	(bob)	dAH:ktTH'r	(doctor)
lAH:k	(lock)	dAH:tTHi	(dotty)

hAH:stTHuhEEl (hostile)
kAH:ns'UHn' (constant)
UHpAH:n (upon)

"OH" .... as in "bone," "sew," "dough," etc.

The substitution for long "o" is another very important element in the Irish dialect. Sometimes, it is changed from "OH-OO," as in American, to "AH-OO," as in "kAH-OOl" (cold). This is the sound that is represented in the writings of Kipling, O'Casey, and others as "oul'" (old) and "coul'" (cold). But, like the change for long "i" into "OI," this "AH-OO" substitution for long "o" is not typical. Instead, a more modified substitution is actually made: that of "AW-oo," as in "bAWoon" (bone). It is this substitution, then, that is preferred and used in this chapter.

DRILL WORDS

gAWoo	(go)	lAWood	(load)
nAWoo	(no)	AH:tTHAWoo	(auto)
sAWoo	(so)	mAWootTH'r	(motor)

prAWootTHEHk' (protect)
gAWoold'n (golden)
nAWootTHUHs (notice)

"AW" .... as in "off," "cough," "bought," etc.

This "o" vowel sound is also treated as "AH:," the (:) sign signifiying that elongation is necessary, as in "AH:f" (off).

DRILL WORDS

sAH:f'	(soft)	glAH:s	(gloss)
AH:f'n	(often)	hAH:g	(hog)
grAH:g	(grog)	kAH:rn	(corn)

UHlAH:ng (along)
mAH:rnUHn' (morning)
stTHrAH:ng (strong)

"OO" .... as in "food," "do," "blue," etc.

The double "o" of "good" (oo), is substituted for this long double "o" (OO), as in "doo" (do).

DRILL WORDS

noo	(knew)	stTHoo	(stew)	rood	(rude)
bloo	(blue)	hoo	(who)	loot	(loot)
food	(food)	gloo	(glue)	soon	(soon)

"OO" .... as in "good," "wolf," "full," etc.

The correct substitution for this short double "oo" (oo) is not clear to many actors and writers. Most dialect writers of Irish indicate it with a "u," as in "tuk" (took). But this "u" sound is not specific as to its exact application. It could be the "U" sound of "up," the "u" sound of "food" or the "UH" sound of mute "a." Minute examination proves that actually it is the "UH" sound of mute "a." With Irish elongation, it becomes "UH:," as in "bUH:k" (book).

DRILL WORDS

fUH:t	(foot)	wUH:lf	(wolf)
hUH:k	(hook)	wUH:d	(would)
bUH:l	(bull)	stTHUH:d	(stood)
biyootTHuhfUHl	(beautiful)		
bUH:kEH:s	(bookcase)		
oond'rstTHUH:d	(understood)		

"yOO" .... as in "unit," "cube," "beauty," etc.

The Irish dialect adds an initial short "i" before "yOO" and changes "OO" to "oo," as in "kiyoob" (cube).

DRILL WORDS

iyoonuht	(unit)	iyoonuhEEtTH'd	(united)
fiyoom	(fume)	piyoor	(pure)
hiyoom'n	(human)	iyooslUHs	(useless)
hiyoomUHd	(humid)		
EHksUHkiyoot	(execute)		
rifiyooz	(refuse)		

"U" .... as in "up," "love," "does," etc.

Two substitutions are used for this short "u" sound. The first treats with it as "AW," as in "AWp" (up). The second and preferred substitute vowel sound changes this short "U" sound to "oo," as in "loov" (love).

DRILL WORDS

dooz	(does)	moostTH'd	(mustard)
mooni	(money)	koostTH'm	(custom)
oop	(up)	doostTHi	(dusty)
koontTHri	(country)		
loogUHj	(luggage)		
froostTHrEH:t	(frustrate)		

"ER" .... as in "curb," "earn," "fir," etc.

The vowel sound of this combination, when found in any of the "er," "ir," "or," and "ur" combinations, is always sounded as "UH," as a in: "bUHruhd" (bird). The added "uh" after the "r" and before certain consonants (see under "R") is an "r" aspirate which occurs when this letter is as strongly sounded as it is in the Irish dialect.

DRILL WORDS

UHrn	(earn)	gUHruhl	(girl)
fUHr	(fir)	wUHruhk	(work)
kUHrb	(curb)	dUHrtTHi	(dirty)

sUHrtTH'nli	(certainly)
flUHrtTHEH:sh's	(flirtatious)
oondUHstTHUHrb'd	(undisturbed)

"OW" . . . . as in "out," "cow," "house," etc.

This diphthong, treated as "AH-OO" in American, is pronounced as "uh-OO" in the Irish, as in "duhOOt" (doubt).

DRILL WORDS

tTHuhOOn	(town)	muhOOs	(mouse)
puhOOt	(pout)	muhOOth	(mouth)
kuhOOnt	(count)	UHbuhOOt	(about)

kuhOOtTHuhOO	(kowtow)
huhOOs-hAWoold	(household)
duhOOntTHuhOOn	(downtown)

"OI" . . . . as in "oil," "boy," "noise," etc.

In American, this diphthong is pronounced as "AW-EE." But in the Irish, it can be treated either as "AH-EE," as in "bAH-EE" (boy) or as "uhEE," as in "juhEE" (joy). The latter is preferred and is used in this chapter.

DRILL WORDS

buhEE	(boy)	suhEEl	(soil)
kuhEEn	(coin)	nuhEEz	(noise)
juhEEn	(join)	spuhEEl	(spoil)

ruhEEltTHi	(royalty)
UHnuhEEy'n'	(annoying)
huhEEd'n	(hoyden)

"EN," "EL," "LE," etc., endings

The Irish dialect features an excessive addiction to consonant assimilation. This will be treated more fully in the section on "Consonant Changes." It also tends to assimilate, in words of two syllables and more, the following word-endings: "en," "an," "on," "in," "el," "le," and "et," so that the vowel is dropped and the preceding consonant is joined with the final consonant sound, as in "AH:f'n" (often), "nEH:sh'n" (nation), "bAH:tTH'l" (bottle), and "bAH:sk't" (basket).

"OW"

The "ow" ending, pronounced "OH," is always spoken as "UH" in Irish, as in "fEH:lUH" (fellow) and "yEH:lUH" (yellow).

WORD EXERCISES

Pronounce the following words in the Irish dialect using the material learned from the preceding Vowel Changes.

1.	few	11.	misunderstood
2.	please	12.	girl-guide
3.	long-suffering	13.	foothold
4.	sacrifice	14.	mousetrap
5.	handclasp	15.	rainbow
6.	friendship	16.	crocodile
7.	magnify	17.	revelation
8.	martyr	18.	woman
9.	crucify	19.	sunrise
10.	water-boy	20.	report

When the above words have been tried, refer to the correct pronunciation given below and check the vowels that were incorrectly sounded. Repeat them correctly a number of times until they have been committed to memory.

1.	fiyoo	11.	mUHsoondUHrstTHUH:d
2.	plAY:z	12.	gUHruhlguhEEd
3.	lAH:ngsoof'r'n	13.	fUH:tTHAWool'
4.	sAH:krUHfuhEEs	14.	muhOOstTHrAH:p
5.	hAH:n'klAH:sp	15.	rEH:nbAWoo
6.	frin'shUHp	16.	krAH:kUHduhEEl
7.	mAH:gnUHfuhEE	17.	rEHvUHlEH:sh'n
8.	mA:rtTHUHr	18.	wUH:mUHn
9.	kroosUHfuhEE	19.	soonruhEEz
10.	wAH:tTH'rbuhEE	20.	ripAH:ruht

CONSONANT CHANGES

B and **C**—Pronounced as in American.

D—When "d" is used initially before "u" it is sometimes pronounced as "j," as in "jook" (*d*uke); medially, also, it is sometimes changed to "j," as in "rijoos" (re*d*uce).

But the most important treatment of the Irish "d" comes with the addition to it of the aspirate "uh" when it is followed by an "r," as in "d*uh*rAH:p" (*d*rop), "d*uh*ruhEEv" (*d*rive), and "mUHd*uh*rUHf" (mid*r*iff).

When "d" follows "n" or "l" at the end of a word, it is usually dropped as in "sAH:n'" (san*d*), "bUHl'" (buil*d*), and "pAH:n'" (pon*d*).

When "d" is used at the end of a word and is preceded by a consonant or a mute vowel it is sometimes changed to "t," as in "kUHl*t*" kill*ed*) and "biyAH:n*t*" (beyon*d*).

F—Pronounced as it is in American.

G—The consonant "g" is always dropped when it is used in the participial ending "ing," as in "tTHEH:kUHn'" (taking). The soft sound of "g" is the same as in American.

H—Pronounced as it is in American.

J—This consonant sound, in all its forms, is pronounced as it is in American.

K—The consonant "k" is sometimes dropped finally and medially, as in "AH:s'" (ask) and "AH:s't" (asked).

L—The Irish "l" is sounded more liquidly than the American. Instead of the thin treatment, as in "look," it is given the liquidity of the "l" in "valor."

M—Pronounced as it is in American.

N—The Irish sound their "n" as though it were a series of "n's" as in "kAH:nnn" (can), elongating the sound.

P and **Q**—Pronounced as in American.

R—It is with the pronunciation of the consonant "r" that the Irish dialect achieves much of its consonantal color. As in the Scotch, the "r" should be heavily sounded—rolled—with the tip of the tongue, but not for the same duration as the Scottish "r."

The presence of a vowel before an "r" usually adds an aspirate "yuh" or "wuh" to the vowel.

The vowel sound "EH" before "r" becomes "EH:yuh," as in "THEH:*yuhr*" (there), "h-wEH:*yuhr*" (where) and "EH:*yuhr*" (air). The vowel sound "AY:," when followed by an "r," becomes "AY:yuh," as in "hAY:*yuhr*" (here), "wAY:*yuhr*" (we're) and "nAY:*yuhr* (near). The vowel sound "uhEE," when followed by an "r" becomes "uhEEyuh," as in "*fuhEEyuhr*" (fire), "*luhEEyuhr*" (liar) and "*uhEEyuhr*" (ire).

The vowel sounds "oo" and "iyoo," when followed by an "r," become "oowuh" and "iyoowuh," as in "shoo*wuhr*" (sure) and "ki*yoowuhr*" (cure).

When "r" precedes certain consonants, like "f," "g," "k," "l" and "m," medially or finally, it is treated with a concluding aspirate "uh," as in "wAH:*ruhm*" (warm) and "fUH*ruhm*n's" (firmness).

S—In a thick, countrified Irish dialect, this consonant "s" is usually pronounced as "sh" when it is initial, or when it is followed by a consonant, as in "shli:p" (sleep), and "shmuhEEl" (smile).

Ordinarily, though, it should be pronounced as in American.

T—The consonant "t" is another of the consonant changes that makes the Irish dialect what it is. Initially, medially, and sometimes finally, "t" is pronounced interdentally, with the tongue tip placed between the upper and lower front teeth. However, it should not be so completely dentalized that the pronunciation becomes "th." For, in the Irish dialect, the "t" is pronounced first, but is followed immediately by the "TH" which is pronounced more heavily than the initial "t," as in "tTHruhEE" (try) and "mAH:tTH'r" (matter).

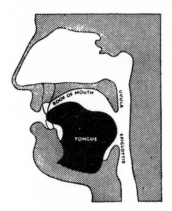

The tongue tip pressed against the backs of the front teeth, introduces into the "t" sound the additional "TH," creating the sound "tTH." The American "t" is produced by touching the gum ridge of the upper front teeth with the tongue tip.

For our purposes, final "t" will be pronounced as "t" although a great many people dentalize it as well.

When "t" follows another consonant, medially or finally, it is usually dropped, as in "wAH:n'd" (wanted), "sAH:f'n" (soften), and "slEHp'" (slept).

V—The consonant "v" is usually pronounced as in American. Sometimes, it is dropped medially, as in "AW-oo'r" (over).

W—Perhaps the most common misspelling of the Irish dialect is found in the treatment of the consonant "w". In books and plays, it is always found to be written as "phw" as in "phwhat" and "phwhy." As a result, a great many actors pronounce it as "*fw*OI" (*w*hy) and "*fw*AHt" (*w*hat). No only that but they give the "fw" pronunciation to all words that begin with a "w." Actually, the Irish people aspirate the initial "w" with "h"—*and only when the "W" is followed by an "h*," as in "h-wuhEE" (why), "h-wi:n" (when), and "h-wEH:yuhr" (where).

X and **Y**—Pronounced as in American.

Z—Pronounced as it is in American.

th—The countrified Irishman sometimes changes the unvoiced "th" to "t," as in "*tw*AH:rt" (*th*wart).

TH—Pronounced as in American.

The consonant sounds "sh," "tch," and "zh" are pronounced as they are in American.

WORD EXERCISES

Pronounce the following words in the Irish dialect using the material learned from the preceding Consonant Changes.

1.	drinking	11.	dutiful
2.	proud	12.	going
3.	earth-worm	13.	tooth
4.	remark	14.	cattle
5.	backyard	15.	child
6.	style	16.	return
7.	wind	17.	aired
8.	shoe-shine	18.	pardon
9.	whip	19.	grandfather
10.	visitation	20.	nowhere

When the above words have been pronounced, refer to the list given below for the correct pronunciation of the words. Check the consonant sounds that were incorrectly pronounced. Repeat them correctly a number of times until they have been memorized.

1.	drUHnkUHn'	11.	jootTHUHf'l
2.	pruhOOd	12.	gAWoon'
3.	UHruhth-wuhruhm	13.	tTHooth
4.	rimA:ruhk	14.	kAH:tTH'l
5.	bAH:kyA:ruht	15.	tchuhEEl'
6.	stTHuhEEl	16.	ritTHUHruhn
7.	wUHnd	17.	EH:yuhrt
8.	shoo-shuhEEn	18.	pA:rd'n
9.	hwUHp	19.	grAH:n'fA:TH'r
10.	vUHzUHtTHEH:sh'n	20.	nAWoohwEH:yuhr

CONTRACTIONS

Most of the contractions used in American speech are also used in the Irish dialect. A typical sentence in the Irish dialect, for instance, would read:

"y'v si:n mini UH' THim tTHEH:k'n t' TH' wAH:tTH'r luhEEk dooks sAWooz y'd thUHnk THEH:'d bUHn bAH:rn wuhTH fUHnz 'stTHEHd UH' A:ruhmz."

"You've seen many o' them takin' t' th' water like ducks so's y'd think they'd been born with fins 'stead o' arms."

There are a number of contractions, though, that are used more in the Irish dialect than in American. They are: "'d" (would), used after any noun or pronoun subject, as in: "pi:pl'd si:" (people would see), "THEH:'d" (they'd), "muhEEk'd" (Mike'd, i.e., Mike would); "g'wEH:" (go away); "j'iv'r" (did you ever?); "d'y" (do you); "g'woop" (go up); "l'gAWoo" (let go); "y'r" (your or you are); "sEHzi:" (says he); "sEHzuhEE" (says I); "h'y'" (have you).

ELISIONS

The Irish dialect also abounds in the elision of letters and syllables from words. Usually, the weakly stressed, unvoiced vowel sounds are completely elided and the consonants are coupled together, with no aspirate "uh," as in "tchEH:yuhr*m'n*" (chair*man*) and "fAYzUHb'l'" (feasi*ble*).

Entire syllables are dropped, as in "prAH:'bli" (probably) and "AH:r'n'ri" (ordinary). But it would be best to avoid these syllabic elisions and use only the consonant elisions.

GRAMMAR CHANGES

The lilt of the Irish dialect can be attributed not only to the musical notes with which the words are endowed, but also to the syntax—the order in which the words are strung together in a sentence. No other dialect uses the word order of the Irish. And it is so much a part of the dialect that, in many cases, it would be possible to simulate an Irish dialect simply by using the word order.

But the most characteristic quality of the speech, perhaps, is its excessive use of highly-colored hyperbole—flowery exaggerations. Phrases like the following abound in the speech of even the lowest scullery-maid and the dialect is surprisingly poetic because of them.

"shoowuhr, AH:n' UHt'd skAH:l' THuh hA:rt uhOOt UH y'!"
(Sure, and it'd scald the heart out of you!)

"hi: wAH:z UHn THuh sooni: loost UH luhEEf"
(He was in the sunny lust of life.)

"THEH:yuhrz UH hoorUHkEH:n UH rEH:j UHn mi:"
("There's a hurricane of rage in me.)

There is almost a Shakespearean quality to the dialect, and the color it sheds endows it with a soulfulness that seems to typify the sentimental Irishman. This same literary quality is furthered by the use of the vivid simile in the dialect, as in:

"luhEEk THuh suhOOnd UH doomzdEH:"
(like the sound of doomsday)

"luhEEk UH shuhEEn'n' shruhOOd"
(like a shining shroud)

"AHz dEH:d AHz UH fUHshmA:rk't mAH:k'r'l"
(as dead as a fish-market mackerel)

It is this feeling for the colorful idiom that forces the Irishman to indulge in the use of old saws, cliché expressions, catch-phrases, tags and poetic fol de rol. The Irishman, too, is an inveterate quoter from the classics and an adapter of catchlines from popular songs using them as an illustration or a comparison.

Aside from the language of the dialect, there is also the consideration of the order in which the words are placed. One of the most common forms uses the conjunction, "after," as an adverb, as in:

"uhEEm AH:ftTH'r ruhEEtTHUHn' UH lEHtTH'r"
(I'm *after* writing a letter.)

"AH:n' THEH:'d joos' bUHn AH:ftTH'r si:ndUHn' UHt"
(and they'd just been *after* sending it)

"uhEEm AH:ftTH'r gEH:tTH'n THuh sAH:k"
(I'm *after* getting the sack.)

"shi:z AH:ftTH'r wEH:yuhr'n' uhOOt h'r wEH:lk'm"
(She's *after* wearing out her welcome.)

Another addition typical of the dialect is the frequent use of "now" where it is not needed, as in:

"si: hAY:yuhr, nuhOO, mi: fuhEEn bookAWoo"
(see here, now, me fine bucko)

"wEHl, nuhOO, UHt'd bi: hA:rd tUH sEH:"
(Well, now, it'd be hard to say.)

"nuhOO, h-wuhEE dUHd yuh sEH: THAH:t?"
(Now, why did you say that?)

Another overworked interjection—repeated almost *ad nauseam* by most who attempt the Irish dialect—is the word "sure." It would be a good rule to confine its use only to those situations in which it is necessary to emphasize a fact, as in "shoowuhr, AH:n' uhEEm nAH:t tTHoo AWool'!" (Sure, and I'm not too old.) Otherwise, give it a well-earned rest.

The use of the interjection, "AH:," sometimes pronounced as "AH:kh" (och!), is quite common in the dialect, particularly when the speaker is disturbed emotionally.

Another interjection used by the Irish is the word "then," inserted for no particular reason other than that it is in the common idiom, as in:

"nuhOO, THin, uhOOt wUHTH UHt!"
(Now, *then*, out with it!)

Still another common interjection is the word "man," thrown into a sentence when the person spoken to is, of course, an adult. When he is a youth, the word "boy," is used, as in:

"gUHv UHt UH tchAH:ns, mAH:n!"
(Give it a chance, *man!*)

"lUHk AH:t UHt, mi: buhEE"
(Look at it, me *boy.*)

Two substitutions occur in the dialect that seem to be typical of all classes of Irishmen. They are "me" for "my" and "be" for "by." It is suggested that these be used as often as possible, for they mirror the Irish dialect perfectly.

"hi: mEH:d mi: loo:z mi: timp'r"
(He made me lose *me* temper.)

"tEH:k mi: nEH:m AH:f THuh lUHs'"
(Take *me* name off the list.)

"bi: THuh lUHk AH:v UHt, hi:z gAH:n"
(*Be* the look of it, he's gone.)

"bi: h-wAH:t ruhEEt AH:r yUH hAY:yuhr?"
(*Be* what right are you here?)
The Irish also substitute "that" for "who" as in:

"THim THAH:t wUHruhks, AY:ts"
(Them *that* works, eats.)

The last example illustrates another error rife in the dialect: the confusion in verb forms. Other examples are:

"hi: riz thuhri: tchUHz'l'rz"
(He *riz* three chiselers.)
(He *raised* three kids.)

"mi: hAH:rt lEHp UHntTHoo mi: thUHrAWoot"
(Me heart *lep* into me throat.)
(My heart *leaped* into my throat.)

"UHzuhn't shi: kAH:m UHn yEHt?"
(*Isn't* she come in yet?)
(*Hasn't* she come in yet?)

"wAH:zn't THuh bAWooth AH:v yUH fuhEEtTHuhn'?"
(*Wasn't* the both of you fighting?)
(*Weren't* both of you fighting?)

There is also present in the dialect a misuse of the reflexive pronoun for the personal pronoun, as in:

"AH:n' UHz UHt y'rsEHlf TH't wAH:ns UHt?"
(And is it *yourself* that wants it?)
(And is it *you* who want it?)

"UHt wAH:z h'rsEHlf TH't wint"
(It was *herself* that went.)
(It was *she* who went.)

"hUHmsEHlf UHt UHz TH't nAWooz bEHs'"
(*Himself,* it is that knows best.)
(It is *he* who knows best.)

The dialect is particularly addicted to the American vulgarism, "youse" (spelled "yez" and "yiz" by writers) instead of "you," as in:

"yooz niv'r sAH: THuh luhEEks AH:v UHt"
(*Youse* never saw the likes of it.)
(You never saw the likes of it.)

"uhEE nAWoo yooz'l tEH:k UHt nuhOO"
(I know *yous'll* take it now.)
(I know you'll take it now.)

The Irish also misuse the plural pronoun "us" for the singular pronoun "me," as in:

"brUHng oos bAH:k wUHrUHd, mAH:n"
(Bring *us* back word, man.)
(Bring *me* back word, man.)

"gUHv oos UH shmuhEEl, nuhOO"
(Give *us* a smile, now.)
(Give *me* a smile, now.)

The substitution of "as" for "who" or "that" is common to the speech, as in:

"AH:n' THEHyuhr'r soom AH:z dAWoont nAWoo"
(and there are some *as* don't know)
(and there are some *who* don't know)

"UH dEH: AH:z wAH:z AH:z nuhEEs AH:z"
(a day *as* was as nice as)
(a day *that* was as nice as)

The substitution of "what" for "why" adds a piquant flavor to the Irish dialect, as in:

"nuhOO h-wAH:t dooz hi: bi: kAH:l'n' f'r?"
(Now *what* does he be calling for?)
(Now, *why* is he calling?)

The substitution of "shall" for "will," and vice versa, accounts for the story of the Irishman who fell into a river and as he was thrashing about in the water, unable to swim, hollered out, "uhEE wUHl duhEE AH:n' nAWoo wAH:n shAH:l hEH:lp mi:!" (I will die and no one shall help me!) The story is apocryphal for no Irishman would say "I will" without contracting it to "I'll," but it does illustrate the tendency.

Another important element in the Irish dialect is the peculiar sentence structure. The commonest habit is the reversal of the usual subject and predicate sequence and the beginning of a sentence with "it," as in:

"UHt's AWoon'i: UH kAH:f uhEE hAH:v"
(It's only a cough I have.)

"UHt's UH gUHd bAY:tTH'n' hi: AH:t tTHuh hAH:v"
(It's a good beating he ought to have.)

"UHt's UH bA:rn hi: sh'd bi: lUHv'n' UHn"
(It's a barn he should be living in.)

Another popular form in the speech uses the same type of reversal without the "it," as in:

"duhOOn UHn THuh vAH:li hi: wAH:z bAH:rn"
(Down in the valley he was born.)

A favored form of syntax indulges in the following sequence:

"AH:n' yoo AWoon'i: joost UHruhEEv'd"
(and you only just arrived)

"AH:n' hi: AH:ftTH'r tTHEHl'n yUH nAWoo"
(and he after telling you no)

"AH:n' THEH: nAH:t wUHl'n tTHUH buhEE"
(and they not willing to buy)

"AH:n' muhEEk joost mAH:ri:d, tTHoo!"
(and Mike just married, too!)

The following odd question form of sentence is also typical:

"UHz UHt UH luhEEyuhr y'r kAH:l'n' mi: ?"
(Is it a liar you're calling me?)

"UHz UHt hoongri y'r AH:ftTH'r bi:UHn?"
(Is it hungry you're after being?)

"AH:m uhEE tTHuh roon nuhOO?"
(Am I to run now?)

"UHz UHt nuhOO uhEEm tTHuh roon?"
(Is it now I'm to run?)

Finally, in this discussion of syntax, we come to what is, perhaps, the most important element in the dialect sentence structure. It is used when an Irishman is telling the story of his conversation with another person. In it, he invariably uses the expressions, "sEHz uhEE" (says I) and "sEHzi:" (says he), as in:

"THEHyuhr wi: wAH:z, stAH:n'n' AH:n THuh kAH:rn'r, A:rgy'fuhEEy'n'
UHbuhOOt pAH:li:tTHuhks. h-wAH:t UHbuhOOt AWoobruhEEin? sEHzuhee.
h-wAH:t UHbuhOOt AWoobruhEEin? sEHzi:. h-wAH:t UHbuhOOt
AWoobruhEEinz rEHkAH:rd? sEHzuhEE. h-wAH:t UHbuhOOt
AWoobruhEEinz rEHkAH:rd? sEHzi:. AH:n' w' THAH:t, uhEE oops AH:n'
kluhOOts THuh mAH:n wAH:n AH:n THuh jAH:!"

(There we was, standing on the corner, argufying about politics. "What about
O'Brien?" says I. "What about O'Brien?" says he. "What about O'Brien's record?"
says I. "What about O'Brien's record?" says he. And, with that, I ups and clouts the
man one on the jaw!)

SENTENCE EXERCISES

Pronounce the following sentences in the Irish dialect making the necessary
changes in grammar and contractions learned from the preceding sections:

1. Yes—my name is Fahey Ryan.
2. I'm the one who knows the real meaning.
3. Are you getting tired?
4. We will be leaving soon.
5. It's all over, by the look of it.
6. I shall get the stout at the pub.
7. Bring me back the good word.
8. He should be working in a fish-market.
9. Hold my hand and follow me.
10. "Did you ever see your father?" I said.

After each sentence, refer to the following versions for the correct changes.
Make the corrections and pronounce the sentence again with the corrected
words. Do this with every sentence.

1. shoowuhr UHn mi nEH:mz fEH:hi: ruhEEuhn.
2. UHts misEHlf THuht nAWooz THuh rAY:l mAY:nuhn'.
3. UHzuht tTHuhEErd yUHr gEHtTHuhn'?
4. wi:l bi AH:ftTHuhr lAY:vuhn' soon.
5. bi: THuh lUH:k UHv UHt, UHt'l AH:l bi: AWoov'r.
6. uhEEl gEHt THuh stTHuhOOt UHt THuh poob.
7. brUHng oos bAH:k THuh gUHd wUHruhd.
8. UHts UHn UH fUHshmA:rkuht hi: shUHd bi: woork'n.
9. hAWool' mi hAH:n' UHn fAH:luh mi:.
10. "jiv'r si: y'r fA:THuhr?" sEHzuhEE.

IRISH MONOLOG

(Adapted from the authors' "Curtain Time" drama, "Passage Through Limbo" on the Mutual Network.)

(The old woman stood at the doorway peering into the darkness. Her eyes were sunk into their sockets. She was mad. She keened out:)

And what business is it of yours that I be awake or no? Be what right do you come snooping after me, following me like a black shadow. Are youse never going to leave me alone? Yous'd be after doing better minding your own business and letting me for to mind mine. For I have an ache in me long-suffering heart and lashin's of pain cutting through me brain like a dull knife. And me eyes is looking at a world that's not of your living. For it's a revelation I'm after having—a view into the banshee world of devils and spirits and the dear departed dead now rotting their whitened bones under the cold, black sod. Ah! sure, now, and it's the likes of you and your friends that call themselves sane, that disbelieves in what I'm after seeing and knowing. But listen, me fine bucko! one of these days, the whole world is going to come toppling down on your heads. Mark me words, man! Remember, it was Bridget O'Rourke as told you. And the heavens'll rain fire, and the rolling waters of the world'll come washing over you to wipe out the sins of the sons and the fathers in Sodom and Gomorrah. And the earth'll crack wide open and swallow up you and all your kind. And only the good'll be left—only the pure in heart and the clean in spirit. Aye—we'll inherit the earth. Remember, man! all this I see in the glass darkly—all this and more. For I have spoke with the feys at the hour of midnight and I have been touched be the moon.

PHONETIC REPRESENTATION
(Syllables in bold-face type are to be accented.)

THAH:t uhEE bi: UH **wEH**:k 'r **nAWoo**? bi: hwAH:t ruhEEt d'yuh koom snoop'n' **AH**:ftTH'r mi:, **fAH**:lUHr'n' mi: luhEEk UH **blAH:k shAH:dUH**. AH:r yooz niv'r gAWoon' tTHuh **lAY**:v mi: UHlAWoon? yuhz'd bi: AH:ftTH'r doo'n **bEHtTH'r** muhEEnd'n' y'r **AW**oon bUHzn's AH:n' lEH:tTH'n' **mi**: f'r tTHuh **muhEEn' muhEEn**. f'r uhEE hAH:v AH:n EH:k UHn mi: **lAH:ng soof**'r'n' **hA**:rt AH:n' **lAH:**sh'nz AH:v **pEH**:n kootTH'n' throo mi: **brEH**:n luhEEk UH **dool** nuhEEf. AH:n' mi: **uhEEz** UHz **luhk**'n' AH:t UH **wUH**ruhl' THAH:ts **nAH:t**

AH:v **y'r** lUHv'n'. f'r UHts UH rEHvUHlEH:sh'n uhEEm AH:ftTH'r hAH:v'n'—
UH **vyoo** UHntTHoo THuh **bAH:**nshi: wUHruhl' AH:v **div**'lz AH:n'
spUHrUHts AH:n THuh **dAY:**yuhr dip**A:**rtTHuhd **dEHd** nuhOO rAH:tTH'n'
THEHr **h-wuhEE**tTH'nd **bAW**oonz oond'r THuh **kAW**ool' **blAH:**k **sAH:**d. **AH!**
shoowuhr, nuhOO, AH:n' UHts THuh luhEEks AH:v **yoo** AH:n' y'r **frin'**z
THAHT:t kAHl: THimsEHlvz **sEH:**n, THAH:t **dUH**sbili:vz UHn h-wAH:t
uhEEm AH:ftTH'r **si:**yuhn' AH:n' **nAW**oowuhn'. boot **lUH**s'n, mi: **fuhEE**n
bookAWoo! **wAH:**n AH:v THi:z **dEH:**z, THuh **hAW**ool **wUH**ruhl' UHz
gAWoowuhn' tTHuh koom **tTHAH:**pl'n' duhOOn AH:n y'r **hEH**dz. **mA:**rk mi:
wUHruhdz, m**AH:**n! **rimim**b'r, UHt wAH:z **brUH**j't AW'**roo**ruhk AH:z **tTHA-**
Wool: yuh. AH:n' THuh **hivUH**nz'l rEH:n **fuhEE**yuhr, AH:n' THuh **rAW**ool'n'
wAH:tTH'rz AH:v THuh **wUH**ruhld'l koom **wAH:**sh'n **AW**oo'r yuh tTHuh
wuhEEp uhOOt THuh **sUH**nz AH:v THuh **soon**z AH:n' THuh **fA:**TH'rz UHn
sAH:d'm AH:n' **gUH**m**AH:**rUH. AH:n' THuh **UH**rth'l krAH:k **wuhEE**d
AWoop'n AH:n swAH:lUH oop **yoo** AH:n' **AH:**l y'r **kuhEE**n'. AH:n' **AW**oon'i:
THuh **gUH**d'l bi: lEH:ft—**AW**oon'i: THuh **piyoo**wuhr UHn hA:rt AH:n' THuh
klAY:n UHn spUHrUHt. uhEE—**wi:l** UHnhEHruht THi: UHrth. **rimim**b'r,
mAH:n! **AH:**l THuhs uhEE si: UHn THuh glAH:s **dA:**rkli—**AH:**l THuhs AH:n'
mAWoo:r. f'r uhEE hAH:v **spAW**ook wuh' THuh **fEH:**z AH:t THi: **uhOO**wuhr
AH:v **mUH**dnuhEEt AH:n' uhEE hAH:v bUHn **tTHoo**tch'd bi: THuh **moon.**

CHAPTER FIVE

The Scottish Dialect

THE SCOTTISH LILT

"uh duhnuh/luhEEk tuh thuhnk sAW."
(I do not like to think so.)

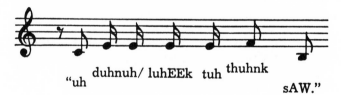

The word "thuhnk" receives slightly more stress than the rest of the words. The pitch is the same as in American, and the rise in pitch is about half a tone. Another sentence to show the moderation of lilt is:

"hwoo/suhr/ oov uh mOn i:z THO/?"
(What sort of a man is that?)

meaning, "What sort of a man is that who would do such and such?"

Naturally, not all Scottish people speak with the same emotion, or lack of it. These examples must be considered only as generalizations.

EMPHASIS

The Scotsman accents his words as we do in America. As for the general stress in a sentence, it will be found that important words receive both tonal and stress emphasis.

Much of the emphasis is created through the use of the glottal stop which is not restricted solely to certain consonants, but is suggested also in many of the vowel sounds which are rarely glided.

THE GLOTTAL STOP

In this chapter the (/) will indicate the glottal stop. The physical characteristic of the glottal stop is the sudden opening and closing of the glottis. Try saying the word "glottal" as "glAW/l." After saying "glAW" close the glottis, then say "l" (not "el" but only the *sound* of "l") as you open it, and that's all there is to it. Also, practice saying "took," "cut," and "fruit," being careful to close the glottis quickly, cutting off all sound of the final consonant, as in "too/," "kU/" and "frOO/."

The glottal stop must be mastered before you proceed further with the Scottish dialect. For, even with a light dialect, this characteristic is part of the Scot. It may be used only occasionally, but it should never be dropped completely.

> 1.   *THE GLOTTAL STOP SHOULD REPLACE MEDIAL DOUBLE "t,"*
>   *AND MEDIAL AND FINAL SINGLE "t," EXCEPT AFTER "f," "k,"*
>   *"l," "n," "p," AND "s."*

The word "bottle" would be pronounced "bAW/l," the sign (/) indicating that the double "t" (tt) has been dropped for the glottal stop. Only the sound of "l" should be given and not the pronunciation of the letter, as "el." It is as though there were a slight aspirate "uh" before the "l." Until the glottal stop is perfected, this "uh" may be used for practice, as "bAW/uhl."

When "t" is final, as in "fluhr/" (flirt), it also is dropped and replaced by the glottal stop. If the "r" is burred, as it should be, the flavor of the word will be more true. It is impossible to say "fluhr" without the glottal stop and still have it sound like a Scottish word. The opening to the throat must be closed off quickly and quickly reopened.

The glottal stop colors a great many vowel sounds in this dialect. When "uh" is indicated as a vowel change and the suggestion is made to keep the sound short, this "uh" is, actually, almost a glottal. It should be as short as the mute "a" in "about." Throughout the following drill words, this should be kept in mind. The "uh" should be treated as little more than a sharp bridge from one consonant to the next.

Be sure to make the glottal stop clean and distinct. It should not be drawn out, as it is the sharp cutting off of all sound for only a minute period of time.

DRILL WORDS

gAW/	(got)		thuhr/i	(thirty)
kuhr/	(curt)		spAW/s	(spots)
lEH/uhr	(letter)		nAW/	(not)
grEHi/	(great)		tuhr/	(tart)

duh-OO/	(doubt)
lAW/	(lot)
prEH/i	(pretty)
ruh-EE/	(right)

In practicing the glottal stop, pronounce the word as though the "t" were to be sounded. Then when you get to the "t," replace it with the glottal. Do not pronounce the word too slowly, or the effect will be lost. The tempo of Scottish speech is slow and measured, but the words sound clipped because of the glottal attack.

Generally speaking, the glottal used with consonants other than "t," tends to make the dialect too thick. It is suggested, therefore, that only the "t" be replaced with the glottal stop. If a thicker dialect is desired, the consonant "k" may also be glottalized—if it is final or medial and between vowels. Rather than replace "k" completely with a glottal stop, the flavor and authenticity will be better retained if the glottal stop is used just before the "k" and the "k" is lightly sounded, as in: "loo/ki" (lucky), "tEHi/k" (take), and "tO/k" (talk).

VOWEL CHANGES

"AY" .... as in "take," "break," "they," etc.

When broken down, this American "AY" sound becomes "AY-EE." The Scots change it to "EHi." The "EH" is like "e" in the American word "get," and the "i" is like the "i" in "it." These two vowel sounds are blended to form "EHi" and must not be sounded separately or unduly elongated.

DRILL WORDS

tEHi/k	(take)		pEHi	(pay)
brEHi/k	(break)		stEHi	(stay)
THEHi	(they)		plEHi	(play)

grEHi/	(great)
mEHibi:	(maybe)
ri:lEHi/	(relate)

"UH" .... as in "alone," "sofa," "final," etc.

The "UH" sound of the unaccented vowel "a" is much shorter in the Scottish dialect than it is in the American. It will be represented by "uh." When used initially, its treatment is similar to the glottal stop. In some cases where the "uh" is lost completely, an apostrophe (') will be used.

DRILL WORDS

uhlAWn	(alone)	b'nOnuh	(banana)
sAWfuh	(sofa)	uhgAW	(ago)
fuhEEn'l	(final)	mOd'm	(madam)
luhpi:l	(lapel)		
puhrEHid	(parade)		
uhbuhOO/	(about)		

"AH" .... as in "father," "arm," "park," etc.

The preferred change for this "AH" is a short "uh." This "uh" is especially short before "r," although a variation is "AY," used only before the "r," as "AYrm" (arm) and "pAYrk" (park).

DRILL WORDS

fuhTHuhr	(father)	buhrn	(barn)
uhrm	(arm)	kuhm	(calm)
puhrk	(park)	kuhrv	(carve)
duhrli:ng	(darling)		
spuhrkl	(sparkle)		
tuhr/	(tart)		

"A:" .... as in "ask," "draft," "laugh," etc.

The Scots shorten this vowel to "O" as in the American word "rod."

DRILL WORDS

Osk	(ask)	tOsk	(task)
lOf	(laugh)	lOst	(last)
drOft	(draft)	bOskuh/	(basket)
mOstuhr	(master)		
pOs	(pass)		
brOntch	(branch)		

"A" .... as in "bad," "am," "fact," etc.

The same "O" is given to this shorter "A."

DRILL WORDS

bOd	(bad)	stOb	(stab)
Om	(am)	mOluhs	(malice)
fOkt	(fact)	lOd	(lad)
grOnd	(grand)		
mOn	(man)		
mOji:k	(magic)		

"AW" .... as in "ball," "falter," "shawl," etc.

This sound is pronounced the same as it is in American, only it is shorter and narrower. Any other pronunciation would tend to thicken the dialect unnecessarily.

"EE" .... as in "he, "treat," "people," etc..

This long "EE" sound in American is shortened to "i:," which is halfway between long "EE" and short "i."

DRILL WORDS

hi:	(he)	ri:mi:mbuhr	(remember)
tri:/	(treat)	pri:tchuhr	(preacher)
pi:pl	(people)	i:guhr	(eager)

gri:n	(green)
fri:	(free)
shi:	(she)

"EE" .... as in "very," "thirsty," "worry," etc.

When final "y" is pronounced as "EE" in American, it becomes "i" in Scottish. This "i" is very short.

DRILL WORDS

vuhri	(very)	duhr/i	(dirty)
thuhrsti	(thirsty)	doosti	(dusty)
wuhri	(worry)	frOnkli	(frankly)

lEHidi	(lady)
nOsti	(nasty)
i:zuhli	(easily)

"EH" .... as in "bet," "said," "head," etc.

The "EH" sound in the above, and similar words, remains the same as in American. See "EH" following for other changes.

"EH" .... as in "where," "dare," "square," etc.

When the short "EH" sound is followed by "r," the vowel sound changes to "uh." This "uh" is very short and acts more as a glide between the two consonant sounds than as an actual vowel sound itself.

DRILL WORDS

hwuhr	(where)	shuhr	(share)
duhr	(dare)	puhr	(pair)
skwuhr	(square)	wuhr	(wear)

vuhri:/uhb'l	(veritable)
tuhri:b'l	(terrible)
kuhr	(care)

"EH" .... as in "tell," "seven," "remember," etc.

If short "EH" is followed by the consonants "l," "n," "ll," "g," "m," or "v," it becomes "i:," which is the sign for a lengthened short "i." This is not to be sounded as a full "EE" but only as a shorter version of it.

DRILL WORDS

ti:l	(tell)	spi:l	(spell)
si:v'n	(seven)	ri:ji:stuhr	(register)
ri:mi:mbuhr	(remember)	di:li:kuh/	(delicate)
	di:v'l	(devil)	
	wi:lkoom	(welcome)	
	uhnti:luhji:nt	(intelligent)	

"I" .... as in "ice," "aisle," "guile," etc.

The Scots change this "I" (AH-EE) sound to "uh-EE." The "uh" is more of an aspirate than a full vowel sound. It is similar in sound to the mute "a" in the American word "about," but is of much shorter duration.

DRILL WORDS

uh-EEs	(ice)	fuh-EEn	(fine)
uh-EEl	(aisle)	ruh-EE/	(right)
guh-EEl	(guile)	duh-EE	(die)
	luh-EEnuhr	(liner)	
	uhnsuh-EEd	(inside)	
	kuh-EEnd	(kind)	

"i" .... as in "it," "women," "familiar," etc.

There are two pronunciations for this short "i" and both are used, depending upon the word involved. One of these changes makes short "i" slightly longer as "i:." This is halfway between "i" and "EE."

Since there are exceptions to all rules, the following rules must be regarded only as general.

> 2. *WHEN SHORT "i" IS FOLLOWED BY A SINGLE CONSONANT SOUND PLUS A VOWEL, OR BY A SINGLE FINAL CONSO-NANT, IT IS ELONGATED TO "i:."*

DRILL WORDS

i:t	(it)	i:vi:l	(evil)
wi:muhn	(women)	mi:nuh/	(minute)
fuhmi:lyuhr	(familiar)	pi:ti	(pity)
	fi:gyoor'd	(figured)	
	bi:/uhr	(bitter)	
	tri:p	(trip)	

"i" .... as in "which," "mister," "indiscreet," etc.

The second change for short "i," which should also be used, is the substitution of "uh." This has the quality of an aspirate "uh" and should be very short. A general rule for its use is:

> 3. *WHEN SHORT "i" IS FOLLOWED BY TWO OR MORE DIFFER-ENT CONSONANTS, IT CHANGES TO "uh."*

DRILL WORDS

hwuhtch	(which)	fuhfti	(fifty)
muhstuhr	(mister)	fuhlthi	(filthy)
uhnduhskri:/	(indiscreet)	suhmpuhthi	(sympathy)
mi:nuhstuhr	(minister)		
uhnstuhnt	(instant)		
duhstuhrb'd	(disturbed)		

Note: For a lighter dialect, the "uh" treatment of short "i" may be lessened but not dropped completely.

"O".... as in "on," "bond," "John," etc.

The preferred change for this "O" is "AW." This "AW" should be shorter and narrower than it is in American. A variant is a short sounded "uh."

DRILL WORDS

AWn	(on)	prAWspuhr	(prosper)
bAWnd	(bond)	kAWndi:sh'n	(condition)
jAWn	(John)	sAWli:d	(solid)
mAWdEHst	(modest)		
shAWp	(shop)		
nAW/	(not)		

"OH".... as in "bone," "sew," "dough," etc.

Although a number of Scottish people change this "OH" to "AY," as in the American word "take," this would tend to make the dialect too thick, as in "hAYm" (home), "sAYr" (sore) and "stAYn" (stone). The preferred change is a short sounded "AW," which may be used for a heavy or a light dialect.

DRILL WORDS

bAWn	(bone)	nAWsh'n	(notion)
sAW	(sew)	lAWuhr	(lower)
dAW	(dough)	klAWz	(close)
tAWld	(told)		
gAW	(go)		
AWnli	(only)		

"AW".... as in "off," "cough," "water," etc.

When the American "AW" sound precedes a consonant, other than "r," it changes to "O," as in the American word "rod." The sound should be produced farther forward in the mouth than the American pronunciation, and the "O" should be round and clear.

DRILL WORDS

Of	(off)	kOst	(cost)
kOf	(cough)	brO/	(brought)
wO/uhr	(water)	tOk	(talk)

klOth   (cloth)
gOn   (gone)
sOft   (soft)

"AW" . . . . as in "force," "court," "portion," etc.

When "AW" precedes "r," the preferred change of the vowel is to "oo." This "oo" is similar in sound to the "oo" of "good"; however, it should be pronounced farther up in the mouth, closer to the teeth and lips.

DRILL WORDS

foors   (force)   hoorn   (horn)
koor/   (court)   uhboord   (aboard)
poorsh'n   (portion)   soor/   (sort)
              soord   (sword)
        muhsfoortyoon   (misfortune)
              poor   (pour)

"OO" . . . . as in "food," "do," "blue," etc.

Long "OO" changes to the short "oo" of the American word "good," or the American "OO" sound may be retained.

DRILL WORDS

food (food)   yoo   (you)   moon   (moon)
doo   (do)   trooth (truth)   tchooz (choose)
bloo (blue)   groop   (group)   spoon   (spoon)

"oo" . . . . as in "good," "wolf," "full," etc.

The long "OO" of "food" should be used for this short "oo."

DRILL WORDS

gOOd   (good)   bOOk   (book)
wOOlf   (wolf)   kuhrfOOl   (careful)
fOOl   (full)   kOOd   (could)
              pOOl   (pull)
              wOOd   (wood)
            wOOmuhn   (woman)

"yOO" . . . . as in "unit," "cube," "beauty," etc.

The "y" is retained and the long "OO" changed to the short "oo" by the Scots, making the combination "yoo."

DRILL WORDS

yooni:/   (unit)   fyoo   (few)
kyoob   (cube)   hyoomuhn   (human)
byoo/i   (beauty)   myoozi:k   (music)
              fyoo/1   (futile)
              yooz   (use)
              pyoor   (pure)

"U" . . . . as in "up," "love," "does," etc.

This short "U," as in the American word "up," is changed to the "oo" of the American word "soot." The word "soot" is used to show this change, rather than "good," which receives a similar sound, because the "oo" of "soot" is pronounced farther forward in the mouth. The "oo" which replaces the short "U" should also be sounded from the forward part of the mouth.

DRILL WORDS

oop	(up)	kroost	(crust)	froont	(front)
loov	(love)	roob	(rub)	noombuhr	(number)
dooz	(does)	shoov	(shove)	kroom	(crumb)

"ER" . . . . as in "curb," "work," "fir," etc.

Before "r," any vowel or combination of vowels (except "e" or a combination with "e") is changed to "uh," as in "kuhrb" (curb), "wuhrd" (word) and "fuhr" (fir).

DRILL WORDS

puhrtchuhs	(purchase)	kuhrs	(curse)
wuhrshi:p	(worship)	wuhrm	(worm)
thuhrsti	(thirsty)	fuhrst	(first)
kuhruhj	(courage)		
uhrksoom	(irksome)		
tchuhrtch	(church)		

"ER" . . . . as in "earn," "herb," "certain," etc.

If "e" or a vowel combination with "e" comes before "r," the vowel is sounded "AY," as in the American word "take." This refers only to those words which take the "ER" sound and it does not refer to those words which are spelled with an "e" before "r" but pronounced "EH," as in "where" and "there." These were discussed earlier and it is suggested that they be reviewed now in order to avoid confusion. Final "er" is always pronounced "uhr" as in: "lEHituhr" (later).

DRILL WORDS

AYrn	(earn)	AYrthli	(earthly)
AYrb	(herb)	pAYrfEH/k'	(perfect)
sAYr/uhn	(certain)	AWbzAYrv	(observe)
sAYrtch	(search)		
klAYr	(clear)		
hAYrmi:/	(hermit)		

"OW" . . . . as in "out," "cow," "house," etc.

Although this American "OW" sound is often written "OO" (as in "food") by some interpreters of the Scottish dialect, there is in reality a very short "uh" sound preceding it. This makes the actual sound "uh-OO."

DRILL WORDS

uh-OO/	(out)		duh-OO/	(doubt)
kuh-OO	(cow)		uhbuh-OO/	(about)
huh-OOs	(house)		kruh-OOd	(crowd)

	huh-OO	(how)
	luh-OOd	(loud)
	muh-OOth	(mouth)

"OI" .... as in "oil," "boy," "noise," etc.

The American sound "OI" changes to "uh-EE" with the "uh" very short.

DRILL WORDS

uh-EEl	(oil)		tuh-EEl	(toil)
buh-EE	(boy)		spuh-EEl	(spoil)
nuh-EEz	(noise)		i:njuh-EE	(enjoy)

	i:mbruh-EEduhr	(embroider)
	luh-EE/uhr	(loiter)
	vuh-EEs	(voice)

WORD EXERCISES

Pronounce the following words in the Scottish dialect using the material learned from the preceding Vowel Changes:

1.	sinful	11.	relation
2.	haggis	12.	taskmaster
3.	tartan	13.	minister
4.	bagpipes	14.	little
5.	pitiful	15.	careless
6.	housemaid	16.	boiler
7.	gorse	17.	remember
8.	bloody	18.	oatmeal
9.	poor	19.	water-pump
10.	barnyard	20.	stomach-ache

When the above words have been tried, refer to the list below and check the vowels that were incorrectly sounded. Repeat the corrections a number of times.

1.	suhnfOOl	11.	rilEHish'n
2.	hOgi:s	12.	tOs'mOstuhr
3.	tuhr/uhn	13.	mi:nuhstuhr
4.	bOgpuhEEps	14.	luh/uhl
5.	puh/i:fOOl	15.	kuhrluhs
6.	huhOOsmEHid	16.	buhEEluhr
7.	goors	17.	ri:mi:mbuhr
8.	bloodi	18.	AW/mi:l
9.	pOOr	19.	wO/uhrpoomp
10.	buhrnyuhrd	20.	stoomuh/EHi/

CONSONANT CHANGES

B, C, D, F, and **G**—The same as in American.

H—The same as in American. When used *after* "w," as in "why," it is pronounced *before* the "w," as in "h-wuhEE" (why).

J—The same as in American.

K—The same as in American when used initially and medially. It may be dropped when final, as in "tEHi'" (take), "bEHi'" (bake), but this will tend to make the dialect too thick. It is suggested that the pronunciation of final "k" be very light.

L—The same as in American when used initially and medially. When final and preceded by "AW" as in "call," or "oo" as in "full," the "l" may be dropped, as "kAW'" (call), "fOO'" (full), "AW'" (all) and "wi:shfOO'" (wishful).

M, N, P, and **Q**—The same as in American.

R—The Scottish "r" is not at all like the American. It is commonly referred to as the "burred r," but this is nothing more than the trilled "r" and need not be viewed with alarm. It is produced by holding the tongue forward in the mouth and then bringing the tip quickly upward and exhaling through the mouth as the "r" is sounded. The air passing through the narrow opening made by the tip of the tongue and the roof of the mouth, causes the tip to vibrate. The "r" in Scottish dialect should be burred whether it be an initial, medial, or final letter. Not only is it a characteristic of the Scottish dialect, but it also governs the change of most of the vowel sounds. Perfection in the production of this burred "r" is essential to an authentic Scottish dialect.

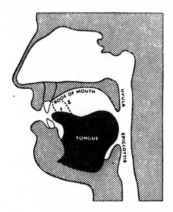

The black area indicates the position of the tongue as it begins trilling the Scottish "r." The dotted line shows the tongue curling upward to touch the forward part of the roof of the mouth. An extended series of this rapid interchange of positions causes the trilled Scottish "r."

S—The same as in American.

T—The same as in American when used initially. Under certain conditions when "t" or "tt" is medial or final, it is replaced by the glottal stop. (Refer to the section on "The Glottal Stop.")

V—For a light dialect, "v" should be treated as in American. It may be dropped occasionally when final. But, for a thicker dialect, drop final "v" consistently, as in "hO'" (have).

W, X, Y, and **Z**—The same as in American.

SH—The same as in American.

TCH—This should be treated the same as in American and "church" should be pronounced "tchuhrtch" not "kuhrk."

TH—The same as in American. It may be dropped from the word "with" (wi:').

th—The same as in American.

GH—The treatment of "gh" in words like "light," "daughter," and "might," is the same as in American and should not be changed to a guttural "kh." A great many Scotsmen substitute this "kh" but the effect results in a dialect that is as thick and as indigestible as Scottish haggis.

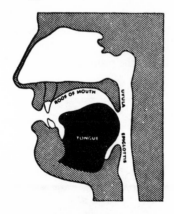

The back of the tongue is raised to touch the uvula at the end of the soft palate. When the breath is brought up past this conjuncture, it is roughened and voiced, producing the Scotch "kh" sound. Neither the tongue nor the uvula vibrates when this sound is produced.

CONTRACTIONS

Because of the habit of eliding or glottalizing certain final consonants, and also because the Scots prefer short words, there are a great number of contractions in their dialect. The verb phrase "can not" (kOn nAW/) thus becomes "canna" (kOnuh/). It will be noticed that the glottal stop changes the "o" of "not" from "AW" to "uh."

In the verb phrase "dare not," the two words are run together and become "darena" (duhrnuh/).

Aside from the numerous verb phrase contractions, there is the important change in the word "it." The "i" is usually dropped when "it" is used as a subject, as "twould" (twOOd).

WORD EXERCISES

Pronounce the following words in the Scottish dialect using the material learned from the preceding Consonant Changes and Contractions:

1.	have	11.	roarer
2.	bitter	12.	cannot
3.	with	13.	it is
4.	careful	14.	wishful
5.	where	15.	wherefor
6.	bakeshop	16.	little
7.	brewery	17.	beggar
8.	battle	18.	daughter
9.	did not	19.	light
10.	bloater	20.	not

When the above words have been tried, refer to the list below for the proper pronunciation. Check the mistakes and correct them, repeating each correction until it has been memorized. The bold-face "**r**" indicates the heavily trilled "r."

1.	hO'	11.	roo**r**uh**r**
2.	bi:/uh**r**	12.	kOnuh'
3.	wi:'	13.	uhts or tuhz
4.	kuh**r**fOO'	14.	wuhshfOO'
5.	h-wuh**r**	15.	h-wuh**r**foor
6.	bEHikshAWp	16.	luh/uhl
7.	b**r**OOuh**r**i	17.	buhguh**r**
8.	bO/uhl	18.	dAW/uh**r**
9.	dinuh'	19.	luhEE/ or likht
10.	blAW/uh**r**	20.	nAW/

GRAMMAR

From reading the poems of Robert Burns and the dialect examples of most writers, one assumes that the dialect is replete with such words as "forby" (except for), "fell" (very), "hod" (hid), "muckle" (much), and "greet" (cry). Words of this type should be used sparingly and only when the context makes the meanings obvious. For example, in the sentence "doo yoo muh-EEnd THuh tuhEEm wi: li:v'd THuhr?" (Do you mind the time we lived there?), the word "mind" would seem to have the meaning of "object to" rather than "remember." The use of this word, then, would depend on the preceding and following dialog.

The adjective "bAWni" (bonny) meaning first-rate, or lovely, is fairly well known as in, "ti:z uh bAWni drEHs yoor wuhrin'," ('Tis a bonny dress you're wearing).

The past tense ending is often added to the present tense of a verb, as "telled" for "told." "uh tild i:/ wi: si:k i:mAWsh'n, i:/ mEHid THi:m kruh-EE." (I telled it with sic emotion, it made them cry.) In this sentence the word "sic" is used in place of the American word "such." Another Scottish word which might have been used in this sentence is "greet" for "cry." However, unless the word had been used previously and was well established, "cry" would be preferred.

The word "ken" (ki:n) for "know" is fairly well known, or, as the phrase would be in Scottish, "wi:l ki:nt."

A change in grammatical construction is not a typifying characteristic of the Scottish dialect. It is, rather, the glottal stop, burred "r," vowel changes and contractions which give the dialect its individuality.

SCOTTISH MONOLOG

(Adapted from a character in the authors' "Curtain Time" show, "Public Enemy Number 2," produced on the Mutual Network.)

(An old Scottish woman is busily working some yarn as she talks to a young woman and her little boy.)

I s'pose you know you're a very lucky woman. Ay! To have a laddie of your own. And to have watched him grow up. That's the lucky part. To take him home when he's a wee one—a little red bit, all kickin' and cryin' and yawnin' at the same time. An' then to see that first smile, an' to hear the first laugh. An' to feel those warm wet hands pattin' against your face. An' to know the best is yet to come—the best and the worst. 'Tis the growin' up that's hard to watch. Ay. When they're grown, they're not the same laddie anymore. They're big an' bristly an' will not cry though their heart is greetin'. I know a lot about the big lads. I got thousands of 'em. Ay, thousands! These socks I'm makin'—they're for John. He's not Scottish, but I dinna worry about that. My lads are all of different religion but their faith is the same. They're soldiers in the army of democracy.

PHONETIC REPRESENTATION

(Syllables in bold-face type are to be accented.)

"uhEE s'pAWz yoo^{nAW} yoor _{uh}vuh _{ri} looki wOO^{muhn.} _{uh} ^{EE!}"

t' hOv uh lOdi uhv yuhr **AWn**. 'n tuh hOv **wOt**cht hi:m grAW **oop**. **THO/s** THuh **loo**ki puhr/. tuh **tEH**ik hi:m **hAWm** hwi:n hi:z uh **wi:** wAHn—uh **li:/l** rEHd **bi:/**, AWl **ki**-k'n 'n **kruh-EE**'n, 'n **yOn**'n O/ THuh **sEHim tuh**-EEm. 'n THi:n tuh si: THO/ **fuh**rst **smuh**-EEl, 'n tuh hi:r THuh **fuh**rst lOf. 'n tuh fi:l THAWz **woo**rm **wEH/ hO**ndz **pO/**n uhgi:ns' yuhr **fEH**is. 'n tuh nAW THuh **bEHs'** i:z **yEH/** tuh **koom**—THuh **bEHs'** 'n THuh **wuh**rs'. ti:z THuh grAWin **oop** THO/s huhrd tuh **wOt**ch. **uh**-EE. hwi:n THEHir grAWn, THEHir nAW/ THuh sEHim lOdi i:nimoor. THEHir **bi:g** 'n **bruh**sli 'n wi:l nAW/ **kruh**-EE THAW THuhr **hOr/** i:z **gri:/**'n. uh nAW uh **lAW/** uhbuh-OO THuh **bi:g** lOdz. uh gAW/ **thuh**-OOzuhnz uhv'm. **uh**-EE, **thuh**-OOzuhnz! THi:z **sAW**ks uh-EEm **mEH**k'n—THEHir foor **jAWn**. hi:z nAW/ **skAW/**i:sh, boo/ uh di:nAW/ wuhri uhbuh-OO **THO/**. muh-EE lOdz'r AWl'v **di:**f'ri:n ri:**li:**joon boo/ THuhr **fEH**ith i:z THuh **sEH**im THEHir **sAW**ldyuhrz i:n THuh **Or**mi'v di:**mAW**kruhsi.

CHAPTER SIX

The German Dialect

THE GERMAN LILT

Strictly speaking, there is little lilt in the German language or dialect. The definition of lilt is "a rhythmical swing or cadence." Neither the language nor the dialect has these qualities. But in this book, lilt is used as a label for the inherent music in the speech. And, as such, the lilt of the German dialect is slow, plodding and pedestrian. Its lengthened vowel sounds are the result of deliberate thought processes evolving methodically into sonant speech. It is only in these vowel glides—which do not rise or fall but are simply attenuated on the same note—that the German dialect achieves a semblance of lilt.

On the whole, the speech is guttural with little music to be found in these harsh tones. It would be only a rabid Germanophile who could find "beautiful music" in the rasping gutturalness of "Ach!," "nacht," and "buch" with their gargled "ch's." The absence of long words in the dialect—although the language abounds in long, windy words—tends to brighten the plodding lilt that borders on the monotonous.

The keynote of the German pitch is somewhat below that of normal American. The high points and low points are usually reached with limited vowel-glides that are not so varied as, say, the Cockney or Swedish vowel-glide. There is a suggestion of the Swedish sing-song, rise-and-fall quality in German speech— but only a suggestion, for this trait is not so exaggerated as it is in Swedish.

This rise-and-fall motif is noticeable, particularly in the question form of sentence, as in:

<blockquote>
"vI: yOO: bplAY: vidt him?"
(Why you play with him?)
</blockquote>

"vI: yOO OO bplAY AY
                        vidt
                              him?"

The simple declarative sentence shows a similar, but more limited, rise-and-fall speech pattern, as in:

"I: kAHn O:lvAY:s gOH: hOH:m"
(I can always go home.)

                                    Ol   hOH:
                                                         OH
"I: kAHn O   vAY:s gOH: m"

These intonations, of course, change with the meaning to be conveyed and, naturally, the rise-and-fall would occur in other words if they were to be emphasized to suit the meaning intended. But there is a definite, if slight, rise and fall in German speech, and it should always be present in the dialect, too.

EMPHASIS

There is not much difference between the American and the German method of inner syllable and word emphasis. As a rule the German follows the American except that, in the German, the musical emphasis is used in the glide vowels in combination with some stress emphasis. There is a tendency, too, in the German, to make more definite separations between the various word syllables, as in "mAW nEE:" (money) and "rEH dtish" (radish). In American, these syllables would be run together so that there would be an even flow of sound instead of a momentary halt between syllables. Another variance occurs in the German tendency to emphasize the noun in an adjective-noun combination, as in "nI:s *dt*AY:" (nice day) whereas in American, we would give both words equal emphasis.

Many Germans retain the initial-syllable emphasis of their native tongue. Thus, they would say "**bp**OH:lI:dt" (polite) and "**EH**ntchOI:" (enjoy). It should be mentioned here that in the word "enjoy," and in all words beginning with a vowel, the German prefixes a sort of glottal stop. This sound can best be heard by forcefully whispering initial-vowel words like "imp," "enter," or "always."

But the fact remains that the emphasis in the German dialect should be a bit heavier than in the American. It should be further noted that the vowel-glide governs the tonal emphasis in all inner-word emphasis. This will be discussed further in the "Vowel Change" section following.

VOWEL CHANGES

Note: For such unusual consonant combination sounds as "bp" and "dt," refer to the corresponding American consonant sounds listed under Consonant Changes.

"AY" . . . . as in "take," "break," "they," etc.

The long "a" vowel sound is retained in the German dialect—as are all the other long vowel sounds—but it is given a more attenuated treatment. Whereas, in American, we would pronounce it as "AY-EE," with emphasis on the "AY" and a vanishing glide on the "EE," the German gives each part its full emphasis and draws out each sound to almost twice the duration that the American would. The same practice applies to all the other long vowel sounds.

DRILL WORDS

bpAY:	(pay)	sAY:ndt	(saint)
dtAY:	(they)	bprAY:	(prey)
nAY:	(neigh)	vAY:	(way)

vAY:lAY:	(waylay)
mAY:bpEE:	(maybe)
vfAY:gkAY:dt	(vacate)

"UH" . . . . as in "alone," "sofa," "final," etc.

Used initially, this mute "a" is treated in the German dialect as "A" (as in "bat") or "AH" (as in "alms"). Medially and finally, it is given the same pronunciation as the American "UH." The sound, "UH," can also be given to the mute "a" initially without disturbing the dialect, for a great many Germans use the "UH" sounds in such words as, "UHlOH:n" (alone) and "sOH:vfUH" (sofa).

"AH" . . . . as in "father," "arm," "park," etc.

Some Germans pronounce this "a" as it is in American. But, again, it is of almost double duration and with the lips more widely separated, the sound coming from deeper in the throat—as when, after the mouth has been widely opened, the doctor orders an "AH." Here, the attenuation will be indicated, as it always is throughout this book, with the sign (:), as in "AH:." Other Germans give this "AH" the "A" sound of "bad."

DRILL WORDS

vfAH:r	(far)	tchAH:r	(jar)
gkAH:rvf	(carve)	bpAH:rn	(barn)
AH:rmEE	(army)	dtAH:rdt	(tart)

shbpAH:rgk'l	(sparkle)
dtEE:bpAH:rgk	(debark)
dtAH:rlingk	(darling)

"A:" .... **as in "ask," "draft," "laugh," etc.**

The "AH:" of "father" is given to this "A:," as in "AH:sk" (ask). This "AH:," like the "AH:" of "father," is drawn out and throated. (The "A" of "bad" may also be used.)

DRILL WORDS

lAH:sdt	(last)	shdtAH:vf	(staff)
lAH:vf	(laugh)	mAH:sdtUHr	(master)
lAH:sdt	(last)	nAH:dtsEE:	(Nazi)
gkAH:zOH:lEEn	(gasoline)		
bpAH:sgk't	(basket)		
hAH:vfvAY:	(halfway)		

"A" .... **as in "bad," "am," "guarantee," etc.**

This "a" sound, when used before all consonant sounds except "f," "n," "s" and "t," is pronounced as "EH," in the German, as in "bpEHdt" (bad). This vowel sound is not lengthened. A variant is "AH" as in "bpAHdt" (bad).

DRILL WORDS

sEHdt	(sad)	dtEHmbp	(damp)
bpEHdt	(bad)	shdtEHbp	(stab)
bpEHdt	(pat)	mEHlEEs	(malice)
bpEHgkitch	(baggage)		
vfEHbprEE:gk	(fabric)		
vfEHgkdtAW:rEE:	(factory)		

"AW" .... **as in "ball," "water," "shawl," etc.**

The Germans substitute "O" (as in "rod") for this "a," as in "bpOl" (ball). The lengthening process of vowels applies also to this vowel sound. The "AW" sound may be used if the lips are tightly pursed.

DRILL WORDS

gkOl	(call)	vfOldtUHr	(falter)
hOl	(hall)	shOl	(shawl)
shdtOl	(stall)	vOdtUHr	(water)
dtOdtUHr	(daughter)		
nOdtEE:	(naughty)		
OlvAY:s	(always)		

"EE" .... **as in "he," "treat," "people," etc.**

This long "e" is pronounced as it is in American but, of course, it is given the Germanic coloring by lengthening so that it becomes "EE:," as in "hEE:" (he).

DRILL WORDS

bpEE:	(be)	gkAW:vfEE:	(coffee)
bpEE:n	(bean)	nEE:s	(niece)
sEE:n	(scene)	gkrEE:s	(grease)

                    bpEE:lEE:vf   (believe)
                    bpEE:bp'l   (people)
                    EE:vf'ningk   (evening)

"EH" .... as in "bet," "said," "friend," etc.

This short "e" retains its "EH" sound as in American with no appreciable lengthening.

"I" .... as in "ice," "aisle," "guile," etc.

Long "i" is one of the vowels that typify the extreme lengthening of vowel sounds in the German dialect. Where, in American, we give "AH-EE" (the phonetic version of long "i") equal emphasis on both parts of the vowel sound, the German lengthens the first part, "AH," to almost three times its normal duration; he also lengthens the second part, "EE." The result is a very long "I:" sound.

DRILL WORDS

I:s	(ice)		rI:dt	(right)
bpI:	(buy)		shbpI:dt	(spite)
dtrI:	(try)		vI:vf	(wife)

                    bpOH:lI:dt   (polite)
                    sI:gklOH:n   (cyclone)
                    hI:vflI:UHr   (high-flyer)

"i" .... as in "it," "women," "busy," etc.

This short "i" is pronounced as it is in American with no appreciable lengthening.

"O" .... as in "on," "bond," "John," etc.

In the German dialect, this "o" is broadened to "AW" as in "AWn" (on), but the lengthening is not so exaggerated as it is in the long vowels.

DRILL WORDS

bpAWndt	(bond)		gkrAWbp	(crop)
bprAWdt	(prod)		tchAWnEE:	(Johnny)
rAWdt	(rod)		AWnEHsdt	(honest)

                    bpAWzib'l   (possible)
                    hAWsbpidt'l   (hospital)
                    AWbpAWn   (upon)

"OH" .... as in "bone," "sew," "dough," etc.

Like the long "i," this long "o" is pronounced as it is in American. But, in the lengthening process, what is "OH-OO" in the American with equal length given to both parts, becomes, in the German, "OOOOH-OOOO." Here, it will be designated as "OH:," as in "bpOH:n" (bone).

DRILL WORDS

sOH:	(sew)		hOH:m	(home)
tchOH:	(Joe)		dtOH:	(dough)
gkOH:	(go)		vfEHlOH:	(fellow)

bprOH:dtEHgkdt   (protect)
gklOH:dtingk   (clothing)
mOH:ningk   (moaning)

"AW" .... as in "off," "cough," "bought," etc.

This sound is pronounced as it is in American but it, too, is lengthened and should be brought up from deeper in the throat, as in "AW:vf" (off).

DRILL WORDS

dtAW:vf	(doff)	gkAW:vf	(cough)
AW:vf	(off)	sAW:dt	(sought)
AW:dt	(ought)	lAW:rdt	(lord)

tchAW:rtch   (George)
AW:vfisUHr   (officer)
mAW:rningk   (morning)

"OO" .... as in "food," "do," "blue," etc.

The American pronunciation of long double "oo," (OO), is retained in the dialect except that it, too, is given the same elongated treatment, as in "vfOO:dt" (food).

DRILL WORDS

mOO:n	(moon)	sgkOO:l	(school)
sOO:bp	(soup)	sUHlOO:n	(saloon)
nOO:	(knew)	mOOvfEE:	(movie)

sOO:dtUHb'l   (suitable)
nOO:sbpAY:bpUHr   (newspaper)
bpOO:dtlEHgkUHr   (bootlegger)

"oo" .... as in "good," "wolf," "full," etc.

This short double "o" (oo) is pronounced as long double "o" (OO), as in "gkOOdt" (good). Again, the sound should be drawn out to obtain the vowel elongation of the German dialect.

DRILL WORDS

bpOO:dt	(put)	shOO:dt	(should)
hOO:dt	(hood)	vOO:lvf	(wolf)
lOO:gk	(look)	gkrOO:gk	(crook)

bpyOO:dtEE:vfOO:l   (beautiful)
bprOOgklin   (Brooklyn)
hOOdtvingk   (hoodwink)

"yOO" .... as in "unite," "cube," "beauty," etc.

Because the German dialect treats long double "o" (OO) as "OO:," it also uses this long "u" as "yOO:," as in "yOO:nidt" (unit). The vowel sound is, of course, drawn out.

DRILL WORDS

gkyOO:	(cue)	myOO:sigk	(music)
vfyOO:	(few)	gkyOO:bp	(cube)
bpyOO:	(pew)	bpyOO:dtEE:	(beauty)
	yOO:nEE:vfAW:rm	(uniform)	
	yOO:nI:dtEHdt	(united)	
	gkyOO:bpidt	(cupid)	

"U" .... as in "up," "love," "does," etc.

This vowel sound is always pronounced as "AW:" in the German, as in "AW:bp" (up), with the vowel sound drawn out.

DRILL WORDS

gkAW:bp	(cup)	bpAW:bpEE:	(puppy)
bplAW:ndt	(blunt)	slAW:gk	(slug)
gkAW:m	(come)	dtAW:s	(does)
	lAW:vflEE:	(lovely)	
	hAW:sbpUHndt	(husband)	
	sAW:sbpEE:shAW:s	(suspicious)	

"ER" .... as in "curb," "earn," "fern," etc.

Next to the elongation of the long vowels, the pronunciation of this vowel sound is one of the most important in the dialect. Up to this point, nothing has been said about the German *umlaut* sound. A discussion of this peculiarity will be found on page 130 in the section on "The German Umlaut." It is this *umlaut* treatment that affects the "ER" vowel sound more than it does any of the other vowel sounds and, for that reason, should be used to color this vowel sound. It can be achieved simply by pursing the lips, placing the tongue in a position to sound the vowel and, instead, sounding "EH." Actually, as in the case of the vowel sound "ER," the pronunciation would be as follows: "dtEHrdtEE" (thirty). It is the pursing of the lips and the gutturalizing of the "EH" substitute for "ER" that will provide the umlaut effect. Remember, always, to sound the following "r" as though it were being gargled with the uvula vibrating. Variations are "EE," with the lips pursed in the umlaut position, as in "vEErdt" (worth); and the normal American "ER" sound of these words, with the lips pursed, as in "vERdt" (worth).

DRILL WORDS

gkEHrbp	(curb)	vEHrdt	(worth)
vfEHr	(fur)	dtEHrdt	(dirt)
hEHr	(her)	lEHrn	(learn)
	dtEHrsdtAY:	(Thursday)	
	vflEHrdtAY:shAWs	(flirtatious)	
	dtisdtEHrbp	(disturb)	

"OW" .... as in "out," "cow," "house," etc.

Although this diphthong is pronounced as it is in American, both parts of it are, according to the German tendency of vowel attenuation, drawn out considerably, as in "AH-AH-OO-OOdt" (out). This elongation cannot, for obvious reasons, be reproduced in phonetics, so we shall designate it by "OW:," as in: "hOW:s" (house).

DRILL WORDS

nOW:	(now)	shdtOW:dt	(stout)
gkOW:	(cow)	lOW:dt	(loud)
hOW:	(how)	gklOW:dts	(clouds)
	dtrOO:OW:dt	(throughout)	
	dtOW:sUHndts	(thousands)	
	mOW:ndtUHn	(mountain)	

"OI" .... as in "oil," "boy," noise," etc.

This diphthong is also pronounced as it is in American but it is elongated to almost three times its duration, as in "AAAW-EEEl" (oil). However, because this phonetic spelling would be awkward, the vowel sound will be designated by "OI:," with the (:) sign indicating the elongation, as in "bpOI:" (boy).

DRILL WORDS

tchOI:	(joy)	rOI:UHl	(royal)
sOI:l	(soil)	UHnOI:	(annoy)
OI:l	(oil)	shbpOI:l	(spoil)
	EHntchOI:	(enjoy)	
	gkOI:dtUHr	(goiter)	
	EHmbprOI:dtUHr	(embroider)	

WORD EXERCISES

Pronounce the following words in the German dialect using the material learned from the preceding Vowel Changes:

1.	Europe	11.	losses
2.	homeland	12.	supper
3.	butcher shop	13.	operation
4.	market basket	14.	crawl
5.	policeman	15.	submarine
6.	sauerkraut	16.	German
7.	oil burner	17.	American
8.	electric	18.	ocean
9.	prize fight	19.	beautiful
10.	stupid	20.	understood

After attempting to pronounce the preceding words, refer to the phonetic list below for the proper pronunciation. Check the mistakes made, correct them and memorize.

1.	yOO:rAWbp	11.	lAW:sUHs
2.	hOH:mlEHndt	12.	sAW:bpEHr
3.	bpOO:tchEHrshAWbp	13.	AWbpEHrAY:shUHn
4.	mAH:rgkuhdtbpAH:sgk'dt	14.	gkrOl
5.	bpOH:lEE:smUHn	15.	sAWbpmUHrEE:n
6.	sOW:UHrgkrOW:dt	16.	tchEHrmUHn
7.	OI:IbpEH:rnUHr	17.	AHmEHrigkUHn
8.	EElEHgkdtrigk	18.	OH:shUHn
9.	bprI:svfI:dt	19.	bpyOO:dtivfOOl
10.	sdtOO:bpidt	20.	AW:ndtEHrsdtOO:dt

THE GERMAN UMLAUT

The German language has three vowel sounds that are not found in American. These are the umlauted "a," "o," and "u," the "a" and "u" seldom occurring in American. The umlaut "o," however, does occur in the pronunciation of "ER," as in "fur," "dirt," and "hurt." Naturally, German immigrants vary in their ability to acquire the American sound, so the use of the umlaut must remain a personal decision. But, if it is to be used in the "ER" words, the lips must be pursed and the vowel sound pronounced as "EH," "EE," or "ER."

CONSONANT CHANGES

The German dialect is affected more by its consonant changes than by its vowel changes. With the exception of elongation, practically all the vowels are pronounced in German as they are in American. But with the consonants come a series of changes that endow the dialect with its most characteristic variations. Most of these changes will be listed below. Not all of them need be used to present an authentic German dialect. As a rule, the Northern German tends to have a cleaner consonantal attack, closer to the American, than does the Southern German.

It will be noticed that a number of consonants have been combined to produce one sound, as "dt," "bp," and "gk." These combination sounds are common to many Germans. Some, however, pronounce a clear "b," "d," "g," "p," "t," and "k" initially and change "b," "d," and "g" to "p," "t," and "k," respectively, when final, as in "mEHt" (mad). "b," also, is often changed to "p" when it is the final letter in a prefix or is followed by "s," as in "ApsAWlvf" (absolve) and "kEHps" (cabs).

B—This consonant receives a combination "bp" treatment. The only way to achieve this peculiar pronunciation is to sound the "b" hard and hit the "p" lightly, so that it does not receive the aspirate "uh." If the sound is difficult to get, use the softened "p" substitute. With this combination, the following words would read as "*bp*OH:n" (bone), "lAY:*bp*'l" (label) and "nEH*bp*" (nab). Although this "bp" or "p" substitution is common to many Germans, others are likely to use a clearer "b" sound.

C—For hard "c," see "K." For soft "c," see "S."

D—This is another combination consonant. The German pronounces it as "dt" and, as a result, both letters appear to be interchanged. The fact is, however, that it is the combination that causes the deception. To obtain the combination sound, hit the "d" hard and the "t" softly. If the effect is difficult, merely stress the "t" softly, as in "dtAY:l" (dale), "lAH:rdtUHr" (larder) and "mEHdt" (mad).

F—The German combines this consonant "f" with a "v," as in "vf." Again, to achieve this combination, stress the "v" and soften the "f." If the effect is difficult, sound the "v" substitute softly, as in "vfl:n" (fine), "nEHvfdtUH" (naphtha) and "lAH:vf" (laugh). This "vf" sound may be achieved by pronouncing it like the "h" in the correct pronunciation of the American word "h-wI" (why).

G—For soft "g," see "J." Hard "g" is still another of the combination consonants for its carries with it the sound of "k," as in "gkAY:l" (gale). Again, the only way to approximate this sound is to pronounce the "g" hard and the "k" softly. If the effect cannot be achieved, simply stress the "k" substitute softly, as in "gkrOH:" (grow), "mEHgkUHdt" (maggot) and "nEHgk" (nag).

H—This consonant is pronounced as it is in American.

J—Some Germans, usually Southerners, substitute "tch" for this "j" sound, as in "tchAW:tch" (George), "bpEHtchUHr" (badger) and "tchAW:tch" (judge). Other Germans pronounce this "J" sound as we do in American.

K—The double consonant sound with which this single consonant is endowed, is in the German dialect, "gk." To achieve it, lay more stress on the "g" and less on the "k." If the effect is difficult, simply substitute a "g" sound softly stressed, as in "gkrEHbp" (crab), "bpEHgkgkrOW:ndt" (background) and "lAWgk" (lock). The second example, "background," illustrates a word in which both "k" and "g" come together. To pronounce them both correctly, first sound the "g" softly and then the "k" softly, as though the word were written "bpEHgkrOWndt." Some Germans pronounce "K" as "K" but with more force than do the Americans.

L—The German "l" should be sounded with the tip of the tongue flattened against the back of the upper front teeth.

M and **N**—The same as in American.

P—This consonant is combined with "b," as was explained under "B," to make the consonant sound "bp" in the German dialect. To accomplish this combination, soften the "p" stress and emphasize the "b." If the effect cannot be accomplished, simply substitute a softly stressed "b," as in "bpEHk" (pack), "nE-Hbpingk" (napping) and "hOH:bp" (hope). Germans also pronounce "p" like the Americans. But when they do, the "p" is overstressed so that an aspirate "uh" follows.

Q—Ordinarily the consonant "q" is sounded, in American, as "kw," as in "kwik" (quick). But, because of the peculiar consonant changes in the German dialect, the combination is changed to "gkvf," as in "*gkvf*igk" (quick), "bpEE:*gkvf*EE:dt" (bequeath) and "rEE:*gkv*EHsdt" (request). A simplification of "q" is "kv" as in "kvigk" (quick). (See "F.")

R—This is one of the most characteristic sounds in the German dialect, and there are several ways of pronouncing it. The first is the trilled "r," typical of the Scotch burr, with the tip of the tongue vibrating against the forward part of the roof of the mouth. The second method is the uvular "r," in which the uvula is vibrated against the soft palate—the back part of the roof of the mouth—in a sort of gargle. This is the preferred method and can be used initially, medially and finally. If, however, this vibration is too difficult to accomplish it can be dispensed with. The rough rasp of the breath grating against the semi-closed throat passage is all that a great many Germans can achieve and it can serve almost as well as the rolled uvular "r." This latter method is the one used by radio and burlesque comedians *ad nauseum* so, if it is to be used at all, it should be used only for a broad comedy effect.

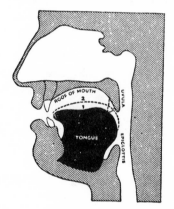

The German rolled "r" is pronounced with the tongue, in the position of the dotted line (2), rising slightly and vibrating against the uvula, then returning to its normal position (1). The dotted uvula line indicates the simultaneous vibration of the uvula. In pronouncing the normal guttural "r," the position of the tongue and uvula is the same as in the rolled "r" but neither the tongue nor the uvula is vibrated.

S—The consonant "s" is another high spot in the German dialect. Ordinarily, it is pronounced as it is in American except that, when it is used to begin a word, it is given a slight "z" flavoring. Too, it should be more sharply hissed than the American "s."

The Austrian German always gives "s" its usual treatment, as in "sUn" (sun). But the German substitutes a "z" sound, as in "zAWn" (sun) and "bpAWzib'l" (possible) when "s" is initial or between vowels. Although this sound may be a definite "z," it is usually a strongly hissed "s" with a "z" flavor. For this reason it has been written as "s" in this chapter. Final "s" is pronounced as "s" and not "z," as in "gkOW:s" (cows).

A great many Germans substitute "sh" for "s," initially, especially when it comes before "l," "m," "n," "p," "t," or "w," as in "*sh*lOH:" (*s*low), "*sh*mOH:gk" (*s*moke), "shnEHbp" (*s*nap), "*sh*prAY:" (*s*pray), "*sh*tEE:l" (*s*teel) and "*sh*vim" (*s*wim). For a broad effect, this substitution can be used, but, ordinarily, it is suggested that the initial "s" be pronounced with a faint suggestion of "z."

T—This consonant, in the German dialect, receives a combination "dt" treatment. To pronounce it, stress the "d" harder than usual and the "t" much more softly. If the effect cannot be accomplished, simply substitute a softly sounded "t," as in "d*t*l:m" (*t*ime), "mEHd*t*UHr" (ma*tt*er) and "sEHd*t*" (sa*t*). It is also permissible to sound the "t" as in American but it should be aspirated more forcefully.

V—This is another consonant that is treated with a double consonant sound, as in "vfI:*vf*" (fi*v*e). In this example, the initial "f" adds a softly stressed "v," while the final "v" is substituted by a softly stressed "f" sound. To accomplish it, try to sound the "v" weakly and the "f" more strongly. If the effect cannot be achieved, simply substitute a weakly stressed "f," as in "*vf*AY:l" (*v*eil), "li*vf*ingk" (living) and "li*vf*" (live).

W—The consonant "w" receives a "v" substitute in the dialect, which, in turn, is treated as "vf." In this case, the "v" is stressed hard while the "f" is softened. If, however, the combination cannot be accomplished, substitute the softened "v" sound, as in "*v*itch" (which), "lEE:vAY:" (leeway) and "*v*EHr*v*OOlv*f*" (werewolf).

X—This consonant, in American, has two pronunciations, "ks," as in "EH*k*splAYn" (e*x*plain) and "gz," as in "EH*gz*Agkt" (e*x*act). In the "ks" pronunciation, the German dialect substitutes a "gz," as in "EH*gzb*plAY:n" (e*x*plain), "lEH*gz*" (la*x*) and "dtEH*gz*EE" (ta*x*i). In the "gz" pronunciation, the dialect substitutes "ks," as in "EH*ks*AHgkdt" (e*x*act), "EH*ks*EHmbpOOl" (e*x*ample) and "EH*ks*isdt" (e*x*ist).

Y—The same as in American.

Z—There are three pronunciations given to this consonant sound. Initially, it is quite often treated as "ts," as in "*ts*id*t*UHr" (*z*ither), "*ts*ingk" (*z*inc) and "*ts*OH:n" (*z*one). Medially, when it is spelled "s," as in "reason," or when it is spelled "z," as in "lazy," it is pronounced as a sibilant "s," as in "rEE:*s*AWn" (rea*s*on) and "lAY:*s*EE:" (la*z*y). When it is used as the end of a word, it is *always* treated as a sibilant "s," no matter if it is spelled "s," as in "has," or "z," as in "daze." Some examples are: "hEHs" (ha*s*), "I:s" (eye*s*) and "sERbprI:s" (surpri*z*e).

SH—This sound is usually the same as in American, and should remain so. Some Germans, however, substitute a "zh" sound as in "azure." Thus, they say "zhOO:dt" for "should," etc.

TH—This voiced "th" is ordinarily treated as "*dt*" in the German dialect, with the "d" receiving the emphasis, as in "*dt*is" (this), "*dt*UH" (the) and "fAH:*dt*UHr" (father). There are though, a great many Germans, who substitute, instead, the French "z," as in "*z*OH:s" (those), "vfEH*z*UHr" (feather) and "bAY:*z*" (bathe). Although the former pronunication is preferred, the latter can be used to vary a characterization.

th—This unvoiced "th" is treated in the German dialect, as "*dt*" with the stress on the "t," as in "*dt*in" (thin), "mid*t*" (myth) and "bpOH:*dt*" (both). The same Germans who pronounce the voiced "th" as "z," treat the unvoiced "th" as "s," as in "*s*in" (thin), "mi*s*" (myth) and "bOH:*s*" (both). The two variations should never be mixed. Either "t" and "d" are used together or "s" and "z."

TCH—This sound is usually the same as it is in American. Some Germans substitute an "sh" but the customary treatment is preferred.

ZH—This thickened "z" sound found, for example, in "azure," is changed to "sh" in the dialect, as in "EH*sh*OO:r" (azure), "rOO*sh*" (rouge) and "vfyOO:*sh*UHn" (fusion).

WORD EXERCISES

Pronounced the following words in the German dialect using the material learned from the preceding Consonant Changes:

1.	crab apple	11.	thirty-three
2.	laughing	12.	racket
3.	wagonload	13.	examination
4.	lifesaver	14.	absolute
5.	weather	15.	with
6.	execution	16.	airplane
7.	zebra	17.	starve
8.	pleasure	18.	people
9.	ragged	19.	protection
10.	require	20.	Constitution

After pronouncing the above words, refer to the phonetic list below for the proper pronunciation. Check the mistakes made, correct them and memorize.

1.	gkrEHbpEHbpUHl	11.	dtEH:rdtEEdtrEE: or
2.	lAH:vfingk		sEH:rdtEE srEE:
3.	vfEHgkAWnlOH:dt	12.	rEHgkEHdt
4.	lI:vfsAY:vfUHr	13.	EHgkzEHminAY:shUHn
5.	vfEHdtUHr or vfEHzUHr	14.	EHbpsOH:lOO:dt
6.	EHgkzUHgkyOO:sh'n	15.	vfidt or vfis
7.	tsEE:bprUH	16.	EHrbplAY:n
8.	bplEHshOO:r	17.	sdtAH:rvf
9.	rEHgkEHdt	18.	bpEE:bp'l
10.	rEEkvfl:r	19.	bprOHdtEH:gkshUHn
		20.	gkAWnsdtidtOO:shUHn

GRAMMAR CHANGES

Perhaps the most typical grammar change in the German dialect occurs with the inversion of sentence structure so that the verb is placed at the end of a sentence, instead of somewhere in the middle, as in:

"vEHr dtUH bpOI: is?"   "hEE: vOs dtEHr gkOH:ingk?"
(Where the boy *is*?)   (He was there *going*?)
(Where is the boy?)   (He was *going* there?)

dtidt hEE:vAWs dtEH*dt* rI:dt dtOO:ingk?"
(Did he was that right *doing*?)
(Was he *doing* that right?)

Another example of this inversion is found in the German's habit of placing adverbs at the end of sentences instead of next to the verb they modify, as in:

"hEE: vAWs bpI: dtUH hOWs AWbpshtEHrs."
(He was by the house *upstairs*).
(He was upstairs in the house.)

"idt is bpI: dtUH sEHlUHr dtOWn."
(It is by the cellar *down*.)
(It is *down* in the cellar.)

"dtUH EHrbplAY:n vAWs in dtUH EHr AW:bp."
(The airplane was in the air *up*.)
(The airplane was *up* in the air.)

This habit of verb and adverb inversion creates sentence structures in which prepositional phrases are used to begin sentences that end with the verb, as in:

"in dtUH hOWs, dtAY: vAWs dtUH mEHn dtAY:gkingk."
(*In the house*, they were the man taking.)
(They were taking the man *into the house*.)

"in dtUH vOdtUHr, dtUH vfish vAWs svimingk."
(*In the water*, the fish was swimming.)
(The fish were swimming *in the water*.)

"bpI: dtUH hOWs, dtUH mAH:mAH: is."
(*By the house*, the mama is.)
(Mama is *in the house*.)

Of course, as do all foreigners, the Germans have difficulty in relating the subject to the proper verb form, as in:

"dtAY: vAWs Ol dtEHr."
(They *was* all there.)
(They *were* all there.)

"is dtUH bpAY:bpEHrs dtEHr?"
(*Is* the papers there?)
(*Are* the papers there?)

"dtUH tchAWbp vAWs *gk*OO:dt dtidt."
(The job was good *did*.)
(The job was *done* well.)

Sometimes, the verb or its auxiliary is entirely dropped in the dialect, as in:

"hEE: bpEE: sOO:n OW:dt."
(He be soon out.)
(He *will* soon be out.)

"dtAY: OlvAY:s lAY:dt."
(They always late.)
(They *are* always late.)

"vEE: nEHvfUHr sEE dtUH bpOI:ndt."
(We never see the point.)
(We *could* never see the point.)

The unnecessary addition of the definite article "the" is noticeable in such sentences as:

"bpI: dtUH shtAWr, dUH mAH:mAH: is."
(By the store, *the* mama is.)
(Mama is at the store.)

"dtUH AW:ngk'l bpI: dtUH dtrAY:n is."
(*The* uncle, by the train is.)
(Uncle is at the train.)

"dtUH lI:vf, vEHrEE: vfAWnEE: is."
(*The* life, very funny is.)
(Life is very funny.)

There is a common misuse of the preposition "by," when it is substituted for the prepositions "in" and "at," as in:

"bpI: dtUH AW:ngk'l, I: vAWs shdtAY:ingk."
(*By* the uncle, I was staying.)
(I was staying *at* my uncle's house.)

"shEE: vAWs bpI: dtUH mEE:dtingk."
(She was *by* the meeting.)
(She was at the meeting.)

"dtUH mEHn bpI: dtUH dtAWrvAY: vAWs."
(The man *by* the doorway, was.)
(The man was *in* the doorway.)

There are a number of other grammatical changes, but the foregoing will give sufficient dialectical coloring. Most of the changes can be used quite often, but the verb and prepositional phrase inversions should not be overdone.

SENTENCE EXERCISES

Pronounce the following sentences in the German dialect using the material learned from the preceding Grammar Changes:

1. Where is the man walking?
2. Her sister is in the country.
3. They were running in all directions.
4. Are the apples good for eating?
5. I would like to go but Mama says no.
6. Mankind should be more understanding.
7. All the children are going to a picnic.
8. There will always be democracy.
9. I will be waiting at the house.
10. They were going to the concentration-camp.

After making the changes, refer to the phoneticized sentences below. Check the mistakes made, correct them and repeat to memorize.

1. vfEHr dtUH mEHn is vfOgkingk?
2. bpI: dtUH gkAWndtrEE hEHr sisdtUHr is.
3. in Ol dtirEHgkshUHns dtAY: vfAWs rAWningk.
4. is dtUH EHbpUHls vfAWr EE:dtingk gkOO:dt?
5. I: ll:gk dtOO: gkOH: bpAWdt dtUH mAHmAH sAY: nOH:.
6. dtUH mEHngkI:ndt shOO:dt mAWr AWndtEHrsdtEHndtingk bpEE.
7. Ol dtUH shildtrUHn is dtOO dtUH bpigknigk gkOH:ingk.
8. OlvfAY:s dtEHr vfil dtUH dtEHmAWgkrUHsEE bpEE.
9. I: vfil bI: dtUH hOW:s vfAY:dt.
10. dtOO dtUH gkAWnsEHndtrAY:shUHn gkEHmbp dtAY: vfAWs gkOH:ingk.

TYPICAL PHRASES AND INTERJECTIONS

There are a number of interjections used in the German dialect. One of these is "AHkh" (ach!), with the gargled "kh" used as in "AHkh, nOH:!" (oh, no!) when surprise, disgust, amazement or any other strong emotion is felt.

There is also a tendency to end a question sentence with the interjections "nOH:" (no) or "yAH:" (yes), as in "I: vAWs rI:dt, nOH:?" (I was right, no?) or "yOO: gkOH: nOW:, yAH:?" (you go now, yes?).

When such emotions as indignation, amazement, surprise, protest, etc., are experienced, many Germans respond with a hurt "bplEEs!" (please!), which is a carryover from the language's "bpidtuh" (bitte), of the same meaning and use.

GERMAN LANGUAGE CARRYOVERS

There are a number of German words that are carried over into the dialect speech. These can be used occasionally but only enough to flavor the dialect. They should never be used if confusion of meaning would result.

auf wiedersehen	OW:vf vEE:dtEHrzAY:n	goodbye
bittebpidtuh	please	
entschuldigen Sie	EHndtshOOldtigkEHn zEE:	excuse me
danke	dtAHngkuh	thank you
sehr gut	zAY:r gkOOdt	very good
warum	vAHrOOm	why?
setzen Sie sich	zEHdtzEHn zEE: zikh	sit down
warten Sie	vAHrdtEHn zEE	wait
wie gehts	vEE: gkAY:dts	hello
wie gehts es Ihnen	vEE: gkAY:dt EHs EE: nEHn	how do you do
ya, mein Herr	yAH mI:n hEHr	yes, sir
ya, madam	yAH mAHdtAHm	yes, madam
nein, Fraulein	nI:n frOWlI:n	no, miss
seien Sie ruhig	zI:EHn zEE: rOOhEEgk	be quiet
vorsicht	vfAWrzikhdt	take care
was sagen Sie	vAHs zAHgkEHn zEE:	what do you say
was vAHs	what?	

GERMAN DIALECT MONOLOG

(Adapted from a character in the authors' broadcast radio drama, "Earth Hunger.")

(It is twilight. On a knoll, overlooking a wide expanse of farm land, a young girl—a German refugee—sits on the ground and stares entrancedly over the spread of land. Then she looks up at her newly-wedded husband and says breathlessly:)

The air, here, it is so clean. Not like in the city. Hans—all this big farm and all this stuff growing, it was yours, no? It was ours. Oh! I am so happy. The city, it was something bad to remember. The tall buildings, the crazy people—it is all behind me. I was being born over again. Now life is in front of me. Once I drink champagne. Now, when I breathe the fresh air, I feel like when I had the champagne—light and silly-like in the head—and, oh! so happy in the heart! Look! I lay down on the ground and stretch the arms in the grass. I have for years dreamed I could lay so with the arms in the grass stretched. Listen! when I put the ear to the earth, I can hear things growing. I can hear the earth breathing. Oh! it is because I am of the earth that I know and feel these things. For years, I starved myself and I was hungry for the earth. Now I have her, all of her. Look! I take the shoes and stockings off. So. I want to dig the feet into the earth . . . so! . . . like this . . . home! . . . home!

PHONETIC REPRESENTATION

(Instead of the double-consonant substitutes, the single consonant substitute is used for easier reading. Syllables in bold-face type are accented).

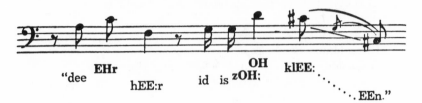

nAWd lI:g in dUH **zid**EE:, **hAH**ns—Ol dis pik **fAH**:rm oo:nt Ol dis shdAWf **krOH**:ink, id vAWs **yOOrs, nOH?** id vAWs **OW:rs. OH:!** I: AHm zOH! **hAH**bee:. dUH **zid**EE, id vAWs zAWmtink **bAH:t** tOO: rEE:mEHmpUHr. dUH tOl **pil**tinkss dUH **grAY**:zEE: bEE:b'l—id is Ol pEE:**hI**:nt mEE:. I: vAW, pEE:ink pAW:rn **OH**:fUHr AHkEHn. nOW: lI:f is in **frAW**nd AW:f mEE:. vAW:ns, I: tring tchAHm**bAY**:n. **nOW:**, vEHn I: prEE:t dUH frEHsh **EHr,** I: vEE:l lI:g vEHn I: **hEHt** dUH tchAH:m**bAY**:n—**lI:d** oo:nt zilEE: lI:g in dUH **hEHt**—oo:nt, **OH:!** **zOH: hEH**:bee in dUH **hAH**:rd! **lOO:g!** I: lAY: tOW:n AWn dUH **krOW**:nt oo:nt shdrEHtch dUH AH:rms in dUH krAH:s. I: hAH:f vAWr **yEE**:rs trEE:mt I: gOO:t **lAY:** zOH: vit dUH **AH**:rms in dUH **krAH:s** shdrEHtcht. **lis'n!** vEHn I: bOO:d dUH EE:r tOO: dUH EHrt I: gAH:n hEE:r tinks **krOH**:ink. I: gAH:n **hEE:r** dUH EHrt **brEE**:tink. Oh:! id is pEE:**gOH**:s I: AH:m AW:f dUH EHrt dAH:d I: **nOH:** oo:nt v EE:l dEE:s tinks. vAWr **yEE**:rs I: **shdAH**:rf mI:zEHlv oo:nt I: vAWs **hAW**nkrEE: vAWr dUH **EHrt.** nOW: I: **hAH:f** hEHr—**Ol**: AW:f hEHr! **lOO:g!** I: dAY:g dUH **shOO:s** oo:nt shdAWginks AWv. **zOH:!** I: vAWn dOO: tik dUH **vEE:d** indOO: dUH **EHrt** . . . **zOH:** ! . . . lI:g **dis** . . . **hOH:m!** . . . **hOH:m!**

CHAPTER SEVEN

The French Dialect

THE FRENCH LILT

The French language is spoken in a pitch that is the highest of all the Romance languages. Italian and Spanish both have the same excitable quality which tends to make the voice shrill—but they possess certain other features which soften them. The Italians, for instance, lengthen their vowels and introduce the aspirate "uh" abundantly. The Spanish people soften their consonants and use the aspirate "uh" occasionally. The French use none of these softening features.

Consequently, the French dialect is brisk and sharp and is spoken with almost staccato effect. This does not mean that they race through their words. On the contrary, they give each word its full, clear value. But they do break off each word cleanly and they do not linger on the vowel sounds. To achieve this staccato effect, it is necessary to break the sentences into small groups of words, for the French will vigorously stress several words in a sentence while the Americans will, possibly, stress two and those lightly. For example, the sentence, "All right, you change the dress" (OHl rAH-EE', yu shAHuzh dEE drA:s) would be spoken as follows:

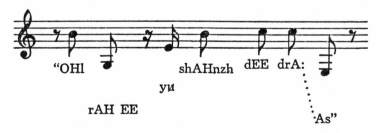

Although, in the above example, the last word "drAs" (dress) seems to follow the Italian habit of lengthening the vowels, such is not the case. The Italian draws out the vowels while the Frenchman simply changes the note on which it is sung. The French make this change rapidly.

In interrogative sentences, the Frenchman sings a rising song, as in the sentence "You like to go, eh?" (yʉ lAH-EEk tʉ gAW, EH?), in which the music pattern would be:

But in most other types of sentences, as in the typical first example, a rising-falling song is sung, as in the sentence, "Oh, no! Steffi, no! not that!" (AW nAW, stAfEE, nAW! nAWt dAHt!)

Although the general pitch level is often higher than it is in American, the French range is wider, but with the voice notes reaching the extreme lower registers.

EMPHASIS

One of the most characteristic habits in the French dialect is the Frenchman's insistence on accenting the last syllable in a word. There are times, in fact, when so very little dialect is required that the use of this quality alone can suggest the dialect sufficiently. Thus, in a word of four syllables, the first three would receive equal emphasis while the fourth would get this identifying overemphasis. The word "AHrtEEkyʉlEHT" (articulate), for example, illustrates this rule as does the two-syllabled word "rEElEE" (really), in which words the emphasis is on the last syllable instead of on the first, as it would be in American. Do not overdo this peculiarity in French dialect but, as often as possible, *accentuate the last syllable in a word.*

The French employ this final emphasis not only in the word unit but also in the sentence unit. The word which receives sentence emphasis is almost always the last word, but in the sentence "Now you in for it" (nAH yOO EEn fAWr EEt), the "in" reaches the highest pitch and thus gets equal stress with the "it." The sentence would be spoken as:

"nAH yOO **EEn**

fAWr **EEt!"**

All the words in the above sentence, with the exception of the last word "it," would receive equal but slightly more stress than in American. This word would get a shade more emphasis, not so much in stressed emphasis, achieved by exerting an extra amount of breath, but in tonal emphasis, achieved by changing the note on which the vowel is sung. Thus, the word emphasis is not hit hard but is merely suggested.

THE FRENCH NASAL

Before dealing with the vowel changes, it is necessary to give an explanation of the nasal treatment often given French vowels. Under certain conditions, vowel sounds are sent up into and through the nasal passages, instead of up from the chest and through the throat and mouth. To learn how to reproduce this quality, raise the back of the tongue until the throat passage is closed and the sound will be forced up through the nose. Do not hold the nose because the resulting sound will in no way be similar to a French nasal. Such a sound will be nothing more than that caused by the universal cold-in-the-head. A good word to practice with is "song." Pronounce only the first two letters and let the "ng" be a flavor but not a sound. The "ng" should be absolutely silent.

All the vowels do not take the same nasal sound, but "song" or "rang" or any short word ending in "ng" may be used for practice. The nasals must not be forced or unduly stressed or they will throw the whole dialect out of focus. The vowel sounds are not always nasalized as it is often and erroneously believed. The vowels are nasalized only under certain conditions and certain definite changes take place when the nasalization occurs.

1. *WHEN THE VOWEL SOUND IS NASALIZED THE "m" OR "n" IS DROPPED COMPLETELY.*

For example, in the word "AWnlEE" (only), the "o" changes to a nasal "AW" and the "n" is not sounded. Other examples are "pEHnt" (paint), "blAHnd" (bland) and "prEHnt" (print). The crossed "m" or "n" indicates that the consonant is dropped and the preceding vowel sound is nasalized.

2. *VOWEL SOUNDS ARE NASALIZED ONLY BEFORE A SINGLE "m" OR "n" FOLLOWED BY ANOTHER CONSONANT.*

If the vowel sound is to be nasalized, the vowel must be followed by "m" or "n" plus another consonant other than "m" or "n." Some examples are "blAWn̸d" (blonde), "AHm̸ptEE" (empty) and "EHn̸vIt" (invite). Thus, if a vowel is followed by "mm," "mn," "nm," or either "m" or "n" plus a vowel, there is no nasalization, as in "AHmnEEzyAH" (amnesia), "AWmEEt" (omit) and "drAHmAHtEEk" (dramatic).

3. *WHEN A WORD ENDS WITH "n" AND THE FOLLOWING WORD BEGINS WITH A VOWEL, THE "n" IS RETAINED AND THE VOWEL PRECEDING IT IS NOT NASALIZED.*

This rule applies only to "n" and need not be used for "m" unless a lighter dialect is needed. Some example phrases are, "yŪnyAWn AWfEEs" (union office), "stEHsyAWn AzhAHn̸'" (station agent) and "sERtEHn ERv" (certain of). It will be noticed that, in the first words, the final "n" is always retained because the following word begins with a vowel. But, if the following words had begun with consonants, the phrases would have read, "yŪnyAWn̸ dEEpAW" (union depot), "stEHsyAWn̸ mAHstEHr" (station master) and "sERtEHn̸ kAWn̸dEEsyAWn̸" (certain condition).

A further discussion of this rule will be found in the section called "The French Glide Rule."

As was mentioned before, there is no one set sound for all the nasalized vowels. Particular combinations have particular sounds and these sounds should be maintained. The following list should be learned thoroughly.

AHn̸" . . . . for "change," "plant," "pound," "plenty," etc.

The above words follow the rules for nasalization of the vowels and thus become "shAHn̸zh," "plAHn̸t," "pAHn̸d" and "plAHn̸tEE." The "AH" is like the "a" of the American "father" but it is given the French nasal sound. According to the above rule, then, all words with "an" followed by another consonant, or "oun" followed by another consonant or "en" followed by another consonant become "AHn." For a lighter dialect, long "a" (AY) and short "e" (EH) words may take a nasal "EH" sound, as in "shEHn̸zh" (change) and "plEHn̸tEE" (plenty). Final "en" usually takes "EH," as in "gAHrdEHn̸" (garden). Short words too, with medial "en," often take the nasal "EH" sound, as in "sEHn̸d" (send).

"AHm̸" . . . . for "sample," "embrace," "tremble," etc.

These words receive the same treatment as the words above and get the nasal "AH" with the "m" dropped, as in "sAHm̸pluh" (sample), "AHm̸brEHs" (embrace) and "trAHm̸bluh" (tremble). This nasal sound will be found in all "am" and "em" combinations which follow the previously listed rule. For a lighter dialect, "em" words may take a nasal "EH" sound, as in "EHm̸brEHs" (embrace) and "trEHm̸bluh" (tremble).

AWn̸" . . . . for "upon," "launder," "motion," etc.

The above words, and words with similar vowel-consonant combinations, receive the nasal "AW," as in "ERpAWn̸," "lAWn̸dEHr" and "mAWsyAWn̸."

"AWɱ" .... for "romp," "promptly," "pomp," etc.

These words, and words with similar vowel sounds, take the nasal "AW" as "rAWɱp," "prAWɱptlEE" and "pAWɱp."

"EHɲ" .... for "invite," "painter," "print," "syntax," etc.

All "in" nasal combinations take a nasal "EH." Thus, the above words are "EHɲvIt," "pEHɲtEHr," "prEHɲt" and "sEHɲtAHks."

"EHɱ" .... for "important," "imprint," "symbol," etc.

These combinations receive the nasal "EH" and are pronounced "EHɱpAWr-tAHɲt," "EHɱprEHɲt," and "sEHɱbAWl."

"ERɲ" .... for "until," "plunder," "blunt," etc.

The "ER"—which is similar to the "ur" sound in "curb" with the "r" silent—is nasalized for "un" in the French dialect, as in "ERɲtEEl," "plERɲdEHr" and "blERɲt."

"ERɱ" .... for "plump," "number," "stumble," etc.

The "um" nasal combinations receive the same treatment as the "un" nasal combinations. The vowel sound is like the "ur" of "curb" with the "r" silent. The example words would be "plERɱp," "nERɱbEHr" and "stERɱbluh."

The above vowel changes are only for the nasalized vowel, although some of them are similar to their normal dialect sound, as will be seen in studying the following non-nasalized vowels. It is suggested that short words, like "man," "am," and "ran," should not usually be nasalized.

WORD EXERCISES

Pronounce the following words in the French dialect using the material learned from the French Nasal section:

1.	France	11.	bonbon
2.	concert	12.	criminal
3.	dinner	13.	rainfall
4.	saint	14.	casino
5.	Monday	15.	charming
6.	bundle	16.	understand
7.	import	17.	prince
8.	country	18.	dominate
9.	invite	19.	transport
10.	romantic	20.	America

When the above words have been pronounced, refer to the list below for corrections. Check the mistakes, correct them and repeat the corrections until they have been memorized.

1.	frAHɲs	11.	bAWɲ bAWɲ
2.	kAWɲsEHrt	12.	krEEmEEnAHl
3.	dEEnEHr	13.	rEHɲfAWl

4. sEHn̥t	14. kAHsEEnAW
5. mAWn̥dEH	15. shAHrmEEng
6. bER̥n̥dER̥l	16. ER̥n̥dEHrstAHn̥d
7. EHm̥pAWrt	17. prEHn̥s
8. kAHn̥trEE	18. dAWmEEnEHt
9. EHn̥vlt	19. trAHn̥spAWrt
10. rAWmAHn̥tEEk	20. AmArEEkAH

VOWEL CHANGES

"AY" . . . . as in "take," "break," "they," etc.

The French often shorten this vowel sound into "EH," as in "tEHk" (take). Many Frenchmen, however, substitute "A" (as in "bat") when "AY" is the initial letter of a word, as in "AmEE-AHbluh" (amiable). This vowel retains its "EH" sound for a lighter dialect when it is nasalized before "m" or "n" although the usual nasal change should be "AH."

DRILL WORDS

brEHk	(break)	AWbEH	(obey)
dEHt	(date)	tEHstEE	(tasty)
dEH	(day)	mEHbEE	(maybe)

shEHn̥zh	(change)
strEHt	(straight)
Ady̆ukEHt	(educate)

NOTE: The "AY" sound may be retained, but if it is, it must be short and clean with no trace of diphthongization. Americans usually break down this "AY" sound into "AY-EE" while the Frenchmen would use only the "AY," which would be sounded sharply and distinctly.

"UH" . . . . as in "alone," "sofa," "final," etc.

This mute sound of "a" is changed by many Frenchmen into "AH," as in "sAW-fAH" (sofa). Ordinarily, when it is the initial letter of a word, it is dropped, as in "'lAWn̥'" (along). But when it is used initially, most Frenchmen change it to "A" (of "bat"), as in "AlAWn" (alone).

When this "a" comes before "m" or "n" in the same syllable, it is changed to "EH" and is nasalized, as in "kAHptEHn̥" (captain). See "The French Nasal."

A variant for this "a" is the "oo" of "good," as in "sAWfoo" (sofa), "fInool" (final) and "oobEElEEtEE" (ability).

DRILL WORDS

AsI'	(aside)
AkwEHn̥t	(acquaint)
fInAHl	(final)

bAHnAHnAH	(banana)
AbEElEEtEE	(ability)
sAWfAH	(sofa)

pAHrEHd	(parade)
sAHly̆t	(salute)
mAHlEEshER̥s	(malicious)

"AH" .... as in "father," "arm," "park," etc.

Although the French treat the sound of this vowel with the American "AH," there is a difference between the two in that the French version is much shorter. It is actually a sound that falls between the "AH" of "father" and the "O" of "rod" but, for our purposes, it will be designated as "AH."

DRILL WORDS

pAHrk	(park)	fAHdEHr	(father)
lAHrzh	(large)	bAHrn	(barn)
AHrmEE	(army)	kAHrnAHl	(carnal)

rEEgAHrd	(regard)
spAHrkluh	(sparkle)
sEEgAHr	(cigar)

"A:" .... as in "ask," "draft," "laugh," etc.

The same "AH" as in "father" is given to this flat "a" of "ask," as in "AHs'" (ask). Here, too, the "AH" should be much shorter than it is in American.

DRILL WORDS

lAHf	(laugh)	lAHs'	(last)
hAHf	(half)	dAHɲs	(dance)
mAHt	(mat)	pAHtEHr	(patter)

fAHsEEnEHt	(fascinate)
stAHɲdEHr'	(standard)
bAHskAT	(basket)

NOTE: In the word "fAHsEEnEHt" (fascinate), it will be observed that the "i" in the second syllable was not nasalized and that its following "n" was not dropped. The rule states that the "n" must not be followed by a vowel—hence the treatment as given here.

"A" .... as in "bad," "am," "guarantee," etc.

This vowel sound is also pronounced as "AH" and it, too, must not be drawn out but must be cut short.

DRILL WORDS

AHd	(add)	bAHzh	(badge)
stAHb	(stab)	lAHmp	(lamp)
sAHd	(sad)	sAHmpluh	(sample)

kAHlAHɲdAHr	(calendar)
pAHrAHfEHɲ	(paraffin)
gAHrAHɲtEE	(guarantee)

"AW" .... as in "ball," "falter," "shawl," etc.

Instead of the usual "AW" sound given this "a," the French substitute a long "o" (OH), as in "bOHl" (ball). Here, again, it must be remembered that the French tend to shorten their vowel sounds so that this long "o" is given sharply, with the lips tensed, and not with the vanishing "OO" glide given it by Americans.

DRILL WORDS

kOHl	(call)	shOHl	(shawl)
stOHl	(stall)	brOHl	(brawl)
hOHl	(hall)	skOHld	(scald)

fOHltEHr	(falter)
bOHld	(bald)
mOHlt	(malt)

"EE" .... as in "he," "treat," "people," etc.

This vowel sound is treated as it is in American but is more pronounced. The corners of the mouth should be pulled back sharply and the teeth should almost be touching.

"EH" .... as in "bet," "said," "friend," etc.

This short "e" vowel sound is often treated as "A" as in "bAd" (bad). It may also be sounded as "AY," as in "bAYt" (bet), "sAYd" (said) and "frAYnd" (friend). The "A" change is preferred.

DRILL WORDS

kAg	(keg)	dAstEEnEE	(destiny)
hAd	(head)	sAd	(said)
gAt	(get)	spEHɲd	(spend)

frAnd	(friend)
lAsAWɲ	(lesson)
mAlAWdEE	(melody)

NOTE: When short "e" (EH) is nasalized, the "EH" sound, according to the nasal rule, changes to a nasal "AH." However, for a lighter dialect, the "EH" sound may be retained but it must be nasalized.

"I" .... as in "ice," "aisle," "guile," etc.

As is the case with most Romance language dialects, this long "i" vowel sound receives an exaggerated treatment. Pronounced in American, the long "i" is treated as "AH-EE" with both parts of the vowel given equal stress and duration. But in the French dialect, the last part of the vowel, "EE," is stressed more than the first part, "AH." It is *not* lengthened, though, and should be treated as long "e" is always treated in French with the corners of the mouth pulled back sharply and with the teeth almost touching. Another important point to remember is that the two parts of the long "i" vowel sound, "AH-EE," are not run together, as in American, but are separated as though they are two different vowel sounds, as in "nAH-EEs" (nice). The phonetic symbol, though, will be "I."

DRILL WORDS

Is	(ice)	Il	(aisle)
rIt	(right)	gIl	(guile)
spIt	(spite)	lInEHr	(liner)

krIm	(crime)
sAWsIAHtEE	(society)
pAWlIt	(polite)

"i" . . . . as in "it," "women," "busy," etc.

This is another vowel sound that receives the same treatment in all the Romance language dialects. Short "i" is *always* pronounced as long "e" (EE), as in "sEEt" (sit). Here, also, the French method of pronouncing long "e" is used with the lips well retracted, the mouth slightly open and the sound treated sharply and clearly.

When this short "i" comes before either an "m" or an "n" which is followed by a consonant, it is changed to "EH," as in "prEHɲtEHr" (printer). In these instances where nasalization is called for it will be noticed that it is the *spelling* of the word rather than its *pronunciation* that determines the change. Ordinarily, short "i" calls for a long "e" treatment which, in the French dialect, does not require nasalization. But the Frenchman considers the spelling of the word, as well, and because the "i's" in the original French language are nasalized under certain conditions, he carries this habit over into his dialect.

DRILL WORDS

fEEt	(fit)	wEEmEHɲ	(women)
sEEn	(sin)	prEHɲs	(prince)
EEt	(it)	bEEzEE	(busy)
	pEElAW	(pillow)	
	prEEtEE	(pretty)	
	sEElvEHr	(silver)	

NOTE: If a lighter dialect is to be used, the "EE" sound for "i" may occasionally, but not consistently, be changed to "i." This "EE" sound is almost habitual with most Frenchmen.

"O" . . . . as in "on," "bond," "John," etc.

This "o" is always pronounced as "AW" in the French dialect, as in "AWɲ" (on).

DRILL WORDS

sAWrEE	(sorry)	kAWɲtEHɲ	(contain)
bAWrAW	(borrow)	zhAWɲ	(John)
frAWlEEk	(frolic)	lAWk	(lock)
	kAWlEEk	(colic)	
	kAWɲvEEkt	(convict)	
	tAWlEHrEHt	(tolerate)	

"OH" . . . . as in "bone," "sew," "dough," etc.

This long "o" is also pronounced as "AW" in the French dialect, as in "bAWn" (bone) and "sAW" (sew).

DRILL WORDS

dAW	(dough)	sAWfAH	(sofa)
mAWs'	(most)	OHldAW	(although)
pAWl	(pole)	mAWn	(moan)
	tAWbAHkAW	(tobacco)	
	hAWbAW	(hobo)	
	fAWtAWgrAHf	(photograph)	

"AW" .... as in "off," "cough," "soft," etc.

This is another vowel sound that receives the same treatment as in American. But here, again, it should be shortened and cut off cleanly with the lips more pursed than they are in the American pronunciation.

Many Frenchmen change this "AW" sound to "OH." See "AW" as in "ball."

"OO" .... as in "food," "do," "blue," etc.

Many French people use the same "OO" sound as Americans do, but their lips are more pursed and tense. A variation is what is known as the French "u." It is achieved by rounding the lips as though to sound "OO" and then, with the lips still in that position, sounding long "e" (EE) instead. Practice will be required to pronouce this sound correctly. This French "u" will be represented phonetically as "ʉ." Both "OO" and "ʉ" may be used in one dialect characterization. If this is done, the "ʉ" sound should be reserved for words which are spelled with a "u" and pronounced "OO" in American. The use of "OO" and "ʉ" will be shown in the following drill words.

DRILL WORDS

dOO	(do)		skOOl	(school)
nOO	(new)		sAHlOOn	(saloon)
mOOvEE	(movie)		dOOmzdEH	(doomsday)
		zhʉn	(June)	
		prʉn	(prune)	
		tʉn	(tune)	

"oo" .... as in "good," "wolf," "full," etc.

The French usually give this short "oo" the "ER" treatment. This "ER" sound is present in the American word "curb" when it is pronounced without the "r." The sound comes from deep within the throat with the lips slightly pursed. The crossed out "R" indicates that the "R" is dropped, but that the "E" retains the "r" flavor. Words like "curb," "fir" and "purr" should be practiced without sounding the "r."

DRILL WORDS

pERt	(put)		shERd	(should)
bERk	(book)		stERd	(stood)
rERf	(roof)		fERl	(full)
		wERlf	(wolf)	
		pAHrtERk	(partook)	
		wERdshAd	(woodshed)	

"yOO" .... as in "unit," "cube," "beauty," etc.

The French give this "u" the same treatment as they do their ordinary long "OO" sound except that they add to it the consonantal "y" sound, as in "yʉnEEt" (unit) and "fyOO" (few). Again, the "u" is produced by rounding the lips as though to pronounce "OO," but sounding long "e" (EE) instead. Also remember to cut the sound off sharply and clearly.

DRILL WORDS

yOO	(you)	myμzEEk	(music)
pyOO	(pew)	Amyμs	(amuse)
myμt	(mute)	fyμtEEl	(futile)

byOOtEEfERl   (beautiful)
yμnEEfAWrm   (uniform)
kyμpEEd   (cupid)

"U" .... as in "up," "love," "does," etc.

There are two substitutes used by the French for this vowel sound. The first treats it simply as "AW" (the sharp, clear version), as in "AWp" (up) and "lAWv" (love). But the preferred and more nearly correct version treats it as "ER." This is again like our sound of the "u" in "curb" but *the "R" is not pronounced.* This sound must not be given its full vowel length, as it is in American, but must be treated sharply and clearly, as should all the French vowels. When this vowel sound comes before "m" or "n," either of which is followed by another consonant, it retains its "ER" sound but is nasalized and the "n" or "m" is dropped, as in "ERńtEEl" (until).

DRILL WORDS

slERg	(slug)	sERpEHr	(supper)
bERg	(bug)	lERvlEE	(lovely)
nERt	(nut)	dERs	(does)

sERspEEsyERń   (suspicion)
wERɲdEHrfúl   (wonderful)
sERɲdEH   (Sunday)

In words where the "u" is followed by a pronounced "r," as in "kEREE" (curry), and "hEREEkEHn" (hurricane), the symbol "ER" will be used to indicate that the "r" is sounded.

"ER" .... as in "curb," "earn," "fir," etc.

This sound is given the same "ER" treatment as the "u" in "up." Again, it must be cut short and sounded sharply and cleanly. But since the "r" is sounded here, the symbol "ER" will be used rather than "ER."

DRILL WORDS

nERs	(nurse)	lERn	(learn)
fER	(fir)	dERtEE	(dirty)
wERt	(worth)	bERn	(burn)

pERT   (pert)
flERtEHsyAWɲ   (flirtation)
mERdEREHr   (murderer)

NOTE: The phonetic representation of the last word, "mERdEREHr" (murderer), brings up an important point that should be discussed and clarified here. Ordinarily, a recently arrived Frenchman would give his "er" sounds an "EHr" pronunciation because that is the usual treatment given it in the French language, as in "fAHdEHr" (father) and "mERdEHr" (mother). But when he becomes acquainted with the American language he will try to approximate the American "er" sound, which is "ER," as in "fAH-TH-ER" (father). The closest he comes to it, though, is the same "er" but of a deeper quality, more forceful and, of course, sharper and clearer. It is still the "EHr" ending, however, that is best suited for the dialect, unless a change in characterization is required.

"OW" .... as in "out," "cow," "house," etc.

This diphthong is shortened in the French dialect from "AH-OO" to "AH," as in "hAHs" (house). This is a closer "AH" than in American and it follows the French habit of pronouncing vowel sounds sharply and crisply.

When used before either "m" or "n" followed by a consonant, this vowel sound retains its "AH" sound and is nasalized, as in "mAHntEHn (mountain).

DRILL WORDS

kAH	(cow)	flAHńdEHr	(flounder)
dAHt	(doubt)	AbAHt	(about)
kAHɲt	(count)	mAHt	(mouth)

tAHzAHɲz (thousands)
AstAHɲd (astound)
prAHd (proud)

"OI" .... as in "oil," "boy," "noise," etc.

Because this diphthong is not in the original French language, the French people tend to separate the two parts of the diphthong, "AW-EE," as though they were two distinct vowels, treating the last part, "EE," as they usually do the long "e."

DRILL WORDS

bAW-EE	(boy)	AnAW-EE	(annoy)
sAW-EEl	(soil)	rAW-EE-AHl	(royal)
nAW-EEs	(noise)	ApAW-EEnt	(appoint)

brAW-EEl (broil)
AHɱbrAW-EEdEHr (embroider)
AHɲzhAW-EE (enjoy)

WORD EXERCISES

Pronounce the following words in the French dialect using the material learned from the preceding Vowel Changes:

1.	adore	11.	pipe-cleaner
2.	mistake	12.	tune
3.	absolute	13.	current
4.	communicate	14.	memory
5.	distance	15.	suffer
6.	graduate	16.	spoil
7.	order	17.	loud
8.	already	18.	cube
9.	foil	19.	curl
10.	toast	20.	party

When these words have been pronounced, refer to the list below for corrections. When the words have been learned correctly, repeat the corrections until they have been memorized.

1.	AdAWr	11.	pIp-klEEnEHr
2.	mEEstEHk	12.	tμn
3.	AHpsAWlμt	13.	kEREHɲt
4.	kAWmyμnEEkEHt	14.	mAmAWrEE
5.	dEEstAHɲs	15.	sERfEHr or sAWfEHr
6.	grAHdyμEHt	16.	spAW-EEl
7.	AWrdEHr	17.	lAHd
8.	AWlrAdEE or OHlrAdEE	18.	kyμb
9.	fAW-EEl	19.	kERl
10.	tAWst	20.	pAHrtEE

CONSONANT CHANGES

B — This consonant is ordinarily sounded as it is in American. But when it comes in the middle of a word, before a voiceless consonant sound — any consonant sound *except* "b," "d," hard "g," "m," "n," and "ng" — it is often changed to "p," as in "AWptEHń (obtain). When "b" is given the "b" pronunciation, greater force should be used than in American.

C — The same as in American.

D — The French "d" is pronounced with the tip of the tongue placed against the rear surface of the *lower* front teeth, instead of up against the front part of the roof of the mouth. This makes for a thicker sounding "d" than in American. Initially and medially, "d" is used as it is in American. But when it is at the end of a word, it may be dropped, unless it follows a vowel. If the word following begins with a vowel, then the "d" is changed to a "t," as in "sAH tǀz" (sad eyes). (See the "French Glide Rule" section for the transposition of the "t" from the end of "sad" to the beginning of "eyes.") When a word ending in "d" is followed by a word beginning with a consonant, the "d" is dropped, as in "bAH' tIm" (bad time). The "French Glide Rule" section will explain this elision also.

The pronunciation of "d" may also be made with the tongue far forward in the front of the roof of the mouth. This "d" should be used for the *lingual* "r"; the "d" mentioned before should be used for the *uvular* "r."

F — The same as in American, except in liaison (see the "French Glide Rule" section), where it changes to "v" when final and is followed by an initial vowel word.

G — Although a great many French people sound "g" so far forward in the mouth that it often resembles weak "k," this consonant may be pronounced as in American. But at the end of a word, the "g" is changed to a weak "k," if the following word begins with a vowel, as in "drAH kEEt" (drag it).

H — The elision of the consonant "h" is a characteristic change in the dialect.

The Frenchman seldom pronounces it, initially or medially, as in "'EE 'Iks ERp'EEl" (*he hikes uphill*). Many Frenchmen are sensitive about this elision and they use "h" correctly but with such grim determination that it is sounded almost twice as heavily as it ordinarily would be.

J — Both in the normal use of "j" and the soft "g" the French dialect substitutes a "zh," as in "*zh*ERmp" (jump), "*zh*AWb" (job) and "stEH*zh*" (stage).

K — The same as in American.

L — Initially and medially, the consonant "l" receives the same treatment as it does in American. It is pronounced a bit thicker, though, with the tip of the tongue more to the front of the roof of the mouth, as in the pronunciation of "d." The results is an "l" that is *almost* the Spanish "ll" (ly), as in "bi*l*ous." When "l" is used at the end of a word and is preceded by a weakly sounded vowel (for example "people," "table," and "apple"), the weak vowel sound, "uh," is made an aspirate "uh" by transposing it from before the "l" to after the "l" as in, "pEEpluh," "tEHbluh" and "AHpluh." This aspirate may be lessened or dropped for a light dialect.

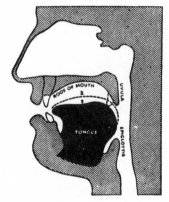

The dotted line (2) indicates the tongue raised against the uvula to pronounce the French *uvulaire* "r." The breath, in passing the conjuncture of the tongue and the uvula, produces the intermittent rough sound of "r." Both tongue and uvula vibrate slightly when this "r" is sounded. This rolled French "r" is not rolled as long as the German.

M and **N** — Initially, the consonants "m" and "n" are given the same pronunciation as in American. But medially and finally, they are affected by certain usages in the French language which will be found in this chapter under the section "The French Nasal."

P and **Q** — The same as in American.

R — The consonant "r" is always pronounced in the French dialect. But there are two types of "r" that can be used. The first, used in Paris and in the larger cities of France, is the *uvular* "r," which is gargled with the uvula at the back of the tongue. The second type, used in the provinces, is the *lingual* "r," trilled with the tip of the tongue against the roof of the mouth. The type of Frenchman to be portrayed can be authentically limned with the proper use of either of these "r"s, although the *uvular* "r" is preferred. (See illustration, page 158.)

S — Initially, the consonant "s" is used as it is in American with, perhaps, a more distinct hiss. Medially, "s" is pronounced as "z" when it comes between two vowels, as in "pAWzEEbluh" (possible), "IzEE" (icy) and "bAHzOOn" (bassoon). Finally, "s" is always pronounced as "s," even when it is sounded as "z" in American, as in "rAWs" (rose), "Amyus" (amuse) and "plEEs" (please).

T — Initially and medially, the consonant "t" is treated as it is in American. But, like the consonant "d," the "t" is often dropped when it comes at the end of a word and is preceded by a consonant, as in "kAWntAHk" (contact). When the word following a word ending with a "t" begins with a vowel, the final "t" is *not* dropped, as in "kAWntAHkt 'EEm" (contact him).

V — The same as in American.

W — The letter "w" is seldom found in French. When it is, it is usually pronounced as "v." However, the French people have a sound which is similar to the American "w" and it is this sound which they carry into their dialect. When pronouncing "w," simply raise the tip of the tongue toward the hard palate and round the lips.

X and **Y** — The same as in American.

Z — See "S."

TCH — This consonant combination is changed to "SH," as in "shAHrm" (charm), "kEEshEHn" (kitchen) and "bAHsh" (batch). The "sh" sound, however, should be sounded more vigorously than it is in the American. For a lighter dialect, "tch" may be used occasionally or completely.

SH — The substitutions made for "sh" are important variants in the French dialect and should always be used. Initially, the "sh" retains its normal pronunciation of "sh," as in "shOHl" (shawl). But medially, when it is followed by an "i," it changes its pronunciation to "sy," as in "AHmbEEsyERs" (ambitious), "fAHsy AWn" (fashion) and "AWfEEsyAHl" (official). In the word "anxious," too, the "ksh" pronunciation of "x" becomes "gsy" so that the word, in the French dialect, becomes "AHngsyus."

TH — To the run-of-the-mine actors, the substitution of "z" for "th" — voiced or unvoiced — represents the last word in presenting the French dialect. They merely have to say "zee man ovair zair" and, presto chango!, they have become Gaston Duval. As a result, the mass audience has come to expect all its stage Frenchmen and French maids to speak with "z"s. Actually, all French people do not substitute "z" for voiced and unvoiced "th." Granted, a great many do treat the *voiced* "TH" (in "the") as "z." But, at the same time, they do *not* give the "z" change to the *unvoiced* "th" (in "think"). They would sound it, rather, as a hard, sibilant "s," as in "*s*EEnk" (*th*ink) and "bAH*s*" (ba*th*). But this pronunciation is representative of only *one* group of Frenchmen. For a considerable number of them, especially those who live in the northern and northeastern provinces, treat it as do most foreigners — as "d" for the voiced "TH," as in "*d*AHt" (*th*at), "*d*AWs" (*th*ose) and "bEH*d*" (ba*th*e); and as "t" in the unvoiced "th," as in "*t*EEnk" (*th*ink), "mEE*ts*" (my*th*s) and "tru*t*" (tru*th*).

Perhaps because audiences have come to expect their stage Frenchmen to talk with "z's" it may be difficult to convince them that a "d" and "t" speaking French-man is authentic. But if the other important characteristics of the French dialect are used in addition to "d" and "t," the characterization will be quite effective. It is for this reason that the "d" and "t" are used in this section almost exclusively. However, the student may take his choice of either treatment. But a word of cau-tion: DO NOT COMBINE THE TWO! Remember, also, that too much dialect — like too much seasoning in a good French soup — can spoil the effect.

ZH — Ordinarily, this "zh" sound, found in such words as "azure," "seizure" and treasure," is treated as "zy" by the French so that the words become "AH*zy*úr," "sEE*zy*úr" and "trA*zy*úr."

ING — When "ing" is used at the end of a word in participial form, as in "walk-ing," "running" and "keeping," the "i" is *not* nasalized and the "n" is *not* dropped. It should be given its full pronunciation of "EEng," as in "wAWkEEng," "rERnEEng" and "kEEpEEng." A great many French people do, however, drop the final "g," so this can be done occasionally.

WORD EXERCISES

Pronounce the following words in the French dialect using the material learned from the preceding Consonant Changes:

1.	abstract	6.	this	11.	Abner	16.	refuse
2.	reason	7.	pathway	12.	blind	17.	French
3.	cage	8.	thrill	13.	mishap	18.	father
4.	happy	9.	treasure	14.	assist	19.	stitch
5.	illusion	10.	obstinate	15.	mission	20.	strict

When the above words have been pronounced, refer to the list below for corrections. Study the phonetic representations and practice the above material again.

1.	AHpstrAHk'	6.	dEEs or zEEs	11.	AHbnEHr	16.	rEEfyús
2.	rEEzAWn	7.	pAHtwEH or pAHswEH	12.	blIn'	17.	frEHńsh
3.	kEHzh	8.	trEEl or srEEl	13.	mEEz'AHp	18.	fAHdEHr or fAHzEHr
4.	'AHpEE	9.	trAzyúr	14.	AsEEs'	19.	stEEsh
5.	EElúzyAWń	10.	AWpstEEnAHt	15.	mEEsyAWń	20.	strEEk'

THE FRENCH GLIDE RULE

Like the Cockney, the French use a glide technique to connect related words. This glide lends flavor and a leavening effect to the staccato tendency.

1. *WHEN A WORD ENDS WITH A VOICED CONSONANT AND THE FOLLOWING RELATED WORD BEGINS WITH A VOWEL, THE CONSONANT IS CARRIED OVER.*

Take, for example, the sentence, "dEE plEHt, AHv yOO gAW tEEt?" (the plate, have you got it?). The word "plate" ends with a voiced consonant (t), the final "e" being silent. Although, in the French dialect, the next word begins with a vowel sound (AH), the final "t" of plate is not carried over because "plate have" is not a related phrase. If the phrase had been "plEH tAWv fOOd" (plate of food), the "t" of "plate" would have carried over to "of." But, in the first example sentence, there is a definite pause after the word "plate" which sets it apart from "have."

In the phrase "gAW tEEt," however, the "t" of "got" is carried over to "it" because the two words are closely related.

Another example sentence is "mEH kEH bEE kAHrmEE" (make a big army). The "k" of "make" is carried over to "a." And the "g" of "big" is changed to "k" and carried over to begin the initial vowel word (army). The general treatment of "g" will be found in "Consonant Changes." Ordinarily, this final hard "g" is slighted or dropped, but when it precedes an initial vowel word, it becomes "k."

A few other consonants are affected noticeably by the glide. The final "s" of the French dialect normally gets the "s" of the American word "sun." Thus, the word "his" would become "EEs." But, if the final "s" is preceded by a vowel, and the next word begins with a vowel, the "s" becomes "z," as in "EEs dEH" (his day), "EE zAHkAHńt" (his account), "AHs dEE" (has the) and "AH zEE" (has he).

If "s" is preceded by "k" or "g" and followed by an "s" sound, the first "s" is dropped. Thus in the phrase, "mAWńk' sAl" (monk's cell), the possessive "s" of "monk's" is not sounded at all because the following word (cell) begins with an "s" sound.

When a final consonant "t" is followed by a similarly pronounced consonant, "th," the final consonant "t" is dropped. That is, when the mouth is in the same position for both consonants, the first is dropped in favor of the second, as in, "nAW dEE" (not the), "kER brAWk" (cup broke), "EE zEEbrAH" (his zebra), "brA dEEpt" (bread dipped) and "brA tuᵘ " (bread to). These final consonant changes apply only when the glide rule is used and care must be taken not to accentuate them unduly.

For example, in the sentence, "I wAHńt mI brAt, dAWń yuᵘ?" (I want my bread, don't you?) it will be noticed that "bread" and "don't" are not related words. There is a definite pause between them and they are not necessary to each other.

Words ending in two voiced consonants usually drop the final consonant, as in "wERl'" (world), "fERs'" (first) and "drAHf'" (draft). Thus, in applying the glide, the dialect pronunciation must be used rather than the actual spelling of the word. This will be seen in the following examples where the first of the final consonants is used to carry over to the next related word which begins with a vowel, as in, "wERr lERv" (world of), "fERr sAHńd" (first hand), "drAH vAW nEEm" (draft on him). Notice that in the last example the word "draft" dropped the "t" and changed final "f" to "v." Final "f" is changed to "v" when the next word is related and begins with a vowel.

Naturally, the sense of some words would be completely destroyed if the final of two voiced consonants were dropped. This must be watched carefully. Words like "pERl" (pearl) and "mAHrk" (mark) retain both consonant sounds. Similarly, two consonants which produce one sound, like "sh," must be kept. Words in which the next-to-the-last consonant is "n" (and this "n" is dropped because of nasalization) must of necessity keep the last consonant, as in "prEHńt" (print) and "plAHńt" (plant). Using the last two words in glide examples, the phrases would be "prEHń tEH bOOk" (print a book) and "plAHń tEH gAHrdEHń " (plant a garden).

Under "The French Nasal," Rule 3, words ending in "n" and followed by initial vowel words are discussed. Since they govern and are governed by the glide rule, it is advisable to discuss them further here. It will be remembered that words like "EHń " (in), "sERtEHń " (certain) and "ERpAWń " (upon) nasalize the vowel preceding the "n," and the "n" is dropped. But, if within a sentence, a word ending in "n" is followed by an initial vowel word, the "n" is sounded and no nasalization occurs. Take, for example, the phrases, "EHń dEE kAHr" (in the car), "sERtEHń dAH tEE wERs dAr" (certain that he was there) and "ERpAWń dEE dAsk" (upon the desk). All the words ending in "n" are nasalized because the following words begin with consonants. But in "EE nEH bEE' kAHr" (in a big car), "sERtAH nAW fEEt" (certain of it) and "ERpAW nEH brI' dEH" (upon a bright day), the "n" is not dropped and the preceding vowel is not nasalized, because the next word begins with a vowel and the "n" is needed to carry the glide to this next word.

The final "v" sound may change to "f" if the next related word begins with a vowel, as in the above example, "certain of it."

Here are some example sentences showing how the glide is used:

"tEH *k*EE *t*AWm" (Take it home.) The "k" of "take" is carried over to the next word "it," which begins with a vowel. But the "t" of "it" is also carried from its own word to begin "home." The "h" of "home" is dropped in the French dialect and the word then begins with a vowel.

"lA *t*EEm gAW" (Let him go.) Again, the "h" is dropped in the word "him," so the "t" of "let" is glided over to begin "EEm."

"mI sER *n*EE zEEr" (My son is here.) The "o" of "son" is not nasalized because the "n" must be carried over to begin the word "is." The "s" of "is" changes to "z" because it is between vowels, and this "z" is carried over to begin "here."

"nAH EEs dEE rI' tIm" (Now is the right time.) It will be noticed that "now" ends with "AH" and "is" begins with "EE." There is no consonant to glide from "now" to "is." "ow" words are pronounced "AH," which eliminates the possible use of the consonant "w." In the word "right," the final "t" is dropped because the next word begins with a "t." But, it would also be absorbed before any other similarly pronounced consonant, as in "rI' drAs" (right dress), and may be dropped completely before a dissimilar consonant such as "rI' plEHs" (right place).

GRAMMAR CHANGES

The French, like most foreigners, have trouble with American verb forms. For that reason, and because the French language uses very few contractions, a great many French people prefer to leave auxiliary verbs out of sentences entirely, as in:

"AH yOO lIk dEE sEEtEE?"	"shEE gAW EEf shEE kAHn."
(How you like the city?)	(She go if she can.)
(How *do* you like the city?)	(She *will* go if she can.)
"I lIk tOO stEH'EEr."	I sEH EET wAn I lIk.
(I like to stay here.)	(I say it when I like.)
(I *would* like to stay here.)	(I'll say it when I like.)

Another characteristic change in grammar is a direct carry over from the French language. The French almost always insert a definite or indefinite article before each noun, as in:

"wEE 'AHv dEE bOOk AHn' dEE pEHpEHr
fAWr dEE prEHńtEEng."
(We have *the* book and the paper for *the* printing.)

Another custom taken over from the language inserts a definite article before a place name when the place name is used as the subject or indirect object of a verb or a preposition, as in:

"dEE kAHnAHdAH EEs bEEg."
(*The* Canada is big.)
(Canada is big.)

"'EE EEs EEn dEE kAHnAHdAH."
(He is in *the* Canada.)
(He is in Canada.)

The only exception to this usage occurs in an answer to the question, "where?," as in "Where is he?" The answer would be made as follows:

"'EE EEs EEn kAHnAHdAH."
(He is in Canada.)

Although most interrogative sentences are constructed in the American form, variations are also heard where the subject noun, ordinarily used after the verb, is placed before the verb instead, as in:

"dEE dAWg, 'AH zEE nAW' dEE bAWn?"
(The dog, has he not the bone?)
(Hasn't the dog a bone?)

NOTE: In the above sentence, there will be noticed in the words "has he," a peculiar change. In the first place, the normal "s" sound given to final "s" has been changed to "z." Secondly, the "s" sound has been transferred from the end of the word "has," to the beginning of the word "he." The section in this chapter under "The French Glide Rule" will explain this transposition. The "s" sound was changed to "z" because the "h" was dropped in the word "he." This brought the consonant "s" between two vowels which, in turn, caused it to be changed to "z," following the rule for such a change.

Other examples of this subject noun change are as in:

"mI 'AHt, dOO yOO nAW wA rEE tEEs?"
(My hat, do you know where it is?)
(Do you know where my hat is?)

"mI kAWt, wA rEE zEEt?"
(My coat, where is it?)
(Where is my coat?)

The Frenchman errs also in the use of forms of the comparative and superlative degree.

"dEE gERl EEs mAWr nIs dAn yOO."
(The girl is *more nice* than you.)
(The girl is *nicer* than you.)

"shEE EEs dEE mAWs' nIs gERl I nAW."
(She is the *most nice* girl I know.)
(She is the *nicest* girl I know.)

TYPICAL EXPRESSIONS AND INTERJECTIONS

eh! — This interjection is used at the end of a sentence and takes on the meaning of "don't you?," "wouldn't you?," etc. For example, "yOO wAHɲ tOO gAW, EH?" (You want to go, eh?) In this sentence the "eh" would stand for "don't you?"

eh bien! — The combination "EH byEHɲ" (eh bien) is similar to the American "well, how about it?" It may be used alone or with a sentence, as in, "EH byEHɲ! I AHm rAdEE." (Well! I am ready.)

zut! — This is definitely a slang expression and is similar to the American "darn it!" "shEE wAWs nAW *t*AWm. zʉt!" (She was not home. Darn it!)

oui! — A very well known and much abused word is "wEE" (oui). It is one of several French words for "yes." "yOO lIk mEE? wEE?" (You like me? yes?)

non! — This word "nAWɲ" is one of the French words for "no" and is used like this: "yOO dAWɲ' lIk mEE, nAWɲ ?" (You don't like me, no?)

n'est-ce-pas — The phrase "nEHs pAH" is used like "eh," thus, "EE *t*EE zEH wERɲdERfERl dEH, nEHs pAH?" (It is a wonderful day, isn't it?)

chéri, chérie — The word "shEHrEE" means "dear" or "darling." Although the pronunciation is the same, the word, when spelled "chéri," refers to a man, when it is spelled "chérie," it refers to a woman.

chic — This word has been carried over from the French to the English. It means fine or in good taste or smart. The pronunciation is "shEEk" and not "tchik" or "tchiker" as has been heard from some misinformed Americans. In forming the comparative or superlative, refer to the section on "Grammar."

c'est la vie — A phrase which is universal is "sEH lA vEE" or, in American, "That's life!"

bien! — The word "byEHń," is used for "good" or "fine" or "excellent," when these words are interjections, as in, "byEHń! dAH tEEs wAW tl wAWń tOO 'EEr." (Good! that is what I want to hear.)

madame—mAdAm.
mademoiselle—mAdmwAzEHl.
monsieur—muhsyER.

SENTENCE EXERCISES

Pronounce the following sentences, paying special attention to the glide rule and grammar changes.

1. This animal is smaller than that.
2. Good! We will go right away.
3. Can you remember Paris?
4. Well then, we must appeal the case.
5. Can you get the passport right now?
6. Madame, you must understand, *c'est la guerre.*
7. I would like to have the bread dipped in a glass of wine.
8. Life can be very cheap, can't it?
9. He would like to go to America when the war is over.
10. Is my hat fashionable?

After pronouncing the above sentences, refer to the following phonetics. Check them for verification or corrections, then practice the above list again.

1. dEE zAHnEEmAHl EEs mAWr smAWl dAHń dAHt.
2. byEHń ! wEE wEEl gAW rI tAwEH.
3. pArEE! kAHń yOO rEEmEHmbEH rER?
4. EH byEHń , wEE mER zApEEl dEE kEHs.
5. dEE pAHspAWr,' kAHń yOO gA tEEt rI' nAH?
6. mAdAm, yOO mER zERńdERstAHńd sEH lA gEHr.
7. I lIk tOO 'AHv dEE brA dEEp tEE nEH glAH zERv wIn.
8. dEE lIf kAHń bEE vArEE shEEp, nEHs pAH?
9. 'EE lIk tOO gAW tOO dEE AmArEEkAH wEHń dEE wAW rEE zAWvEHr.
10. mI 'AHt, EE zEEt shEEk?

FRENCH DIALECT MONOLOG

(It is Christmas Eve. In the dim twilight of a monk's cell, Brother Alex kneels near his cot, praying. As he hears the monastery bells ring out from the tower, he lifts his face to the barred light streaming in from the window and says:)

I am grateful, on this eve for the solitude of my monk's cell. The world of woe is in the past. Once, I am of the world. I create the words for the false people and I believe they are wise. I write the plays and they are popular. I become rich. Then I fall in love. I build the happiness on the shifty sands of the worldliness — but know it not. Until, on the Christmas Eve, five year ago, I hurry home with the present for her. The streets are soft with the white snow. The Christmas spirit is in every face. My heart is full with the joy of my wife, the most dear in the world. I open the door. I shout the "Merry Christmas!" Oh, she is there, yes — with the eyes full of love, the arms anxious, the lips warm. . .for another man. They are in the deep embrace. My Christmas present from her! Then the great rage choke me. I want to kill them both. But I run out on the street. The whole night I walk. I do not know where I go or what I do. But, all at once, a great peace fill me. I am born into the new life of humility. Yes — she give me the most real Christmas present, after all. But she know it not. She reveal to me the light of my soul's salvation. *Panis angelicus. . .fit panis hominum. . .dat panis coelicus . . . .*

PHONETIC VERSION

(Syllables in bold-face are to be accented)

"I AHm grEHt fERl AWɳ dEE sEE fAWr dEE sAW lEE tu

tAWv mI **mAWɳk' s**Al. dEE wER lAWv wAW EE zEEn dEE **pAHs**'. wER**ɳ**s, I AHm AWv dEE **wERl**'. I krEE-**EH**' dEE wERds fAWr dEE **fOH**ls pEE**pool** AHn' I bEEl**EE**v dEH AHr **w**Is. I rI' dEE pl**EH** zAHn' dEH AHr pAWp**ú**l**AHr**. I bEEk**AW**m r**EE**sh. dA nI **fOH** lEEn l**ER**v. I **bEE**l' dEE 'AHpEEnA zAWɳ dEE shEEft**EE**ng s**AH**n' sAWv dEE wERl'EEn**A**s — bERt **nAW** EEt nAWt. ER**ɳ**t**EE**l, AW**ɳ** dEE krEEsm**AH** s**EE**v, flv yEE r**A**g**AW**, I 'EREE '**AW**m wEEt dEE prAz**AH**ɳt fAW **rER**. dEE str**EE**t s**AH**r s**AW**f' wEEt dEE w**I**' sn**AW**. dEE krEEsm**AH**' sp**EE**r**EE** tEE z**EE** n**A**vr**EE fEH**s. mI '**AH**r tEEs **fER**l wEE' dEE zh**AW**-**EE** AWv mI w**I**f, dEE m**AW**s' dEE rEH**ɳ** dEE **wERl**'. I AWp**EH**ɳ dEE d**OH**r. I sh**AH**' dEE "m**A**r**EE** krEEsm**AH**s!" **AW**! sh**EE** **EE**s d**A**r, y**A**s—wEEt dEE Is f**ER** lAWv l**ER**v, dEE **AH**rm s**AH**ɳgsy**ER**s, dEE l**EE**ps w**OH**rm ... f**AW**

rAnAWdEHr mAHn. dEH AH rEEn dEE dEEp EHɱbrEHs. mI krEEsmAHs
prAzAHɳt frAW mER. dAn dEE grEHt rEHzh shAWk mEE. I wAHɳ' tOO kEEl
dAm bAWt. bER tI rER nAH tAWɳ dEE strEEt. dEE 'AWl nI tI wOHk. I dOO
nAWt nAW wA rI gAW AWr wAW tI dOO. bERt, OH lAHt wERɳs EH grEHt
pEEs fEEl mEE. I AHm bOHr nEHɳtOO dEE nOO ll fAW fyɥmEElEEtEE.
yAs—shEE gEEv mEE dEE mAWs' rEEl krEEsmAHs prAzAHɳ tAHftEH rOHl.
bERt shEE **nAW** EEt nAWt. shEE rEEvEEl tOO mEE dEE ll tAWv mI sAWl
sAHlvEHsyAWɳ. "pAHnEEs AHnjAYlEEkoos . . . fEEt pAHnEEs OHmEEnoo . . .
dAHt pAHnEEs kAYlEEkoos . . . . "

CHAPTER EIGHT

The Italian Dialect

Like the language, the Italian dialect is melodic and warm. The language has a great many vowel sounds which are carried over into the dialect. In fact, about 99 percent of the Italian lexicon ends with some vowel sound. The reason may be that, in singing, a vowel sound serves as a connecting glide between words which, in turn, provide a melodic, rhythmic flow of sound rather than a staccato jumping. To compensate for the lack of vowel-sound word-endings, Italians, in speaking English, insert an aspirate "uh" between their words when the first word ends with a consonant and the following word begins with a consonant. This is, perhaps, the most important distinguishing characteristic in the entire Italian dialect. A more detailed discussion of this aspirate "uh" sound will be found further on in this chapter in the section titled "The Aspirate 'UH.'"

THE ITALIAN LILT

Lilt is an important factor in any dialect. It would be possible to simulate the feel of a dialect with lilt alone, if all that was spoken was gibberish. A story is told of a famous Russian actress who was asked to entertain at a party. Because she was unprepared, she recited the Russian alphabet with great feeling and pathos. No one understood what she was saying but the rhythm of the language conveyed the emotion.

The Italian lilt is very important in the reproduction of the dialect. It calls for, first, a complete relaxing of all the throat muscles. For the sound of Italian speech is warm and musical—and relaxed. The open throat is always used, both in speaking and in singing. This is the famous *bel canto* method which produced Caruso.

Following are a few sample sentences in which the lilt has been approximated:

"uh-wI: dAW:n-uh yOO: sEE: fAW:r-uh yOOsA:-OOf?"
(Why don't you see for yourself?)

It can be seen, then, that the vocal pattern of the question is spoken with a rising inflection. In an imperative sentence, the rising inflection is still retained but the tempo is faster, as in:

"dAW:n'-uh yOO tO:tch-uh!"
(Don't you touch!)

An example of the vowel attenuation can be noticed in the above example sentence where the vowel "O" was used as a falling tone, dropping from the high spot in the pattern all the way down to the low spot. The range in Italian speech is much greater than it is in American and the note on which the speech begins is usually three or four notes higher than that of the corresponding word in an American sentence. More of the rising-falling inflection is to be observed in the following sentence in which sarcasm is intended. This attitude would be evident in the following coloration of tones:

"EE:z-uh vA:r-uh suhmAH:rd-uh fA:lAW!"
(He's a very smart fellow!)

A somewhat similar tonal pattern is observed in the following sentence of gentle admonishment where the emotion has again affected the lilt:

"uh-wI: fAW:r-uh yOO dOO: dAH:d-uh?"
(Why for you do that?)
(Why did you do that?)

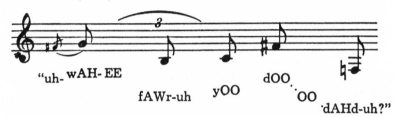

In the above sentence, the vowel glide can be observed in action in the first word "wAH-EE," which was separated into its component parts to effect the glide from the lower note on "AH" up to the higher note on "EE" which two notes, when joined, make the long "I" sound. In the second to the last word, "dOO," the vowel glide was shown by the addition of the extra "OO." The aspirate "uh," before the "w" in the first word is explained in the "The Aspirate 'UH'" section.

The internal-syllable lilt in a word is as important to the dialect as the internal-word lilt is to a sentence. Usually, the emphasis falls on the next-to-the-last syllable in a word. The vowel sound in this syllable is given considerable tonal emphasis but it should always be drawn out as a monosyllable — never as a diphthong. Take for example the word "vA:r-uh" (very). Actually, the Italian pronounces it as "vAAAr-uh." It would not be spoken in one tone but, instead, as:

The commonplace contraction "dAW:n'-uh" (don't) would be pronounced as:

The above examples, although the vowels are split up, should not be pronounced as though each part were sounded separately, as in Chinese or Japanese.

Rather they should be fused in an even, smooth, rhythmic flow of sound, gliding easily down from high to low and gliding evenly up from low to high. Choppy elongation of the vowels will throw the entire dialect out of focus.

EMPHASIS

With such a musical dialect, it is obvious that much of the syllabic and word emphasis is obtained from a tonal treatment rather than from a stressed treatment — that is, from a change of musical note rather than from an increased expulsion of breath. But the emotional nature of the Italians causes them to add the stressed emphasis to the tonal emphasis, which accounts for an additional liveliness of the emphasis treatment.

In syllabic emphasis, the Italian dialect generally allows the emphasis to fall on the next-to-the-last syllable. But in words of three or more syllables, the emphasis is given both to the next-to-the-last syllable and to the first syllable as well, as in "**OH**rdEEnA:r'" (ordinary) and "rAkAWmAndEHsh'" (recommendation). The (') sign indicates that a syllable has been dropped. Since the spelling of the entire original word is considered in the above rule, the seeming discrepancy in the examples is explained by the sign (') indicating that a syllable has been dropped.

THE ASPIRATE "UH"

In the preceding material, and in all the material that follows in this chapter, it will be noticed that an aspirate "uh" has been added to most words ending with a consonant. The inept actor who essays the Italian dialect usually hits this sound very hard and, as a result, audiences have come to expect an Italian dialect to be heard as "wAWtsAH mAHrAH wEEtAH dAHtAH mAHnAH?" (What's the matter with that man?) This sound is never treated as hard as "AH;" neither is it to be treated even as hard as "uh," as it is indicated in this book. The sound is simply that extra puff of air which is exploded after certain consonants. For example, pronounce the word "take" to yourself. Notice that when you complete the pronunciation of the final "k" a *very slight* puff of breath is expelled. That is the aspirate "uh." And it should be *only* that treatment, and no more, that should be given to any aspirate "uh" indicated in this book and especially in this Italian dialect chapter where it is such an important consideration.

This aspirate "uh" is frequently used at the beginning of a word, the first letter of which is "r," as in "uh-rI:'" (right), "uh-rAT-uh" (red) and "uh-rI:p-uh" (ripe). A great many Italians drop the initial mute "a," sounded as "AH," as in "'lAWn-uh" (alone) and "'bOWt-uh" (about). But in words like "around," although the initial mute "a" is dropped, the aspirate "uh" is added again because of the following "r." This, then, would make the pronunciation of the word "uh-rOWn'-uh" (around).

The aspirate "uh" is also used medially, between two consonants, the first of which, in most cases, is either "r" or "l," as in "bAHr-uh-buh" (barber) and "bEEl-uh-dEEng" (building).

The use of the final aspirate "uh," which most students attack with energetic enthusiasm, should be treated as lightly as the initial and medial "uh."

> *THE FINAL ASPIRATE "UH" IS USUALLY FOUND AFTER ALL CON-*
> *SONANT SOUNDS, EXCEPT THE "ING" ENDING, WHEN THE*
> *CONSONANT IS FINAL OR FOLLOWED BY A WORD THAT BEGINS*
> *WITH ANOTHER CONSONANT.*

"tchAW:p*uh* duh wOO:t*uh*."
(Chop the wood.)

"tEH:k*uh* duh dOH:g*uh* bI: d*uh* pOH:*uh*."
(Take the dog by the paw.)

"EE:z*uh* nAW: plEH:z*uh* fAWr*uh* yOO: tuh gAW:?"
(Is no place for you to go?)
(Is there no place for you to go?)

It will be noticed, in the above examples, that in the word "paw," the aspirate "uh" was added although "OH" is a vowel sound. The reason is that the lips are in position to form the unvoiced "w" sound, so the Italian sometimes adds the aspirate "uh."

The rule states that the aspirate "uh" is added *only* when a word ends with a consonant sound and is followed by a word beginning with a consonant. Therefore, in such cases where the succeeding word begins with a vowel, the aspirate "uh" is *not* added to the final consonant, as in:

"tEH:k EEt EEnsI:tuh."
(Take it inside.)

"OH:luh duh nI:z AH:pOOlzuh"
(all the nice apples)

The aspirate "uh" is the most important identification tag in the Italian dialect and one which is easily overdone because of its simplicity. If the vowel sound preceding the final consonant is drawn out it should aid in shortening the aspirate "uh." For example, pronounce "is" as "EEEEEEzuh" and "get" as "gAAAAAduh" and continue this practice throughout. This not only keeps the aspirate "uh" in line but it also follows the Italian method of drawing out all the vowels. Use this system in the drill words suggested in the following sections on vowel and consonant changes and your Italian dialect will be infinitely the better for it.

VOWEL CHANGES

Note: Although most of the vowel sounds receive elongation, the (:) sign will be used only when the vowel is stressed. In the following drill words the aspirate "uh" must not be sounded as "AH" or "U." It is merely a slight puff of air which results when the preceding consonant is struck forcefully.

"AY" .... as in "take," "break," "they," etc.

This long "a" receives an "EH" substitution in the Italian dialect. This should be a clear monosyllable with no vanishing "EE" or "i" sound attached, furthermore, it should be drawn out to about twice the length of the American "EH" in "get," as in "tEH:k" (take). The (:) sign will indicate the need of vowel attenuation.

DRILL WORDS

stEH:	(stay)	rEElEH:duh	(relate)
dEH:	(day)	mEH:bEE	(maybe)
'wEH:	(away)	tEH:stEE	(tasty)

AHvEH:luh   (avail)
bEH:zuhbOH:luh   (baseball)
stEH:bOOluh   (stable)

"UH" .... as in "alone," "sofa," "final," etc.

This mute "a" becomes "AH" in the dialect. But, as was explained previously, it may be dropped when it comes at the beginning of a word, as in "'bOWduh" (about).

DRILL WORDS

sAW:fAH	(sofa)	sAHlOO:duh	(salute)
fI:nAHluh	(final	AHgAW:	(ago)
lAHpA:luh	(lapel)	pAHrEH:tuh	(parade)

bAHnAH:nAH   (banana)
mAHlEE:shOzuh   (malicious)
sAHlOO:nuh   (saloon)

"AH" .... as in "father," "arm," "park," etc.

This "a" retains the same sound as is given to it in American. But, remember, it should be lengthened considerably.

"A:" .... as in "ask," "draft," "laugh," etc.

This "a," usually found before the consonants "f," "n," "s," and "t," is changed to "AH:" in the Italian, as in "AH:s'uh" (ask). Again, the lengthening process should be applied.

DRILL WORDS

lAH:fuh	(laugh)	fAH:s'uh	(fast)
lAH:s'uh	(last)	mAH:stuh	(master)
pAH:suh	(pass)	'AH:zuh	(has)

dAHnsuh   (dance)
duhrAH:f'uh   (draft)
grAH:suh   (grass)

"A" .... as in "bad," "am," "guarantee," etc.

This shorter "a" receives the same "AH:" as in "ask," in such words as "bAH:tuh" (bad). It, too, should be lengthened. A variant is "EH:."

DRILL WORDS

sAH:tuh	(sad)	'AH:pEE	(happy)
mAH:puh	(map)	fAH:brEEkuh	(fabric)
fAH:k'uh	(fact)	mAH:lEEsuh	(malice)

bAH:gEEtchuh	(baggage)
sAH:vAHtchuh	(savage)
fAH:ktAWrEE	(factory)

"AW" .... as in "ball," "falter," "shawl," etc.

The common substitution for "AW" in the Italian is "OH:," as in "bOH:luh" (ball). Sometimes an "AH:" or "AW:" is substituted but the "OH:" is preferred. There should be no suggestion of a diphthong and the sound should be drawn out.

DRILL WORDS

'OH:luh	(hall)	wOH:duh	(water)
kOH:luh	(call)	shOH:luh	(shawl)
stOH:luh	(stall)	fOH:luhtuh	(falter)

kOH:duh	(caught)
OH:luhwEHzuh	(always)
skwOH:luh	(squall)

"EE" .... as in "he," "treat," "people," etc.

The long "e" vowel sound is retained in all the Romance languages and their dialects. But in Italian this sound should be more intense and of longer duration, as in "trEE:duh" (treat).

"EH" .... as in "bet," "said," "friend," etc.

Short "e," in Italian, is changed to the "A" of "bad," as in "bA:duh" (bet). The sound should be flat and broad.

DRILL WORDS

sA:tuh	(said)	bA:l'uh	(belt)
uhrA:tuh	(red)	fuhrA:n'uh	(friend)
mA:nuh	(men)	bA:s'uh	(best)

kuhrA:dEE:duh	(credit)
uhrA:tEE	(ready)
spAHgA:duh	(spaghetti)

"I" .... as in "ice," "aisle," "guile," etc.

Although the Italian tries not to diphthongize his vowel sounds, he cannot help himself sometimes, as with his treatment of long "i." He often retains the "AH-EE" pronunciation but sustains the "AH:" and throws off the final "EE" sound, as in "*AH*-EEsuh" (ice). For instance, the personal pronoun, "I," throws off the "EE" completely and is treated as "AH:." In this book, the phonetic symbol for long "i" is always "I:" but the correct pronunciation (AH-EE) should be remembered and applied whenever this "I:" is seen in the phonetic symbols. A variant is "AH:," as in "AH:suh" (ice), "trAH:" (try) and "bAH:duh" (bite).

DRILL WORDS

nI:zuh	(nice)	uhrI:duh	(right)
fI:nuh	(fine)	stI:luh	(style)
mI:	(my)	dI:muh	(dime)

pAWlI:duh	(polite)
lI:nuh	(liner)
fI:duh	(fight)

"i" .... as in "it," "women," busy," etc.

Again, as in all Romance languages, the Italian substitutes long "e" (EE) for this short "i" vowel sound, as in "EE:duh" (it). Remember, this long "e" sound must be pronounced vigorously and clearly and, furthermore, must be drawn out.

DRILL WORDS

sEE:duh	(sit)	wEE:duh	(with)
flEE:duh	(flit)	tEE:nuh	(thin)
mEE:luhkuh	(milk)	vEE:zEE:duh	(visit)

uhrEE:bAWnuh	(ribbon)
sEE:gAH:ruh	(cigar)
lEE:vuh	(live)

"O" .... as in "on," "bond," "John," etc.

There are two substitutions made for this "O" sound in the Italian. Sometimes it is pronounced as "AW," as in "AWnuh" (on). At other times it is pronounced as "O," as in American, as in "gOtuh" (got). The former is preferred because it is richer and more melodious.

DRILL WORDS

sAW:tuh	(sod)	bAW:dEE	(body)
'AW:duh	(hot)	jAW:nuh	(John)
pAW:duh	(pot)	bAW:n'uh	(bond)

AW:nAs'uh	(honest)
OpAWnuh	(upon)
krAW:puh	(crop)

"OH" .... as in "bone," "sew," "dough," etc.

The usual substitution for this long "o" vowel sound is a drawn out "AW:," as in "bAW:nuh" (bone). But a great many Italians retain the long "o" although they do not give it the full color of the American long "o." Again, the first pronunciation is preferred.

DRILL WORDS

sAW:	(so)	fA:lAW	(fellow)
tAW:l'uh	(told)	dAW:n'uh	(don't)
nAW:	(know)	'AW:muh	(home)

                          klAW:suh   (clothes)
                          OH:luhdAW: (although)
                          mAW:'ruh   (motor)

"AW" . . . . as in "off," "cough," "bought," etc.

This "AW" vowel sound receives a long "o" (OH) treatment, as in "OH:fuh" (off). This "OH:," as the (:) indicates, should be lengthened much more than it is in American and should be richly colored.

DRILL WORDS

kOH:fuh	(cough)		klOH:tuh	(cloth)
sOH:f'uh	(soft)		bOH:duh	(bought)
nOH:duh	(nought)		gOH:nuh	(gone)

                          OH:fuh   (off)
                       kOH:stEE:ng   (costing)
                          fOH:duh   (fought)

"OO" . . . . as in "food," "do," "blue," etc.

This vowel sound is given the same treatment as in American. It should, however, be lengthened considerably, as in "fOO:tuh" (food).

"oo" . . . . as in "good," "wolf," "full," etc.

For this short double "oo" the Italians substitute the long "oo" of "food" (OO), as in "gOO:tuh" (good). Remember to lengthen it.

DRILL WORDS

pOO:duh	(put)		wOO:lfuh	(wolf)
fOO:duh	(foot)		pOO:shuh	(push)
shOO:tuh	(should)		lOO:kuh	(look)

                          rOO:fuh   (roof)
                        bOO:tchuh   (butcher)
                    fOH:ruhsOO:kuh   (forsook)

"yOO" . . . . as in "unit," "cube," "beauty," etc.

This vowel sound is pronounced as it is in American. Like the "oo" in "fOO:tuh" (food), it should be lengthened and enriched with a full, throaty quality, as in "yOO:nEEduh" (unit).

"U" . . . .as in "up," "love," "does," etc.

There are two pronunciations given this short "u" sound in the Italian dialect. In the first it is sounded like the "O" in "rod," as in "O:puh" (up). The second pronunciation changes it to "AW," as in "lAWvuh" (love). The first is preferred and is used here.

DRILL WORDS

lO:vuh	(love)		dO:s'uh	(dust)
uhrO:nuh	(run)		bO:s'uh	(bust)
wO:nsuh	(once)		puhlO:muh	(plum)

kO:duh   (cut)
'O:suhbAHn'uh   (husband)
krO:muh   (crumb)

"ER"....as in "curb," "earn," "fern," etc.

This sound receives the long double "o" of "food" (OO), as in "kOOruhbuh" (curb). Sometimes it is shaded a bit flatter and is sounded as "UH," as in "fUHruh" (fir). The latter pronunciation is preferred in this chapter. The same treatment is given to all the vowel "r" combinations—"er," "ir," "ur," and "or." Many Italians give "ur" words an "OOr" sound, as in "kOO:ruhbuh" (curb); "er" words the sound of "EHr," as in "pEHruhmEE:duh" (permit); "or" words the sound of "AWr," as in "wAW:ruhkuh" (work); and "ir" words the sound of "EEr," as in "dEE:ruhtEE" (dirty).

DRILL WORDS

gUHruhluh	(girl)	stUHruh	(stir)
nUHruhsuh	(nurse)	hUHruh	(her)
wUHruhtuh	(worth)	dUHr'EE:	(dirty)
	sUHruht'n	(certain)	
	tUHruhztEH:	(Thursday)	
	lUHruhnuh	(learn)	

"OW"....as in "out," "cow," "house," etc.

This diphthong is pronounced as it is in American except that it is richer and fuller. A variation is "AH:," as in "AH:duh" (out) and "dAH:nuh" (down).

"OI"....as in "oil," "boy," "noise," etc.

This diphthong, too, is pronounced as it is in American but with a richer and fuller treatment.

WORD EXERCISES

Pronounce these words using the material learned from the vowel and aspirate "uh" sections.

1.	army	11.	customer
2.	group	12.	crowd
3.	gondola	13.	boil
4.	soprano	14.	uniform
5.	ravioli	15.	hospital
6.	bombshell	16.	letter
7.	football	17.	olive-oil
8.	hate	18.	passport
9.	mile	19.	antipasto
10.	fern	20.	foreman

After pronouncing the above words, refer to the following phonetic list. Check it for verification or corrections, then practice the above list again.

1. AHruhmEE	11. kO:stO:muh
2. grOO:puh	12. krAH:tuh
3. gAW:ndAW:lAH	13. bOIluh
4. sAW:prAH:nAW:	14. yOO:nEEvfOH:ruhmuh
5. rAH:vEE-AWlEE	15. 'AW:spEEtAHluh
6. bAW:muh-shA:luh	16. lA:tuh
7. fOO:duhbOH:luh	17. AW:lEEvuh-OIluh
8. 'EH:tuh	18. pAH:suh pOH:ruhduh
9. mI:luh	19. AH:ntEEpAH:stAW
10. fUHruhn or fEHruhn	20. fOH:ruhmAH:nuh

CONSONANT CHANGES

B—The same as in American.

C—For the soft sound, see "S"; for the hard sound, see "K."

D—This consonant, in the Italian dialect, is sounded with the tip of the tongue placed against the back of the upper front teeth, instead of at the forward part of the roof of the mouth as in American. This makes for a dentalized "d" that is thicker than the American.

Initially, "d" is pronounced as "d." Medially, though, "d" is often changed to "t," between vowels, by southern Italians and by Sicilians, as in "mAW*t*UHnuh" (mo*d*ern). The Neapolitans, however, and a great many Italians from central Italy change "d" to "r," medially, as in "mAW*r*uhnuh" (mo*d*ern) and "mAW*r*As'uh" (mo*d*est).

When final "d" is pronounced—when preceded by a vowel sound —it is so close to "t," because of its dentalization, that the phonetic change has been made in this chapter. However, when final "d" is preceded by a consonant, it is usually dropped, as in "fuhrAn'uh" (friend). The (') sign indicates that the "d" has been dropped and the "n," being final now, takes the usual aspirate "uh." Medial "d" is also elided occasionally, as in "shOO'nuh" (shouldn't), "uh-wOO-'nuh" (wooden) and "fEE:'luh" (fiddle), but the elision is not typical and should not be used too often.

F—Initially, "f" is pronounced as it is in American, but medially and finally, "f" takes on a combination "vf" sound, as in "kAW:*vf*EE:" (co*ff*ee) and "skAH:uhr*v*-*f*uh" (scar*f*). At all times, though, the "f" sound should predominate.

G—Both sounds of "g," as in "get" and "George," are pronounced as they are in American.

H—When used initially and when the word is the first in a sentence, "h" is dropped completely, as in:

"'EE uh-wAWzuh lEH:duh."
(*He* was late.)

However, when "h" is used initially in a word that comes in the middle or end of a sentence, it is often, but not always, dropped. When it is dropped, it affects the preceding word, if that word ends with a consonant, by causing it to drop its aspirate "uh," as in:

> "dEH: uh-wAn' 'AW:muh."
> (They went home.)

When the "h" is not dropped initially, the above sentence would read:

> "dEH: uh-wAn' *uh* *h*AW:muh."
> (They went home.)

In the middle of a word, "h" is quite often dropped, as in "On'AH:pEE" (unhappy) and "puhr'AH:pzuh" (perhaps).

Occasionally, the consonant "h" is added to a word that begins with a vowel, as in "*h*AH:pOOluh" (apple) and "*h*AWrAHnjuh" (orange). It is more natural to the Italian to drop the "h," but if it is used, it should be given greater force than in American.

J—The same as in American. Some Italians, however, give this "J" sound a "zh" treatment. This "zh" is sounded as in the American word "azure." In the Italian, it would be used in "*zh*AW:buh" (job).

K—The Italian "k" sound is actually a combination of "gk." Ordinarily, the "k" sound predominates and therefore it is designated as "k," in this book. But if the character to be portrayed is from Rome, he would give his "k's" an actual "g" pronunciation as in "*g*uhlEE:*g*uh" (click) and "fAH:*g*tAWrEE" (factory). Ordinarily, however, the "k" sound should prevail.

L—The consonant "l" is dentalized by the Italians with the same mouth position as "D." This will make for a thicker "l" than is pronounced in American.

Initially, "l" is sounded as "l." But, medially, it is sometimes dropped, as in "'EE:msA-OO'fuh" (himself). It is also dropped finally when the following word begins with an "r," as in "AW':rIduh" (*all* right) and "AW'rA:dEE" (all ready). Medially, it is usually given the aspirate "uh" when it is followed by another consonant, as in "bEE:l*uh*dEE:ng" (building).

M—The same as in American.

N—This consonant is dentalized by the Italians so that the tip of the tongue touches the back part of the upper front teeth instead of the forward part of the roof of the mouth, thus making a thicker "n."

P—The Italian "p" should not be pronounced more explosively than is the American. There is a suggestion of a "b" in it but the "p" sound predominates so it is given as "p" here.

Q—The same as in American.

R—In Italian, the "r" is always trilled.

Initially, "r" is often given an initial aspirate "uh," as in "uh-rAW:luh" (roll), "uh-rI:duh" (right) and "uh-rEE:tchuh" (rich).

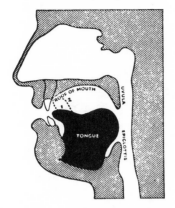

The black area indicates the position of the tongue as it begins trilling the Italian "r." The dotted line shows the tongue curling upward to touch the forward part of the roof of the mouth. An extended series of this rapid interchange of positions causes the trilled Italian "r."

In the middle of a word, when "r" is followed by another consonant, it may be given the usual final aspirate "uh," as in "pAH:r*uh*tAW:nuh" (pardon) and "pUHr*uh*mEE:duh" (permit). When used at the end of a word, "r" is often dropped, as in "uh-wOH:dUH'" (water) and "'fl:UH'" (fire).

S—At the beginning of a word, the consonant "s" is treated as it is in American. But medially and finally, the consonant "s" is often changed to "z." It is changed when it is preceded *and* followed by a vowel sound, as in "bEH:*z*EEnuh" (basin) and "pAW:*z*EEbOOluh" (possible). It is changed finally, as in "bAz'uh" (best), where the final "t" is dropped, making "s" the final letter and thus changing it to "z." Double "s" (ss) may retain the "s" sound, as in "glAHsuh (gla*ss*).

T—The consonant "t" is another of the dentalized Italian consonants. (See "D" for mouth position of dentalized consonants.) There are a number of variations in the pronunciation of "t." Some southern Italians, for example, retain the "t" sound between vowels but change the "t" to "d" when it is preceded by an "n" or an "r," as in "pIn*d*uh" (pin*t*) and "pAH:ruh*d*uh" (par*t*). Northern Italians change "t" to "d" between vowels, as in "mEE:*d*UH'" (meter) but retain the "t" sound after "n" or "r."

The following suggestions, however, can be followed as a general rule in making the proper changes. Initially, give "t" its usual American treatment. Medially, and especially if the Italian is a Neapolitan, change the "t" to "r," as in "pEE:*r*EE:" (pi*t*y), "mAH:*r*UH'" (ma*tt*er) and "byOO:*r*EE:fOOluh" (beautiful). This change is also made when the "t" is final, the following word begins with a vowel, and the words are run together so that the "t" becomes medial, as in "pOO*r*EE:dOWnuh" (put it down). The "r," here, should never be fully trilled. There is always a tendency to drop the final "t" when it is preceded by a consonant—especially "s" and "n"—as in "dAW:n'uh" (don't). "bA:z'uh" (best) and "sOH:f'uh" (soft). When final "t" is preceded by a vowel sound, it is changed to "d," as in "bAH:*d*uh" (ba*t*). "fOH:*d*uh" (fough*t*) and "sEE:*d*uh" (si*t*). The fact must be remembered, when substituting "d" for "t," that the "d" sound of "d" is not sounded so strongly as it is in American, as in "dark," for example. Because it is dentalized, it carries with it a suggestion of the "t," just as the substituted "t" for "d" carries with it a suggestion of the "d."

There is also a tendency to drop the "t" completely in certain contractions, as in "dAH'zOH:rI" (that's all right), "uh-wAW:'z-UHyOOzuh" (what's the use?) and "EE:'zAW:kEH:" (it's O.K.).

W—The Italian "w" receives a very slight initial aspirate "uh," when it is used at the beginning of a word, as in "*uh*-wEE:luh" (*w*heel), "*uh*-wAW:nuh" (won) and "uh-wAnuh" (when). The last example illustrates another habit in the Italian. The combination, "wh," is always pronounced simply as "w" (with the initial aspirate, of course) instead of "huh-w," as in "huh-wEHn" (when), as it is sometimes pronounced in American. Since there is no "w" in the Italian language, the Italians make a forced effort to pronounce the American "w" correctly. The aspirate "uh" must, therefore, be very short.

X—This consonant, which is actually pronounced "ks," as in "six" and "gz" as in "example," in American, has its two consonants separated by an aspirate "uh" in the Italian dialect, as in "sEEk*uh*zuh" (six) and "Ag*uh*sAHmpOOluh" (example). It will be observed, in the above examples, that the "s" in the "ks" sound of "six" has been changed to "z," following the Italian custom of substituting "z" for "s" when it is at the end of a word. You should further observe that the "z" in "gz," of "example," has been changed to "s" because of the Italian usage. The "ksh" of "luxury" becomes "lO*kuhsh*UHrEE." The aspirate "uh" must be very slight.

Y—The same as in American.

Z—The Italian quite often substitutes an "s" for a "z," as in "EE:suh" (hi*s*). This can be done in the dialect but care must be taken that the usage does not conflict with the substitution of "z" for "s," when "s" comes between two vowel sounds, as in "bEH:zEEnuh" (basin).

SH—The same as in American.

th—The unvoiced "th" (of "thin") is changed to "t," as in "*t*EE:nuh" (*th*in) and "bEH:*t*uh" (ba*th*). Remember, however, that the "t" is thickened by dentalization.

TH—The voiced "th" (of "they") is changed to "d," as in "*d*EH:" (*th*ey), "bEH:*d*EEng" (ba*th*ing) and "bEH:*d*uh" (ba*the*). This "d" is also thickened by dentalization.

ZH—This consonant sound is pronounced as it is in American. But, following the Italian custom, the final syllable is usually dropped from such words as "azure," leisure" and "pleasure," in which the consonant sound appears. The words would then be pronounced as "AH:zh-uh," "lEH:zh-uh" and "plAzh-uh," with the aspirate "uh" only barely suggested.

DOUBLE CONSONANTS

The Italian dialect often treats double consonants in an unorthodox manner.

The double "c" (cc) combination is often pronounced as "s," instead of "ks," as in "AH'*s*EE:tuh" (accede) and "vAH'*s*EE:nEHduh" (vaccinate).

The double "g" (gg) combination is pronounced as "j," not "gj," as in "sO'-jAs'uh" (su*gg*est). Some Italians, especially those from Tuscany, sometimes give this "j" a "zh" sound, as in "sOzhA:s'uh."

Contrary to general usage in the dialect, the double "s" (ss) combination is always pronounced as "s"—never as "z"—when it is sounded as "s" in American, as in "bEH*s*OOnuh" (bassoon). This is done despite the fact that the "s" sound comes between two vowel sounds. When double "s" (ss) is treated as "sh" in American, as in "passions," the "sh" sound remains in the Italian dialect.

WORD EXERCISES

Pronounce the following words using the material learned from the preceding consonant section.

1.	habit	11.	find
2.	united	12.	one
3.	silk	13.	milk
4.	is	14.	exist
5.	treasure	15.	path
6.	accident	16.	easy
7.	satisfy	17.	face
8.	winter	18.	the
9.	hope	19.	steelworker
10.	warm	20.	without

After pronouncing the above words, check them with the phonetic list below. When the correct changes have been noted and learned, practice the above words again.

1.	'AH:bEEduh	10.	uh-wOH:ruhmuh
2.	yOO:nI:ruhtuh or	11.	fI:n'uh
	yOO:nI:duhtuh	12.	uh-wO:nuh
3.	sEEluhkuh	13.	mEEluhkuh
4.	EEzuh	14.	A:guhsEEs'uh or
5.	trA:zhuh		A:guhsEEstuh
6.	AH:sEEdA:n'uh	15.	pAH:tuh
7.	sAH:rEEzfI: or	16.	EEzEE
	sAH:dEEzfI:	17.	fEH:zuh
8.	uh-wEEnduh or	18.	duh
	uh-wEEntuh	19.	stEEluhwUHruhkuh
9.	AWpuh	20.	uh-wEEdAH:duh

GRAMMAR CHANGES

One of the most important changes wrought by the Italian in his use of the American language is his lopping off of the final syllable in multi-syllabled words, as in:

"AH gAW:duh bEE:guh sOspEE:shuh."
(I got big suspic'.)
(I am very suspic*ious*.)

"uh-wAWzuh tOO: mOtch AkuhsI:duh."
(Was too much excite'.)
(There was too much excite*ment*.)

"EE:zuh tOO bAHt EE:z OH:l uh-rEHnj'uh."
(Is too bad is all arrange'.)
(It's too bad it is all arrang*ed*.)

The Italian is prone to use "more" and "most" instead of the suffixes "er" and "est" for the comparatives and superlatives of adverbs and adjectives, as in:

"uh-rAW:zuh, shEE: EEzuh mAW:ruh nI:z'uh."
(Rose, she is *more* nice.)
(Rose is *nicer*.)

"EE:zuh dUH mAW:zuh fO:nEE: fAlAW!"
(He's the *most* funny fellow!)
(He's the *funniest* fellow!)

But the most important errors in grammar are due to the confusion arising from verb forms. American conjugations are so difficult for Italians—and for all foreigners—that they prefer to drop them rather than try to use them. Some of the most frequent misusages are:

"uh-wEE: gAW:."
(We go.)
(We *shall* (or *will*) go.)

"'EE: sEH: hEE: bEE: hEE:ruh, 'EE: bEE: hEE:ruh."
(He say he be here, he be here.)
(If he says *he'll* be here, *he'll* be here.)

NOTE: The above sentence illustrates an interesting case in which the consonant "h" is dropped and retained to suit the demands of the aspirate "uh." The "h" in the first word, "he," is dropped according to rule. But the "h" in the third word, "he," is retained because its preceding word, "say," is a final vowel sound and so requires a consonant beginning in its following word. The "h" in the fifth word, "here," is retained for the same reason because the fourth word, "he," closes with a final vowel. But the "h" in the sixth word, "he," is dropped because it is preceded by a consonant that receives the aspirate "uh," necessitated by an obvious pause in the speech. Thus the sixth word "he" begins a new breath and a new thought and drops the "h." The "h" in the eighth word, "here," is retained, though, because the preceding word, "he," closes with a final vowel sound. Thus it can be seen that the aspirate "uh" is a very important adjunct to the dialect and is the reason for a great many of the dialect characteristics.

To continue with more of the examples of verb misusage in the dialect:

"uh-wEE nAW: hO:ngrEE."
(We *no* hungry.)
(We *aren't* hungry.)

"nAW: fAW:ruhgAduh dUH pEH:p'uh."
(*No* forget the pap'.)
(*Don't* forget the paper.)

"uh-wAW:ruhyOO:kA?"
(What you care?)
(What *do* you care?)

The second sentence above illustrates another common failing in the dialect: the substitution of "no" for the negative contractions, "don't" or "do not," and "wasn't" or "was not," as in:

"yOO: nAW: gAW:dA:ruh."
(You *no* go there.)
(*Don't* you go there.)

"AH nAW: b'lEE:vuh 'EE gAW:."
(I *no* believe he go.)
(I *don't* believe he went.)

"nAW sOtchuh tArEE:bOOluh tEE:nguh."
(*No* such terrible thing.)
(It *was not* such a terrible thing.)

The last example above illustrates another popular elision in the dialect: the dropping of "it," as in:

"uh-wAW:zuh bAH:tuh."
(Was bad.)
(*It* was bad.)

"EE:zuh nAW: hEE:ruh."
(Is no here.)
(*It* is not here.)

"EE:zuh nAW: sAW: hEE:zEE lI:kuh yOO tEE:nkuh."
(Is no so easy like you think.)
(*It* is not as easy as you think.)

The Italian is confused by the necessity in American for making the parts of speech agree in number and gender, as in:

"EE:zuh sEE:kuhzuh yEEruh frAW:muh nOW."
(Is six year from now.)
(It is six years from now.)

"dEH: uh-wAW:n'uh hAH:pOOluh."
(They want *apple*.)
(They want *apples*.)

When the possessive "your" is to be used in a sentence, the Italian often substitutes "you," as in:

"I: AHmuh yOO frA:n'uh."
(I am *you* friend.)
(I am *your* friend.)

"EEzuh fOH:ruh yOO: drA:zuh."
(Is for *you* dress.)
(It is for *your* dress.)

"gAW: uh-wAW:shuh yOO fEH:zuh."
(Go wash *you* face.)
(Go wash *your* face.)

One of the commonest errors is the use of the double subject, as in:

"mAHrEE:AH, shEE: gAW: nOW."
(Maria, *she* go now.)
(Maria is going now.)

"tAW:nEE: hEE: mEH:kuh mEE:stEH:kuh."
(Tony, *he* make mistake.)
(Tony made a mistake.)

"duh bOH:luh EE:duh rAW:luh dA:ruh."
(The ball, *it* roll there.)
(The ball rolled there.)

Another popular substitution uses "whyfor" instead of "why," as in:

"uh-wI:fAW:ruh yOO gAW: sAW: sOO:nuh?"
(*Whyfor* you go so soon?)
(*Why* are you going so soon?)

"uh-wI:fAW:ruh yOO mEH:kuh sAW: mOtchuh tOH:kuh?"
(*Whyfor* you make so much talk?)
(*Why* do you talk so much?)

The phrase, "from when," is often substituted for "since," as in:

"EEzuh lOH:nguh tI:muh frOH:m uhwA:nuh yOO kO:muh."
(Is long time *from when* you come.)
(It's a long time *since* you came.)

The American habit of running words together falls in with the Italian method of connecting word endings and beginnings with the aspirate "uh." Consequently, he may run together not only two words, but three and four and sometimes five words, as in:

"OH:'rI:duh, AH: kO:muh."
(*Allright*, I come.)
(*All right*, I come.)

"uh-wAW:ruhyOOgAW'n'uhdOO:?"
(*Whatareyou goingtodo?*)
(*What are you going to do?*)

"AHzOH:luhrI:duh-wEEdOsuh."
(*That'sallrightwithus.*)
(*That's all right with us.*)

The Italian not only runs words together, he occasionally elides letters, substitutes one letter for another, performs true contractions (in which whole syllables are omitted) and even concocts run-together one-word phrases. One of the most common examples is "son-of-a-gun," which the Italian pronounces as: "sOnOmuhgOnuh." It will be noticed that the "f" of "of" changes to "m."

Another example which contains an unusual change is "gArOpuh" for "get up" where the "t" changes to "r" following the Neapolitan custom of substituting "r" for "t" between vowels.

And another is "mOO'eembEEtchuh'" for "moving picture" where the "v" is dropped, the "ing" is changed to "m" and the "p" is changed to "b."

Other contractions and typical phrases are "bAtchuhmI:lI:fuh" (you bet my life!), "shOrOpuh!" (shut up!), "uh-wAW:zuhmAHruh" (what's the matter?), and "AHzOH:rI:" (that's all right).

TYPICAL EXPRESSIONS AND INTERJECTIONS

come sta? . . . . This phrase "kAWmEH stAH" is used as the American "How do you do?" The reply is *"sto bene, grazie"* (stAW bAYnEH, grAHtsEE-EH), "I am well, thank you."

grazie . . . . Many Italians prefer their own "grAHtsEE-EH" to the American "thank you."

si . . . . This word "sEE" may be used exactly like the American word "yes."

no .... The word "nAW" means "no" and is used like the American.

scusi .... A number of Italians use "skOO:zEE" rather than the American words "Excuse me." "Scusi" takes care of both "excuse" and "me" and need not be written "scusi me."

basta! .... The word "bAHstAH" is used for "enough," "that's all," etc., when these words or word phrases are used as interjections.

SENTENCE EXERCISES

Pronounce these sentences paying special attention to the grammar changes.

1.   It's been three years since I went there.
2.   Giovanni is all right.
3.   Why are you giving me your picture?
4.   It isn't right for you to go.
5.   I've worked harder than you.
6.   I don't believe what you say.
7.   He doesn't have any ambition.
8.   Signorelli has a fine bambino.
9.   Why don't you take your coat?
10. I don't want you to go there any more.

After pronouncing the above sentences, refer to the following phonetics. Check them for verification or corrections, then practice the above list again.

1.   EEzuh trEE yEEruh frAW:muh wA:n I: gAW: dA:ruh.
2.   jAWvAH:nEE, 'EEz OH:'rI:duh.
3.   uhwI:fAW:ruh yOO gEEvuh mEE yOO pEEtchuh?
4.   EEzuh nAW rI:duh fOHruh yOO tOO gAW.
5.   I:muh wUHruhkuh duh mOH:ruh hAH:ruhtuh dA:nuh yOO.
6.   I: nAW b'lEEvuh wAWruhyOOsEH:.
7.   EEzuh nAW gAWruh nAW AH:mbEEsh.
8.   EEzuh fI:nuh bAH:mbEEnAW sEEnyAWrAYlEE gAW:duh.
9.   uhwI:fAW:ruh yOO nAW tEH:kuh yOO kAWduh?
10. I: nAW uhwAW:n'uh yOO gAW dA:ruh nAW mOH:ruh.

ITALIAN MONOLOG

(*A young Italian immigrant nervously paces the floor in a hospital waiting room. He looks at the clock, he looks at his nails, he looks at the nurse. Finally, he gathers up enough courage, approaches her and blurts out:*)

My wife, she make the bambino and the doc he tell me to wait right here. Is all right with you? I no can sit still. I no can stand still. Oh! I no afraid, oh, no! Is just I kind of nervous, that's all. Is not I think anything she happen to my Rosa. She so strong like the horse. She no got no operation—she no sick all her life—you bet my life, no! Say! what's the most kids born? the boy or the girl? I want the boy. You bet my life! Rosa, she want the girl. Son of a gun! what if she be twin? When is more is all right, too. Oh! excuse me! please no mind! is because this is my first one. Is make me excite. Say! is lots . . . what I mean . . . sometime, something happen . . . they . . . they die, no? Sometime . . . no! my Rosa, she no die! is no good she die! I go in, nurse! We so happy all the time! whyfor we want the bambino? let me go in, nurse! that's all right! I go in! help my Rosa! whyfor she must got all that hurt? She very fine woman! I no let her die! you got to let me in to her, nurse! she hurt! she want me! she need me! . . . eh! what's that? you hear that? is bambino crying! son-of-a-gun! is my bambino! Is my kid! some yell, no? what he is, nurse? boy or girl? I think is boy! what the difference? is girl, so we get the boy next time! oh boy! I'm papa! here, nurse, have a cigar!

PHONETIC REPRESENTATION

(Syllables in bold-face type are to be accented.)

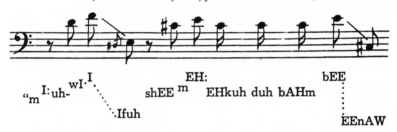

AHnuh dUH **dAW**:kuh, hEE tAluh mEE tOO wEH:duh **rI**:d 'EE:ruh. EEz OH:luh **rI**:duh wEE:tuh **yOO**:? AH nAW kAHnuh **sEE**:duh stEE:luh. AH nAW kAHnuh **stAH**nuh stEE:luh. AW:! AH nAW '**frEH**:tuh, AW **nAW**:! EEzuh jOOz AH kI:nuh **nUH**:ruhvO:zuh, **AHz**OH:luh. EEzuh **nAW**:d AH tEE:nk AnEE-tEE:ng shEE **hAH**:pAnuh tOO mI: uh-rAW:zuh. shEE sAW **strOH**:ng lI:kuh dUH **hAW**:rzuh. shEE nAW gAW:duh **nAW** hAWpUH**rEH**:shuh—shEE nAW sEE:k **OH**:luh hUH **lI**:fuh—**bA**:tchuhmI:**lI**:fuh' **nAW**:! **sEH**:! uh-**wAW**:dzuh dUH **mAW**:s'uh kEE:tsuh **bAW**:ruhn? dUH **bOI** hOH:ruh dUH **gUH**:ruhl? AH wAW:nuh dUH **bOI**:. **bA**:tchuhmI:**lI**:fuh! uh-**rAW**:zuh, **shEE** wAW:nuh dUH **gUH**ruhl. uh-**sOn**Om**UH**g**On**uh! uh-**wAW**:d EE:fuh shEE bEE tuh**wEE**:nuh? uh-wAn EEzuh **mAW**:r EEz **OH**:luhrI: **tOO**! **AW**:! **skOO**zEE! **plEE**:zuh nAW **mI**:n'uh! EEzuh bEEkAWzuh **dEE**:z EEzuh mI: **fUH**rz' uh-wOnuh. EEzuh mEH:kuh mEE hAks**I**:duh. **sEH**:! EEzuh lAW:tsuh . . . . uh-wAWrI:**mEE**:nuh . . . . **sOm**uht**I**:muh **sOm**uhtEE:ng **hAH**: pAnuh . . . . dEH: . . . . dEH: **dI**:, **nAW**:? sO-muht**I**:muh, **nAW**:! mI: uh-**rAW**:zuh, shEE **nAW dI**:! EEzuh nAW **gOO**:tuh shEE **dI**:! AH gAW **hEE**:nuh, nUHruhz! uh-wEE sAW **hAH**:pEE hOH:luh dUH

tI:muh! uh-**wI**:fAW:ruh wEE wAW:nuh dUH bAHm**bEE**:nAW? lAduh mEE
gAW **hEE**:nuh, nUHruhz! AHzOH:l uh**rI**:'! AH gAW **hEE**:nuh! hAlpuh mI:
uh-**rAW**:zuh! uh-wI:fAW:ruh shEE mO:zuh gAWr**OH**:luhdAHduh **hUH**ruh-
duh? shEE **vArEE fI**:n uh-**wOO**:mAHnuh! AH **nAW** lAruh **dI**:! yOO **gAW**:ruh
lAmEE **hEE**:nuh tOO hUHruh, **nUH**ruhz! shEE **hUH**ruhtuh! shEE
uh-**wAW**:n'uh mEE:! shEE **nEE**:tuh mEE:! . . . . A:! uh-wAW:suhd**AH**:duh? yOO
hEE:ruh **dAH**:duh? EEzuh bAHm**bEE**:nAW kr**I**:EEng! sOnOmUH**g**Onuh!
EEzuh **mI**: bAHm**bEE**:nAW! EEzuh **mI**: **kEE**:tuh! sOmuh **yAl**uh, nAW:?
uh-wAW:r**EE hEE**:zuh nUHruhz? **bOI** hAWruh **gUH**ruhl? AH tEE:nkuh
hEE:zuh **bOI**:! uh-wAW:zuh dEE:f'uh! EEzuh **gUH**ruhl sAW wEE gAruhdUH
bOI dUH **nA**kzuh tI:muh! **AW bOI**:! **AH**muh **pAH**:puh! '**EE**:ruh, nUHruhz!
'**AH**:vuh sEE**gAH**:ruh!

CHAPTER NINE

The Spanish Dialect

THE SPANISH LILT

One of the outstanding speech characteristics that contributes much toward the Spanish dialect lilt is the habit of enunciating each vowel clearly, sharply and distinctly. This is a speech habit of all the Romance languages. There are no fuzzy edges around a Spaniard's vowel pronunciation. Each vowel is attacked separately and diphthongs are rarely used. When they do occur in the dialect, as in the American "OW," and "OI," each separate vowel-part of the diphthong is pronounced as a distinct vowel. The only times when vowel glides are used in the Spanish dialect are when a statement is heavily emphasized or when an emphasized syllable, which marks the high note of a sentence, comes at the end of a sentence, as in:

"uhwAH' dTHEEdTH I: dTHAWn?"
(What did I done?)
(What did I do?)

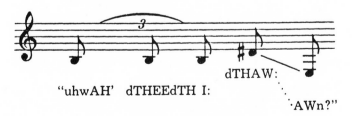

In the above sentence, the high note came with "dTHAWn," which was at the end of the sentence and the vowel sound, "AW," was glided downward.

The pitch in such an emotional people would naturally be much higher than in American. And because of the Spaniard's emotional volatility, his pitch-range varies considerably—sometimes, in great emotional stress, taking in almost two octaves. It might be expected, then, that the speech patterns would show a definite rising inflection. But, strangely, the reverse is the case: the general inflection is a falling one—except in a questioning sentence which calls for a "yes" or "no" answer, in which exception the intonation rises.

In short simple statements of fact, for instance, this falling inflection will be observed:

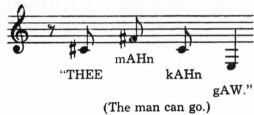

(The man can go.)

In sentences that begin with a one-syllable interrogative word, such as "who," "why," or "when," the question word begins on the high note of the sentence and the balance of the sentence trails off in a falling intonation, as in:

"uhwI: dTHEEdTH 'EE gAW THAr?"
(Why did he go there?)

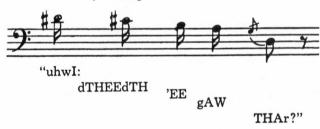

However, as was mentioned previously, in question sentences that call for a "yes" or "no" answer, the general falling intonation is reversed to a rising inflection, as in:

"'AHbv yoo sEE THEE lAtTHEHr?"
(Have you see the letter?)
(Have you seen the letter?)

EMPHASIS

The Spaniard's habit of sounding vowels clearly results also in his separating syllables sharply. There, is, in this respect, a slight similarity to the German. But the German dialect is less distinct because the German elongates his vowels and uses them as the emphasis glide in his words. Thus in the word "officer," the Spaniard would say "AW fEE sEHr." This vowel separation is a factor in making the dialect staccato.

In the syllabic emphasis, the Spaniard usually places a stressed emphasis, rather than a tonal emphasis, on the last syllable of a word. This tonal—or musical—emphasis would naturally be missing in a dialect that features clipped vowels, because it is on the elongated vowels that musical emphasis is carried. Exceptions to this rule of emphasizing the last syllable are to be found in certain words that end with "n" or "s" sounds, as in "**bEH** kAWn" (bacon) and "**AW** fEEs" (office). In words of three syllables ending with an "n" or "s" sound, the emphasis is placed on the next-to-the-last syllable, as in "pAW **tTHEH** tTHAWs" (potatoes) and "sAW **loo** shAWn" (solution). In words of four or more syllables, the emphasis should be placed on two or more syllables with equal intensity. This emphasis may, however, fall on syllables that are not emphasized in the American, as in "**kAWn** tTHEHm plEH **shAWn**" (contemplation).

In the word emphasis, as it affects the word pattern in a sentence, Spanish is again at odds with American custom. We impart different implicated meanings to the same words, simply by laying the emphasis on another word in the sentence, as in "I want it," where the implication is that the person speaking desires the object, "it." The implication of the sentence can be changed completely by emphasizing "want," instead, as in "I **want** it," where the meaning is changed to indicate that the subject is quite certain about his desire. The Spaniard, though, makes no such distinctions in his word emphasis. He avoids the use of such pronouns as "he," "she," "it" or "they" and refers to the subject specifically, as in "I: uh-wAHn' THAHtTH bOOk" (I want that book), giving each word almost equal emphasis and thus contributing to the even, unemphasized flow of the dialect stress. When, however, a word is stressed in a sentence it is, as is true with syllables, usually given the stress emphasis rather than tonal emphasis.

The Spanish dialect should, however, be liquid and mellifluous at all times, with no glottal stops such as are found in American speech. The tongue laxity results in the dentalization by the Spaniard of his "d's" and "t's" explained in the section "Consonant Changes." The lip and mouth-muscle activity results in his widening his mouth to pronouce the long "e" (EE) substitution for short "i." With these facts in mind, an examination of the various other vowel changes, in the section following, should contribute greatly to the reproduction of an authentic Spanish dialect.

VOWEL CHANGES

"AY" .... as in "take," "break," "they," etc.

In American, we pronounce this long "a" as "AY-EE." But the Spaniard, following his custom of avoiding double sounds in vowels and treating them cleanly and sharply, cuts this double sound down to a clean "EH," as in "lEHk" (lake). A variant is "AY" as in "lAYk" (lake). This "AY" sound, if used, must not be the American diphthong "AY-EE," but merely a short monothong "AY."

DRILL WORDS

fEHtTH	(fate)	uhwEH	(way)
mEHl	(male)	stTHEH	(stay)
THEH	(they)	brEHk	(break)
	mEHbvEE	(maybe)	
	uhwEHlEH	(waylay)	
	bvEHkEHtTH	(vacate)	

"UH" .... as in "alone," "final," "sofa," etc.

This mute "a" is pronounced as "AH" in the Spanish dialect, as in "fI:nAHl" (final). When it is used initially, as in "along," it is sometimes dropped when it follows a word that ends with a vowel, as in "gAW 'lAWn'" (go along).

DRILL WORDS

sAWfAH	(sofa)	kAHnArEE	(canary)
AHmAWng	(among)	lAHpAl	(lapel)
AHgAW	(ago)	bAHnAHnAH	(banana)
	AHbvrEHsEEbv	(abrasive)	
	mAHlEEshAWs	(malicious)	
	pAHrEHdTH	(parade)	

"AH" .... as in "father," "arm," "park," etc.

This vowel sound is pronounced as it is in American.

"A:" .... as in "ask," "draft," "laugh," etc.

This broadened "a" is treated as "AH" in the dialect, as in "AHsk" (ask).

DRILL WORDS

tTHAHsk	(task)	bAHskAtTH	(basket)
dTHrAHftTH	(draft)	mAHstTHEHr	(master)
lAHf	(laugh)	grAHf	(graph)
	fAHstTHEHr	(faster)	
	dTHAHns	(dance)	
	pAHth	(path)	

"A" .... as in "bad," "am," "narrow," etc.

This short "a" is also pronounced "AH," as in "AHdTH" (add).

DRILL WORDS

sAHdTH	(sad)		khAHs	(has)
mAHdTH	(mad)		mAHlEEs	(malice)
kAHtTH	(cat)		stTHAHb	(stab)

bAHg   (bag)

fAHbvrEEk   (fabric)

fAHktTHAWrEE   (factory)

"AW" .... as in "ball," "falter," "shawl," etc.

In American, we treat this sound as "AW-UH." But the Spaniard, with his tendency to sharpen vowels, cuts it down to the "O" of "rod," as in "bOl" (ball).

DRILL WORDS

kOl	(call)		fOltTHEHr	(falter)
uhwOr	(war)		shOl	(shawl)
khOl	(hall)		kOtTH	(caught)

OluhwEHs   (always)

nOtTHEE   (naughty)

skuhwOl   (squall)

"EE" .... as in "he," "treat," "people," etc.

Pronounced as in American. Remember, the mouth is spread into a wide grin.

"EH" .... as in "bet," "said," "friend," etc.

This short "e" is changed to the "A" of "bat," as in "mAn" (men).

DRILL WORDS

tTHAl	(tell)		bAn'	(bend)
sAtTH	(set)		sAlf	(self)
sAl	(sell)		lAtTHEHr	(letter)

AbvEHrEE   (every)

spAndTHEEn'   (spending)

dTHEEpAn'   (depend)

"I" .... as in "ice," "aisle," "guile," etc.

Long "i" is pronounced as in American except that the last part of the sound "EE" is lengthened somewhat because of the Spanish habit of widening the mouth for the sound.

"i" .... as in "it," "women," "busy," etc.

This is a most important vowel change in the Spanish dialect, as it is in all the Romance languages. This short "i" is changed to long "e" (EE) and the Spanish give it a broadened attack, with the lips spread wide, as in "EEf" (if).

DRILL WORDS

lEEbv	(live)		mEEstTHEHk	(mistake)
mEElk	(milk)		fEEdTHOOl	(fiddle)
flEEtTH	(flit)		lEEtTHOOl	(little)

tTHEEdTHbvEEtTH   (tidbit)
bEEtTHEHr   (bitter)
pEEpEEn   (pippin)

"O" .... as in "on," "bond," "John," etc.

Since all the Spanish dialect "o's" are changed to "AW," this "o" is pronounced as in "AWn" (on).

DRILL WORDS

rAWdTH	(rod)	zhAWn	(John)
nAWtTH	(not)	khAWlEE	(holly)
sAWdTH	(sod)	fAWlAW	(follow)

khAWbvOOl   (hobble)
AWnAs'   (honest)
AWpAWn   (upon)

"OH" .... as in "bone," "sew," "dough," etc.

This long "o," too, is treated as "AW," following the vowel shortening habit of the dialect, as in "bAWn" (bone).

DRILL WORDS

rAWdTH	(road)	dTHAW	(dough)
khAWm	(home)	fAlAW	(fellow)
sAW	(so)	mAWtTHAWr	(motor)

pAWlItTH   (polite)
klAWs   (clothes)
mAWnEEn'   (moaning)

"AW" .... as in "off," "cough," "bought," etc.

This vowel sound is pronounced as in American.

"OO" .... as in "food," "do," "blue," etc.

The Spanish dialect pronounces this long double "o" (OO) as short double "o" (oo), as in "foodTH."

DRILL WORDS

moon	(moon)	soop	(soup)
dTHoo	(do)	moobvEE	(movie)
bloo	(blue)	dTHootTHEE	(duty)

sootTHAHbvOOl   (suitable)
noospEHpEHr   (newspaper)
sAHloon   (saloon)

"oo" .... as in "good," "wolf," "full," etc.

This short double "o" (oo) is reversed, in the dialect, to the long double "o" (OO), as in "gOOdTH" (good).

DRILL WORDS

fOOl	(full)	uhwOOlf	(wolf)
lOOk	(look)	pOOtTH	(put)
khOOdTH	(hood)	kOOdTH	(could)

> uhwAWndTHEHrfOOl (wonderful)
> AWndTHEHrstTHOOdTH (understood)
> bOO'kEHs (bookcase)

"yOO" .... as in "unit," "cube," "beauty," etc.

Because the Spaniard reverses the long double "o" (OO) sound into short double "o" (oo), he reverses the same sound in this long "u" and he does *not* retain the initial consonant "y" sound, as in "oonEEtTH" (unit). For a lighter dialect, this change may be used occasionally.

DRILL WORDS

koo	(cue)	bootTHEE	(beauty)
poo	(pew)	moosEEk	(music)
kootTH	(cute)	oonItTH	(unite)
	oonEEfAWrm	(uniform)	
	footTHEEl	(futile)	
	foowEHr	(fewer)	

"U" .... as in "up," "love," "does," etc.

This vowel sound can be given one of two pronunciations. Some Spaniards treat it as "AH," as in "AHp" (up). Others give it an "AW" sound, as in "lAWbv" (love). The latter is preferred but the former can be used for a character variance.

DRILL WORDS

mAWs'	(must)	tTHrAWk	(truck)
bAWg	(bug)	pAWpEE	(puppy)
nAWtTH	(nut)	pAWbvlEEsh	(publish)
	khAWsbvAHn'	(husband)	
	sAWspEEshAWs	(suspicious)	
	sAWpEHr	(supper)	

"ER" .... as in "curb," "earn," "fern," etc.

Most dialects give this "ER" sound in all the "er," "ir," "or" and "ur" combinations the same treatment—that is to say, they do not vary in the same dialect. But, in the Spanish, there seems to be a tendency to pronounce the sound according to its spelling.

The combination, "er," for example, is always pronounced as "EHr," as in "uhwOtTH*EHr*" (wat*er*), "*EHr*nAs'" (*ear*nest) and "b*EHr*lEEn" (B*er*lin).

The combination "or" is always pronounced as "AWr," as in "uhw*AWr*k" (w*or*k), "uhw*AWr*THEE" (w*or*thy) and "lEHbv*AWr*" (lab*or*).

The combination "ir" is always pronounced as "EEr," as in "b*EEr*dTH" (b*ir*d), "th*EEr*dTH" (th*ir*d) and "stTH*EEr*" (st*ir*).

The combination "ur" would always be pronounced as "OOr," as in "dTHEEstTH*OO*rb" (dist*ur*b), "f*OO*r" (f*ur*) and "AWk*OO*r" (occ*ur*).

"OW" .... as in "out," "cow," "house," etc.

The American version of this diphthong is "AH-OO." But the tendency in the Spanish is to separate the double sound, whereas the American runs them together to form "OW." Phonetically, then, this diphthong will be represented as "AH-OO," as in "AH-OOtTH" (out).

DRILL WORDS

nAH-OO	(now)	AHbvAH-OOtTH	(about)
khAH-OO	(how)	khAH-OOs	(house)
lAH-OOdTH	(loud)	sAH-OOndTH	(sound)
	mAH-OOntTHEHn	(mountain)	
	thAH-OOsAndTHs	(thousands)	
	klAH-OOdTHEE	(cloudy)	

"OI" .... as in "oil," "boy," "noise," etc.

Again the Spaniard separates this diphthong, pronounced in American as "AW-EE" and run together to form the diphthong "OI," so that his treatment is "AW-EE," as in "AW-EEl." Remember, the long "e" sound is formed by setting the lips in a wide grin.

DRILL WORDS

bAW-EE	(boy)	nAW-EEs	(noise)
bvAW-EEs	(voice)	rAW-EE-AHl	(royal)
sAW-EEl	(soil)	AHnAW-EE	(annoy)
	AnzhAW-EE	(enjoy)	
	gAW-EEtTHEHr	(goiter)	
	AmbrAW-EEdTHEHr	(embroider)	

WORD EXERCISES

Pronounce the following words in the Spanish dialect making the necessary changes learned from the preceding Vowel Section:

1. homeland	6. royalty	11. waterway	16. canary
2. bullfight	7. starving	12. following	17. murderer
3. duty	8. dictator	13. romance	18. friendship
4. airplane	9. house	14. first	19. worker
5. factory	10. country	15. uniform	20. master-plan

When the above words have been tried, refer to the list below for the proper pronunciation. Check the mistakes and correct them, repeating the corrections until they have been memorized.

1.	khAWmlAHn'	11.	uhwOtTHEHruhwEH
2.	bOOluhfItTH	12.	fAWlAWEEn'
3.	dTHootTHEE	13.	rAWmAHns
4.	ArplEHn	14.	fEErs'
5.	fAHktTHAWrEE	15.	oonEEfAWrm
6.	rAW-EE-AHltTHEE	16.	kAHnArEE
7.	stTHAHrbvEEn'	17.	mOOrdTHEHrEHr
8.	dTHEEktTHEHtTHAWr	18.	frAn'shEEp
9.	khAH-OOs	19.	uhwAWrkEHr
10.	kAWntTHrEE	20.	mAHstTHEHrplAHn

CONSONANT SOUNDS

Before discussing the individual consonant sounds, it is necessary, first, to deal with certain general rules regarding them.

Ordinarily, the Spaniard separates two consonant sounds when they come together in a word, as in "AWn*uht*THEEl" (until), the separation being effected by the aspirate "uh." The same treatment can be observed in such words as "sAW-m*uh*thEEn" (something), "kAHn*uh*dTHEE" (candy) and "lIk*uh*lEE" (likely). This applies only when both consonants are not similar in their production.

WHEN TWO SIMILARLY PRODUCED CONSONANTS COME TOGETHER IN THE SAME WORD, THE WEAKER-PRODUCED CONSONANT IS DROPPED WHILE THE STRONGER-PRODUCED CONSONANT IS RETAINED AND THE ASPIRATE "UH" IS NOT APPLIED, AS IN "AW-'buhrEHdTH" (*upbraid*).

A similar rule applies to consonant word endings. When a word ends with a consonant and is followed by a word beginning with a similarly produced consonant, the first consonant is dropped, as in "bEE' kAWrn" (big corn) and "buhlAH' gAWldTH" (black gold).

There is also a tendency to drop certain final consonants when they are preceded by another consonant, as in "sAHn'" (sand), "kAWmEEn'" (coming) and "fuhrAWn'" (front). But these elisions will be considered more in detail under the consonants that are so treated.

The words used in many of the preceding and following examples have not included the aspirate "uh" that separates double consonants. Since a smooth and authentic reproduction is difficult to achieve, this aspirate "uh" can be dropped for a lighter Spanish dialect. The aspirate "uh" between dissimilar consonants is preferred, however, if the effect can be achieved without forcing.

CONSONANT CHANGES

B—Although "b" should be pronounced as "b" when used initially and finally, it becomes "bv" medially, unless it is preceded by "m" or "n." This exception will be found in a word such as "'AWmbAWg" (humbug). To achieve the "bv" sound, the lips should be slightly open with the lower lip protruding; and the sound of "b" should be attempted without touching the lips together completely.

Americans pronounce "b" with the lips completely closed. Thus it can be seen that the sound substituted for "b" is a difficult one to approximate. It is important to the dialect, however, and should be learned. In the phonetic version it has been designated as "bv," as in "AH*bv*EHs" (abase), "kAH*bv*AHzh" (cabbage) and "kAH-*bv*EE" (cabby).

C—For the hard sound of "c" see "K"; for the soft sound, see "S."

D—The Spaniard dentalizes the consonant "d" by placing the tip of his tongue at the under cutting edge of the upper front teeth, not at the forward part of the roof of the mouth, as the Americans do for their clear "d" sound. What the Spaniard actually produces is a combination of "d" and the voiced "TH" of "the."

The phonetic spelling for this consonant will, therefore, be "dTH," as in "*d*THrI" (*d*ry), "mEE*d*THOOl" (mi*dd*le) and "mAH*d*TH" (ma*d*).

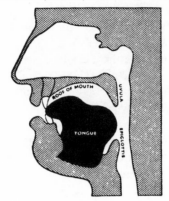

The tongue tip, pressed against the backs of the front teeth, introduces into the "d" sound the additional "TH," creating the sound, "dTH." The American "d" is produced by touching the gum ridge of the upper front teeth with the tongue tip.

When final "d" is preceded by a consonant it is often dropped, as in 'FrAn'" (friend), "stTHAHn'" (stand), and "FIn'" (find).

Final "d" is also dropped before initial "t" as in "sAH' tTHIm" (sad time).

F—Pronounced as it is in American.

G—The normal American hard sound of "g" should be retained in the Spanish dialect. However, the hard sound of "g" may become a gutteralized "kh" before "e" and "i." This refers to the American spelling of a word, so that "kh" may be found in "khAtTH" (get).

When final "g" is preceded by a consonant, especially in the "ing" combination, it should be dropped, as in "rAWn'" (wrong), "AHlAWn'" (along) and "mEHkEEn'" (making). Final "g" may be kept ordinarily to thin out a thick dialect but the "g" should always be dropped from the "ing" ending, since this habit is one of the most identifying characteristics of the Spanish dialect.

For the soft sound of "g," see "J."

H—The consonant "h" contributes a great deal toward the reproduction of an authentic Spanish dialect. Used initially, it is often dropped, as in "'AWdTH" (*h*od), "'AWm" (*h*ome) and "IuhwEH" (*h*ighway).

But when "h" is used initially or medially it may also be treated with the gutteral "kh" sound heard in the Scotch "loch" and the German "ach." This sound is a sort of gargle with the uvula not vibrating as the breath is brought up past it. This sound is quite difficult to produce for a great many people, but it can and should be done if the Spanish dialect is to be treated authentically. Words with a medial "h," would then, be pronounced as "AnEE*kh*AH-OO" (any*h*ow), "mEE*skh*AHp" (mis*h*ap), and "fool*kh*AHrdTHEE" (fool*h*ardy).

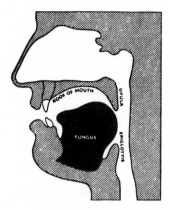

The back of the tongue is raised to touch the uvula at the end of the soft palate. When the breath is brought up past this conjuncture, it is roughened and voiced, producing the Spanish "kh" sound. Neither the tongue nor the uvula vibrates when this sound is produced.

J—In the original Spanish language, this consonant is treated with the gargled "kh." But there is no comparable usage in American so it need not be discussed. But when the soft "j" is used, as in "jar" or in any of the other word combinations that are pronounced as soft "j," such as "cabba*ge*" and "sol*dier*," the Spanish substitute the "zh" sound of "z," as in "azure." This substitution is made initially, medially and finally, as in "*zh*EHrmAHn" (German), "prAW*zh*Ak'" (pro*j*ect) and "kAWrAH*zh*" (courage).

K—This "k" sound, which includes hard "c," is pronounced as it is in American.

L—The consonant "l" is pronounced as it is in American, except that it is treated liquidly, more drawn out. (See illustration below.)

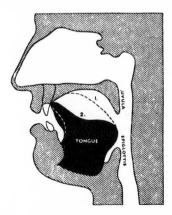

The black area indicates the position of the tongue when a clear American "l" is produced. The center part of the tongue is *not* depressed, as shown by the dotted line, when the Spanish "l" is sounded.

M—This consonant sound also is treated as it is in American. Sometimes, though, it is changed to "n," as in "frAW*n*'" (fro*m*) but this change is a minor one.

N—This sound remains unchanged from the American. Here, too, there is a tendency, at times, to reverse "m" and "n," as in "grEE*m*bAHk" (gree*n*back).

P—This is pronounced as it is in American.

Q—In American, we pronounce this consonant, which is really the double consonant of "kw," by running both consonants together, as in "quick." But, in the Spanish the "k" and the "w" are separated by an aspirate "uh" so that the treatment becomes "kuhw," as in "k*uh*wEEk" (*q*uick), "k*uh*wEEn" (*q*ueen) and "k*uh*wAs'" (*q*uest). This is done only when "q" is used at the beginning of a word; otherwise, it is pronounced as it is in American, as in "lAH*k*EHr" (lac*q*uer), "lEE*k*AWr" (li*q*uor) and "klAH*k*" (cla*q*ue).

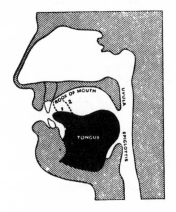

The black area indicates the position of the tongue as it begins trilling the Spanish "r." The dotted line shows the tongue curling upward to touch the forward part of the roof of the mouth. An extended series of this rapid interchange of positions causes the trilled Spanish "r."

R—As in the other Romance languages, the consonant "r" is always rolled vigorously. It should never be dropped. When it follows another consonant, it is rolled only slightly, as in "b*rr*EEn'" (b*r*ing). When it is followed by a consonant, it is also trilled slightly, as in "pAH*rr*lEE" (pa*r*ley). But when it comes between two voiced vowels, as in "narrow" and "around," it is rolled very heavily, as in "nAH*rrrr*AW" (na*rr*ow) and "AH*rrrr*AH-OOn'" (a*r*ound).

S—The consonant "s" is always hissed out in Spanish. Initially, medially and finally it is always sounded more sibilantly than in American. If a word is spelled with an "s," it will be pronounced with an "s" even though the correct American pronunciation may be "z," as in "EE*s*EE" (ea*s*y), "uhwAW*s*" (wa*s*) and "uh*s*AWm" (*s*ome).

In the example word "some" it will be noticed that an aspirate "uh" precedes the "s." This treatment is usually given to the initial "s" of a word if the preceding word in the same sense group has ended with a consonant sound, as in "shEE kAWm uh-soon" (she come soon) and "I lIk uhsuhwEEmEEn'" (I like swimming).

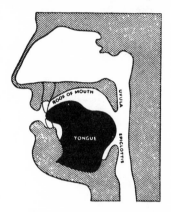

The tongue tip, pressed against the backs of the front teeth, introduces into the "t" sound the additional "TH," creating the sound, "tTH." The American "t" is produced by touching the gum ridge of the upper front teeth with the tongue tip.

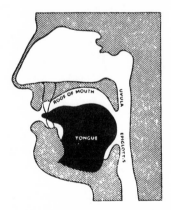

The voiced "TH" is sounded in the throat with the tongue tip extending between the upper and lower front teeth as illustrated in the American "TH." The voiceless "th" is made with the tongue in this position but with no sound being made in the throat. The throat vibrates if the voice is being made there.

T—Like the "d," the consonant "t" is dentalized by the Spaniards so that the sound produced is actually "tTH," the "TH" being similar to the voiced "th" of "the." See "D" for the method used in achieving this sound. It should be stressed here, though, that the "tTH" sound is *not* the same "th" of "the." This "t," (tTH) like the "d," is used initially, medially and finally.

When a word ends with a "t" and is followed by another word beginning with a "d," the "t" is dropped and only the "dTH" sound is pronounced, as in "sAH' dTHAH-OOn" (sat down).

When "t" comes at the end of a word and is preceded by *any* consonant, it is usually dropped, as in "skrEEp'" (script), "uhwAHn'" (want) and "uhwEHs'" (waste).

TH—This combination is pronounced more forcefully in the Spanish dialect than in the American.

"th"—The unvoiced "th," as in "thin," is also pronounced with greater force in the Spanish dialect.

TCH—This consonant sound of "tch," as in "church," is pronounced as it is in American.

V—This consonant sound is treated with the same "bv" substitution given to "b." See "B" for its proper pronunciation. Thus, initially, medially and finally, it becomes "bvArEE" (very), "lAWbvEHr" (lover) and "AHbvAWbv" (above). Even for a light dialect, this "bv" should be used instead of "v."

W—This consonant sound is pronounced as it is in American except that it is treated with an initial aspirate "uh," like the "s," as in "uhwEHk" (wake), "uhwEEn" (win) and "uhwAr" (where).

X—This consonant is pronounced as "s" when it precedes a consonant, as in "Askoos" (excuse). But, between vowels, the "x" becomes "ks" or "gs" according to the American pronounciation, as in "AksAHkootTH" (execute) and "AgsAH-mEEn" (examine). Two exceptions are the words "A'sAHk'" (exact) and "O'sEElyAHrEE'" (auxiliary), where the "k" sound is dropped.

Y—This consonant sound is always pronounced as it is in American. When used as a vowel, it is always treated as "EE."

Z—The hissed "s" is used exclusively by the Spanish. In the original language the consonant "z" is pronounced as "th." But in the dialect, the Spaniard imparts a hissed "s" to his "z's," as in "pAWsOOl" (puzzle), "lEHsEE" (lazy), "sEEnk" (zink) and "fAWs" (fuzz).

SH—The "sh" sound, in Spanish, is sometimes changed to "tch," as in "tchAHl" (shall), "pAHtchAWn" (passion) and "rAWtch" (rush). But, ordinarily, it can be pronounced as it is in American.

ZH—This "z," as in "azure," is pronounced as it is in American.

LE—When final "le" is preceded by a consonant, it is pronounced as "OOl" as in, "tAWmbOOl" (tumble), "fEHbvOOl" (fable), and "AHpOOl" (apple).

WORD EXERCISES

Pronounce the following words in the Spanish dialect using the material learned from the preceding Consonant section:

1.	home	11.	strong
2.	German	12.	bonbon
3.	quiet	13.	lovely
4.	bad times	14.	excuse
5.	somewhere	15.	see some
6.	dazzling	16.	does
7.	sadder	17.	stabbing
8.	execution	18.	anyhow
9.	olive	19.	South America
10.	capable	20.	exactly

When the above words have been tried, refer to the list below for the proper pronunciation. Check the mistakes and correct them, repeating the corrections until they have been learned.

1.	'AWm or khAWm	11.	stTHrAWn'
2.	zhEHrmAHn	12.	bAWnbAWn
3.	kuhwI-AtTH	13.	lAWbvlEE
4.	bAH' tTHIms	14.	Askoos
5.	sAWmuhwAr	15.	sEE sAWm
6.	dTHAHslEEn'	16.	dTHAWs
7.	sAHdTHEHr	17.	stTHAHbvEEn'
8.	AksAHkooshAWn	18.	AnEE'AH-OO or
9.	AWlEEbv		AnEEkhAH-OO
10.	kEHpAHbvOOl	19.	sAH-OOtTH AHmArEEkAH
		20.	A'sAHklEE

GRAMMAR CHANGES

The avoidance of the pronoun in the dialect has been discussed in the section on "Emphasis." But there are a number of other changes in syntax and grammar that give the dialect its flavor. The confusion in verb forms is common to a great many Spaniards as it is to most other foreigners. The present tense is used rather than the past, as in:

"yoo khAHbv mEHk THEE mEEstTHEHk."
(You *have make* the mistake.)
(You have *made* a mistake.)

Other verb confusions typical to the dialect are:

"uhwAW dTHEEdTH I dTHAWn?"
(What did I *done*?)
(What did I *do*?)

"khoo EEs tTHAWldTHEEn' yoo THAHtTH?"
(Who is *tolding* you that?)
(Who *told* you that?)

"uhwEE gAW nAH-OO tTHoo THEE bOOluhfltTH."
(We *go* now to the bullfight.)
(We *shall* now *go* to the bullfight.)

"'EE'AHs nAWtTH rIdTH 'EEs 'AWrs yAtTH."
(He has not *ride* his horse yet.)
(He has not *ridden* his horse yet.)

There is tendency in the dialect to substitute "be" for some of the verb forms, as in:

"khEE nAWtTH bEE gAW yAtTH."
(He not *be* go yet.)
(He *has not* gone yet.)

"khEE bEE stTHEEl khEEr."
(He *be* still here.)
(He *is* still here.)

Confusion in the tense of verbs is also prevalent, as in:

"THEE gEErl uhwOk EEn THEE pAHrk."
(The girl *walk* in the park.)
(The girl *walks* in the park.)

"THEE fEEl' EEs kAWbvEHr uhwEETH grEHn."
(The field is *cover* with grain.)
(The field is *covered* with grain.)

"khEE kAWm frAWm THEE nAWwAr."
(He *come* from the nowhere.)
(He *comes* from nowhere.)

The last example illustrates another error common to the dialect in the tendency to substitute "the" for "a" or "an" for no purpose other than to make the designated object or action more specific. As in:

"tTHEHk THEE AWrAHnzh!"
(Take *the* orange!)
(Take *an* orange!)

"dTHoo yoo wAHn' THEE fltTH?"
(Do you want *the* fight?)
(Do you want to fight?)

"mAnEE gEErls lIk THEE wOkEEn'"
(Many girls like *the* walking.)
(Many girls like *to* walk.)

"uhwEE gAH' THEE nEHbvAWrs."
(We got *the* neighbors.)
(We have neighbors.)

"THEE lAWbv rools THEE wAWrl'"
(*The* love rules the world.)
(Love rules the world.)

The preposition, "to," in infinitives, is dropped by a great many Spaniards, as in:

"I AHm gAWEEn' bI THEE dTHrAs."
(I am going buy the dress.)
(I am going *to* buy the dress.)

"THEE mAHn EEs gAWEEn' zhAWmp."
(The man is going jump.)
(The man is going *to* jump.)

There is also a definite pronoun confusion, as in:

"uhwAWtTH EEs THAWs nAW-EEs?"
(What is *those* noise?)
(What is *that* noise?)

"khoo EEs THEEs mAHn?"
(Who is *these* man?)
(Who is *this* man?)

The Spaniard also substitutes the impersonal "what" for the relative pronoun, "who," as in:

"I AHm THEE mAHn uhwAWtTH nAWs."
(I am the man *what* knows.)
(I am the man *who* knows.)

"THAWs AHr THEE fAlAW wAW' dTHEEdTH EEtTH."
(Those are the fellow *what* did it.)
(That is the fellow *who* did it.)

The dialect also bogs down in the use of comparative and superlative adverbs, as in:

"shEE wAWs THEE mAWr bEEootTHEEfOOl gEErl."
(She was the *more* beautiful girl.)
(She was the *most* beautiful girl.)

"I wOOdTH mAW' rAHTHEHr uhsEEn.'"
(I would *more* rather sing.)
(I would rather sing.)

The double negative is as much a stumbling block for the Spaniard as it is for most other foreigners. But the Spaniard is pecularily addicted to another error in negatives. When he becomes acquainted with the idiom and the use of contractions, especially "don't," he tries to use it always and, as a result, misuses it quite often, as in:

"khEE dTHAWn' bEE glAH' tTHoo sEE yoo."
(He *don't* be glad to see you.)
(He is *not* glad to see you.)

"THEH dTHAWn' kAHn dTHoo THAH' tTHoo mEE."
(They *don't* can do that to me.)
(They *can't* do that to me.)

SENTENCE EXERCISES

Pronounce the following sentences in the Spanish dialect making the necessary changes in grammar learned from the preceding section:

1. You can't tell him a thing.
2. I do not like to fight.
3. We would rather work hard.
4. We shall now see who is right.
5. Honor is man's greatest virtue.
6. Is he the fellow who pays salaries?
7. She has tried to make nice things.
8. I am not a lazy fellow.
9. Is he still going to see her?
10. Where will you try to buy it?

After each sentence, refer to the following versions for the correct changes. Make the corrections and pronounce the sentence again with the corrected words. Do this with every sentence.

1. yoo dTHAWn' kAHn tTHAI 'EEm nAWthEEn'.
2. I nAWtTH lIk THEE fItEEn'.
3. uhwEE mAW' rAHTHEHr uhwAWrk 'AHrdTH.
4. uhwEE nAH-OO sEE khoo EEs rItTH.
5. THEE AWnEHr EEs THEE mAHns mAWr grEHtTHAs' bvEErtTHyoo.
6. EEs 'EE THEE fAlAW uhwAWtTH pEH THEE sAHlAHrEE?
7. shEE tTHrI THEE mEHkEEn' THEE mAWs' nIs thEEn'.
8. I dTHAWn' bEE THEE lEHsEE fAlAW.
9. khEE bEE stTHEEl gAW sEE khEHr?
10. uhwAr yoo bI EEtTH?

SPANISH LANGUAGE CARRYOVERS

buenos dias	bOOAYnAWs dTHEE-AHs	good day or hello
adios	AHdTHEE-AWs	goodbye
por favor	pAWr fAHbvAWr	please
perdoneme	pAYrdTHAWnAYmAY	pardon me
gracias	grAHthEE-AHs	thanks
de nada	dTHAY nAHdTHAH	don't mention it
si	sEE	yes
no	nAW	no
hasta mañana	AHstTHAH mAHnyAHnAH	until tomorrow

SPANISH MONOLOG

(*Lolita is very much put out about things. She confronts her boyfriend with her eyes flaming, her teeth gleaming, her little fists clenched, and, as she stamps her foot, she screams out:*)

No! no! you have make the mistake. I don't be gland to see you. And I don't be want see you no more. You are always asking me I should go with you. But you never, never say: "All right, Lolita! we go now to the friend's house." Oh, no! never you say that! For you, I am like the beautiful doll—something you can show so the people they can say, "Oh! is he not the lucky fellow!" But I am not the doll! I am the woman! I am the woman you are loving—no? And I would more rather see you no more! You don't can make me for the fool no more. Because I don't be see you no more! never! never! never!

PHONETIC REPRESENTATION

(*The syllables in bold-face type are to be accented*)

"nAW! n   yoo   'AHbv **mEHk THEE mEE** st**THEH**

AW!   k!"

I **dTHAWn'** bEE glAH' tTHoo sEE yoo. AHn' I **dTHAWn' bEE** uhw**AWn'** uhsEE yoo **nAW mAWr.** yoo AHr **Ol**bvEHs AHskEEn' mEE I shOOdTH gAW w**EETH** yoo. bAWtTH yoo **nAbvEHr, nAbvEHr** uh-sEH, "Ol **rIt**TH, lAWl**EE**tTHAH! uhwEE gAW nAH-OO tTHoo THEE **frAn's** 'OWs." AW, **nAW! nAbvEHr** yoo sEH

THAHtTH! fAWr **yoo**, I AHm lIk THEE bEE-**oot**THEE**fOOl dTHAWl**— uh-**sAW**mthEEn' yoo kAHn **shAW** sAW THEE pEEpOOl, THEH kAHn sEH, "**AW**! EEs 'EE nAW' THEE **lAWkEE fAlAW**!" bAWtTH I AHm **nAW'** THEE **dTHAWl**! I AHm THEE **wOO**mAHn! I AHm THEE **wOO**mAHn yoo AHr **lAW**-bvEEn'—**nAW**? AHn' **I** wOOdTH mAW' rAHTHEHr uhsEE yoo **nAW mAWr**! yoo dTHAWn' kAHn mEHk mEE fAWr THEE **fool** nAW mAWr. bEEkAWs I dTHAWn' bEE sEE yoo nAW mAWr! **nAbvEHr**! **nAbvEHr**! **nAbvEHr**!

SUPPLEMENTARY STUDY

BOOKS

1. Cable, George. *Grandisimes.* New York, Charles Scribner's Sons, 1880.

PLAYS

1. Brown, Robert E. "The Bad Man" *in Best Plays of 1920-21*, edited by Burns Mantle. New York, Mead & Co., 1922.

THE MEXICAN DIALECT

For ordinary purposes, the Spanish dialect can be used for all Spanish-speaking peoples such as Mexicans, Central Americans and for all South Americans except Brazilians, who speak Portuguese. But the perfectionist who desires to use some of the Mexican dialect variants may refer to the following material.

VOWEL CHANGES

AMERICAN VOWEL SOUND	WORD	SUBSTITUTE	DIALECT
AY	take	EH	tEHk
UH	along	AH	AHlAWng
AH	father	AH	fAHtEHr
A:	ask	A or AH	Ask or AHsk
A	bad	A or AH	bAt or bAHt
AW	ball	OH	bOHl
EE	he	EE	khEE
EH	bet	AY:	bAY:t
I	ice	I:	I:s
i	sit	EE	sEEt
OH	bone	OH or AW	bOHn or bAWn
AW	off	AW	AWf
O	on	OH or AW	OHn or AWn
OO	food	OO	fOOt
oo	good	OO	gOOt
yOO	unit	yOO	yOOnEEt
U	up	AH or AW	AHp or AWp
ER	curb	OOr	kOOrb
	girl	EEr	gEErl
	work	AWr	uhwAWrk
	her	EHr	khEHr
OW	out	OW	OWt
OI	oil	OI	OIl

CONSONANT CHANGES

The initial aspirate "uh" preceding both "s" and "w" is used in the Mexican dialect. The Spanish substitution of "s" for the "z" sounds is also made in the Mexican. But the dentalized "d" and "t," of Spanish, are *not* carried through in the Mexican. Some Mexicans, especially those with a Spanish background who are proud of their pure Castilian pronunciation, may do so but, as a rule, the Mexican peon does not. Two different consonants that come together are often separated with an aspirate "uh," as in "kuhwEEk" (quick) and "tuhwI:n" (twine), and "AHnuh-tEEl" (until). The "zh" sound substituted for "j," in Spanish, becomes "tch" in Mexican. The "tch" substituted sometimes by the Spanish for "sh" is treated in the same way by the Mexican, as in "tchAl" (shall). The important gargled "kh" given to the Spanish "h" is similarly treated in the Mexican.

A peculiarity of the Mexican dialect is the substitute "tAY" for the word "the." This is odd, not only because of the "AY" substitution for "EE," but also because of the "t" substitution for the voiced "TH" of "the." It is this "t," then, that is given to both the voiced and unvoiced "th," as in "tAY" (the), "tAYs" (these), "tEEnk" (think), "bEHt" (bathe) and "pAt" (path).

THE FILIPINO DIALECT

In some respects, because of the use of bare key-words in the speech, the Filipino dialect resembles Pidgin English. In fact, it has, for this reason, been called Bamboo English. But the pronunciation is based mostly on the Spanish with some infiltrations of Malaysian. The aspirate "uh," for instance, is used before initial "s," as in Spanish.

The emphasis in the dialect shifts from the first syllable, as in American, to the second syllable, as in "kAHrAHktEHr" (character) and "kAHmfAWrtAHbOOl" (comfortable). The dialect features a monotonously intoned pitch—similar to the Chinese—which is varied only under emotional stress.

VOWEL CHANGES

VOWEL SOUND	WORD	SUBSTITUTE	DIALECT
AY	take	EH	tEHk
UH	along	AH	AHlAWng
AH	father	O	pOdEHr
A:	ask	O	Osk
A	bad	O	bOdTH
AW	ball	OH	bOHl
EE	he	EE	khEE
EH	bet	AY	bAYtTH
I	ice	I:	I:s
i	sit	EE	sEEtTH
OH	bone	AW	bAWn
AW	off	AW	AWp
O	on	AW	AWn
OO	food	oo	poodTH
oo	good	OO	gOOdTH
yOO	unit	OO	OOnEEtTH
U	up	AW	AWp
	curb	OOr	kOOrb

	girl	EEr	gEErl
ER	work	AWr	wAWrk
	her	EHr	khEHr
OW	out	AHoo	AHootTH
OI	oil	AWi	AWil

Because the Filipino speaks so that his lower lip does not make the proper contact with the cutting edge of his upper front teeth, he has difficulty in pronouncing our "f" properly. The result makes for one of the most characteristic changes in the dialect: that of substituting "p" for "f," as in "pEElEEpEEnAW" (Filipino). The same speech habit accounts for his pronouncing "v" as "bv," as in the Spanish. For a more understandable dialect it is suggested that the "h" of the correctly pronounced American word "h-wI" (why) be used instead of using the "p" for "f." This "h" sound should not come from the back of the throat, as in the word "how," but should be the slight puff of air projected from the front of the mouth which is found in the "h" of "why." Other consonant changes are:

D—dropped finally when following a consonant, as in "uhsOn'" (sand). When sounded, it is usually given the Spanish dentilization, as in "dTHAWs" (does).

H—sounded as the gargled "kh" in Spanish, as in khOtTH (hat).

J—changed to "tch," in soft "j," as in "tchAWtch" (judge).

R—trilled strongly especially after "d" and "t."

SH—changed to "s," as in "sAW" (show).

T—pronounced "tTH," as in the Spanish, as in "bOtTH" (bat).

TT—given a double "t" sound with the first "t" receiving the aspirate "uh," as in "lEEtTHuh-tTHOOl" (little).

TH—the voiced "TH" of "the" becomes "dTH," as in "dTHEE" (the).

th—the unvoiced "th" of "thin" remains the same as in American.

Z—changed to "s," as in "khOs" (has), "EEs" (is) and "pAWsOOl" (puzzle).

The Filipino dialect gets along with practically no prepositions. A few other common departures in grammar occur in the following:

"dTHEE dTHAWg EEs dTHI:."
(The dog is *die*.)
(The dog is *dead*.)

"wEE wAYntTH EEn mAWndTHEH."
(We went *in* Monday.)
(We went *on* Monday.)

"yoo tTHEHk tTHoo mAYnEE tTHrAWbOOl."
(You take too *many* trouble.)
(You take too *much* trouble.)

THE PORTUGUESE DIALECT

The Portuguese language is spoken by two general groups of people: by the natives of Portugal and its possessions and by the Brazilians in South America. Although there are a number of language differences between the two groups, the foreign dialects of both groups are virtually the same. But, in this section, a number of these variations will be listed to enable the actor to present as close a dialect conception of each as is possible.

Generally speaking, the following variations are to be observed:

1. The Brazilian version of the Portuguese dialect is slower and less forceful than the native Portuguese.

2. The Brazilian vowel sounds are not drawn out as much as the Portuguese.

3. The changes in consonants, in Brazilian, are not as radical as they are in Portuguese, nor are the consonants treated as forcefully in Brazilian.

4. Brazilians, more than Portuguese, insert an aspirate "uh" between consecutive consonants in the same word.

There is a common misconception among actors who believe that a Spanish dialect can successfully portray a Portuguese character. Actually, the Portuguese dialect differs from Spanish in a great many respects. The following are the most important:

1. The Portuguese dialect, like the French, features a nasalization of certain vowel and diphthong sounds that the Spanish does not have.

2. The Portuguese dialect (both versions) is spoken with a liaison (like the Cockney Glide) while the Spanish is clear-cut.

3. The Portuguese "r" is trilled considerably longer and more forcefully than is the Spanish "r."

In addition, of course, there are a number of vowel and consonant changes that differ. A comparison of those listed below (both Portuguese and Brazilian) with those listed in the Spanish chapter should be revealing.

VOWEL CHANGES

VOWEL SOUND	AMERICAN WORD	CHANGED TO	PORTUGUESE WORD
AY	take	EH	tEHkuh
UH	sofa	AH	sAWfAH
AH	arm	AH	AHrm
A:	ask	AH	AHskuh
A	cab	EH	kEHbuh
	cab	AH	kAHbuh
AW	ball	AW	bAWluh
	ball	O	bOluh
EE	he	i:	khi:

EH	bet	A	bAtuh
	fell	EH	fEHluh
	meant	AY	mAYnt
I	nice	I	nIs
	nice	AHi	nAHis
i	sit	i:	si:tuh
O	hop	AH	khAHpuh
	hop	AW	khAWpuh
OH	hope	AW	khAWpuh
AW	off	O	Ofuh
	off	AW	AWfuh
OO	food	oo	fooduh
oo	good	oo	gooduh
yOO	unit	yoo	yooni:tuh
	popular	oo	pAWpoolAHr
U	up	AW	AWpuh
	up	AH	AHpuh
ER	curb	ER	kERbuh
OW	cow	OW	kOW
	house	OWuh	khOWuhsuh
OI	boy	AWi	bAWi
	boy	OHi	bOHi

A few vowel sound changes in the above list must be explained in more detail. In the substitutes given for "EH," the "EH" sound is usually used only before "l," as in "fEHlAW" (fellow). The "A" substitute is used before other consonants, as in "vAri:" (very) and "gAtuh" (get). The "AY" substitute is used before "m" or "n" and is nasalized, as in "AYmti:" (empty) and "plAYnti:" (plenty). The same "EH" sound is changed to "i" when it is in a prefix, as in "i:ksplAYn" (explain) and "ri:plAHi" (reply). The "i" sound is very short and is almost not sounded.

The "oo" substitute for "OO" in "food" should be made with the lips tenser than in American and should be produced from a more forward position in the mouth.

The "yoo" substitute for the American "yOO" does not seem to follow any general rule. Sometimes it is pronounced as "yoo," as in "yooni:fOrm" (uniform) retaining the "y" and, again, as "oo" as in "pAWpoolAHr" (popular), in which the "y" is dropped.

When "OW" comes in the middle of a word, it is often pronounced as "OWuh," the "uh" sound apparently being an aspirate "uh," as in "sOWuhs" (South). However, when "OW" is used finally, it is usually pronounced as "OW," as in "nOW" (now).

Long "i" (I) is usually pronounced in Portuguese as "AH-EE," as in American. But, in Brazilian, following the tendency to make vowel sounds closer, the pronunciation usually is closer to "AHi," as in "nAHis" (nice).

CONSONANT CHANGES

Note: Crossed out "m" (m̶) or "n" (n̶) indicates that the preceding vowel is nasalized and the "m" or "n" dropped.

B—When "b" is initial, it is usually pronounced as in American. But it is pronounced as a combination "bv" when it is:

1. between vowels, as in "khAH*bv*i:tuh" (ha*b*it) or
2. when it is preceded by "s" between vowels, as in "khAWs-*bv*AHnduh" (hus*b*and) or
3. when it is followed by "d," "l," "r," "s," or "t," as in "AH*bv*di:kEHtuh" (a*b*dicate), "tAH*bv*lAtuh" (ta*b*let), "fAH*bv*ri:kuh" (fa*b*ric), "AH*bv*sAYn̶tuh" (absent) and "AW*bv*tEHn̶ " (o*b*tain).

See "B" in the Spanish chapter for its pronunciation. Although it is not shown in the above examples, as aspirate "uh" should always separate the "bv" and the consonant so that the word would actually be pronounced as "AW*bvuh*tEHn̶ (o*b*tain). This aspirate "uh," it must be remembered, is only a puff of air expelled after certain consonants have been forcefully sounded, and should not be given a full "UH," "AH" or "U."

D—Initial "d" and medial "d" after "n," "l," or "r" remain the same as in American, as in "*d*oo" (*d*o), "kAHr*d*ER" (car*d*er) and "kAWl*d*ER" (col*d*er). The tongue, though, should be more forward in the mouth than in the American treatment.

But when "d" is by itself between vowels or when it is followed by "r" between vowels, it is pronounced as "dTH," with the tongue tip pressing against the backs of the front teeth, as in "lEH*dTH*i:" (la*d*y) and "AH*dTH*rAs" (a*d*dress).

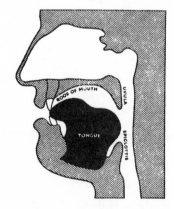

The tongue tip, pressed against the backs of the front teeth, introduces into the "d" sound the additional "TH," creating the sound "dTH." The American "d" is produced by touching the gum ridge of the upper front teeth with the tongue tip.

H—Initially, "h" is sometimes dropped, as in "'AWm" (*h*ome) or is given the gargled "kh" treatment, as in "*kh*i:" (*h*e). See the Spanish "H" for this sound. Medially, "h" is also dropped or treated as the gargled "kh."

J—This sound is pronounced as an energetic "zh," (the "z" of "azure") as in "dEH*ń*zhERuhs" (dangerous).

L—Generally, "l" is sounded as in American except that it is pronounced a little farther forward in the mouth. Sometimes, the silent "l" is sounded in American words, as in "tAW*l*kuh" (talk).

M—Initially or between vowels, "m" is usually pronounced as it is in American. But when it is final, or is followed by a consonant, it makes the preceding vowel sound nasalized. If, in this case, the consonant that follows "m," is either "b" or "d," then the "m" is pronounced, although the preceding vowel is nasalized, as in "AHmbER" (amber), "khAWmdrAW*ḿ*" (humdrum) and "si:mpuhluh" (simple). Finally, "m" is seldom pronounced unless the next word begins with either "b," "d," "g," "k," "p" or "t," as in "tri:*ḿ* khER" (trim her), when it is dropped, and "sAWm tAWtAHl" (sum total), when it is pronounced. It is suggested, however, that the dropped final "m," would make a dialect entirely too thick.

N—This consonant is treated in exactly the same way as the above "m." Thus, "plAYnti:" (plenty) retains the sound of "n" although the "AY" sound here is nasalized while in the word "sAYns" (sense) it is dropped.

R—The Portuguese "r" is always trilled. It is trilled with extra force when it is initial or when it follows "n," "l," or "s" or when it is doubled. But when it comes between vowels it is given a short trill.

S—When "s" is initial, is double, or follows a consonant, it is treated as in American. Also, when it follows a prefix, it is pronounced as "s," as in the verb "pri:sAYnt" (present).

When "s" comes between vowels, it is pronounced as "z," as in "bEHzi:*ń*" (basin).

When "s" is the final letter in a word which comes before a pause, it is usually given a slight "sh" sound, and also when it is the final letter in a word and the next word begins with "k," "f," "p," "s," or "t."

When "s" is the final letter in a word and the next word begins with "b," "d," "g," "l," "m," "n," "r," or "v," it is treated with a slight "zh" sound. This also applies to "s" when it is medial and is followed by any one of the above consonants.

Again, the suggestion must be made that too many of these changes would make a dialect too thick. A few of them are advisable particularly because the Portuguese is full of these "sh" and "zh" sounds. Brazilians, however, seldom use the "sh" or "zh" substitutions for "s." When they do use them, the sounds are very slight.

T—This consonant is pronounced as it is in American except that the tongue is placed farther forward in the mouth in Portuguese than in American. When used as the final letter of a word, it is slightly aspirated.

V—In Brazil, and in Southern and Central Portugal, "v" is pronounced as in American. But in some northern sections of Portugal, "v" is sometimes pronounced as "b" or both are used interchangeably.

W—There is no "w" in the Portuguese language except in loan words from other languages. But when it is pronounced in the dialect, it can be either "v," as in "vAHgAHn̉" (wagon) or "uh-w," as in "uh-wAHi" (why).

X—When "x" is used as "gz" in American, it may be pronounced as "z" in the dialect, as in "i:zAHktuh" (exact).

When "x" is preceded or followed by a consonant, it may be pronounced as "sh" in the Portuguese as in "i: shpAWrtuh" (export). This pronunciation, however, cannot be used in the Brazilian.

When "x" is used in "ks" American words, it retains the "ks" sound as in "i: kstrAH" (extra).

Z—When "z" is preceded and followed by a vowel, it is pronounced as in American. Otherwise, it is treated as "sh" or "zh." At the end of a word before a pause, "z" is pronounced as "sh." Or, if the next word begins with "c," "f," "k," "p," "s," or "t," it is often pronounced as "sh." If the next word begins with "b," "d," "g," "l," "m," "n," "r," or "v," it is pronounced as "zh." Remember, as with the "s," that Brazilians do not use the "sh" and "zh" sounds as much as the Portuguese. Remember, also, that if these radical changes are made, the sound must be very slight.

TH—This voiced "TH" is pronounced as either "d" or "z," as in "di:" (the) or "zAHtuh" (that). The former pronunciation is preferred.

th—This unvoiced "th" is pronounced either as "t" or "s." Usually, "t" is reserved for initial "th," as in "tAHnk" (thank) and "s" is used for final "th," as in "sOWuhs" (South).

LIAISON

As in the Cockney and French dialects, the liaison, that is, the linking together of words, is characteristic of the Portuguese dialect. When a word ends in a consonant and the next word begins with a vowel, the final consonant of the first word is carried over to begin the next word as in "nAWr sAHmAri:kAH kAH nAWpAY nAWp trEHduh." (North America can open up trade.) Here it will be seen that the final "s" of "nAWrs" was carried over to the next word which began with the vowel sound "AH." Then, in the word "kAHn," the "n" was carried over to the next word, "AWpAYn," which began with a vowel. Similarly, in the word "AWpAYn," the "n" was a final consonant and it, too, was carried over to begin the word "AWp," which began with a vowel. With the Portuguese, however, vowels are also merged together. But because this vowel liaison would make a dialect too thick, it should not be used.

CHAPTER TEN

The Japanese Dialect

THE JAPANESE LILT

The lilt of the Japanese dialect is very much like that of the Chinese. Japanese is spoken in a high falsetto voice, the keynote starting almost an octave above the keynote of American speech. There is a tendency in the Japanese to separate its syllables, as in the Chinese. In the original Japanese language the vowel sounds are lengthened somewhat but they are pronounced sharply and clearly. The individual syllables are not overly emphasized. The same treatment is found in the Japanese dialect. There is little vowel elongation and there is a clipped quality given to the separated syllables that sets the dialect apart from the Chinese sing-song. The effect is almost staccato but it should be a staccato quality with a slow tempo.

An example of the tonal pattern would be as follows:

"AW! puhrissuh nAHtuh tAHtchuh mi!"
(Aw! please not touch me!)
(Aw! please don't touch me!)

"AW! puhrissuh   nAHtuh tAH..tchuh mi!"

There is very little rise or fall in the inflection and the only rise in tone comes with the emphasized word, "tAHtchuh." In the following example, the same pattern is to be observed:

"AHi sEH yOO hAH wAHss."
(I say you how was.)
(I'll tell you what happened.)

The tonal range is as limited as the Chinese. Like the Chinese, the Japanese is an unemotional character. He is not demonstrative, especially when coming into contact with people other than intimate friends. He is evasive. He tries to hide his true emotions. Therefore, there is very little tonal rise or fall found in the Japanese speech and dialect, especially the utterances brought about by extremes of emotion and temperament. The words of a sentence are delivered with very few note changes—in what is almost a monotonous, dead quality relieved only occasionally by the emphasizing of a key-word.

THE ASPIRATE "uh"

The use of this aspirate "uh" can give authenticity to the Japanese dialect or mar it beyond recognition. The aspirate "uh" is an imperceptible puff of air released after voicing certain consonants. In Japanese most of the consonants, except "n," receive this treatment nearly all the time. This is a carry-over from the original language. But it cannot be stressed too often that this aspirate must not be broad.

Words which contain the aspirate should be studied mentally first. That is, for example, look at the word "kAHtuh" which is the phonetic spelling for the Japanese pronunciation of "cat." The "uh" is the aspirate. It is not to be sounded as "AH" or "UH" nor as the "u" in "up." It simply indicates that the final "t" is followed by a slight puff of air.

The aspirate will also be found medially, as in "kuhrimuh" (cream). Here, too, there is a break between "c" and "r" because the Japanese do not like to pronounce two consonants together. They separate them slightly with the aspirate.

For a lighter dialect, the aspirate treatment may be lessened but it should not be dropped completely, especially at the end of a word that is followed by another word beginning with a consonant. In some sections of this chapter, however, the aspirate "uh" will be designated only when it comes between two consonants. But it must be remembered that the aspirate "uh" should be added, only slightly, wherever needed.

This aspirate has confused many reporters of the Japanese dialect. That is, we believe, why it may sometimes be found written as "o," as in "good-o-morning." This "o" is obviously the aspirate "uh" and should not be pronounced as "o" or any other vowel, in spite of the fact that most Japanese verbs end with either a "u" or an "i." For other examples of the use of the aspirate "uh," within a sentence, see the section "Grammar Changes."

MOUTH POSITION

The shape of the mouth and the position of the jaws and lips are very important in the reproduction of the Japanese dialect. The jaws must be practically closed at all times. The mouth must be slightly open and the lips broadened into a wide grin. Most important, the upper front teeth should extend beyond the line of the lower front teeth and touch the forward part of the lower lips. The restricted area of the mouth is used as a sounding chamber for the speech, rather than the lower passages of the throat and the upper nasal chamber. It is by duplicating this typical mouth position of the Japanese that the Japanese dialect variances can be mastered.

EMPHASIS

There is practically no tonal emphasis in the Japanese dialect. Syllabic emphasis usually follows the American and it relies strictly on a modified stress emphasis. Word emphasis in the sentence has already been treated in the section on lilt. The words of a sentence are usually delivered with the same very slight stress emphasis, which is the result of the Japanese habit of separating the syllables by producing the aspirate "uh," and by giving a more energetic treatment to the final consonants. Only the key-word of a sentence is treated with a slight over-emphasis.

VOWEL CHANGES

"AY" .... as in "take," "break," "they," etc.
This long "AY" sound becomes "EH" in Japanese as in the word "tEHk" (take).

DRILL WORDS

bvuhrEHk	(break)	dEHt	(date)
ssEH	(they)	EHp	(ape)
EHt	(ate)	ssuhtEH	(stay)
	tEHssuhti	(tasty)	
	mEHbvi	(maybe)	
	Ss' uhrEHt	(straight)	

"UH" .... as in "alone," "sofa," "final," etc.
The short "UH" sound in American becomes "AH," as in "AHrAWn" (alone).

DRILL WORDS

ssAWfAH	(sofa)	pAHssifik	(pacific)
fAHinAH'	(final)	AHnAHssAH	(another)
bvAHnAHnAH	(banana)	AHbvAHt	(about)
	AHbvAHd	(aboard)	
	AHbvAHbv	(above)	
	pAHrEHd	(parade)	

"AH" . . . . as in "father," "arm," "park," etc.

This sound remains the same as in American.

"A:" . . . . as in "ask," "draft," "laugh," etc.

This "A:" becomes "AH," as in "AHssuhk" (ask).

DRILL WORDS

duhrAHf'	(draft)	ssuhtAHf	(staff)
rAHf	(laugh)	kuhrAHssuhp	(clasp)
pAHss	(pass)	pAHss	(path)

rAHssuh'   (last)
dAHnuhss   (dance)
kAWmAHnuh'   (command)

"A" . . . . as in "bad," "am," "guarantee," etc.

This receives the same "AH" as above.

DRILL WORDS

tchAHtAH	(chatter)	ssAHd	(sad)
fuhrAHtAH	(flatter)	puhrAHn	(plan)
tuhrAHp	(trap)	mAHd	(mad)

bvAHd   (bad)
AHm   (am)
gAHrAHnuhti   (guarantee)

"AW" . . . . as in "ball," "falter," "shawl," etc.

This sound remains the same as in American, as in "bvAWoo" (ball), "fA-WootAH" (falter), "shAWoo'" (shawl). The "oo" sound of "good" which follows the "AW" is a result of the dropped "l." This dropped "l" will be discussed in the consonant changes.

"EE" . . . . as in "he," "treat," "people," etc.

The long "EE" becomes a very short "i" in the Japanese dialect. This "i" is weakly sounded in the original Japanese language and should receive the same weak treatment in the dialect.

DRILL WORDS

hi	(he)	shi	(she)	nidoo'	(needle)
tuhrit	(treat)	mi	(me)	ssim	(seem)
pipoo'	(people)	ti	(tea)	guhrin	(green)

"EH" . . . . as in "bet," "said," "friend," etc.

The American short "EH" sound changes to "A" as in the American word "bad." Thus, the American word "bet" becomes "bvAt" in the Japanese dialect.

DRILL WORDS

ssAd	(said)	bvAtAH	(better)
fuhrAn'	(friend)	fArAW	(fellow)
tAr	(tell)	ssAr	(sell)

rAtAH (letter)
bvAri (very)
rAt (let)

"I" .... as in "ice," "aisle," "guile," etc.

The American "I" becomes "AH-EE" when broken down. The Japanese retain the "AH" and change "EE" to "i" making the sound "AHi" as in "AHiss" (ice).

DRILL WORDS

AHioo'	(aisle)	rAHit	(right)
gAHioo'	(guile)	tAHit	(tight)
AHi	(I)	nAHiss	(nice)

ssuhmAHioo' (smile)
tuhrAHi (try)
mAHi (my)

"i" .... as in "it," "women," "busy," etc.

This sound remains the same in the Japanese dialect, although it may be changed to long "EE," as in "EEt" (it).

"O" .... as in "on," "bond," "John," etc.

The "AH" sound of the "a" in "father" is given to this "O" in Japanese, as in "AHn" (on).

DRILL WORDS

bvAHn'	(bond)	hAHt	(hot)
jAHn	(John)	bvAHdi	(body)
jAHbv	(job)	rAHt	(lot)

kAHmAHn (common)
shAHt (shot)
AHpAHn (upon)

"OH" .... as in "bone," "sew," "dough," etc.

This long "OH" sound is changed to "AW" as in "bvAWn" (bone).

DRILL WORDS

ssAW	(sew)	tAWoo'	(told)
dAW	(dough)	AHrAWn	(alone)
AW	(O!)	shAW	(show)

hAWp (hope)
pAWssishAWn (position)
pAWtEHtAWss (potatoes)

"AW" .... as in "off," "cough," "water," etc.

This retains its American sound of "AW."

"OO" .... as in "food," "do," "blue," etc.

This sound remains the same in the Japanese dialect. However, it should be weakly stressed.

"oo" .... as in "good," "wolf," "full," etc.

This "oo" changes to the weakly stressed "OO" of "food."

DRILL WORDS

gOOd	(good)	bvOOk	(book)
wOOf	(wolf)	shOOd	(should)
fOOr	(full)	ssuhtOOd	(stood)

fOOt	(foot)
pOOr	(pull)
rOOk	(look)

"yOO" .... as in "unit," "cube," "beauty," etc.

This retains the same sound, but the treatment is weaker than in American.

"U" .... as in "up," "love," "does," etc.

This "U" changes to "AH," as in "AHp" (up).

DRILL WORDS

rAHbv	(love)	kAHnuhtuhri	(country)
dAHss	(does)	ssAHnuhbvAHn	(sunburn)
ssAHm	(thumb)	tuhrAHbvoo'	(trouble)

kAHm	(come)
tAHtch	(touch)
rAHsh	(rush)

"ER" .... as in "curb," "earn," "fir," etc.

The "ER" sound drops the "r" and changes to "AH" as in "kAHbv" (curb).

DRILL WORDS

AH'n	(earn)	bvAHtAH'	(butter)
fAH'	(fir)	shAH't	(shirt)
hAH'	(her)	wAH'ss	(worth)

ssuhkAH't	(skirt)
hAH't	(hurt)
AH'bv	(herb)

"OW" .... as in "out," "cow," "house," etc.

This sound remains the same as in American. A variant is "AH," as in "AHt" (out), "kAH" (cow), and "hAHss" (house).

"OI" .... as in "oil," "boy," "noise," etc.

This sound remains the same as in American. A variant is "AWi," as in "AWioo" (oil), "bvAWi" (boy) and "nAWiss" (noise). This sound should not be pronounced as "AW-wi"; but should merely be given the "AW" sound of "off," with the "i" of "it" glided on.

WORD EXERCISES

Pronounce the following words in the Japanese dialect using the material learned from the preceding section on Vowel Changes:

1.	better	11.	honorable
2.	Russia	12.	oil
3.	please	13.	action
4.	face	14.	password
5.	kindly	15.	military
6.	careful	16.	nicely
7.	worship	17.	hopeless
8.	Pacific	18.	Chinese
9.	command	19.	treaties
10.	American	20.	general

After pronouncing the words on preceding page, refer to the following list for the correct pronunciations. Check the mistakes, repeat the corrections and memorize.

1.	bvAtAH'	11.	AHnAHrAHboo'
2.	rAHssiAH	12.	AWioo'
3.	puhriss	13.	AHkuhssAHn
4.	fEHss (see "F")	14.	pAHssuhwAHd
5.	kAHinuhri	15.	miritAri
6.	kA'foo'	16.	nAHissuhri
7.	wAH'ssip	17.	hAWpuhrAss
8.	pAHssifik	18.	tchAHiniss
9.	kAWmAHn'	19.	tuhritiss
10.	AHmArikAHn	20.	jAnAHrAHoo'

CONSONANT CHANGES

B—It is difficult for the Japanese to distinguish between "b" and "v," so that whenever either of these consonants occur, a combination "bv" is sounded. The lips should be slightly parted almost in position for the "b" sound but "v" should be pronounced without the lower lip touching the upper teeth, as in "*bv*OI" (*b*oy) and "*bv*itAH" (*b*itter).

C—When hard, the "c" retains the American "k" sound as in "*k*AHtuh" (*c*at).

When soft, the "c" changes from the "s" sound to the "ss" hiss of Japanese, as in "*ss*iti" (*c*ity). See "S."

D—The actual pronunciation of "d" is the same as in American. However, it is often dropped following another consonant, as in "fAHin'" (fin*d*).

F—The Japanese approximates but does not actually pronounce this consonant. The American "f" requires that the lower lip touch the cutting edge of the upper teeth. But the Japanese pronounce "f" by bringing the lower lip almost into contact with the upper lip and sounding what is similar to the "h" of "hwl" (why).

G—Initial hard "g" is pronounced the same as in American. Medial and final hard "g" often take a nasal treatment as though the spelling were "ng." Thus, the Japanese would say "bvAH*ng*" (bag) and "tchikAH*ng*AW" (Chicago). As a general rule, this nasal treatment should not be used.

Soft "g" may retain its "j" sound or it may be changed to "tss," as in "bvAH*j*" (badge) or "bvAH*tss*."

H—This is the same as in American.

J—This is usually the same as in American, although it may be changed to "tss."

K—This is the same as in American.

L—This consonant gives the most characteristic variance of the Japanese dialect. It is well known that "l" is a very difficult sound for the Japanese to pronounce. Even with a light dialect, the "l" will give occasional trouble. Throughout this section, "r" has been used for "l" because, when trying to pronounce "l," the Japanese make a sound very similar to "r."

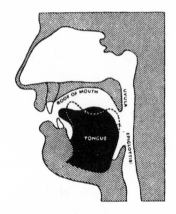

In pronouncing the Japanese dialect "l," the tongue does *not* touch the roof of the mouth (compare with the Russian "l," page 000). The dotted line indicates the tongue position after the sound has been produced. Note that the upper front teeth extend well past the lower, a typical characteristic affecting Japanese speech.

When trying to sound "l," do not touch the roof of the mouth with the tip of the tongue. Pronounce this sound far up in the front of the mouth and say "life." The sound produced is similar to "r" and even to "w." But a simple "r" or "w" must not be used. A great deal of practice must be given to this "l" sound as the authenticity of the dialect may be determined by it.

Final "l" is often dropped and replaced by the "oo" of "good," as in "pipoo'" (people). When it is not followed by a mute "e," as in the previous example, it is often changed to the "r," as in "hAWr" (hall), or dropped, as in "hAW'" (hall). The Japanese are extremely sensitive about their pronunciation of "l" and avoid it as often as possible.

M, N, and **P**—The same as in American.

Q—Although this sound may be pronounced as in American, there are two other possibilities. One is to place the aspirate "uh" between the "k" and "w" sounds of "q" as in "kuhwAHit" (quite). The other is to drop the "w" and retain only the "k," as in "k'AHit" (quite).

R—A weak version of the American "r" is used—it is never rolled or trilled. When final, it is dropped or replaced by "AH," as in "ri'" (rear) and "bvAT*AH*" (better).

S—This consonant is actually a combination of "s" and "sh" with the "s" predominating. It should be heavily accentuated with a hiss and can be achieved by shaping the lips for "sh" but hissing out "s" instead, as in "ssin" (sin) and "fEHss" (face). It will be noticed that this "s" is written phonetically as "ss."

The "s" is sometimes dropped when it is not thought to be essential to the word, as in "bvifuh'tEHk" (beefsteak).

T—The preferred sound for this consonant is its regular American sound of "t." However, some Japanese change "t" to "k" as in "pEHnuh*k*" (pain*t*. This, obviously, will make a dialect too thick. Others change "t" to "tch" as in "kAHssuh-mA*tch*ik" (cosme*t*ic). Neither is this change recommended. Still others will drop the "t" whenever possible, as in "puhr'i" (pretty).

V—This sound is interchanged with "b" to form a "bv" combination, as in "*bv*Ari" (*v*ery). For further details see "B."

W—The same as in American.

X—This consonant sound gives the Japanese a great deal of difficulty. He usually separates two consonants with the aspirate "uh." But here finding one symbol for two sounds, he becomes confused, and prefers "ss" rather than attempt "x," as in "ssi*ss*" (si*x*) and "mi*ss*" (mi*x*).

Y—The same as in American.

Z—Like the "s," this sound also becomes "ss" and takes an aspirate "uh" after it, as in "mEH*ss*uh" (ma*z*e).

SH—Although the Japanese can pronounce this sound, it should be colored by the "ss."

TCH—This "tch" sound is less forceful than in American and is colored by the hissing "ss" sound.

TH—the voiced "TH" changes to the hissed "ss" as in "*ss*i" (*th*e).

th—The unvoiced "th" changes to the hissed "ss," as in "pAH*ss*" (pa*th*).

ZH—This sound becomes "ss," as in "rOO*ss*" (rouge). For a lighter dialect, this sound may remain the same.

WORD EXERCISES

Pronounce the following words in the Japanese dialect using the material learned from the preceding section on Consonant Changes:

1.	understand	11.	father
2.	save	12.	battle
3.	trouble	13.	cruiser
4.	incident	14.	airplane
5.	soldier	15.	headquarters
6.	Philippine	16.	communique
7.	evacuate	17.	sniper
8.	think	18.	Emperor
9.	rifle	19.	ancestor
10.	quietly	20.	order

After pronouncing the above words, refer to the following list for the correct pronunciations. Check the mistakes, repeat the corrections and memorize.

1.	AHn'AH'ssuhtAHn'	11.	fAHssAH'
2.	ssEHbv	12.	bvAHtoo'
3.	tuhrAHbvoo'	13.	kuhroossAH'
4.	inuhssidAn'	14.	AruhpuhrEHn
5.	ssAWruhjAH'	15.	hAduhkuhwAH'tAHss
6.	firipin	16.	kAHmyoonikEH
7.	ibvAHkuhyooEHt	17.	ssuhnAHipAH'
8.	ssinuhk	18.	AmpAHrAH'
9.	rAHifoo' (see "F")	19.	AHnuhssAssuhtAH'
10.	kuhwAHituhri	20.	AH'dAH'

GRAMMAR CHANGES

(The aspirate "uh" has been added in the following examples to indicate how it is used. Remember not to sound it as "AH" or "U" or "EH" but simply as a puff of breath after a hard-hit consonant. The aspirate "uh" should not be used too often or it will blur the dialect.)

Perhaps the best way to illustrate the changes in grammar that the Japanese give to their dialect is to cite an example of a sentence in the Japanese language as it would be translated literally:

"Adams Mister of hat that closet in is."

The meaning of this sentence in American is:

"Mr. Adams' hat is in that closet."

It would be impossible to go to such extremes in the dialect. No Japanese could hope to transfer his grammatical structures intact into the American language. But some peculiarities will be carried over and these will be lessened as his knowledge of American increases. A few of these grammar changes can give a great deal of authenticity to the dialect, and they will be dealt with here.

The Japanese seldom endow a neuter noun with active qualities. Instead of saying, for example, "The bullet hit him," they will say, "He was hit by the bullet" (hi wAHssuh hituh bvAHi ssi bvOOrAtuh).

In the Japanese language, verbs have neither person nor number. It is for this reason that Japanese confuse the plural with the singular in American nouns and verbs, as in:

"AH' kAssuhtchAHnuh fAW mi?"
(*Are* question for me?)
(*Is* the question for me?)

"ituh hAHbv AHrAHibvuh."
(It *have* arrive.)
(It *has* arrived.)

"AH' hi nAHtuh nAHissuh?"
(*Are* he not nice?)
(*Isn't* he nice?)

Sometimes the verb or auxiliary is dropped completely, as in:

"hOO ssAHtuh?"   "wAH' yOO minuh?"
(Who that?)   (What you mean?)
(Who *is* that?)   (What *do* you mean?)

There is no neuter pronoun in the Japanese language and this makes for considerable confusion when the Japanese undertakes the American language.

"AHi tAruh yOO hAH wAHssuh."
(I tell you how was.)
(I'll tell you how *it* was.)

"hi' issuh."
(Here is.)
(Here *it* is.)

"tEHkuh kAHpuh bvAHi hissuh iAH."
(Take cup by *his* ear.)
(Take the cup by *it's* handle.)

"mAHi AHissuh ssAW bvAHduh, hi kuhrAHi."
(My eyes so bad, *he* cry.)
(My eyes are so weak, *they* are watering.)

The absence of articles in the original Japanese accounts also for the following usages:

"AHtuh ssEHmuh tAHimuh."
(At same time.)
(At *the* same time.)

"yOO wAHnuh' dAWguh?"
(You want dog?)
(Do you want *a* dog?)

"mEHkuh ssuhtApAHpuh tOO tchAruh."
(Make step-up to chair.)
(Get up on *the* chair.)

A characteristic error in grammar is the confusion of adverbs, and of adjectives:

"AHbvuh ssAHdAnuhri, AHi gAW."
(Of *suddenly*, I go.)
(I'll go right away.)

"wAHnuhssuhri AHi wAHssuh pOOAH."
(*Oncely*, I was poor.)
(*Once*, I was poor.)

"ituh wAHssuh rAHduhri nAWissuh."
(It was *loudly* noise.)
(It was a *loud* noise.)

There seems to be stubborn insistence on misplacing the negative:

"nAHtuh AHi dOO."
(*Not* I do.)
(I *didn't* do it.)

"AW! nAHtuh tOO dOO, puhrissuh."
(Oh! *not* to do, please.)
(Oh! please *don't* do it.)

The Japanese seem to make no distinction between "tell," "say" and "talk":
"AHi tAWkuh ssAHmuhssin' AHbvAHt ituh."

(I *talk* something about it.)
(I'd like to *say* something about it.)

"AHi sEH yOO nAW."   "hi tAruh hi gAW."
(I *say* you no.)   (He *tell* he go.)
(I *told* you no.)   (He *said* he would go.)

A common Japanese substitution stems out of the Japanese excessive politeness. Not being satisfied with the respectful, though short word "please," he uses other words and phrases:

"kAHinuhri kAHmuh tOO fAtchuh."
(*Kindly* come to fetch.)
(*Please* bring.)

"ssAHnuhkuh yOO nAHtuh tOO dOO sAW."
(*Thank* you not to do so.)
(*Please* don't do that.)

A complete disregard for the proper adjective is typical:

"hAH puhrAssOO' AHi firuh!"
(How *pleasure* I feel!)
(How happy I feel!)

Like the Chinese, whose idea-letter alphabet they adopted, the Japanese are addicted to compound words. In their own language they have such combinations as "kami-kiru" (to cut by biting) and "arukikuduru" (to descend by walking). This habit is carried over into their dialect.

"mEHkuh tchEHnuhjuh kAH."
(Make change-car.)
(Transfer cars.)

"dAW' gAW bAHnguh ssuhrAHmuh."
(Door go bang-slam.)
(The door slammed.)

"hi fAHi' shOOtuh gAHnuh."
(He fire shoot-gun.)
(He fired the gun.)

"mEHkuh bAHng AHtuh fuhrAHmuh dAW."
(Make bang-out from door.)
(He slammed the door.)

SENTENCE EXERCISES

Pronounce the following sentences in the Japanese dialect using the material learned from the preceding section on Grammar Changes:

1. Is your name John Mercer?
2. Do you want to fight the Japanese army?
3. I told him not to go.
4. Please obey the order I have given to you.
5. They did not do what they know is right.
6. The air in this room is very bad.
7. It is good to be alone here.
8. Oh! please don't take the honorable life of the prisoner.
9. It has been good to visit you here.
10. Will you tell me who is that man?

After pronouncing the above sentences, refer to the sentences below giving the correct treatment. Check the mistakes, repeat the corrections and memorize.

1. AH' nEHm jAHn mAH'ssAH'?
2. yoo wAHn' fAHituhfAHit jAHpAHniss AH'mi?
3. AHi ssEH him nAHt gAW.
4. kAHinuhri AWbvEH AH'dAH' AHi gibv yoo.
5. nAW' ssEH doo wAH' ssEH nAW AH' rAHituhri.
6. A' inroom bvAri bvAHduhri.
7. iss puhrAssoo' bvi AHlAWn hi'.
8. AW! nAW' too tEHk AHnAHrAHbvoo' puhrissAHnAH' rAHif.
9. it hAHbv bvi puhrAssoo' bvissit yoo hi'.
10. ssEH mi hoo ssAHt mAHn.

JAPANESE LANGUAGE CARRYOVERS

hello	*konnichi wa*	kAWnuh *ni*tchi wAH
goodbye	*sayonara*	sAHyAW*nAH*rAH
goodnight	*O yasumi nasai*	AW yAH*soo*mi nAH*sI*
excuse me	*gomen kudasai*	*gAW*mEHn koodAH*sI*
thank you	*arigato gozaimasu*	AHrig*AH*tAW gAWsI*mAH*soo
please	*dozo*	dAW*sAW*
Oh! or Ah!	*ei*	AY!
I see	*ha-ha*	hAH hAH
you don't say	*hate na*	hAH*tAY* nAH
yes	*ikanimo*	ikAH*nim*AW
no	*iya*	i*yAH*
regrettable	*oshii*	AW*ssi:*

JAPANESE MONOLOG

Oh! please not touch me! kindly take hand from arm. Oh! please not make fight-fight with me. I are Japanese born so you think I are enemy. Oh! not so, I say you—Oh! not so! I say you how was. I are from Japan greatly number year. I depart Japan of suddenly. I are not like military officer. Firstly, he take father for army. Then he take two brother. Then he want take me. Of suddenly, I go. Oh! not I stay where poor man not have right for to live. So I come to America. Oh! Are not he nicely country, I question me! Oh! he are, I make reply. So I stay. I work hardly. Oh! very muchly hardly! But I are pleasure—very muchly pleasure. I make marry with Japan girl. I are have two children. And I are in America—not in Japan—where military army men make poor man muchly slave. Oh! oncely I try be citizen—American citizen. Not I do. Japanese man not be citizen, postoffice man tell. But I still muchly like America. Greatly more now. America now fight with Japan. And when America win then Japan poor man not be slave no more. Oh! Lincoln free slave here. Maybe Roosevelt free Japan slave. That why I are not enemy. I are American. Oh! good American! Oh! please believe I are truth reporting. Oh! yes, please!

PHONETIC REPRESENTATION

(The syllables in bold-face type are to be accented.)

Note: Remember that the aspirate "uh" is not sounded broadly. It is simply a slightly perceptible puff of air.

"AW! puhrissuh   nAHtuh ^tAH..tchuh mi!"

kAHinuhri tEHkuh **hAHn**'uh fuhrAHm **AH**muh. AW! puhrissuh nAHtuh mEHkuh **fAH**ituh **fAH**ituh wissuh mi. AHi AH' jAHpAHnissuh **bAW**nuh ssAW yOO **ssin**uhk AHi AH' AnAmi. **AW! nAH**tuh ssAW, AHi sEH yOO—AW! **nAH**tuh ssAW! AHi sEH yOO hAH **wAH**ss. AHi AH' fuhrAHmuh jAHpAHnuh guhrEHtuhri nAHmuhbAH yi'. AHi dip**AH**tuh jAHpAHnuh AHbvuh ss**AH**d**A**nuhri. AHi AH' nAHtuh **rAH**ikuh miritAri AWfiss**AH**. f**AH**suhri, hi tEHkuh **fAH**ssAH fAW' **AH**'mi. **ss**Anuh hi tEHkuh **tOO** bvuhr**AH**ss**AH**. **ss**Anuh hi w**AH**nuh' tEHkuh **mi**. AHbvuh **ssAHd**Anuhri, AHi **gAW. AW! nAHt** AHi ssuhtEH w**A' pOO'** mAHnuh nAHtuh hAHbvuh **rAH**ituh fAW' tOO **ribv**uh. **ss**AW AHi kAHmuh tOO AHm**A**rik**AH**. **AW! AH' n**AHtuh hi **nAH**issuhri **kAH**nuhtuhri, AHi **kAs**suhtchAHnuh mi! **AW!** hi' **AH'**, AHi mEHkuh ripuhr**AH**i. ssAW AHi ssuhtEH. AHi wAHkuh **hAH**duhri. **AW! bvA**ri mAHtchuhri **hAH**duhri! bvAHtuh AHi AH' puhr**A**ss**AH**—**bvA**ri mAHtchuhri puhr**A**ss**AH**. AHi mEHkuh **mAH**ri wissuh jAHpAHnuh **gAH**ruh'. AHi AH' hAHbvuh **tOO** tchiruhduhr**A**nuh. AHn AHi AH' in AHm**A**rik**AH**—**nAH**t in jAH**pAH**nuh—wA' miritAri **AH'**mi mAnuh mEHkuh **pOO'** mAHnuh mAHtchuhri ssuhr**EH**bvuh **AW! wAH**nuhssuhri AHi tuhr**AH**i bvi **ss**itissAnuh—AHm**A**rik**AH**nuh **ss**itissAnuh. **nAH**t AHi dOO. jAHpAHnissuh mAHnuh nAHtuh bvi **ss**itissAnuh, pAWss'**AW**fissuh mAHnuh **tAr**OO'. bvAHt AHi ssuht**iOO' mAH**tchuhri rAHik AHm**A**rik**AH**. guhr**EH**tuhri **mAW'** nAH. AHm**A**rik**AH** nAH f**AH**ituh wissuh jAHp**AH**nuh. **AH**nuh w**A**nuh AHm**A**rik**AH win**uh **ss**Anuh jAHp**AH**nuh **pOO'** mAHnu nAHtuh bvi ssuhr**EH**bvuh **nAW mAW'**. **AW! rink**AHnuh fuhri ssuhr**E**Hbvuh **hi**AH'. mEHbvi **rAW**ssuhbv**A**-OOtuh fuhri jAHp-**AH**nuh ssuhr**EH**bvuh. **ss**AHtuh wAHi AHi AH' nAHt A**n**Ami. AHi AH' AHm**A**rik**AH**nuh. **AW! gOO**d AHm**A**rik**AH**nuh! **AW!** puhr**i**ssuh bviribv AHi AH' tuhr**OO**ssuh rip**A**Wtin'. **AW!** y**A**ss, puhr**i**ssuh!

CHAPTER ELEVEN

The Chinese Dialect

Although the various branches of the Chinese language are derived from one common stock, all are quite different. There are, for example, Cantonese, Kwangtung, Amoy, Swatow, Ningpo, Foochow, Menchow and Mandarin, which is the official Chinese language and has itself a number of sub-dialects. Therefore it would be absurd to expect the following material to reproduce *the* Chinese-American dialect. For there is no *one* Chinese dialect, just as there is no one Chinese language commonly used by all Chinese.

Each native of a separate district has his own special version of the Chinese language. Thus he would speak his version of the American language differently. Therefore, the rules given in this chapter for learning the Chinese dialect cannot be absolute, but are representative only of the Chinese dialect as we know it.

THE CHINESE LILT

The Chinese sing-song can be attributed to the fact that, in his own language, the Chinese has only four tones. It is for this reason that, in English, his speech is sometimes a series of monotones rising and falling in a droning manner. The Chinese dialect student may find it valuable to listen to some Chinese records and get a good idea of this limited tonal range.

Naturally, if the character is educated in America, and has lived in his adopted country for a long period of time, the sing-song will not be so noticeable. It should never be dropped completely, but it may be lightened generally and thickened only under emotional stress.

The typical foreign-born Chinese speaks in a high-pitched, nasalized voice and the public has somehow come to expect that all Chinese must speak so or else they are impostors. However, the American-born Chinese who has mingled freely with Americans will speak like an American. His voice may be slightly higher, but he will have a greater range than the foreign-born Chinese. On the other hand, the speech of the Manchu Chinese is deliberate and soft. The enunciation is meticulous and the sentences end with a downward inflection as though the thought were unfinished. Nevertheless, for general purposes a high, nasal quality should be approximated.

Because of the lack of possibilities in the speech tones, the sentence "AHi nAW lAHi' gAW dEH'" (I no like go there) would read:

"AHi   nAW   lAHi'   gAW   ^{dEH:}   EH!"

Start this sentence about an octave higher than in American.

The sentence "yoo tEH-oo' mi wAHt AHi doo" (you tell me what I do), which means "You tell me what to do," would read:

"yoo   tEH-oo'   mi   wAHt   AHi   doo: ..oo."

In the above sentence it will be found that "doo" (do) takes more tonal emphasis than the other words.

EMPHASIS

The emphasis in the Chinese dialect is more on tone than on stress. Thus there are only four accents one could give a word and each must be an accent of pitch. A Chinese would be a poor subject for the dialect coach who required that a student give the word "yes" some twenty different interpretations. He, being Chinese, would stop at four, achieving only a question, disbelief, a curt response and a whine.

Another point to remember is that in the Chinese language each word is only one syllable, and each syllable has its own accent. Therefore, when speaking American, the Chinese has a tendency to break the words into their component syllables and pronounce each part separately.

For example, take the following sentence:

<pre>
                        ki   tuh?"
              wi-ssuh-   ssaw-
     "yoo lAHi'   EHnuh
              (You like whiskey and soda?)
</pre>

The word "wi-ssuh-ki" (whiskey) is broken up into three syllables and "ssAW-tuh" (soda) retains its two syllables, but they are made more distinct.

In the sentence "hi wOn' yoo too gAW nAH." (he wants you to go now), the word "go" (gAW) would receive tonal stress and would be spoken a note higher than the rest of the sentence. The Americans would be apt to give "go" a stress, rather than a tonal, emphasis.

THE ASPIRATE "uh"

The Chinese language uses the aspirate "uh" which is a natural carry-over into the dialect. This should never be sounded as broadly as the "U" in "up." It is an imperceptible puff of air and nothing more. It will be used between two voiced consonants, as in "ssuhtoopit" (stupid). It will also be found after the final voiced consonant in a word when the beginning letter of the next word is a consonant. The aspirate must not be broad.

VOWEL CHANGES

(*Although the Chinese sing their vowels, they do not elongate them as much as do the Swedish or Italian people. The vowel sounds must, therefore, be kept short.*)

"AY" .... as in "take," "break," "they," etc.

This long "AY" sound is changed to a short "EH" as in the American word "get," thus "take" becomes "tEHk."

DRILL WORDS

buhlEHk	(break)	kEHss	(case)	tEHk	(take)
dEH	(they)	bvEHkEHt	(vacate)	hEHt	(hate)
fEHss	(faith)	lEHt	(late)	lilEHt	(relate)

"UH" .... as in "alone," "final," "sofa," etc.

Either the "A" of the American word "had" or the "AH" of the American word "father" may be used. The latter is preferred.

DRILL WORDS

AHlAWn	(alone)	pAHssifik	(pacific)
fAHinAHl	(final)	AHnAHdAH	(another)
ssAWfAH	(sofa)	pAHlEHt	(parade)
	AHbAHt	(about)	
	lAHkoon	(lagoon)	
	bAHnEHnAH	(banana)	

"AH" .... as in "father," "arm," "park," etc.

This American "AH" sound is shortened to "O" in the Chinese dialect. The "O" is the same as in the American word "rod" and should be short and clear.

DRILL WORDS

fOdAH	(father)		kOm	(calm)
Om	(arm)		hObAH	(harbor)
pOk	(park)		Omi	(army)
	dOk	(dark)		
	fO	(far)		
	ssOp	(sharp)		

"A:" .... as in "ask," "draft," "laugh," etc.

This elongated American "A:" becomes a short "AH."

DRILL WORDS

AHss'	(ask)		tAHss'	(task)
duhlAHf	(draft)		lAHss'	(last)
lAHf	(laugh)		pAHss	(path)
	tssAHnuht	(chant)		
	buhlAHnuhtss	(branch)		
	mAHssuhtAH'	(master)		

"A" .... as in "bad," "am," "guarantee," etc.

This short "A" changes to "EH." For a lighter dialect it may remain the same in short words, as "mAt" (mad) or "bAt" (bad).

DRILL WORDS

bEHt	(bad)		ssEHt	(sad)
EHm	(am)		puhlEHn	(plan)
gEHlAHnuhti	(guarantee)		tssEHtAH	(chatter)
	mEHt	(mad)		
	lEHm	(lamb)		
	pEHn	(pan)		

"AW" .... as in "ball," "falter," "shawl," etc.

The American "AW" changes to "AH." But another change which must be noticed here is that the "l" is often dropped and replaced by "oo" (as in "good"). This "l" may be studied further in the consonant changes. Other "AW" words without the "l" will be found under "AW" as in "off."

DRILL WORDS

bAHoo'	(ball)		kAHlAH	(caller)
fAHoo'tAH	(falter)		hAHoo'	(hall)
ssAHoo'	(shawl)		AHoo'	(all)
	AHoo'wEHss	(always)		
	fAHoo'	(fall)		
	ssuhmAHoo'	(small)		

"EE" .... as in "he," "treat," "people," etc.

The Chinese dialect changes "EE" to "i," although for a lighter dialect the "EE" may be retained.

DRILL WORDS

hi	(he)		mi	(me)
tuhlit	(treat)		ssi	(she)
pipoo'	(people)		nitoo'	(needle)

	ssuhlip	(sleep)
	ssuhli	(three)
	wi	(we)

"EH" .... as in "bet," "said," "friend," etc.

This "EH" sound remains the same as in American.

"I" .... as in "ice," "aisle," "guile," etc.

When broken down, this American "I" becomes "AH-EE." The "AH" is retained by the Chinese, but the "EE" is changed to short "i." Although written together as "AHi," the two sounds "AH" and "i" should be pronounced distinctly and separately. The sound of "i" should not be lost.

DRILL WORDS

AHiss	(ice)		AHissuhkuhlim	(ice-cream)
AHioo'	(aisle)		pAWlAHi'	(polite)
gAHioo'	(guile)		puhlAHiss	(price)

	lAHit	(light)
	tAHi	(tie)
	kuhlAHi	(cry)

"i" .... as in "it," "women," "busy," etc.

The short "i" should remain the same, although some Chinese substitute "AY" for it.

"O" .... as in "on," "bond," "John," etc.

The sound of this "O" remains the same, as in "On" (on), "bOn'" (bond), "tssOn" (John) and "kOmOn" (common).

"OH" .... as in "bone," "sew," "dough," etc.

When the American sound "OH" is broken down, it becomes "OH-OO." This is changed by the Chinese to "AW" as in the American word "saw." The Chinese "AW," however, is shorter and sharper.

DRILL WORDS

bAWn	(bone)		ssuhtAWn	(stone)
ssAW	(sew)		bAWss	(both)
dAW	(dough)		dAWss	(those)

	mAWtAH	(motor)
	gAW	(go)
	ssAW	(show)

"AW" .... as in "off," "cough," "water," etc.

The American "AW" sound becomes "AH" in Chinese.

DRILL WORDS

AHf	(off)	bAHss	(boss)
kAHf	(cough)	kAHss'	(cost)
wAHtAH	(water)	lAHss	(loss)

fuhlAHss'	(frost)
kuhlAHss	(cross)
ssAHf'	(soft)

"OO" .... as in "food," "do," "blue," etc.

The "OO" of "food" is replaced by the "oo" of "good." For a lighter dialect this sound may remain the same as that in "food."

DRILL WORDS

foot	(food)	moon	(moon)	ssuhtoopit	(stupid)
doo	(do)	yoo	(you)	noo	(knew)
buhloo	(blue)	ssoop	(soup)	poo'	(poor)

"oo" .... as in "good," "wolf," "full," etc.

The "oo" of "good" remains the same.

"yOO" .... as in "unit," "cube," "beauty," etc.

This "yOO" sound is changed to "yoo." The "oo" is like that of "good." The aspirate "uh," should, of course, be inserted between any preceding consonant and the "y," as in "p*uh*yoo'" (pure).

DRILL WORDS

yoonit	(unit)	kOmuhyooniti	(community)
kuhyoob	(cube)	yoonifAWm	(uniform)
buhyooti	(beauty)	muhyoossik	(music)

huhyoomAHn	(human)
yooss	(use)
puhyoo'	(pure)

"U" .... as in "up," "love," "does," etc.

Although this sound may remain the same, it is preferable to change it to "AH."

DRILL WORDS

AHp	(up)	AHnuhkoo'	(uncle)
lAHbv	(love)	lAHbvuhli	(lovely)
dAHss	(does)	ssAHmuhssin'	(something)

ssAHnuhtEH	(Sunday)
AHnuhtioo'	(until)
dAHss'	(dust)

"ER" .... as in "curb," "earn," "fir," etc.

Since few Chinese can pronounce the "r," and those few only after considerable practice, this sound becomes "ER." The crossed "r" (R) means that the "r" is not sounded, but that the preceding vowel is treated as though it were. For example, "kERb" is pronounced the same as in American except that the "r" is dropped.

DRILL WORDS

ERn	(earn)	hER	(her)	dERti	(dirty)
fER	(fir)	lERn	(learn)	ssERt	(shirt)
wERss	(worth)	pERpoo'	(purple)	litER'li	(literally)

"OW" .... as in "out," "cow," "house," etc.

This "OW" sound which, when broken down, becomes "AH-OO," is changed to "AH" in the Chinese dialect.

DRILL WORDS

AHt	(out)	dAH'foo'	(doubtful)
kAH	(cow)	AHbAH'	(about)
hAHss	(house)	ssuhkAHt	(scout)
mAHnuhtin	(mountain)		
ssuhtAHt	(stout)		
ssAHt	(shout)		

"OI" .... as in "oil," "boy," "noise," etc.

This sound becomes "AH-yi" in the Chinese. The "AH" is like the "a" in "father" and the "yi" like that of "yip."

DRILL WORDS

AH-yioo'	(oil)	ssAH-yi	(soy)
bAH-yi	(boy)	tssAH-yiss	(choice)
nAH-yiss	(noise)	tAH-yi	(toy)
EHnuhjAH-yi	(enjoy)		
lAH-yitAH	(loiter)		
lAH-yioo'	(loyal)		

WORD EXERCISES

Pronounce the following words in the Chinese dialect using the material learned from the preceding section on Vowel Changes:

1.	collar	11.	always
2.	street car	12.	shrimps
3.	save face	13.	again
4.	airplane	14.	murder
5.	water pan	15.	until
6.	good-bye	16.	cry
7.	somewhere	17.	starve
8.	outside	18.	coughing

9. doing	19. sewing machine
10. soy bean	20. upstairs

After pronouncing the above words, refer to the following list of correct pronunciations. Check the mistakes made in the vowels, repeat the corrections and memorize.

1.	kOlAH	11.	AHoo'wEHss
2.	suhli'kO'	12.	ssuhlim'
3.	ssEH' fEHss	13.	AHgEH'
4.	EHpuhlEH'	14.	mERdER
5.	wAHtERpEH'	15.	AHnuhtioo'
6.	goo'bAHi	16.	kuhlAHi
7.	ssAHmuhwEH'	17.	ssuhtO'bv
8.	AH'ssAHi'	18.	kAHfin'
9.	dooin'	19.	ssAWin'mAHssin
10.	ssAHyibin	20.	AHpuhssuhtEHss

CONSONANT CHANGES

B—A number of voiced consonants become voiceless in the Chinese dialect. This means that the lips, teeth and tongue are in position for the letter, but it is not sounded or given voice. Final "b" is an example. In the word "kEHb" (cab), the "b" is shaped with the mouth and receives sound only as long as the mouth is in the process of forming the letter. Once the letter "b" is formed, the mouth freezes in that position until the next word is pronounced. The aspirate "uh" which usually follows "b" is not found in the Chinese final "b." Initially and medially, the "b" retains the aspirate as in American.

C—The same as in American.

D—This is one of the most difficult letters for many Chinese to pronounce. Although, for a simplified effect, the symbol for initial "d" remains the same throughout this chapter, it may change to "t." Medially, it should change to "t." And finally, it is either changed to "t," is dropped, or is voiceless. It is usually dropped when preceded by another consonant, as in "bihAHin'" (behind). When final after a vowel, it may be voiceless as in "bEHd" (bad), so that the shape of "d," but not the sound, is given. Or it may be changed to "t" as "bEHt" (bad).

F—The actual sound of this consonant is the same as it is in American. However, when it is medial and before another consonant, it is usually dropped, as in "fi'tin" (fifteen).

G—Initial "g" should remain the same as in American, although some Chinese pronounce it as "w." This "w" pronunciation, however, would be entirely too thick for general purposes.

Medially "g" usually changes to "k." However, for a light dialect, it may remain the same as in American.

Final "g" is either changed to "k" or made voiceless. But, in words which end with "ng," as "young" and "thing," the "g" is dropped completely and the "n" is sounded as the final consonant, as in "yAHn" (young) and "ssin" (thing).

Again when "ng" is medial the "g" is dropped in favor of the "n," as "lEHn'ss" (length) and "dooin'ss" (doings).

Some Chinese will add an extra "g" after a final "n," as "ting" (tin). This will make the dialect too thick and should not be used.

H—This consonant is sounded very distinctly by the Chinese. It is more forced than the "h" in "have" and comes closer to the "h" in "a*ha*."

J—The "j" also is more forced than it is in American. There should be a slight "d" sound before the "j" making it actually "dj." If a thicker dialect is needed, the "ss" may be used. See "S."

K—Unless "k" comes before "s," it should be pronounced as in American. A number of Chinese have difficulty with this sound and substitute a strong "h" for it. This "h" substitution may be used for a thicker dialect.

When "k" comes before "s," as in "bakes," the "k" is dropped, and the pronunciation becomes "bEH'ss." "K" is hard enough for the Chinese to reproduce, but when they have a "ks" combination, they throw the "k" out completely. Even the educated foreign-born Chinese find this sound very difficult. Final "k" is sometimes dropped, especially if the preceding letter is a consonant, or if the initial letter of the next word is a similarly sounding consonant.

L—Although the Chinese could feel superior to the Japanese in that the Chinese can pronounce "l," they don't seem to appreciate their speech advantage for they are very negligent with this consonant. So unless the "l" is absolutely essential to the word, it should be dropped in the light as well as in the heavy dialect. Initially, it would have to be used, and medially between vowels it should be sounded. Although some Chinese say "minyAHnss" (millions) and substitute "n" for the "l" sound, this change is not recommended. If the "l" which is followed by a "y" sound, as in "million" or "civilian," is to be dropped, it is best to offer no substitute, as, "mi'yAHnss" (millions) and "sibvi'yAHn" (civilian).

When "l" is the final sound in a word it should be dropped, and "oo" as in "good" should be substituted, as "pipoo'" (people), "mAHlEH-oo'" (morale). The "l" substitution for "r" is discussed under "R." For a light dialect, the final "l" may be retained occasionally, but not often, and should be sounded only in common words.

M—The same as in American.

N—The same as in American, but it should be dropped when unimportant, as in "mAH'ss" (months) and "kOmAH'" (common).

P—This becomes an unaspirated consonant when it is final in a word. The mouth, then, is shaped for its pronunciation but the sound is not completed.

Q—Since this consonant is a combination of the disliked "k" plus "w," the Chinese will try to avoid it as much as possible. When there is no avoiding it, he will usually pronounce it so that it sounds like a forceful "h." Sound "k" (the sound, not the letter) farther back in the mouth with the back of the tongue raised and you will get a grating sound. This is the sound that should be used for "q," and the "w" should be dropped.

R—Many an actor's Chinese dialect is based on the belief that a high voice and the substitution of "l" for "r" is all that is required for an authentic representation. As a matter of fact, the "r" may be retained and the dialect will still be authentic. A great many Chinese, particularly the Northern Manchus, pronounce the "r" gutturally, as the Germans do. And the educated Chinese pronounce the "r" almost as well as we do. The only difference is that their attack is lighter and they use "r" only when necessary. They would not include it in words like "kERb" (curb), but they would sound it quickly in "kEHrit" (carried).

The less educated Chinese, however, would change the "r" to a sound resembling "l." Instead of drawing the tongue back and raising it in the middle so that it touches the roof of the mouth, the Chinese flattens his tongue. The sound of "l," as we know it, is not usually pronounced for "r." What we hear is an attempt to pronounce "r" with the tongue in position for "l." Care must be used with this change so that the dialect does not become unintelligible. It is suggested that words using "r" be changed to synonyms with less radically changed consonant sounds. The final "er" is always "AH."

S—The Chinese "s" should be used for both a light and heavy dialect. It is a hiss produced with the lips shaped for "sh" but actually sounding a hard "s."

T—This consonant is unaspirated when final, although the mouth, lips and tongue are in position for "t," the actual sound is not heard.

Medial "t" is often dropped when the sense of the word is obvious without it, as in "fERss'li" (firstly). Initial "t" remains the same as in American.

V—This letter often is sounded like "bv." The lips are slightly parted and an attempt is made to sound both consonants at the same time. The lips do not close but remain half open until the sound is completed. This "bv" should be used for both thick and light dialect.

Although the "bv" is preferred, some Chinese substitute "f" for "v" while others prefer "w" for "v."

W—The same as in American.

X—The "x" is a combination of "k" and "s." Since the "k" is, for many Chinese, a tricky consonant to pronounce, it is dropped in favor of the single sound of hissed "ss," as in "EHssEHmpoo'" (example) or is aspirated as "bAWkuhss" (box).

Y—The same as in American.

Z—The "z" also takes a hissed "ss" treatment, as in "iss" (is) and "ssitiss" (cities).

SH—This sound also receives the hissed "ss" treatment.

TCH—This sound receives the hissed "ss" treatment. It may use a "t" preceding it (tss). For a light dialect, the "tch" may be sounded as in American, but with less emphasis. However, the "ss" should be used for other consonant sounds which take it.

TH—The voiced "TH" may be either "d" or the dentalized "d**TH**."

th—The unvoiced "th" may be either "t" or "ss." The "ss" is preferred, as in "ssAHssEHn'ss" (thousands).

ZH—This sound receives the hissed "ss" treatment.

TS—Many Chinese have difficulty with this sound. They usually drop the "t" and pronounce the hissed "ss," as in "ssi'ss" (sits).

NOTE: Final consonants are often dropped by the Chinese even when they are preceded by a vowel. But if the dialect is too thick because of this elision, use discretion in dropping such consonants.

ELISIONS

Many American words seem too long for even the most educated foreign-born Chinese because the Chinese are used to one-syllable words. So, wherever possible, and without distorting the sense, a word should be shortened. Some examples are: "plEHtuh'li" (practically), "lipiduh'li" (repeatedly) and "litER'li" (literally).

Dropped final, and sometimes medial, consonants are also noticeable and were discussed under "Consonant Changes."

WORD EXERCISES

Pronounce the following words in the Chinese dialect using the material learned from the preceding section on Consonant Changes:

1.	once	11.	juice
2.	shaving	12.	stand
3.	rubber	13.	long
4.	bathe	14.	takes
5.	goes	15.	millions
6.	six	16.	hangs
7.	sits	17.	rouge
8.	rapidly	18.	final
9.	throw	19.	fifteen
10.	fetch	20.	robber

After pronouncing the above words, refer to the following list of correct pronunciations. Check the mistakes made in the consonants, repeat the corrections and memorize.

1.	wAH'ss	11.	djooss
2.	ssEHbvin'	12.	ssuhtEHn'
3.	lAHbvAH'	13.	lAWn'
4.	bEHd	14.	tEH'ss
5.	gAWss	15.	mi'yAHnss
6.	ssikuhss	16.	hEHn'ss
7.	ssi'ss	17.	looss
8.	lEHpi'li	18.	fAHinAHoo'
9.	ssuhlAW	19.	fi'tin'
10.	fEHtss or fEHss	20.	lObAH'

GRAMMAR

If the Chinese vocabulary were not so involved, the Chinese school boy would be eager to study, for there are no formulated grammatical rules.

The Chinese language has no words or word endings to indicate gender, tense, mood, person or number. Words are used as pictures, or symbols of things or ideas. And compound words become actually compound pictures, as "lamp-cage" for lantern, "mix-wine" for cocktail and "milk-skin" for cream.

Another typical word habit derived from their original language is the coupling together of the same verbs, as in "mEHkuh ssituh ssit" (make sit-sit) which actually means "sit down."

The points to remember in going over the script for a Chinese character are that unnecessary words should be eliminated, that the simplest verb form should be used and that short words are preferred. For examples of this treatment, see the following monolog and Sentence Exercises. It will be noticed in the monolog that certain Pidgin English phrases have been used. Refer to the chapter on Pidgin English for more of these phrases.

An example of the verbal shorthand discussed above is the American sentence, "Give the money to that man." The Chinese would say,

"gibv mAHni dEH' mEHn."
(Give money that man.)

The Chinese rely more on the inflection of the voice than on the proper words, as in

"wOnuh' bEHss?"
(Want bath?)
(Do you want a bath?)

Certain common Chinese expressions, if sparingly used, will help give color to the dialect, like "tai lai" (lady), "chop" (quality), "mei-yi fahtzu" (it can't be helped), "tou wang-la" (all finish) and "chan-choh" (stop). It is impractical to include a great many of the phrases here, since their authenticity depends on the tone rather than on the pronunciation.

SENTENCE EXERCISES

Pronounce the following sentences in the Chinese dialect using the material learned from the preceding section on Grammar Changes. Remember to use only those words that are absolutely necessary and remember, also, to avoid multi-syllable words.

1.   I'm going to see the boss.
2.   Why do you do all that work yourself?
3.   I'll have everything done soon.
4.   The other man paid the bill.
5.   Would you like to see how I make this?
6.   I don't make much money at this place.
7.   Maybe I'll go back to China after the war is over.
8.   The Chinese people are an old race.
9.   How would you like to hear some music?
10. I've got a wife and five children to earn money for.

After pronouncing the above sentences, refer to the following sentences for the correct treatment. Check the mistakes, repeat the corrections and memorize.

1.   mi gAW ssi bOss.
2.   wAHi yoo doo AHoo' wER k yoossEHoo'?
3.   mi doo AHoo' soon.
4.   AHdAH' mEH' pEH bioo'.
5.   yoo lAHik ssi hAH AHi mEHk?
6.   nAW mEHk puhlEHn'i mAHni diss puhlEHs.
7.   mEHbi mi gAW bEH' tssAHinAH EHf'AH' wAH'.
8.   tssAHinAH pipoo' AWoo' pipoo'.
9.   yoo lAHik hi' ssin'ssAHn'?
10. mi gAW' wAHif fAHi' tssil'EH' mEHk mAHni fAW'.

CHINESE MONOLOG

(John Lee stands behind the laundry counter grinning widely at a customer.)

Ticket, please? Thank you. Me got wash finish. Ticket say, "Mr. Harris." That you, no? Fifty-five cent please. Thank you. Here change. Thank you. Maybe you put change in China Relief Box, no? That for China people Japan make hurt. That for make world safe for democracy, no? Me got old father, old mother—brother, sister there. Oh, he got no good, there. He got plenty much trouble. He got all-time no eat. China Relief make help them. Maybe soon China people be happy. Maybe long time more. Oh! not matter—long time—little time. China people throw Japan out chop-chop. Then maybe China be good place go home. See old father—old mother. Maybe soon everything be O.K. no! Oh! thank you! thank you! me send letter old father—old mother, they shoot fire-cracker prayer for you. Thank you! thank you!

PHONETIC REPRESENTATION

(The syllables in bold-face type are to be accented)

"tik....EH'

                    puhliss.   ssEHnuhkuh yoo: ·· ·   .oo.

mi gO' wOssuh **fin**iss. tikEH' sEH, "missuh **hEH**liss." dEHt **yoo, nAW**? fi'ti fAHi'
ssEHnuh puhliss. **ssEH**nuhkyoo. hi **tssEH**nuhss. **ssEH**nuhk yoo. mEHbi yoo
poo' **tssEH**nuhss inuh tssAHinAH li**li**fuh bAWkuhs, **nAW**? dEHt fAW
tssAHinuh pipoo' tssAHpEHnuh mEHkuh **hER**t. dEHtuh fAW mEHkuh
wERluh **sEH**fuh fAW dEHmOk'uhssi, **nAW**? mi gO' AWluh' **fO**dAH', AWluh'
mAHdAH'—buh**lAH**dAH, **ssissAH** dEH'. AW, hi gO' nAW **goo'**, dEH. hi gO
puhlEHn'i mAHtssuh tuh**lAH**boo'. hi gO' AHoo' tAHim nAW it. tssAHinAH li**li**-
fuh mEHkuh **hEH**oo'p dEHm. mEHbi soonuh tssAHinAH pipoo' bi **hEH**pi.
mEHbi **lAH**nuh' tAHim mAW'. AW! **nAW' mEHtAH'**—l**AH**nuh' tAHim—li'oo'
tAHim. tssAHinAH pipoo' ssuhlAW tssAHpEHn AH' **tssOp-tssOp**. dEHnuh
mEHbi tssAHinAH bi goo' puhlEHssuh gAW **hAW**muh. ssi AWluh' **fO**dAH'—
AWluh' **mAH**dAH'. mEHbi ssoon EHbvissinuh' bi **AW** kEH **nAW**! AW!
ssEHnuhk yoo! **ssEH**nuhk yoo! mi ssEHn' lEHtAH' AWluh' **fO**dAH'—AWluh'
mAHdAH', dEH ssootuh fAHi' kuhlEHkAH' **puhlEH'** fAW' yoo. **ssEH**nuhk yoo!
ssEHnuhk yoo!

CHAPTER TWELVE

Pidgin English

Strictly speaking, Pidgin English—Chinese Pidgin—is more a jargon than it is a dialect. But it is included here because it is one of the most widely spoken jargons in the world. It has been estimated that more than 50,000,000 people use it as a means of verbal communication. All along the China coast, in the South Seas, on practically all the Pacific Islands, in the Malay Peninsula, on the west coast of Africa, in the Australian bush, in parts of India, Egypt and the Near East and even on the west coast of the United States, some form of Pidgin English is spoken.

The name "pidgin" is supposed to have been derived from the Chinese pronunciation of "business," and it described the language used to transact their business affairs with the English-speaking people. The variations of Pidgin English have been severally called "Beachcomber," "Beche le Mar" and "Sandalwood English." But, basically, they are all the same, no matter where they may be spoken, in that they have a somewhat standard lexicon of words and phrases. Of course, each particular section uses certain words that are peculiar to itself. But, in all forms of Pidgin, there are found roots in Portuguese, Hindustani, Chinese, Japanese, Spanish, Russian, German and, of course, English.

The basic idea of Pidgin is this: English words are treated as though they were Chinese characters and are strung together as the Chinese language is strung together, not in standardized grammatical forms but, rather, with root ideas simply stated in logical sequence.

The Chinese speak Pidgin with their own peculiar methods of pronouncing the English vowels and consonants. The British, on the other hand, when using Pidgin, color their version with their own British dialect. Americans speak it with an American intonation, the Japanese with theirs, and so on. But, fundamentally, the words they use are Pidgin English. And it requires a knowledge of only about 300 words to be able to carry on a creditable Pidgin conversation.

Pidgin could be termed a sort of shorthand language. However, the shorthand sometimes goes into reverse and produces "bel-bel belong me plenty walk-about" which means, simply, "I'm hungry," as used by the Australian bushmen. But a great deal of language can be covered with relatively few words of Pidgin. In China, where so many dialects of the Chinese language are spoken, the people are forced to resort to Pidgin as a medium which is commonly understood among them.

The only way to speak the jargon is to learn the words and phrases. There is no grammar as such. There are a few Pidgin dictionaries and these can be referred to for a more complete treatment of the jargon. Here, in this section, it will be possible to deal only with the fundamentals, to lay out a workable system for a simplified treatment and to list some of the words used.

Here is an example of how Pidgin has been used in an old poem by an anonymous writer:

> "My name blong Norval—topside t'hat too high mountain, my too muchee olo fata pay t'hat sheep he chow-chow. He smallee-heart man; too muchee take care catchee t'hat dollar, galaw! my no wantchee my stop t'his side, countee my his own piecee chilo, my no wantchee—my hab hear talkee talkee t'hat fightee-pidgin, my like fo'long t'hat Mandalin knockee allo man. Littee tim Joss pay me what ting my fata no likee do. Last nightee t'hat moon get up lound, allo same my hat, no get full up, no get square; too muchee quiri man come down t'hat hill; catchee t'hat sheepee catchee long t'hat cow he own take care him away. My go catchee my flin—my own eye hab see whatside t'hat lobber-man walkee. He no care him away—he pocket too muchee fill up, hi yah! my largee heart t'hat tim my hab go home, my no likee take care t'hat sheep long t'hat cow."

That is Pidgin. You may not get much sense out of it from a first reading, but a perusal of the following word list and a few more readings should give you an inkling of the meaning. The poem was written about forty years ago and many of the words have become obsolete. The author must have had a defective sense of hearing and recorded things he had not heard, for the poem, is not, strictly speaking, authentic Pidgin. But it is a fairly good example of the dialect or jargon.

There are a few common usages that may be put into some sort of rule form. For example, "talking," in all forms, can be covered with the word "talkee." It doesn't matter what the actual talking action is—shouting, pleading, asking, whispering or mumbling—it is always "talkee," regardless of tense or number, as in "my talkee he chop-chop" (I'll tell him right away).

Any situation that suggests possessing or receiving can be covered with the word "catchee," as in "my catchee too-much chow-chow" (I've had a lot of food) or "he catchee two piecee dollar belong Missy Hallis" (he found the two dollars Miss Harris lost).

The pronoun "he" in the previous example is used for all the pronouns "he," "she," "it," and "they."

The personal pronoun "my" is used for all the pronouns "I," "me," "my," "mine," "our," "ours" and "we."

The word "belong" ("blong" in the above poem) suggests a certain shade of possession, as in "he belongee top-side joss-house" (it should be on the roof of the church) or, more specifically, (the roof of the church owns the right to carry it).

The words "hab" and "hab got" are similarly used, although with different shades of meaning, as in "my hab got one piecee chit belong you" (I have a letter for you) or "my hab hear talk-talk belong he" (I heard him say).

The expression "can do" is always used to denote power of performance or ability of completion and is used by itself in answering a question, as in "can do washee chop-chop?" (can you finish the washing first?) to which the answer would be, "can do."

The word "piecee," heard so often in Pidgin, is a carryover from the original Chinese and is a sort of noun classifier. In Pidgin, it is always used after a numeral, as in "catchee four piecee chilo house-inside" (there are four children in the house). The phrase "one piecee" is always used in place of "a" or "an," as in "my chow-chow one piecee kumquat" (I ate a kumquat).

Following is an alphabetical word list with sentence examples:

afterward . . . . "by-an'-by," used for afterward or for any future action, as in "My come this side by-an'-by." (I'll come back later.)

affair . . . . "pidgin," as in "This sing-sing one piecee chop pidgin." (This entertainment is a fine affair.)

again . . . . "two time," as in "My walkee two time room-inside." (I went into the room again.)
  "nother-time," as in "Nother time my pay muchee dollar."
(I paid more money again.)

alike . . . . "all same," as in "Pidgin belong my all same coolie." (My work and the coolie's are alike.)

American . . . . "melican"

another . . . . "nother," as in "My go nother time." (I went another time.)

apprentice . . . . "larn pidgin"

approved speech . . . . "good talkee," as in "That man he makee good talkee." (He was right in what he said.)

argument . . . . "bobbery," as in "Chilo makee muchee bobbery inside house." (The children argued a lot in the house.)

arrived . . . . "come this side," as in "Chilo belong Missy Peel come this side house." (Mrs. Peel's children arrived at the house).

ask for . . . . "wantchee," as in "My wantchee more better chow-chow maskee no get." (I asked for better food but I didn't get it.)

bamboozle . . . . "play pidgin," as in "He play pidgin all same bad heart man." (He bamboozles like all bad men.)

beg. . ."chin-chin," as in "Coolie makee chin-chin catchee cumshaw." (The coolie begged for a tip.)

below . . . . "bottom-side," as in "He go bottom-side house makee chop-chop." (He went down to the basement in a hurry.)

beneath . . . . "bottom-side"

be quick . . . . "fai tee," as in "Fai tee! catchee masta chop-chop!" (Be quick! hurry and get your master.)

bottom . . . . "bottom-side"

bow . . . . "kow tow," as in "My makee all-proper kow-tow catchee cumshaw." (I make the right bow to get the tip.)

bring . . . . "pay," as in "He pay piecee chit, makee kow-tow." (He brought the letter and made a bow.)

business . . . . "pidgin," as in "For what he makee pidgin?" (Why did he go into business?)

can't . . . . "no can," as in "No can hab tiffin finishee chop-chop." (I can't have the lunch done now.)

child . . . . "chilo"

Chinese . . . . "chinee"

church . . . . "joss-house"

clergyman . . . . "joss-house-man"

close . . . . "long side," as in "One piecee rickshaw come long-side house." (A rickshaw has pulled up close to the house.)

cold . . . . "colo"

correct . . . . "proper," as in "He pay proper piecee dollar." (He brought the correct change.)

curious . . . . "quiri," as in "For what he makee quiri talk?" (Why did he ask that curious question?)

custom . . . . "cutsom," as in "He had got quiri cutsom makee plentee talkee long time." (She has a strange custom of gossiping for a long time.)

disturbance . . . . "bobbery" (see "argument")

do . . . . "makee," used in all forms of the verb "to do" and always before a verb, as in "Makee that piecee man walkee chop-chop." (Make that man to hurry.)

dollar . . . . "dollar" or whenever money is referred to

done . . . . "finishee," used in any completed action, as in "My finishee pidgin." (I have done the work.)

down . . . . "bottom-side" (see "bottom")

error . . . . "spoil'm," as in "Masta hab got spoil'm one piecee dollar." (The master has made a mistake of one dollar.)

every . . . . "all," as in "My makee spoil'm all time." (I always make mistakes.)

evil minded . . . . "bad heart" (see under "bamboozle")

excellent . . . . "how!" as we use "fine!" or "swell!"

extra-fine . . . . "chop," as in "He hab got plenty fine chop chow-chow." (They have very fine food.)

face . . . . "facee" but when used with "losee," as "losee facee," it means to be put to shame or embarrassed.

false . . . . "look-see pidgin," as in "Bad heart man makee looke-see pidgin makee chinee losee plenty piecee dollar." (The crook made false promises and stole money from the Chinese.)

fashion . . . . "cutsom" (see under "cutsom")

fast . . . . "chop chop" (see under "below")

fine . . . . "how!" (see "excellent")

finest . . . . "first chop-chop," as in "My makee first chop-chop tiffin." (I shall make you the finest lunch possible.)

first class . . . . "number one," as in "He hab got number one joss-house makee joss-pidgin." (They have a first class church for services.)

food . . . . "chow chow"

foolish . . . . "water top side," as in "He makee spoil'm hab got water top-side." (He made the mistake because he's crazy.)

formerly . . . . "before time," as in "My walkee man-man before time." (I formerly walked slowly.)

go . . . . "walkee," used in all forms of "to go," "to walk," etc., as in "He wantchee walkee plenty all time." (He always wanted to go.) When speaking of the future, "go" is always used for active future tense, as in "My go house makee chow-chow." (I shall go home to eat.)

God . . . . "Joss"

good . . . . "proper" (see "correct")

goodbye . . . . "good wind! good water"

great . . . . "largee," as in "He makee largee chop-chop." (He was in a great hurry.)

greenhorn . . . . "griffin" for any "newcomer" or "foreigner"

habit . . . . "cutsom" (see "custom")

has . . . . "hab got," as in "He hab got plenty piecee dollar catchee chop chow-chow." (He has enough money to buy the best food.)

have . . . . "hab," as in "My no hab joss. (I haven't any religion.)

have you . . . . "hab got," as in "Hab got flower-heart makee love-pidgin you missy?" (Have you a faint heart for making love to your girl-friend?)

here . . . . "this side," as in "One piecee coolie come this side house makee bobbery." (A coolie came here and made a disturbance.)

hey! . . . . "ai hai!" a common interjection used as we use, "hey!" or "look!"

house . . . . "houso" or "house."

however . . . . "maskee," used as we use, "O.K.," "though" and "however" and also used as an interjection. (See "ask for")

hurry . . . . "chop-chop" or "faitai" (see "be quick")

husband . . . . "has-a-man"

hypocritical . . . . "look-see pidgin" (see "false")

if . . . . "supposee," as in "Supposee you catchee dollar you catchee chow-chow." (If you get some money, you can eat.)

implore . . . . "chin-chin," to beg for, request, or ask in any form, as in "He makee chin-chin catchee piecee cumshaw catchee chow-chow." (He begged for a tip to buy food.)

impossible . . . . "no can," used as a negative reply to indicate impossibility or inability to perform any action, as in "No can walkee chop-chop." (I can't walk so fast.)

indecision . . . . "flower-heart" (see "have you")

independent . . . . "saucy," also "sassy," proud or independent

inside . . . . "inside," anything that is interior or inside, even thoughts, body organs, or the soul, as in "He hab got plenty smart inside." (He's a smart man.)

know . . . . "savvy," to understand, to know or to think, as in "No savvy" (I don't understand) or "My savvy plenty he inside he heart." (I know everything he's thinking.)

label . . . . "chop"

laborer . . . . "coolie"

later . . . . "by-an'-by" (see "afterward")

little . . . . "littee"

lot . . . . "plenty," very much or a lot of, as in "Hab got plenty masta." (I've had a lot of employers.)

love . . . . "love-pidgin," used for mild love, as distinct from "love-love pidgin," which is used to indicate a torrid love affair.

lovers . . . . "flower-heart"

lunch . . . . "tiffin"

master . . . . "masta"

make-believe . . . . "play-pidgin"

much . . . . "plenty," used to indicate much of or plenty of

near . . . . "long side," as in "For what you makee muchee-muchee bobbery long side my masta house?" (Why are you making such a commotion near my master's house?)

negative . . . . "no can" (see "impossible")

Negro . . . . "moloman"

nice . . . . "proper" (see "correct")

night . . . . "nightee"

no . . . . "na"

noise . . . . "bobbery" (see "disturbance")

not afraid . . . . "no fear," as in "No fear, my makee tiffin all same plenty chop." (Don't be afraid—-I'll make a good lunch as I always do.)

not right . . . . "no belong reason" or "unreasonable" as in "Missy Lee makee my chop-chop walkee that side no belong reason." (It is not right for Miss Lee to ask me to go right over.)

occupation . . . . "pidgin"

odd . . . . "culio"

offer . . . . "pay" (see "bring")

O.K . . . . ."all-proper," "maskee," or "pukka." All three words can be used for the purpose.

old . . . . "olo"

once . . . . "one time," as in "one time he pay chit my masta." (Once he brought a letter to my master.) Also "before time."

once more . . . . "nother time," (see "again")

only . . . . "one time," as in "My makee one time chow-chow." (I make only one meal a day.)

other . . . . "nother," as in "Melican man walkee nother littee joss-house." (The American man went to the other small church.)

pay . . . . "pay"

peculiar . . . . "culio"

place . . . . "side" (see "below")

play . . . . "sing-sing"

possess . . . . "hab got" (see "have")

possession . . . . "belongee" used to indicate possession in all its forms, as in "My catchee dollar belongee my." (The money I earned is mine.)

pray . . . . "chin-chin" (see "beg")

present . . . . "cumshaw"

previously . . . . "before time," used to indicate past action, as in "Before time my walkee man-man." (I used to walk slowly.)

proud . . . . "saucy"

queer . . . . "culio" or "quiri"

quickly . . . . "chop-chop"

quite . . . . "muchee" or "too muchee," as in "He hab got too muchee saucy." (He's too independent.)

religion . . . . "joss-pidgin"

request . . . . "chin-chin" (see "beg")

run . . . . "walkee" (see "go")

same as . . . . "all same" (see "alike")

should not . . . . "not ought," as in "My not ought walkee house." (I shouldn't go to the house.)

slowly . . . . "man-man"

small . . . . "littee"

spoil . . . . "spoil'm" (see "error")

stamp . . . . "chop"

strange . . . . "culio" or "quiri"

suppose . . . . "supposee" (see "if")

that . . . . "that same," as in "He pay that same nightee." (He brought it that night.)

then . . . . "that time," as in "My walkee house that time." (I was walking home then.)

there . . . . "that side," as in "Got plenty chow-chow belong you that side." (There is a lot of your food there.)

there is . . . . "got"

think . . . . "tinkee"

tip . . . . "cumshaw"

twice . . . . "two time"

under .... "bottom-side" (see "below")

understand .... "savvee" or "understand?", as in "You savvee for what melican man makee walkee that side?" (Do you understand why the American went there?)

unreasonable .... "no belong reason," as in "No belong reason why for he wantchee nother chit." (It's unreasonable for him to ask for another check.)

very .... "muchee"

very much .... "muchee-muchee"

very very much .... "too muchee"

walk .... "walkee" used for any action of going, as in "My walkee too muchee." (I went there quite often.)

want .... "wantchee," used in all forms of wanting or desiring or asking for, as in "He wantchee walkee house." (He wants to go home.)

when .... "what time" or "that time," as in "He no hab dollar that time he chow-chow." (They didn't have any money when they ate.)

where .... "what side," as in "What side masta walkee." (Where did your master go?)

who .... "who man," as in "Who man wantchee my?" (Who wants me?)

why .... "for what?" as in "For what masta wantchee my?" (Why did the master ask for me?)

within .... "room inside," as in "Littee chilo room inside house." (The small child is in the house.)

CHAPTER THIRTEEN

The Hawaiian Dialect

M ost people associate Hawaii with hula dancers. They also imagine that the natives speak in some sort of South Seas dialect or language that would be quite foreign to American ears. Actually, though, the ordinary young Hawaiian speaks an American form of English with the exception of a few vowel and consonant variations and a smattering of grammatical changes. Also, there is an infiltration of a slight Portuguese intonation—from which the Hawaiian dialect obtains its lilt and emphasis—as well as some Pidgin English and Beche la Mar.

There was a time, only a few years ago, when Pidgin and Beche le Mar were the Hawaiian dialects. But, with the advent of the United States into the islands, the entire trend of the language has changed and a fairly defined regional dialect of American is spoken. The natives of the French mandated islands, however, still converse in Beche la Mar (see page 000).

However, some of the original Hawaiian language characteristics remain. The intriguing glottal stop—the elision of medial consonants—which charmed so many travelers before Hawaii was civilized, is still evident in the dialect. Because of a lack of consonants in the original language, certain consonants are dropped in the modern dialect. There were only twelve letters in the Hawaiian language— the five pure vowels, "a," "e," "i," "o" and "u" (pronounced "AH," "AY," "EE," "OH" and "OO") and seven consonants, "h," "k," "l," "m," "n," "p" and "w." Two conso- nants never came together in a word. But any number of vowels could, each vowel being pronounced separately, as in "hOO-mOO-hOO-mOO-nOO-kOO-nOO- kOO-AH-pOO-AH-AH" (humuhumunukunukuapuaa), which was the name of a small tropical fish.

In the consonants, "w" sometimes receives a "v" treatment, depending on its position in a word. Initially, in compound words, it receives a soft "w"; medially, it is sounded like a combination of "vw." "K" is substituted for "t" in the Hawaiian language. In that language, there were originally no diphthongs. But, in recent years, combinations of "au" and "ai," instead of being pronounced separately, are run together, as in American.

The Hawaiian is a relatively unstressed language. But whatever stress there is is usually placed on the next to the last syllable, as in "mAH-*h*AH-lOO" (thank you) and wi-ki-*wi*-ki" (hurry up).

For a reproduction of the dialect of very backward natives who are still out of contact with civilization, the following suggestions would apply. The fact must be realized, however, that a strict adherence to these changes would make a dialect entirely incomprehensible. Therefore, they must be used only sparingly, but still enough to establish the dialect.

Because there are only seven consonants in the original language, in the dialect the letter "k" is substituted for "d," "t," and "s" as in "*k*AHlAH" (*d*ollar), "*k*EHl" (*t*ell), and "*k*EHnuhtuh" (*c*ent). The aspirate "uh," it will be seen in the last example, separates the consonants, since no two are spoken together.

Substitution of "p" for "f" and "b" is also made, as in "*p*AWn" (*ph*one) and "kAH*p*ikuh" (ca*bb*age).

As in the Chinese, "r" is pronounced as "l," as in "*l*AWkuh" (*r*od) and "*l*EHkuh" (*r*ed).

The consonant sounds, "zh," "tch," "sh" and "j" become "k," as in "kEHk" (badge), "wAHkuh" (watch), "wAHkuh" (wash) and "kAHk" (judge).

The consonants "d" and "t," when used at the end of a word, and preceded by another consonant, are dropped.

Both the voiced and unvoiced "th" are often pronounced as "t."

All the vowels coupled with "r" drop the "r," as in "EHkAH" (acre), "kAHlAH" (dollar), and "pAHnuh" (burn).

This thick version of the dialect is given in the event that an extremely backward native from the hinterland is to be portrayed. An excellent example of how the dialect reads can be obtained from Stevenson's *In The South Seas*,[1] from which the following example was transcribed:

> Here in my island, I 'peak. My chieps no 'peak—do what I talk; very good. Kanaka 'peak in a big outch. Toppoti mitonary think "good man"; very good. Toppoti he think "cobra"; no good. I send him away ship. I think he good; he no 'peak. I look your eye. You good man. You no lie. Toppoti I see man. I know tavvy good man, bad man. I look eye, look mouth. Then I tavvy. Look eye, look mouth. I and my pamily. Mo betta.

From the use of "tavvy" (savvy) and "mo betta" (more better), it can be seen that there is some Pidgin English used. A reference to the Pidgin English section of this book should, therefore, aid in increasing the dialect vocabulary. The above example from Stevenson is also helpful in that it affords an excellent means of learning how to temper the thick dialect with sufficient changes to make it characteristic and yet not incomprehensible.

Before going into a discussion of the modern Hawaiian dialect, it might be apropos to give a short sketch of the outstanding Hawaiian characteristics. The Hawaiian is traditionally a lazy person. He is essentially calm and unemotional; he can seldom be stirred to anger. At the same time, he can be influenced easily by sadness and despondency. That is why his songs are nearly all in a minor-key. On the whole, the Hawaiian possesses a childlike simplicity, an almost pagan indulgence in things of the flesh, and a carefree attitude toward the past, present, and future.

THE MODERN HAWAIIAN DIALECT

The young people and most of the older people in the large cities of Hawaii speak American with only a few vowel and consonant changes. Some of them are:

VOWEL CHANGES

SOUND	WORD	CHANGE	DIALECT
AY	take	EH	tEHk
UH	sofa	UH	sOHfUH
AH	father	U	fUdUH
A:	ask	EH	EHs'
A	bat	EH	bEHt
AW	ball	U	bUl
EE	he	EE	hEE
	get	A	gAt
EH	get	U	gUt
I	nice	I	nIs
i	sit	EE	sEEt
O	on	U	Un
OH	bone	OH	bOHn
AW	off	U	Uf
OO	food	OO	fOOd
oo	good	OO	gOOd
yOO	unit	yOO	yOOnEEt
U	up	U	Up
ER	curb	U	kUb
OW	out	AH-AW	AH-AWt
OI	oil	AHi	AHil
er	paper	AH	pEHpAH

CONSONANT CHANGES

There is considerable confusion in the pronunciation of the vowel plus "r" combinations. The combination "or" is pronounced "AW," "ar" is pronounced "AH" and "ur" is pronounced "U."

Some of the other consonant changes are:

D—is dropped finally when preceded by another consonant, as in "wEEn'" (win*d*).

B—is nasalized.

P—is nasalized.

T—is dropped finally when preceded by another consonant, as in "kEHn'" (can't).

TH—the voiced "TH" is changed to "d," as in "dEE" (the).

th—the unvoiced "th" is changed to "t," as in "tEEn" (thin).

V—changed sometimes to "w," as in "wOHt" (vote).

THE GRAMMAR CHANGES

It is with the changes in grammar that much of the Hawaiian flavor can be captured. Generally, the Hawaiian is confused by our verbs and has a tendency to leave out certain words he believes to be redundant. In addition, his grammar is affected by Pidgin English which is still spoken in Hawaii to a great extent. The repetition of "talk," for instance, in the following, is an example of the Pidgin influence:

> "shEE Uluh tIm tUk-tUk."
> (She alla time talk-talk.)

See the section on Pidgin English for other examples that can be used.

The word order in the Hawaiian dialect is an important element in its reproduction. The following are some of the principal word-order peculiarities.

The subject is placed before the verb in such direct questions as:

> "wUt I shEHl dOO?"
> (What *I* shall do?)
> (What shall *I* do?)

For emphasis, the adjective is often placed before the noun or article, as in:

> "nIs, dEEs mEHn."
> (*nice*, this man)
> (this *nice* man)

> "tOO fAH dEHt plEHs."
> (*Too far*, that place.)
> (That place is *too far* away.)

The verb usually precedes the subject after "what" and "where," as in:

> "wAr yOO wAn' shEE sEEn."
> (Where you went, she *seen*.)
> (She *saw* where you went.)

"wUt wUn' dEEs mEHn?"
(What *wants* this man?)
(What does this man *want*?)

Adverbs, especially those of time, often come before the subject, as in:

"nAwAH AwAH wEE gOH."
(*Never* ever we go.)
(We *never* go.)

"UlwEHz hEEz hEHpEE."
(*Always*, he's happy.)
(He's *always* happy.)

The simple present tense of verbs is preferred in all the tenses, as in:

"I gOH nAH-AW."
(I *go* now.)
(I'm *going* now.)

"I gOH hEElOH yAs'UHdEH."
(I *go* Hilo yesterday.)
(I *went* to Hilo yesterday.)

The plural form of the verb is used with a singular subject, as in:

"dEE tchA AH hEE nAH-AW."   "mIt shEE AH gOOd."
(The chair *are* here now.)   (Might she *are* good.)
(The chair *is* here now.)   (Maybe she *is* good.)

The use of "might" in the above sentence is typical of the Hawaiian's preference for the word to use of the conditional tense, and to express possibility, probability, etc., as in:

"mIt hEE sEE hEEm."
(*Might* he see him.)
(*Maybe* he saw him.)

The use of "been" with the present tense in order to indicate past action is a common addiction, as in:

"hEE bEEn plAntEE mEHd."
(He *been* plenty mad.)
(He *was* very mad.)

"Us bEEn nOH UlUHtIm."
(Us *been* know allatime.)
(We knew all the time.)

"dEH bEEn sEE plAntEE."
(They *been* see plenty.)
(They *saw* a lot.)

Another verb form used excessively is the Pidgin expression, "no can" for "cannot" or "can't," as in:

"wEE nOH kEHn EEt Ul dEHt."
(We *no can* eat all that.)
(We *can't* eat all that.)

"wI yOO nOH kEHn sEE EEt?"
(Why you *no can* see it?)
(Why *can't* you see it?)

Substitution of "allatime" for "always" is another typical carry over from the Pidgin. The use of "stay" is also characteristic of the dialect, as in:

"Us stEH rUnEEn' UlUHtIm."
(Us *stay* running *allatime.*)
(We ran the entire distance.)

"yOO bEEn gOH stEH hOHm."
(You been go *stay* home.)
(You go home.)

The word "try" is usually substituted for "please," as in:

"jOH, trI sEE EEt mI wEH."   "trI kUm bEHk sOOn."
(Joe, *try* see it my way.)   (*Try* come back soon.)
(Joe, *please* see it my way.)   (*Please* come back soon.)

The word "please" is used only when extreme politeness is necessary. The past tense of "break" is preferred by the Hawaiians, as in:

"hEE nOH kEHn brOHk Ul dAm."
(He no can *broke* all them.)
(He can't *break* all of them.)

The word "broke" is also confused with "tear" and "torn," as in:

"yOO brOHk mI kOHt."
(You *broke* my coat.)
(You *tore* my coat.)

"hEE brOHk dEE bOOk EEn lEE'l pEE suhz."
(He *broke* the book in little pieces.)
(He *tore* the book into little pieces.)

The perfect tense form of "see" (seen) is preferred to the past tense form (saw) as in:

"I sEEn hEEm dOO EEt."   "wEE sEEn Ul dAr wUz."
(I *seen* him do it.)   (We *seen* all there was.)
(I *saw* him do it.)   (We *saw* all there was.)

The tenses of most verbs are similarly misused, as in:

"fU' wUt shEE dEEd drEHnk EEt?"
(For what she did *drank* it?)
(Why did she drink it?)

"wUz yOO UlrIt?"
(*Was* you all right?)
(*Were* you all right?)

"wEE gUt plAntEE mU' flAH-AWz."
(We *got* plenty more flowers.)
(We have many more flowers.)

"wEE bEE plAntEE skAr."
(We *be* plenty scare.)
(We *were* quite scared.)

The preposition "to" is often dropped from sentences, as in:

"hEE trI gOh hOHm."   "trI kUm bEHk sOOn."
(He try go home.)   (Try come back soon.)
(He tried *to* go home.)   (Try *to* come back soon.)

At other times this preposition is added where it does not belong, as in:

"dEH mUs' tOO bI EEt."
(They must *to* buy it.)
(They must buy it.)

At other times "and" is substituted for "to," as in:

"dEH gOH EHn' sEE dImUHn' hAd."
(They go *and* see Diamond Head.)
(They went *to* see Diamond Head.)

Perhaps one of the most important errors in grammar comes with the substitution of "for" for "to" and the use of the phrase "for what," instead of "why," as in:

"fU' mEHk trUb'l"   "fU' wUt yOO gOH 'wEH?"
(*for* make trouble)   (For *what* you go 'way?)
(*to* make trouble)   (*Why* did you go away?)

The phrases "for why" and "why for" are also substituted for "why," as in:

"fU' wI yOO UlUHtIm EHngrEE?"
(*For why* you allatime angry?)
(*Why* are you always angry?)

"wIfU' yOO nOH kEHn hUrEE?"
(*Why for* you no can hurry?)
(*Why* can't you hurry?)

Repetitive pronouns are also the rule in Hawaii, as in:

"mEE, I sEE A'rEEtEEn." "Us, wEE gOOd bAHiz."
(*Me, I* see everything.)   (*Us, we* good boys.)

The misuse of the pronoun is also characteristic, as in:

"mEE plAntEE tIr."
(*Me* plenty tire.)
(I'm very tired.)

The impersonal pronoun, "it," is often dropped, as in:

"yOO trI."   "tEHk UHwEH."
(You try.)   (Take away.)
(Try *it*.)   (Take *it* away.)

The pronoun "what" is often substituted for "that," as in:

"nUtEEn' wUt EEz EEmpUtUHn."
(nothing *what* is important.)
(nothing *that* is important.)

The double negative is another error common in the Hawaiian dialect, as in:

"I nAvAH wUn' nOH trUb'l."
(I *never* want *no* trouble.)
(I *never* want trouble.)

The words "never" and "never ever" are often overly used, as in:

"wEE nAwAH AwAH EEt tchEEk'n nUt AwAH."
(We never ever eat chicken, not ever.)
(We never eat chicken.)

The Hawaiian uses the positive and comparative of an adjective preceded by "more," in place of the comparative and superlative, as in:

"dEHt kIn' mU bAtAH."   "dEE UdAH strEEt mU bEHd."
(That kind *more better*.)   (The other street *more bad*.)
(That kind is the *best*.)   (The other street is *worse*.)

Instead of "always," the Hawaiian substitutes "everytime," as in:

"I EHm nUt A'rEEtIm sEEk."
(I am not *everytime* sick.)
(I am not *always* sick.)

There are a number of typical interjections used in the dialect. When the Hawaiian wishes to get the attention of somebody, he calls out, "EH!" (hey!).

To show pleasure or joy or amazement, he says, "bAHi!" (boy!).

When speaking to another person and trying to gain the other's attention, he will insert, "yOO nOH!" (you know!).

To show surprise or excitement, he will ejaculate a rising intoned, "EE!"

NATIVE HAWAIIAN WORD LIST

The Hawaiians use a number of original language words in their dialect. The following are some of those that would most likely come up in the speech. A few, scattered about, can authenticate and identify an Hawaiian dialect.

ae	"AH-AY"	yes
aloha	"AH-lOH-hAH"	welcome or farewell
aole	"AH-OH-lAY"	no
apopo	"AH-pOH-pOH"	tomorrow
hale	"hAH-lAY"	house
haole	"hAH-OH-lAY"	foreigner
iki	"EE-kEE"	small
ipo	"EE-pOH"	sweetheart
kanaka	"kAH-nAH-kAH"	a person
kane	"kAH-nAY"	a man or husband
kapu	"kAH-pOO"	keep out
huhu	"hOO-hOO"	angry
kaukau	"kAH-OO-kAH-OO"	food
keiki	"kAY-EE-kEE"	child
kope	"kOH-pAY"	coffee
la	"lAH"	the sun or day
mahalo	"mAH-hAH-lOH"	by-and-by
maikai	"mAH-EE-kAH-EE"	good
nani	"nAH-nEE"	beautiful
pau	"pAH-OO"	stop, or, it is finished
pehea oe	"pAY-hAY-AH OH-AY"	how are you?
poi	"pAW-EE"	breadfruit
taro	"tAH-rOH"	plant used to make poi
wahine	"wAH-hEE-nAY"	wife or woman
wikiwiki	"wEE-kEE-wEE-kEE"	hurry! step on it!

THE HAWAIIAN LILT

There is a suggestion of Chinese sing-song in the dialect. A tendency toward a rising and falling intonation followed by a falling and rising intonation is evident. Simple questions usually end on a rise and fall inflection, instead of the usual rising inflection of American. But when a Hawaiian agrees with something, he uses the rising notes, as in: "yOO A'rEEtIm rIt!"

"yOO   A'rEE...ᵗIm   ʳIt!"

(You everytime right.)
(You are always right.)

The keynote of the pitch in Hawaiian is higher than in American, close to the British but not as high as the Chinese. There is little dawdling in the dialect although the vowels in emphasized words are elongated. The sharp treatment given to the consonants adds to the tempo. It is this alternating of fast and slow, for the consonants and the vowels, that gives the dialect its typical color.

1.   *Reprinted by permission of Charles Scribner's Sons, New York.*

CHAPTER FOURTEEN

Beche Le Mar

Beche Le Mar, or Sandalwood Pidgin as it has been called, is much like Chinese Pidgin English and is spoken in the South Sea and other Pacific islands. The form of Beche le Mar is about the same as Chinese Pidgin. It differs in that it uses words that are typical of the island in which it is spoken. Another variation comes with the pronunciation, which is governed also by the native pronunciation and by the various speech difficulties of each.

One of the chief changes comes with the addition of "um" to the verbs used in Beche le Mar. It is added to almost every verb, as in "walkum," "eatum," "callum" and "scratchum."

Another variation from Chinese Pidgin lies in the use of the word "fella" which is usually attached as a modifier, not only of people, but of inanimate things as well, as in "this fella bone him olo." (This bone is old.) It is also used after the personal pronoun "me," as in "Me fella me savvee talk along white fella man." (I understand white man's talk.)

For the Chinese "chow-chow," Beche le Mar substitutes "kai-kai" ("food" or "to eat").

The word "stop" is used to indicate "stay," "remain," exists" or any other similar meaning.

"Waste-time" is used as an epithet and not necessarily in its time sense, as in "Him waste-time, that fella." (He's a no-good bum.)

The most important variance comes with the use of the pronoun. Where Chinese Pidgin uses the personal pronoun "me" exclusively, Beche le Mar falls back on "me" for "we," "me," "I," "my," "mine," "our" and "ours." But for "he," "she," "it" and "they," it uses "him" exclusively. The word "you" is used almost as it is in American.

A number of interjections are peculiar to Beche le Mar, particularly, "what name!," as in "What name you want along me?" (Why do you want me?). It can also mean, "What's the big idea!," "Is it any of your business?" or "What do you want?"

"My word!" is another common interjection. It obviously stems from the British but is used by the Kanakas and others who speak Beche le Mar to indicate surprise, embarrassment, disgust, etc.

"Too much" is always used to indicate great amounts or quantities of anything, as in "Me likum you too much." (I like you a lot.)

"Wassamatta" is used in an ordinary question, but it can be used also in a question indicating disapproval.

The following list comprises a few more words used only in Beche le Mar and not in Chinese Pidgin, with their American equivalents:

BECHE LE MAR	AMERICAN
mary	woman
gammon	to lie
sing out	to call, holler, talk, etc.
fennis	fence
sittor	store
bokkis	box
walk about	any kind of action
long way li'l bit	far
long way big bit	very far
close up	near
fright	fear or afraid
cross	any type of anger

There are, of course, many other words typical of Beche le Mar. Following is a vocabulary list together with sample sentences. From them, it is possible to learn the jargon, at least sufficiently to be able to portray the character of a South Sea native.

BECHE LE MAR VOCABULARY LIST

about . . . . used only in "walk about" and "run about."

adrift . . . . to open anything, as in "Make'm fennis adrift." (Open the fence.)

alive . . . . as in "look alive!" (hurry up!)

all . . . . used to indicate plural, as in "all fella" (everybody).

> Also used as an adverb, as in "White fella man die all finish." (The white man is dead.)

> Also used in "all right," "all same" and "all time."

along . . . . used to indicate possessiveness, as in "head along him" (his head). See "belong" for similar usage.

Also used for "with," as in "Walk about along me." (Come with me.)

Also used for "at," as in "Big fella master stop along door." (The boss stood at the door.)

Also used for "to," as in "Him run about along big fella master." (He went to the boss.)

Also used for "for," as in "Him no catch'm mary along two fella year." (He was unmarried for two years.)

Also used for "out of," "on," "in," "into," "because of," "like," "as" and "with."

altogether .... used as an adjective for "everything," as in "You kai-kai bullama-cow, pisoup, apple altogether." (You ate the meat, the canned food and the apples.)

Also used to indicate definiteness, as in "You fella Kanaka no stop'm kai-kai altogether." (You'd better not stop eating.)

bad .... anything negative such as "unhealthy," "sick," "rotten," etc., as in "Him fella bone him bad." (The leg is broken.) or "him fella coconut him bad" (a headache) or "inside bad" (sorry or sad or grieved).

been .... always used to denote the past tense, as in "Master belong me been die all finish." (My boss is dead.) or "What name! you been drink water altogether." (What's the big idea of drinking all the water?)

before .... used to indicate time past, as in "Me been walk about long way big bit before." (I walked a long distance for some time.)

behind .... used as in American.

belly .... any part of the body below the neck, as in "Belly belong me walk about too much." (I've got a stomach ache.) or "Belly belong me bad." (My side hurts.)

belong .... used to indicate possession, as in "master belong me" (my boss) or "kai-kai belong me" (my dinner) or "You catch'm fella boy belong you?" (Have you found your servant?)

Also used to indicate habitation or membership of, as in "mary belong my house" (my wife) or "Me belong big white fella man." (I live in the white man's house.)

Also used in place of "for," as in "Bokkis belong that fella tobacco." (The box is for tobacco.)

Also used in place of "that has" as in "li'l fella bokkis belong kai-kai" (small box that has the food).

better .... used in the phrase "more better" to indicate "should," as in "More better you belong white fella man belong me." (You should be working for my boss.)

Also used alone, as in "Mary belong me him walk about better." (My wife has improved.)

big . . . . used to indicate a large amount of, or a superlative quality, or anything of magnitude, as in "Him big white fella man." (He's a big shot.) or "Him make'm big cry." (He cried aloud.) or "Me kai-kai big fella bullamacow." (I ate a lot of meat.)

bit . . . . anything small in size, amount, distance, etc., as in "li'l bit bad" (small ache) or "long way li'l bit" (a short distance) or "long way big bit" (much farther).

bite . . . . to stick, punch, pierce, etc.

black fella . . . . uncivilized native.

bloody . . . . used as an intensifying adjective, as in the Cockney, as in "Me bloody tire." (I'm very tired.) or "Him bloody bad fella." (He's a very tough guy.)

boat . . . . any sort of ship that is of foreign make. Native boats are called "canoes." Sometimes "schoona" is used for a foreign boat.

boss . . . . used as in American in both noun and verb forms.

bokkis . . . . a container of any sort, as in "Li'l fella bokkis belong you make'm plenty tire." (Your suitcase is so heavy I'm tired.) or "big fella bokkis, you fight'm him cry" (a piano) or "li'l fella bokkis, you push'm him cry, you pull'm him cry" (an accordion).

boy . . . . used to designate a boy and also any sort of man, usually a servant, as in "Li'l fella boy belong you, him bad, him hurt, him make'm big cry." (Your little boy is hurt and is crying.)

break . . . . to smash, to fall apart in any way, as in "Boat belong cap'n, he break'm altogether." (The captain's boat has capsized.) or "Break'm pisoup." (Open that can.)

broke . . . . used in the past tense of "break," as in "bokkis him broke." (The box burst open.)

brother . . . . used for a brother, a sister, or a cousin.

bullamacow . . . . formerly used for tinned meat but now used for meat of any kind or for a meat-producing animal. See "pisoup."

bush . . . . uncultivated land or wild growth of any sort, as in "White fella man him walk about bush." (The white man went into the country.)

buy . . . . used as in America.

bymby . . . . used to indicate the future of any sort, as in "Me fix'm boat bymby." (I'll patch up the boat later.) or "White fella man belong me walk about bymby." (My boss will come out soon.) or "Bymby him call'm this fella bloody rogue." (Pretty soon, he began to call him names.)

calaboose . . . . jail, as in "You catch'm black fella alongside bush, you throw'm calaboose." (When you catch the native in the jungle you'll throw him into jail.)

calico . . . . any manufactured woven cloth.

call . . . . used as in American, as in "What name you call'm black fella?" (Why did you call that native?) or "Me call'm you too much." (I called you for some time.) or "Me call'm pickaninny kai-kai—him kai-kai too much." (I call my baby kai-kai because he eats too much.)

canoe . . . . any native boat.

capsize . . . . used to indicate sinking, turning over, falling out of, falling down, etc., as in "Water belong mary him capsize altogether." (The woman's jug of water fell over and all the contents spilled.)

catch . . . . indicates possession of any sort, as in "Me catch'm canoe belong black fella man." (I have the native's canoe.) or "That fella man him catch'm money belong mary." (He's got the woman's money.) or "Me catch'm li'l bit bullamacow." (I got only a small piece of meat.) Also used as "to find."

close up . . . . used to signify "almost" or "just about," as in "Him close up capsize." (He almost drowned.)

      Also used for "soon," as in "Close up make'm kai-kai." (We'll soon eat.) or "Me walk about close up." (I'll leave soon.)

coconut . . . . used to signify the fruit, itself, and also the head, as in "Coconut belong him plenty sore." (His head hurts.)

cook . . . . to prepare food in any manner.

cooky . . . . a servant or, specifically, a cook.

cross . . . . anger of any kind, as in "white fella man belong me him plenty cross." (My boss is sore.)

cry . . . . any type of noise or instrumental sound, as in "Him cry bloody hell." (He hollered at me.) or "O! him cry, white fella man him cry him catch'm mary." (The white man sang songs to his girl friend to win her.)

door . . . . used to indicate any sort of hinged flap.

eye . . . . used as in American, as in "Him put'm eye along me too much." (He stared at me.)

fashion . . . . used extensively to signify style, fashion, kind, type, sort, or mode, as in "My word! what name buy'm bokkis this fashion?" (Why did you buy this kind of trunk?) or "What fashion kai-kai belong you." (What kind of food do you serve?)

feel . . . . used as in American, as in "Me feel cross inside coconut." (I'm angry.) or "Him feel plenty bad hurt." (He was very badly hurt.)

fella . . . . See opening part of section.

fight . . . . to strike in any way, as in "Big fella master belong me him fight'm cap'n." (My boss had a fight with the captain.) or "Me fight'm drum too much." (I beat the drum a long time.)

finish . . . . used to indicate completed action of any sort, as in "Him finish kai-kai." (He ate up all the food.) or "Father belong me him finish altogether." (My father is dead.) or "Him finish walk about bush." (He went through the jungle.)

fright . . . . fear of any sort, as in "pickaninny him fright too much." (The child was very frightened.) or "Me fright plenty too much big white fella man belong me him go finish altogether." (I was afraid my boss was going to die.)

gammon . . . . to lie, to deceive or exaggerate in any way, as in "What name you gammon me too much?" (Why do you always lie to me?) or "Him gammon black fella altogether." (He cheated all the natives.)

got . . . . used instead of "to have," as in "Mary belong you not got'm kai-kai." (Your wife has no food.)

him . . . . used indiscriminately regardless of number or gender, as in "Bokkis belong him." (It's his bag.) or "Mary him mak'm cook along fire." (The woman prepared the food on the fire.) or "Him fight'm mary belong him—capsize him." (He beat his wife and knocked her over.) or "Him catch'm two fella boy." (They seized two men.)

he . . . . also used instead of him.

hump . . . . to carry, as in "Mary belong him hump'm pickaninny." (His wife carried the child.)

inside . . . . used to indicate any type of emotional condition or situation, as in "Inside tell'm him." (He considered it.) or "Him plenty fright inside." (He was afraid.) or "Me feel'm inside." (I know.) or "inside bad" (to be sad) or "Inside him cross." (He was very angry.)

kai-kai . . . . from the Chinese, chow-chow—to eat and also to indicate any kind of food, as in "Him kai-kai plenty finish altogether." (He ate everything.) or "Belly belong me no kai-kai." (I'm hungry.)

kill . . . . used not only for "to kill" but also for "to beat," as in "White fella cap'n belong boat him kill black fella man plenty too much him finish altogether." (The white captain beat the native so much he died.)

lik-lik . . . . used for "almost" or "nearly," as in "Me lik-lik finish altogether." (I almost died.)

> Also used to signify smallness, as in "Me like'm lik-lik pickaninny belong white fella mary." (I like the white woman's child.)

look . . . . used for all forms of seeing, as in "Me look'm plenty black fella man walk about bush." (I saw a lot of natives in the jungle.) or "Him look'm daylight long time." (He was not sleepy.)

When used with "around" it means "to seek," as in "Me look'm around plenty too much." (I looked for it high and low.)

make. . . used as in American, as in "Altogether plenty too much black fella man make'm plenty cry." (A lot of natives were making quite a bit of noise.) or "What name white fella man make'm growl?" (Why did the white man holler angrily?)

man . . . . used to designate all men, as in "That fella man him plenty smart." (He's a smart man.) or "All fella man him kai-kai plenty." (They all ate enough.)

Also used as "husband," as in "That fella mary fella man him fight'm mary belong him too much." (That woman's husband beats her a lot.)

mary . . . . used to designate all women.

me . . . . used as the subject of a sentence and also as the object and with "fella," as in "Me no see." (I don't see.) or "Me no growl." (I'm not angry.) or "Me two fella black man me walk about bush plenty." (Two other natives and I remained in the jungle for a long time.) or "Bokkis make'm cry belong me." (The music box is mine.)

mebbe . . . . perhaps or maybe.

moon . . . . a month.

more . . . . used with "better," as in "More better that black fella man him capsize all finish." (That native should die.)

Also used as in American, as in "Me want'm more tobacco." (I want more tobacco.)

no . . . . used as in American and also in place of "not," as in "That fella mary no make'm kai-kai." (The woman didn't eat.) or "No savvy that fella bokkis." (I don't know what's in the box.)

Also used as "do not," as in "No be 'frai'." (Don't be afraid.)

of . . . . sometimes used and pronounced as "o," as in "Man o' bush," or "Man o' war."

one time . . . . used instead of "at one time" or "once" as in "One time me make'm walk about along water." (Once I took a jaunt down the river.)

pisoup . . . . applied to all types of foreign food.

pickaninny . . . . a child of either sex.

pigeon . . . . a bird of any kind.

place . . . . used extensively to indicate position or place, as in "that place" (there) or "this place" (here) or "That fella man him catch'm place. (He arrived.)

plenty .... used for "a lot of" or "very," as in "Plenty kai-kai this place." (There's a lot of food here.) or "Him make'm plenty cry." (He hollered very loudly.) or "Mary belong me him walk about plenty too much." (My wife was gone a very long time.) or "White fella man belong me him gammon black fella man plenty too much." (My boss cheated the natives a lot.)

proper .... used to designate "fitness" or "approval," as in "White fella mary plenty proper." (The white woman is very nice.) or "Him no proper fella man catch'm kai-kai along me." (He's not the kind of person to eat with us.)

rauss .... used instead of "to throw out" or "scram," as in "White fella man belong me him cry rauss." (My boss told me to get out.)

right .... used with "all" to indicate "correctness" or any condition of approval or good as distinct from bad, as in "Black fella man him all right this time plenty all right." (The native has recovered completely.)

Also used as an interjection, as in "All right! me no make'm walk about bush." (O.K. then I won't go into the jungle.)

same .... used with "all" to indicate "like" or "as," as in "Mary belong white fella man him all same fella man." (The white man's wife acts like a man.) or "Me Kanaka fella boy all same you." (I'm a Kanaka native like you.)

Also used in "all along same as" (to resemble) and "all same one" (alike), as in "Pickaninny belong mary belong big white fella man him all same one." (The child of the white boss' wife looks like him.)

savvy .... used in all forms of "to know," "to understand," "to believe," "to be able to," etc., as in "No savvy." (I don't understand.) or "Kanaka fella boy him savvy too much." (That Kanaka knows a lot.) or "Olo fella man him proper savvy." (The old man is wise.)

side .... used to designate "place," as in "this side" (here) "that side" (there).

sing out .... used for any vocal sound, as in "White fella man belong me him sing out growl." (My boss hollered angrily.)

sing sing .... a dance or a song.

small .... used as "little," as in "small talk" (a whisper).

sore .... used for "pain," "ache" or "smart," as in "Me break'm bone me altogether sore." (I broke my leg and it hurts.)

speak .... ordinarily used for all forms of the verb "to say," "speak," "tell," etc., as in "Him speak'm straight." (He tells the truth.) or "Him speak'm him want'm kai-kai." (He said he wanted something to eat.) or "Big fella master belong me him speak'm plenty too much." (My boss gave a long speech.) or "You fella boy you speak'm me all same altogether." (You had better tell me everything.)

stink .... anything with a smell or an odor will "stink" as in "water belong stink" (perfume) and "apple belong stink" (onion).

stop .... in addition to being used as in American, it is also used with forms of the verbs "to be" and "to live," as in "One fella boy him stop topside house belong me." (A boy was on our roof.) or "White fella man him stop along side this place." (The white man lived here.) or "What name you stop that place?" (Why did you stay there?)

tabu .... refers to anything forbidden, as in "That fella bokkis him tabu along side black fella boy." (The natives are forbidden to look into that box.)

take .... used as in "to take" or "to have," "to carry," etc., as in "Me take'm one fella boy alongside bush." (I took another boy with me into the jungle.) or "Me take'm kai-kai belong cap'n. (I took the captain's food.)

talk .... also means "to speak," as in "no talk straight" (lying) or "talk big" (to promise) or "talk plenty bad belong white fella man" (to swear like a white man).

time .... used as in American, as in "all time" (always), "no got time" (to be unable to), "first time" (formerly) and "Two fella boy him make'm plenty too much good time." (The two men had a fine party.)

Also as "long time fashion" (old style) or as "one time" for "once," as in "One time black fella boy him all time walk about along side bush altogether." (Once, the natives roamed the bush alone.)

too much .... refers to superlative degree of anything, as in "Father belong me him savvy too much." (My father is the wisest.) or "Me like'm that fella mary too much." (I like that girl most.)

walk about .... used not only as "to walk" but in all forms of "to go" and many forms of "to do," as in "That white fella man him walk about boat belong cap'n." (The white man went to the captain's boat.) or "That fella pigeon him walk about all time no stop." (The bird flew around without stopping.)

what name .... used as "why" or "what," as in "What name that fella boy him kai-kai plenty too much bullamacow?" (Why did he eat so much meat?) or "What name you cry?" (What did you say?)

Also used for "how" and "who" as in "What name that fella boy him catch'm bokkis belong chief?" (Who was the man who found the chief's box?) or "What name black fella man him run about along calaboose?" (How did the native escape from the jail?)

An excellent example of Beche le Mar—one that should illustrate the manner in which it can be used so that it will not be too thick, is the following excerpt from R. L. Stevenson's *In The South Seas:*[1]

"I got 'melican mate," the chief, he say. "What you go do 'melican mate?" Kekela, he say; "you come tomollow eat piece." "I no want eat 'melican mate!" Kekela he say, "why you want?" "This bad shippee, this slave shippee," the chief he say. "One time a shippee he come from Pelu, he take away plenty Kanaka, he take away my son. 'melican mate he bad man. I go eat him; you eat piece?" "I no want eat 'melican mate," Kekela he say; and he cly—all night he cly. He say chief: "Chief, you like things of mine? you like whaleboat?" "Yes," he say, "You like file-a'm (firearm)?" "Yes," he say. "You like blackee coat?" "Yes," he say. Kekela he take Missa Whela' by he shoul'a, he make him light out house; he give chief he whaleboat, he file-a'm, he blackee coat. He take Missa Whela' he house, make him sit down with he wife and chil'en. Missa Whela' all-same pelison (prison); he wife he chil'en in Amelica; he cly—oh, he cly. Kekela he solly. One day Kekela he see ship. He say Missa Whela', "Ma Whela'?" Missa Whela' he say, "Yes?" Kanaka they begin go down beach. Kekela he get eleven Kanaka, get oa' (oars), get evely thing. He say Missa Whela', "Now go quick." They jump in whaleboat. "Now you low," Kekela he say, "you low quick, quick!" All the Kanaka they say, "How! 'melican mate he go away." "Jump in boat; low afta," Kekela he say, "low quick."

The above example is not an exact reproduction of the Beche le Mar jargon. But it can be used as a model to indicate how the word list given previously can be adapted for American understanding. In passing, it may be of interest to note that the "l" pronunciation of "r" was a throwback to the Chinese merchants from whom the Kanakas learned their Pidgin English which later became Beche le Mar. The following example, from the same source, is also revealing:

"Miss Stlevens he good man, woman he good man, boy he good man; all good man. Woman he smart all same man. My woman he good woman, no very smart. I think Miss Stlevens he big chiep (chief with the "f" changed to "p"). All same cap'n man-o-wa'. I think Miss Stlevens he rich man all same me. All go schoona. I very solly. My patha (father) he go, my uncle he go, my cutcheons (cousins) he go, Miss Stlevens he go: all go. You no see king cly before. King all same man; feel bad he cly. I very solly. Last night I no can 'peak; too much here. Now you go away all same my pamily. My blothers, my uncle go away. All same."

1.   *Reprinted by permission of Charles Scribner's Sons, New York.*

AUSTRALIAN PIDGIN

A list of Australian Pidgin words and phrases follows:

AMERICAN	AUSTRALIAN PIDGIN
abandon	"bin go"
acquaintance	"brother belong me"
acquire	"catchum"
all	"alla"
all right	"awright"
almost	"near finish"
am	"bin"
American, or any white person	"white fella"
anger	"him proper hot inside head"
another	"nudder"
any person	"um"
anything	"fella," "him," or "he"
anywhere	"out all about"
bad man	"snake fella"
break	"breakum"
breakfast	"tucker first time"
been	"bin"
before	"first time"
beside	"longa"—this is used for all designations of place
black woman	"lubra" or "gin"
bold	"cheeky"
bull	"bullamoocow" or cattle of any kind
call	"callum"
camp	"sit down"
change	"turnum nother side"
child	"piccaninny"
cloudy	"sun him go sleep"
come close	"come close up"
continuous	"no stopum"
crabby	"bad growl fella"
dangerous	"that one makum fright me"
dark	"longa sleep time"
dead	"properly close up finish"
desire	"likum hab dat"
discover	"findum"
distance	"little bit long way" or "big bit long way"
done	"bin done"
don't understand	"no savvee"

AMERICAN	AUSTRALIAN PIDGIN
employer	"boss"
evening	"close up sun go"
exhausted	"close up tired"
extra	"nudder"
finish	"no more do"
food	"tucker"
friend	"brother belong me"
frightened	"fright" or "fright belongum inside"
gee whizz	"my word!"
get	"getum" or "catchum"
give	"gib"
good man	"properly fella"
have	"hab"
he	"him" or "that fella"
hide	"tumbee"
high	"longa"
hills	"big fella stone"
horse	"yarraman" or "fellahorse"
house	"mia-mia"
I	"me" or the name of the speaker
is that all?	"no mo?"
it	"him," "he," or "that fella"
kill	"killum"
lake	"big fella watta"
large	"big fella"
later	"byumby"
lazy	"nothing do"
letter	"paper-talk"
like	"likum"
little	"bit" or "li'l"
luscious	"me like 't"
me	"me"
mine	"belongum me"
month	"one fella moon"
months or weeks	"many long time"
my	"belongum me"
nasty	"snake"
natives	"boys"
near	"close up"
no	"no savvee"
not	"nothing"
old	"no more too much strong"
other side	"nudder side"

AMERICAN	AUSTRALIAN PIDGIN
part of	"bit"
people	"mob"
perhaps	"might be" or "mightum"
policeman	"gubmint catchum fella"
preferable	"mo betta"
quickly	"too much quick"
real	"true"
same as	"allasame"
saw nothing	"bin no see"
sea	"big fella watta"
she	"him" or "that fella"
shoot	"shootum"
shriek	"sing out"
sing	"singum"
soon	"close up"
stomach	"belly belong me" or "bel-bel"
stranger	"new fella"
sunset	"sun him go sleep"
take	"takeum"
take it easy	"quiet, fella"
talk	"yabber-yabber"
that's all	"can no mo tell"
their	"that fella mob"
thing	"him" or "fella"
think	"tink"
thirst	"him belly allatime burn"
time	"hab mo plenty time"
understand	"savvee"
water	"watta"
we	"all"
wet season	"big fella rain"
what?	"what name?"
what's the	"wassa?" or "what name?"
where has he gone	"where him go?"
which way?	"what way walk-about?"
who	"what name?"
yes	"yah" or "yass"
yesterday	"day bin gone go"

A good example of Australian pidgin in action was reported by Carleton Kent in the *Chicago Daily Times* when he transcribed the reports of some black fellows who rescued American airplane pilots downed in the bush back-country. According to his report, they said:

Pickaninny daylight we three fella bin leave. We bin go along Blank Island, we bin come along one li'l fella creek, we bin go longa li'l creek; we bin go li'l longway alright. We fella wantum sit down talk talk now. Byumby one fella white man bin sing out alonga mangrove other side creek. We fella bin go alonga that side now. We bin hearum one fella white man singing out alla time alright. We fella bin go follerum up that one white man singing out. We bin find him. He up alonga tree. We fella bin lift him down. That one white man him close up. We fella bin go other side creek now, we bin cookum tucker. That man him properly hungry. He bin eatum tucker no more li'l bit. Alright we fella bin go along boat now. We bin go close up sundown now. We fella bin go alonga boat alright.

As Mr. Kent translated the above: "three aborigines took their boat up the creek quite a ways, then got out for a conference and heard a man shouting from the mangrove swamps across the stream. They found him in bad shape perched in a tree to avoid crocodiles and snakes. They walked him back to the boat, cooked him food which he wolfed down, then delivered him to a small boat."

CHAPTER FIFTEEN

The Swedish Dialect

THE SWEDISH LILT

The Swedish lilt has often been compared with the Chinese. The reason for this is that in Swedish—and in Norwegian—certain words may have two meanings according to the intonation. For example, the Norwegian word "kokken" (kAWkuhn) may mean either a male chef or a female chef. If *kokken* is pronounced with the "simple" intonation, that is with a rising intonation only, it signifies a male chef. But, if the word is pronounced with the "compound" intonation, that is with a short falling and then a rising intonation, it signifies a female chef.

The keynote of the Swedish pitch should be slightly higher than the American. The range, too, is wider because of the generous lilt and the singing quality of the vowels, particularly in the emphasized words. It is in this word emphasis that the Swedish dialect achieves much of its sing-songy lilt. In American, for example, we emphasize those words that are to be given relative importance over the other words in the sentence. The emphasis changes with the meaning intended, as in the sentence, "I'm walking *home*." If the speaker intended to mean that he is going, not to work or the theater but *home*, then he would emphasize home. If, however, he meant that he didn't care what the others were going to do, *he* was going home, then he would emphasize "I'm." And if he meant to say that he was not riding with the group, then he would emphasize the word "walking." Other reasons, of course, would compel these emphasis changes.

The Swede, however, does not use this form of emphasis. Instead, he gives practically all his words the same amount of stressed emphasis (with an extra burst of breath), endows the vowels in those stressed words with tonal emphasis (the emphasis of changing the musical note), and then over-emphasizes the meaning-word or words of the sentence with a combination of both the stressed and tonal emphasis. In the sentence, "I go home," for instance, the Swede would say **"EH gOH: hOH:m,"** emphasizing all three words but giving the last word, "home," over-emphasis, to indicate that he is not going downtown but home.

The lilt and inner-vowel glides can be observed in action from the following graphical representation of the speech pattern. For example, the sentence

"AY: vʊ:t lI:k tʊ: gOH: vi:t yʊ:."

(I would like to go with you.)

The inner vowel glide can easily be observed now. In the first word, "AY:," there was a considerable rise on the elongated vowel sound. In the third word, "lI:k" (lAH-EEk), both the "AH" and "EE" sounds rise. When broken down, the long "I" sound becomes "AH-EE." This "AH-EE" representation is used in the graph because it shows the glide more vividly than "I:." This sound will be discussed further under "Vowel Changes." In the sixth word, "vi:t," the elongated "i:" took a definite upward rise as did the last word, "yʊ:," on the umlaut vowel sound "ʊ ." The sentence was divided into three beats, the first beginning with "AY:," which started about two notes above the normal American keynote. The second beat began with the word "lAH-EEk" and started about one note below the keynote word "AY:." The third beat began with the word "vi:t" and it started about one note below the second-beat opening word, "lAH-EEk."

The combination of these three beats—each starting a note lower than the opening word of the previous beat and then taking a rising inflection, with the end of each beat taking a sudden drop to the lowered note of the opening word of the next beat—constitutes the Swedish sing-song lilt. The sing-song effect would be heightened considerably with the application of the previously mentioned stress and tonal emphasis.

The first word, "AY:," would receive both stress and tonal emphasis. The next word, "vʊ:t" would receive neither stress nor tonal emphasis. The word, "lAH-EEk," would then get the same degree of stressed and tonal emphasis given the first word, "AY:" and the following two words, "tʊ:" and "gOH:" would not be emphasized by stress or tone. But the next word, "vi:t," would receive the stressed and tonal *over*-emphasis. The last word, "yʊ:" would be thrown off with neither stress nor tonal emphasis.

In a simple sentence, the same elements that contribute to the sing-song can be observed. The sentence following, for example, would read:

"syEH: vAW:s yŮ:s dEH: pŮrtEH:As' ti:ng"
(She was just the prettiest thing.)

Again, it will be observed that, in all the four beats of the sentence, the keynote of each beat was begun lower than that of its previous beat. The same combination of falling key notes from which the beats glide upward to make the Swedish sing-song is also noticed in the question form of sentence:

"dOȞ:n yŮ: stEH: hEH:r?"
(Don't you stay here?)

The fact must be remembered, though, that a change in word emphasis, to change the meaning, could create a situation in which the keynote of a beat might not start below the keynote of the preceding beat. But, as a general rule, it does. And it is this rising-falling, sing-song speech pattern that is essential to the dialect even to the point of unendurable monotony. The rising inflection may be tempered slightly but it must always be present, even if it is only barely suggested. The sing-song lilt and the vowel-glide are important characteristics of the Swedish dialect—perhaps the most identifiable of its elements. The vowel glide is a matter of singing out the elongated vowel sound so that it glides from a low note to a high note or vice versa. Even among educated Swedish people there is a tendency to adhere to the speech habits of the commonplace native language. They may try to make a conscious effort to obliterate them from their speech but, in an off moment, the sing-song lilt and the vowel-glide will intrude to betray them.

EMPHASIS

The word emphasis has already been discussed in the preceding section. But in the syllabic emphasis, also, the Swedish dialect is distinctive in that, generally, it is the first syllable of a word that receives the emphasis. Thus, "terrible" would be accented on the American syllable "tEH," as in "**tA:ri:buhl**," and "prettiest" would be pronounced as "**pɄrt**EH:A:s." This habit has a tendency to endow the initial syllable with a lower pitch, which accounts, in part, for the gradual falling of the keynotes in the beat pitch discussed previously. The accented syllable gets considerably more stress than is usually given in American. Keep this stress rule in mind when studying the following sections on "Vowel" and "Consonant Changes," for it will aid considerably in acquiring an authentic Swedish dialect.

THE UMLAUT

Before going into the vowel changes, it will be necessary first to discuss the all-important Swedish umlaut treatment of certain of its vowel sounds. Like the German umlaut and the French "y," the Swedish umlaut is produced by pursing the lips as though to whistle and then making the required vowel sound. Care must be taken to make sure that this sound is not diphthongized. It must be simply an elongation of the same sound. If the vowel sound is long "o" (OH), it would be given the umlaut treatment with the lips pursed and the sound produced may be either "OH" or the vowel sound of the American word "curb." See "OH" in "Vowel Changes." The umlaut vowel sounds will be indicated by a line drawn through the letter, as in "Ʉ " and "OH."

NOTE: The flavor of the Swedish dialect for most sounds can be best achieved by curling the tip of the tongue back toward the center of the roof of the mouth, instead of using the normal American position.

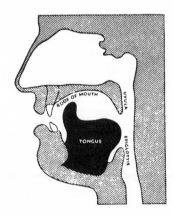

For the Swedish curled tongue effect, notice that the tip of the tongue is curled upward instead of being extended forward. This is the position the tongue takes in pronouncing the Swedish vowels.

VOWEL CHANGES

"AY" .... as in "take," "break," "they," etc.

Long "a," in Swedish, is changed to short "e," "EH." But the sound is elongated so that, actually, the pronunciation becomes "EH-EH," as in "tEH-EHk" (take).

For simplification, however, this elongated vowel sound will be written as "EH:," the (:) sign indicating the elongation, as in "tEH:k" (take). A variation retains this long "a" sound, as it is in American, but elongates it more than the American usually does, so that "take" becomes "tAY:k." Either sound is acceptable although the "EH:" is more typical.

DRILL WORDS

hEH:	(hey)		fEH:s	(face)
nEH:m	(name)		kEH:k	(cake)
sEH:	(say)		dEH:	(they)
	mEH:bEH:	(maybe)		
	pEH:strEH:	(pastry)		
	vEH:kEH:t	(vacate)		

"UH" .... as in "alone," "sofa," "final," etc.

This muted "a," treated as "UH" in American, is changed to **AH** in Swedish, as in "AHlOH:n" (alone). The vowel sound should not be elongated but should be given the same duration as in American. The "UH" may be retained for a lighter dialect.

DRILL WORDS

sOH:fAH	(sofa)		AHbAOOt	(about)
AHvEH:	(away)		pAHrEH:t	(parade)
sAHlℲ:t	(salute)		lAHpA:l	(lapel)
	hℲ:sbAHn'	(husband)		
	bAHnEH:nAH	(banana)		
	mAHli:syℲ:s	(malicious)		

"AH" .... as in "father," "arm," "park," etc.

The Swedish pursing of the lips changes this vowel sound from "AH" to the "A:" of "bad," the (:) sign indicating elongation, as in "fA:duhr" (father). Some Swedish people use the "U" sound of "up" and elongate it, as in "fℲ:r" (far), "fℲ:duhr" (father) and "pℲ:m" (palm). The "A:" is preferred.

DRILL WORDS

A:rms	(arms)	fA:r	(far)	A:rti:kℲ:l	(article)
A:ms	(alms)	dA:rk	(dark)	gA:rduhn	(garden)
pA:m	(palm)	kA:r	(car)	mA:rkuht	(market)

"A:" .... as in "ask," "draft," "laugh," etc.

In the Swedish, this "a" is changed to "EH:," the (:) sign indicating elongation, as in "EH:sk" (ask). A variant is "AH:," as in "pAH:s" (pass). The treatment of this "AH" is different from the American in that the Swedes elongate the vowel on two notes. This is typical of most of the Swedish elongated vowel sounds.

DRILL WORDS

pEH:s	(pass)		drEH:ft	(draft)
pEH:t	(path)		lEH:fi:ng	(laughing)
hEH:f	(half)		lEH:st	(last)

bEH:skuht	(basket)
EH:ftuhr	(after)
grEH:s	(grass)

"A" .... as in "bad," "am," "narrow," etc.

This shorter "a," too, is treated as "EH:" and is elongated, as in "bEH:t" (bad).

DRILL WORDS

bEH:t	(bad)		hEH:pEH:	(happy)
EH:m	(am)		nEH:rOH:	(narrow)
sEH:t	(sad)		pEH:k	(pack)

pEH:duhl	(paddle)
pEH:lAH:s	(palace)
nEH:pi:ng	(napping)

"AW" .... as in "ball," "falter," "shawl," etc.

This rounded "AW" is changed to the "O" of "rod," as in "bO:l" (ball), the (:) sign indicating elongation. Remember to bring up the sound from deep in the throat. For a lighter dialect, the "AW" sound may be retained but the lips should then be pursed more than in American.

DRILL WORDS

kO:l	(call)		O:tOH:	(auto)
syO:l	(shawl)		skvO:l	(squall)
fO:l	(fall)		kO:t	(caught)

O:lvEH:s	(always)
nO:tEH:	(naughty)
tO:t	(taught)

"EE" .... as in "he," "treat," "people," etc.

In Swedish, this long "e" sound is flattened into "EH:," as in "hEH:" (he). But, again, the sound is not the shortened short "e" sound of the American "get" but an elongated treatment so that, actually, the pronunciation becomes "hEH-EH" (he). Here, though, the elongation will be indicated with the (:) sign. For a lighter dialect, the American long "e" sound (EE) may be retained. Another substitution changes long "e" to "AY:," as in "fAY:r" (fear), "kO:fAY:" (coffee), and "klAY:n" (clean) but "EH:" is preferred.

DRILL WORDS

syEH:	(she)		hEH:r	(here)
fEH:r	(fear)		grEH:n	(green)
bEH:	(be)		pEH:puhl	(people)

$$bEHlEH:v \quad \text{(believe)}$$
$$EH:vni:ng \quad \text{(evening)}$$
$$kO:fEH: \quad \text{(coffee)}$$

"EH" .... as in "bet," "said," "friend," etc.

This short "e" is flattened out in the Swedish to the "A:" of "bat," as in "gA:t" (get), the (:) sign indicating elongation. Although "A:" is preferred, "AY:" may also be used, as in "sAY:t" (said).

DRILL WORDS

sA:l	(sell)		frA:nt	(friend)
syA:t	(shed)		mA:nt	(meant)
mA:n	(men)		jA:lOʜ	(yellow)

O:lrA:tEH:	(already)
plA:ntEH:	(plenty)
yA:l℧:s	(jealous)

"I" .... as in "ice," "aisle," "guile," etc.

Ordinarily, the Swedish people do not diphthongize their vowels. But they find it impossible to pronounce long "i" without sounding it as "AH-EE," not with the two vowel sounds run together, as in American, but with the two sounds pronounced separately. Both receive the elongated treatment so that the entire vowel sound is held almost twice as long as it is in American. From now on, though, the phonetic representation for it will be "I:" but the fact must be remembered that the "AH:" and the "EE:" are pronounced separately.

The "U-EE" sound is a variation, in which the light "U" of "up" is used rather than "AH."

DRILL WORDS

I:s	(ice)		rI:t	(right)
I:l	(aisle)		prI:s	(prize)
gI:l	(guile)		stI:l	(style)

kvI:AtlEH:	(quietly)
rEH:mI:nt	(remind)
fI:nduhr	(finder)

NOTE: The Swedish pronunciation of the personal pronoun, "I," as "AY," has given rise to an erroneous belief that all Swedish long "i's" are sounded as long "a." A possible reason for this seeming inconsistency—for many Swedes do sound the pronoun "I" as "AY" and long "i" as "I:"—may be that the Swedes adopted the Norwegian word for the personal pronoun "I," which is "yeg," pronounced "yAY" in Norwegian, and having heard the Norwegians pronounce "I" as "AY" thought it to be correct. Or they may have retained this "AY" sound from their own word, "mig," pronounced "mAY," which means, literally, "me." Although "AY" is often used, "EH:" may also be substituted for the personal pronoun "I" but it should be brought up from deep in the throat, as are most of the Swedish vowel sounds.

"i" .... as in "it," "women," "busy," etc.

This short "i" sound, in Swedish, retains its American pronunciation but it should be elongated so that it becomes "i-i-it" (it). Here, it will be designated simply as: "i:" the (:) sign indicating the elongation.

"O" .... as in "on," "bond," "John," etc.

This short "o" is broadened slightly to "AW:," in the Swedish, as in "AW:n" (on). It should also be elongated. The American "O" sound, in "rod," may also be used but it should be elongated more than usual.

DRILL WORDS

bAW:nt	(bond)	sAW:li:t	(solid)
hAW:t	(hot)	mAW:dɰrn	(modern)
gAW:t	(got)	drAW:p	(drop)
	hAW:li:dEH:	(holiday)	
	kAW:ndi:syɰn	(condition)	
	kAW:li:k	(cholic)	

"OH" .... as in "bone," "sew," "dough," etc.

This long "o" is the first vowel sound that receives a definite umlaut treatment as was explained under the "Umlaut" section. It may retain its usual long "o" sound of "OH" but it is pronounced with the lips tensely pursed and with the sound brought up from deep in the throat. This is the preferred sound. Another accepted substitution of long "o" is "AW:," as in "bAW:n" (bone), "sAW:" (sew) and "dAW:" (dough). The lips should again be pursed for this sound. Remember, also, not to give it the vanishing "OO" glide, but to elongate it.

DRILL WORDS

sO͡H:	(so)	fA:lO͡H:	(fellow)
nO͡H:	(no)	mO͡Htuhr	(motor)
dO͡H:	(though)	kO͡H:t	(coat)
	klO͡H:ding	(clothing)	
	hO͡H:pfɰl	(hopeful)	
	nO͡Hti:s	(notice)	

"AW" .... as in "off," "cough," "bought," etc.

This vowel sound is flattened in the Swedish dialect so that it becomes "O," as in "rod" and is pronounced "O:f" (off). The elongation is applied here, too. The American "AW" may also be used with the lips pursed.

DRILL WORDS

kO:f	(cough)	fO:t	(fought)
bO:t	(bought)	O:f'n	(often)
hO:tEH:	(haughty)	kO:fi:n	(coffin)
	kO:s'	(cost)	
	vO:tuhr	(water)	
	krO:l	(crawl)	

"OO" .... as in "food," "do," "blue," etc.

This long double "o" (OO) is one of the most important vowel-sound changes in the Swedish dialect. It, too, uses the umlaut. The lips are pursed and the sound of "EE" is brought up from deep in the throat. The vowel sound will be designated as "ɰ," as in "fɰ:t" (food). Remember always to elongate.

DRILL WORDS

dƱ:	(do)	mƱ:n	(moon)
hƱ:	(who)	sƱ:t	(suit)
nƱ:	(knew)	syƱ:s	(shoes)

sAHlƱ:n (saloon)
nƱ:spEH:puhr (newspaper)
skƱ:l (school)

"oo" .... as in "good," "wolf," "full," etc.

This short double "o" (oo) is changed to umlaut "Ʊ" as in "gƱ:t (good).

DRILL WORDS

lƱ:k	(look)	vƱ:t	(would)
pƱ:s	(push)	syƱ:t	(should)
kƱ:k	(cook)	fƱ:t	(foot)

kA:rfƱ:l (careful)
spƱ:nfƱ:l (spoonful)
hƱ:dvi:nk (hoodwink)

"yOO" .... as in "unit," "cube," "beauty," etc.

This vowel sound retains its consonantal "y" initial sound but the long double "o" (OO) sound is umlauted and elongated, as in "yƱ:ni:t" (unit).

DRILL WORDS

yƱ:s	(use)	yƱ:nIt	(unite)
myƱ:si:k	(music)	kyƱ:t	(cute)
kyƱ:b	(cube)	pyƱ:r	(pure)

pi:ktyƱ:r (picture)
kAW:styƱ:m (costume)
vAW:lyƱ:m (volume)

"U" .... as in "up," "love," "does," etc.

This vowel sound is also umlauted with the "Ʊ:" substitute, as in "Ʊ:p" (up). A variation uses a deep "AW:" that is elongated, but the former is preferred.

DRILL WORDS

sƱ:n	(sun)	dƱ:s	(does)
dƱ:n	(done)	trƱ:k	(truck)
lƱ:v	(love)	sƱ:puhr	(supper)

pƱ:bli:s (publish)
hƱ:sbAHn' (husband)
sƱ:spi:syƱ:s (suspicious)

"ER" .... as in "curb," "earn," "fern," etc.

The preferred substitution for this vowel sound, which applies to all the "ir," "er," "ur" and "or" combinations, is "Ʊ:," as in "kƱ:rb" (curb), "vƱ:rk" (work), "lƱ:rn" (learn) and "gƱ:rl" (girl). But there are some Swedes who treat it as an umlauted "ER," as in "vERk" (work).

DRILL WORDS

hƱ:rt	(hurt)	syƱ:rt	(shirt)
bƱ:rt	(bird)	tƱ:rst	(thirst)
vƱ:rt	(word)	pƱ:rpuhl	(purple)

sƱ:rtuhn   (certain)
tƱ:rsdEH: (Thursday)
di:stƱ:rb   (disturb)

"OW" .... as in "out," "cow," "house," etc.

This diphthong may remain the same as it is in American but it should be elongated. Both parts of the diphthong are pronounced "AH-OO." However, they should each be pronounced on a different note, and the "AH" should receive greater stress. The diphthong may also be changed to "A-OO." Here the sound should be brought up from deep in the throat and elongated so that the two parts, "A" and "OO," are sounded on different notes. In this combination the "A" receives greater stress.

DRILL WORDS

kAOO	(cow)	mAOOt	(mouth)
nAOO	(now)	lAOOt	(loud)
hAOOs	(house)	syAOOt	(shout)

kAOOn'   (count)
tAOOsuhns   (thousands)
mAOOntuhns   (mountains)

"OI" .... as in "oil," "boy," "noise," etc.

This diphthong, in American, is pronounced as "AW-EE," with both parts of the sound receiving equal stress and elongation. In Swedish, however, the same sound is used but the first part of the diphthong, "AW," is elongated and stressed more than the second part, "EE." Both parts are sounded on different notes. The familiar "OI" symbol will be used to designate this diphthong in the dialect.

DRILL WORDS

bOI	(boy)	rOI-AHl	(royal)
nOIs	(noise)	AHnOI	(annoy)
vOIs	(voice)	spOIuhl	(spoil)

A:nyOI   (enjoy)
gOItuhr   (goiter)
A:mbrOIduhr   (embroider)

WORD EXERCISES

Pronounce the following words using the material learned from the preceding vowel changes:

1. clean
2. doctor
3. housemaid

11. coffeepot
12. June
13. worry

4.	mineral	14.	everything
5.	lunch basket	15.	broil
6.	father-in-law	16.	woman
7.	Japanese	17.	man
8.	German	18.	oil-burner
9.	American	19.	vacation
10.	find	20.	particle

When the above words have been pronounced, refer to the phonetic list below for verification or corrections. Then repeat the words with the correct pronunciation.

1.	klEH:n	11.	kO:fEH:pAW:t
2.	dAW:ktuhr	12.	j𝒰:n
3.	hAOOsmEH:t	13.	v𝒰:rEH:
4.	mi:n𝒰rAHl	14.	A:vrEH:ti:ng or
5.	l𝒰:nshbEH:skuht		AY:vrEH:ti:ng
6.	fA:duhri:nlO:	15.	brOIl
7.	yEH:pAHnEH:s	16.	v𝒰:mAHn
8.	y𝒰rmAHn	17.	mEH:n
9.	AHmA:ri:kAHn or	18.	OIlb𝒰:rnuhr
	AHmAY:ri:kAHn	19.	vEHkEH:syuhn
10.	fI:n'	20.	pA:rti:k𝒰l or
			pU:rti:k𝒰l

CONSONANT CHANGES

Note: All initial consonants, and especially "f" and "h," are pronounced more forcefully than in American.

B—Pronounced as in American. Final "b" is weak and often sounds like a soft "p."

C—Both hard and soft forms pronounced as in American.

D—The Swedish "d" is dentalized, the tip of the tongue being placed against the cutting edges of the upper front teeth instead of at the forward part of the roof of the mouth, as in American. This thickens the pronounciation so that the sound produced is a combination of "d" and voiced "TH." Final "d" often becomes "t," as in "sEH:*t*" (sa*d*), "prAOO*t*" (prou*d*), and "v𝒰rt (wor*d*). (See illustration, page 272.)

F—Pronounced as in American.

G—The hard form of "g" should be pronounced as in American. For the soft form, see "J."

H—Pronounced as in American but more forcefully when it is initial.

J—This is the consonant sound with which most Swedish comedians create their comedy effects. Initially, it is changed to the consonant "y" sound, as in "*y*𝒰:n"

(June) and "yEH:k" (Jack). Medially, it may also become "y," but for a lighter dialect it is suggested that soft "g" or "j" change to "s," as in "dEH:nʃuhr" (danger) and "lEH:syⱰn" (legion). Finally, the consonant "j" is changed to "sh," as in "gAHrA:*sh*" (garage) and "bEH:gi:*sh*" (baggage).

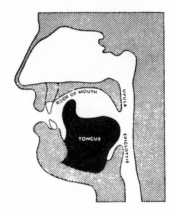

The tongue tip, pressed against the backs of the front teeth, introduces into the "d" sound a very slight additional "TH." The American "d" is produced by touching the gum ridge of the upper front teeth with the tongue tip.

K—Pronounced as in American.

L—Pronounced as in American but with a more energetic attack.

M and **N**—Pronounced as in American.

P—Pronounced as in American but with greater force.

Q—Instead of the usual "kw" treatment given the consonant sound "q" in American, the Swedish dialect sounds it as "kv," as in "*kv*i:k" (*q*uick) or "rEH:*kv*I:r" (re-*qu*ire), initially and medially. Finally, it receives its usual "k" treatment.

R—The Swedish "r" is trilled with the tip of the tongue but it should be very short.

S—The consonant "s" is pronounced as it is in American except that its sibilance should be more energetic and forceful.

T—Like "d," the consonant "t" is dentalized with the tip of the tongue laid against the cutting edges of the upper front teeth, instead of at the forward part of the roof of the mouth, as in American. The dentalization is not very pronounced, as it is in Spanish, so it will not be indicated here phonetically. It is dropped, finally, when it is followed by a word beginning with a "d," "t" or "th," as in "sEH:' *d*AOOn" (sa*t* down), "mI:' *t*rI:" (migh*t* try) and "hEH:' *d*EH:t" (hea*t* that.)

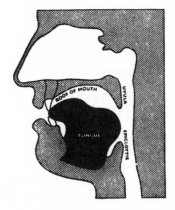

The tongue tip, pressed against the backs of the front teeth, introduces into the "t" sound a very slight additional "TH." The American "t" is produced by touching the gum ridge of the upper front teeth with the tongue tip.

V—Pronounced as in American.

W—The Swedish people pronounce "w" as "v" and this is carried over into the dialect as well, as in "*vⱰ:*rld" (*w*orld), "AH*v*EH:" (a*w*ay) and "nOH:*v*A:r" (no*w*here).

X—Pronounced as in American.

Y—Pronounced as in American. Sometimes, however, it is pronounced as "j," as in "jA:lOH" (*y*ellow).

Z—The consonant "z" is never pronounced as "z" in Swedish. Therefore, when it is spelled "s," as in "has" or "z," as in "puzzle," a sibilant "s" should be used, as in "hEH:*s*" (ha*s*), "bi:*s*EH:" (bu*s*y) and "pⱰ:*s*uhl" (pu*zz*le).

SH—The "sh" combination is often pronounced as "sy," as in "*sy*O:l" (*sh*awl), "pEH:*sy*uhn" (pa*ss*ion) and "rEH*s*" (ra*sh*), the final "sh" being pronounced only as "s." For a lighter dialect it may retain its "sh" sound in words which are spelled with the "sh" such as "shawl," and may remain "sy" for words spelled with "s" such as "passion."

TCH—Many Swedish people substitute an "sh" for this "tch," as in "*sh*Ⱶr*sh*" (*ch*ur*ch*) and "kEH:*sh*" (ca*tch*). Still, there are a great many who give it the normal "tch" sound.

TH—The voiced "TH," in Swedish, is treated as "d" (see "D" at the beginning of this section), as in "dEH:" (*th*e), "bEH:*d*" (ba*th*e) and "bEH:*di*:ng" (ba*th*ing). When it is used finally and comes before a word beginning with "d," "t" or "th," it is dropped, as in "bEH:' *d*EH:t" (bathe *th*at).

th—The unvoiced "th" in Swedish, is changed to "t" (refer back to "T" in this section), and will be found in such words as "ti:nk" (*th*ink), etc. When this unvoiced "th" comes at the end of a word and is followed by a word beginning with "d," "t" or "th," it is dropped, as in "EH: brA:' dEH:t" (a breath that).

ZH—This consonant sound, as found in "azure" and "vision," is treated as "sy" in the dialect, as in "EH:*syƲr*" (azure) and "vi:*syƲn*" (vi*s*ion).

ER—When "er" is used at the end of a word, it does not get the full "U" umlaut sound but usually "uh," as in "vO:tuhr" (water).

LE or **EL**—Words ending with this combination take the aspirate "uh," as in "lEH:buhl" (label) and "pAW:si:buhl" (possible).

PRE and **PRO**—When either "pre" or "pro" is used at the beginning of a word, it usually becomes "pƲr" with the umlaut "Ʋ," as in "pƲrtEH:" (pretty), "pƲrdi:kt" (predict), "pƲrpA:r" (prepare), "pƲrvI:t" (provide) and "pƲrtA:kt" (protect).

WORD EXERCISES

Pronounce the following words using the material learned from the preceding consonant section:

1.	jazz	11.	shipwreck
2.	yet	12.	queer
3.	dungeon	13.	joke
4.	this	14.	kitchen
5.	pathway	15.	mad
6.	purple	16.	without
7.	provoke	17.	wish
8.	bedroom	18.	chicken
9.	treasure	19.	cradle
10.	hotter	20.	porch

When the above words have been pronounced, refer to the phonetic list on the following page for verification or corrections. Then repeat the words with the correct pronunciation.

1.	yEH:s	11.	syi:prA:k
2.	yA:t or jA:t	12.	kvi:r
3.	dƲ:nyƲn or dƲ:nsyƲn	13.	yOHk
4.	di:s	14.	ki:shuhn
5.	pEH:twEH:	15.	mEH:t
6.	pƲ:rpuhl	16.	vi:dAOOt
7.	pƲrvOH:k	17.	vi:s
8.	bA:trU:m	18.	shi:kuhn
9.	trA:syƲ:r	19.	krEH:duhl
10.	hAW:tuhr	20.	pO:rsh

GRAMMAR CHANGES

There are few actual grammar changes in the Swedish dialect that are typical of the Swedish language which is constructed, grammatically, like the American. The errors that are present are similar to those found in the more illiterate American speech. One of the common errors comes with the verb forms. There seems to be a tendency to use the present tense where the past is intended, as in:

"yAH! EH gOH: dA:r."
(Yah! I *go* there.)
(Yes! I *went* there.)

"vEH: hEH:r hi:m lEH:s' nI:t."
(We *hear* him last night.)
(We *heard* him last night.)

"vI: di:'n yʊ dʊ lI:k EH tA:l yʊ?"
(Why didn't you do like I *tell* you?)
(Why didn't you do as I *told* you?)

The above example also illustrates the error of substituting "as" for "like." There is too, a tendency to misuse the verbs "is," "am" and "are," as in:

"syEH A:r dEH: pʊrtEH:As' ti:ng."
(She *are* the prettiest thing.)
(She *is* the prettiest thing.)

"EH A:r sOH: hEH:pEH."
(I *are* so happy.)
(I *am* so happy.)

The above may not be so much an error in grammar as it is a carry over from the Swedish language. For, in the language, the three words, "am," "is," and "are" are all the same "är," pronounced "EHr."

When the past tense of a verb is used, it is sometimes given the wrong number, as in:

"vEH: vAW:s vEH:ti:ng."
(We *was* waiting.)
(We *were* waiting.)

"dEH: vAW:s nAW:t hOH:m."
(They *was* not home.)
(They *were* not home.)

The words "so" and "like" used as comparatives, are often misused, as in:

"syEH: vAW:s sOH: hEH:pEH lI:k AnEHti:ng."
(She was *so* happy *like* anything.)
(She was *as* happy *as* anything.)

"hEH: vAW:s sOH: mEH:t lI:k EH dOH:'nOH: vAW:t."
(He was *so* mad *like* I don't know what.)
(He was *as* mad *as* I don't know what.)

Pronouns are often ignored, as in:

"vAW:t hEH: sEH: i:n lA:tuhr?"
(What he say in letter?)
(What does he say in *his* letter?)

Articles, too, are left out, as in:

"vEH: A:r i:n bi:g bOH:t."
(We are in big boat.)
(We are in *a* big boat.)

"hEH: gOH: tʊ stOH:r."
(He go to store.)
(He went to *the* store.)

At this time, it is necessary to mention the word "bane" which, according to a great many Swedish dialect experts, should be wedged in whenever there is the slightest opportunity. Actually, few Swedes use it. At some time, some comedian may have heard a Swede say, "EH bEHn ti:nki:ng" (I been thinking), which is an error in grammar common to many illiterate Americans. The comedian's assumption was that all Swedes use "been" all the time instead of "am," "was" or "is." Actually, "bEH:n" should be used only when the occasion calls for it and at no other time.

SENTENCE EXERCISES

Pronounce the following sentences in the Swedish dialect, paying special attention to the material learned from the preceding grammar section:

1. I listened to the radio last night.
2. We were wishing you were here.
3. They were as quiet as mice.
4. She went to the store but it was closed.
5. John is as cross as a bear.
6. Lily is waiting for the jam to jell.
7. He said to wait in the house.
8. Why don't you do as he did?
9. They asked me to do it but I told them no.
10. She came to my house with the prettiest hat you ever saw.

When the above sentences have been practiced, refer to the phonetics below for verification or corrections. Then practice the above sentences again using the Swedish grammatical constructions.

1. EH li:suhn tʊ rEH:diOH lEH:s' nI:.
2. vEH: vAW:s vi:syi:ng yʊ vAW:s hEH:r.
3. dEH: vAW:s sOH: kvI:At lI:k mI:s.
4. syEH: gOH: tʊ stO:r bʊ:t i:t vʊ:r klOH:st.
5. yAW:n A:r sOH: krO:s lI:k AH bA:r.
6. li:lEH A:r vEH:ti:ng fOr yEH:m tʊ yA:l.
7. hEH: sEH: tʊ vEH:t i:n hAOOs.
8. vI: dOH:n' yʊ dʊ lI:k hEH: di:t?
9. dEH: EH:sk mEH: tʊ dʊ i:t bʊ:t I: tA:l dA:m nOH:.
10. syEH: kAW:m tʊ mI: hAOOs vi:t duh pʊrtEH: As' hEH:t lI:k yʊ
    A:vuhr sEH:n.

SWEDISH LANGUAGE CARRYOVERS

hello	*god dag*	gʊ *dAH*
goodbye	*adjo*	AH*dyʊ*
excuse me	*ursakta*	ʊrsEH*k*tAH
thank you	*tack*	tUk
yes	*ja*	yAH
no	*nej*	nAY
how do you do?	*hur star det till*	hʊr stAWr dEHt til

SWEDISH MONOLOG

"LULLABY FOR A WAR BABY"

(*Adapted from a character in the authors' scripts for "Your Dream Has Come True" over NBC.*)

(*She bends over the crib and, as she tucks her baby into his bed, she whispers softly to him:*)

Sleep, baby. Soon, mother she will hear your father talk on the radio. Wouldn't that be nice? Maybe you hear him talk too, yah. The papers say they hook up tonight from the island where father is now and maybe the soldiers they say something. My, I hope father will be there. He got big, strong voice. He big man, too, yah sure. Maybe some day you grow up so big like him, yah. Won't he be surprise when he come home. You was two weeks old when he saw you last. Now you almost nine month. My, he be tickle. Yah, I just see him walking in the door. He ... wait! here is the program. Oh, my goodness! I hope they get the right island! The one with your father! Now they hook up. In just a minute, maybe, we hear your father talk. Ssssh! Oley, sssh! Be quiet! Yah! is father! Oh my goodness, it's all over now! Just couple words he say and you got to cry and we don't hear what he say! Oh! Oley! Oley!

PHONETIC REPRESENTATION

(The bold-face syllables are to be emphasized.)

"slEH:· ᵉEHp   EHbEH   sƱ:n   .duhr   vi:l
                  bEH: mƱ:·'   syEH: hEH:r"

yƱr **fA**:duhr tO:k AW:n dEH: **rEH**:diOⱮ:. vƱ:'n dEH:t bEH: **nI**:s? mEH:bEH y**Ʊ**:
hEH:r hi:m tO:k t**Ʊ**: , **yAH**. dEH: **pEH**:puhr sEH: dEH: h**Ʊ**:k Ʊp tƱ**nI**:t frAW:m
dEH: I:lAHn' vA:r **fA**:duhr i:s nAOO EH:n' **mEH**:bEH dEH s**OⱮ**:l' yuhs dEH:
sEH: sƱ:mti:ng. **mI**:, EH h**OⱮ**:p **fA**:duhr vi:l bEH: **dA**:r. hEH: gAW:t **bi**:g,
strO:ng **vOI**s. hEH **bi**:g **mEH**:n, tƱ, **yAH** sy**Ʊ**:r. **mEH**:bEH: s**Ʊ**:mdEH: y**Ʊ**
grOⱮ: Ʊp sOⱮ: **bi**:g lI:k hi:m, **yAH**. vƱ: 'n' hEH: bEH: sƱ:**rprI**:s vA:n hEH: k**Ʊ**:m
h**OⱮ**:m. yƱ: vAW:s t**Ʊ**: vEH:ks **OⱮ**:l' vA:n hEH: sO: yƱ: **lEH**:s'. **nAOO** yƱ:
O:lmOⱮ:s' **nI**:n m**Ʊ**:nt. **mI**:, hEH: bEH: **ti**:kuhl'. **yAH**, EH y**Ʊ**s' **sEH**: hi:m
vO:ki:ng i:n dEH: **dOⱮ**:r. hEH:. . .**vEH**:t! hEH:r i:s dEH: **pOⱮ**:grEH:m. **OⱮ**: **mI**:
g**Ʊ**:**nA**:s! EH: h**OⱮ**:p dEH: gA:t dEH: **rI**:t I:lAHn'! dEH: v**Ʊ**:n vi:t y**Ʊ**:r **fA**:duhr!
nAOO dEH: h**Ʊ**:k **Ʊ**:p. i:n y**Ʊ**:s' EH mi:n**Ʊ**:t, **mEH**:bEH:, vEH: hEH:r y**Ʊ**:r
fA:duhr tO:k. **ssssh! OⱮ**:lEH:, **ssssh!** bEH: kvI:At! **yAH!** i:s **fA**:duhr! OH mI:
g**Ʊ**:**nA**:s, i:ts O:l **OⱮ**vuhr nAOO! y**Ʊ**:s' **kƱ**:puhl v**Ʊ**:rts hEH: sEH: EH:n' y**Ʊ**;
gAW:' tƱ: **krI**: EH:n vEH: **dOⱮ**:n' hEH:r vAW:t hEH: **sEH**: OH:! **OⱮ** :lEH:!
OⱮ:lEH:!

THE NORWEGIAN DIALECT

Although there are definite similarities between the Swedish and the Norwegian dialects, there are also differences. Most actors, though, use the Swedish dialect to cover all Scandinavians—to the natural annoyance of all Scandinavians. But for the actor who is meticulous enough to want to give a reasonably exact replica of the Norwegian dialect, the following changes are listed.

There are three symbols indicating umlauts given below: "OH," "𝒰" and "ER." The "OH" sound is produced with the lips pursed for whistling while "OH" is being sounded. The "𝒰" sound also keeps the lips pursed for the sound of "EE." The "ER" sound retains the pursed lips while the "ir" sound of "fir" is produced.

VOWEL CHANGES

VOWEL SOUND	WORD		SUBSTITUTE	DIALECT
AY	take		EH:	tEH:k
UH	sofa		AH	sOHfAH
	alone		dropped initially	'lOHn
AH	father		AH	fAHdUHr
A:	ask		AH	AHsk
A	bad		AH	bAHd
AW	ball		AW	bAWl
EE	he		EE	hEE
	he	*also*	i	hi
EH	get		A	gAt
I	ice		I:	I:s
i	it		i	it
O	on		AW	AWn
OH	bone		OH	bOHn
AW	off		AW	AWf
OO	food		𝒰	f𝒰d
oo	good		𝒰	g𝒰d
yOO	unit		y𝒰	y𝒰nit
U	up		ER	ERp
	up	*also*	AW	AWp
ER	curb		ER	kERb
OW	now		AW-OO	nAW-OO
OI	oil		AW-EE	AW-EEl

NOTE: Initially, the "yOO" of "unit" is pronounced as "y𝒰." But medially, the pronunciation of this "u" is often governed by the addition or omission of the letter "i." Thus, the word "view" would be pronounced as "vy𝒰" but the word "populate" would be pronounced as "pAWp𝒰lEH:t," without the initial "y."

It must be remembered that in Norwegian—as in Swedish and Italian—the vowels are lengthened. But in the lengthening, do not broaden the mouth. The number of umlauts in the Norwegian language tends to flavor many of the other vowel sounds. To simulate this coloring, try to place your mouth in a puckered position. But do not keep it actually pursed or pouting all the time. Prepare for it mentally and it can be put across orally.

Internal vowels that are weakly sounded in American are usually dropped in the Norwegian, as in "kAWm'n" (common), "s'prAs" (suppress) and "fAHkt'ri" (factory).

Like the Swedish people, the Norwegians do not diphthongize their vowel sounds. When they are lengthened, the elongation must be solely on the original monosyllable.

Following is a list of typical consonant changes:

When "b," "d," "g" or "v" are followed by "s" or "t" they are changed to "p," "t," "k" and "f," respectively, as in "AW*p*tEH:n" (o*b*tain), "g*Ʋt*ss" (goo*d*s), "rAH*k*tI:m" (ra*g*time) and "lAW*f*sik" (lo*v*esick).

D—Usually silent with another consonant, as in "sAHn's" (san*d*s). Usually dropped finally, as in "AHn'" (and).

F—Many Norwegians do not give this consonant a clear "f" sound. Instead, they pronounce it as "h" in the correct pronunciation of the American word "h-wI" (why).

G—Finally, it is formed but not sounded, as in "bi'" (big).

J—Pronounced as "y," as in "yAWs'" (just), or as "zh," as in "zhAW-EEn" (join).

R—Strongly trilled unless it is followed by "l," "n" or "t," when it is not trilled but sounded as in American.

The uvular "r" (or guttural "r") may be used for Norwegians from Stavanger or Bergen.

S—Always hissed.

W—Changed to "v," as in "vEE" (we).

Z—Always a hissed "s," as in "his*s*" (hi*z*).

TH—Changed to "d," as in "*d*EE" (*th*e).

th—Changed to "t," as in "*t*ink" (*th*ink).

The above consonant changes are the most common. However, an interesting variation for the unvoiced "th" of "think" may be "s," as in "*s*ink" (*th*ink and "mAWn*s*" (mon*th*). If the "s" for "th" is used, then the voiced "TH" (of "the") would not be substituted with a "d" but would receive a "z" treatment, as in "*z*EE" (*th*e).

The Norwegian lilt is a modified form of the Swedish lilt. There is not as much sing-song to it but what there is, is delivered with a more forceful emphasis and the rhythm is not as smooth. The pitch range of the Norwegian does not vary as greatly as it does in the Swedish.

Norwegians are among the few groups of people who, as a rule, drop their dialect very quickly. This ready adaptability to American speech must be kept in mind when a Norwegian character is to be portrayed.

CHAPTER SIXTEEN

The Russian Dialect

THE RUSSIAN LILT

Generally speaking, the Russian possesses a rich, warm, throaty voice—much like that of the African American. Like the African American, the timbre of his voice is of the resonant kind that comes up from deep in the chest.

He pitches his voice quite low and the presence of a great many guttural sounds in his language helps to bring the pitch down. Even the women speak in a lower pitch—much lower than American women—which accounts for the preponderance of contraltos over sopranos in Russia.

The Russian's tonal range varies widely, even causing him to become, in moments of excitement, a falsetto tenor. But, in the main, his voice is guttural and in the lower registers. He enriches and broadens his vowels and uses them to carry a slight upward glide for a combination of tonal and stressed emphasis. The glide does not, however, in any way compare with the Italian or Swedish vowel glide. It is of lesser range and is of broader duration, as in the sentence:

I nAWtTH sAW gOOtTH filyEEnk."
(I not so good feeling.)
(I do not feel very well.)

Starting his keynote off about three notes lower than in American, the Russian would sing:

The keynote, it will be observed, is repeated as the opening note of the first three beats in the sentence. Although not shown here in every vowel but the one, in "sAW," there is a rising inflection of about one note, the duration of the note being much longer than in American. It must also be remembered that the emphasis is placed on the high note of each beat with a slight over emphasis on the next-to-the-last vowel, "i," in "filyEEnk."

This tendency of vowel elongation makes for a slower tempo in Russian speech. This slow pace is abetted by the fact that, because he is unsure of the American language, the Russian pauses considerably to grope for the right word.

EMPHASIS

The word emphasis has already been discussed in the above section. But the distinctive method of syllabic emphasis in the Russian dialect contributes greatly to its flavor. The most important change in syllabic emphasis comes with the Russian's insistence on avoiding the stressing of secondarily stressed syllables and endowing the stressed syllable with about double the vigor given it in American. The emphasis is only slightly tonal—as can be observed in the speech-pattern above. Practically, it is an entirely stressed emphasis, made with a vigorous burst of breath. In the word "kAHlyEEfAWrnyAH" (California), for example, the American will place primary emphasis on the "for" syllable and secondary emphasis on the first syllable, "cal." The Russian, however, will heavily emphasize the "for" and will give all the other syllables, including the ordinary secondary syllable, "cal," a decidedly weakened emphasis.

The Russian does this because, in his own language, no definite stress rule is postulated. Only one syllable is ever stressed in a word. It must be remembered, however, that the Russian does not always emphasize the *proper* syllable in an American word. He creates such syllabic errors as "khAWspEEtTHAHl" (hospital), with the emphasis placed on the last syllable instead of on the first, as in American. In "AWdTHAWrvIs" (otherwise), he places the emphasis on the ordinarily weakly stressed "vIs" whereas, in American, it would be placed on the first syllable. This last example illustrates the Russian tendency to emphasize suffixes, prefixes and word endings, as in "mAWnyEEnk" (morning), "rAstTHAWrAHn'" (restaurant) and "pripAr" (prepare).

THE ADDED CONSONANTAL "Y"

A number of example words in the following material will be found to contain an odd addition of the consonantal "y" sound after certain other consonants, as in "nAWtTH*y*EEs" (notice) and "l*y*in" (lean).

THE DISTINCT FLAVOR OF THE RUSSIAN DIALECT CAN BE ACHIEVED BY THE SUBTLE ADDITION OF THIS CONSONANTAL "y" SOUND.

This "y" is a carry over from the Russian language. Most Russian consonant sounds can be pronounced either "hard" or "soft"—that is, with or without the added "y." Its use is governed by the nature of the vowel sound that follows the consonant. The absence of a definite rule governing the use of the "y" makes it one of the most difficult factors in learning the Russian language. This same complexity carries over into the dialect so that *absolute* rules to govern its application cannot be formulated. However, a number of *general* rules can be suggested which, if followed, will make for an understandable Russian dialect that still retains its flavor and authenticity.

NOTE: Never give this added consonantal "y" a full "y" treatment. It should be only barely suggested and should be a sort of connecting glide device between the consonant and the vowel that follows it.

Although consonants other than those listed below also take the consonantal "y," only the "l," "n," "d," "t," "th" and "TH" sounds are listed so as not to make the dialect too thick.

1. ADD THE CONSONANTAL "Y" SOUND TO THE CONSONANT "L" WHEN IT IS FOLLOWED BY THE VOWEL SOUNDS "EE," "i," or "EH."

EXAMPLES

lyEEk	(lick)			bilyif	(believe)
lyEEnk	(link)			lyitTH	(lead)
lyEEf	(live)			lyik	(leak)
		lyEHmp	(lamp)		
		blyEHk	(black)		
		lyEHntTH	(land)		

2. ADD THE CONSONANTAL "Y" SOUND TO THE CONSONANT "n" WHEN IT IS FOLLOWED BY THE VOWEL SOUNDS "EE," "i," "EH" or "A."

EXAMPLES

nyEEtTH	(knit)		nyis	(niece)
yoonyEEtTH	(unit)		nyil	(kneel)
nyEEp	(nip)		nyir	(near)

nyEHkEEtTH	(naked)		nyAKs'	(next)
nyEHl	(nail)		nyAl	(Nell)
nyEHm	(name)		nyAtTH	(net)

3. ADD THE CONSONANTAL "y" SOUND TO THE CONSONANT SOUNDS "d," "t," "th" or "TH" WHEN THEY ARE FOLLOWED BY THE VOWEL SOUNDS "EE" OR "i."

EXAMPLES

tTHyEEn	(thin)		tTHyi	(tea)
dTHyEEm	(dim)		dTHyil	(deal)
AWntTHyEEl	(until)		dTHyi	(the)
dTHyEEs	(this)		tTHyim	(theme)

VOWEL CHANGES

"AY" . . . . as in "take," "break," "they," etc.

The Russian shortens this long "a" into "EH," as in "dTHEH" (day). The "AY" sound is not found in the Russian language so care must be taken to use "EH" and not "AY" in the following words.

DRILL WORDS

pEH	(pay)		dTHEH	(they)
stTHEH	(stay)		vwEH	(way)
mEH	(may)		brEHk	(break)

vwEHlyEH	(waylay)
mEHbi	(maybe)
vEHkEHtTH	(vacate)

"UH" . . . . as in "alone," "final," "sofa," etc.

This mute "a" is changed to "AH" in the Russian, as in "sAWfAH" (sofa).

DRILL WORDS

AHgAW	(ago)		kAHnyAri	(canary)
lAHpAl	(lapel)		bAHnAHnAH	(banana)
AHnoo	(anew)		sAHloon	(saloon)

pAHrEHtTH	(parade)
mAHlyEEshAWs	(malicious)
'sAWshiEHtTH	(associate)

NOTE: In the word "'sAWshiEHtTH" (*a*ssociate), it will be noticed that the initial "AH" was dropped. This is done very often by the Russians, especially in the longer words where the elision would not make word identification difficult, as in "'bAH:tTH" (about) and "'pirAHns" (appearance).

"AH" . . . . as in "father," "arm," "park," etc.

This broadened "a" is shortened into the "O" of "rod," as in "fOdTHAWr" (father).

DRILL WORDS

Orm	(arm)	Oms	(alms)	kOrvwEEnk	(carving)
khOrtTH	(heart)	kOm	(calm)	stTHOrtTH	(start)
pOrtTH	(part)	pOm	(palm)	fOrmEEnk	(farming)

"A:" .... as in "ask," "draft," "laugh," etc.

This broadened "a" receives an "AH" pronunciation as in "AHsk" (ask).

DRILL WORDS

lAHs'	(last)	bAHnk	(bank)
tTHAHsk	(task)	lAHf	(laugh)
khAHs	(has)	stTHAHf	(staff)
pAHspAWr'	(passport)		
mAHstTHAWr	(master)		
bAHskAtTH	(basket)		

"A" .... as in "bad," "am," "narrow," etc.

This flat "a" also receives an "AH" change, as in "AHtTH" (add). A variant, "EH," can also be used, as in "bEHtTH" (bad) and "fEHbrEEk" (fabric).

DRILL WORDS

sAHtTH	(sad)	stTHAHp	(stab)
kAHp	(cap)	bAHgi	(baggy)
fAHtTH	(fad)	tTHAHps	(tabs)
bAHgAHtch	(baggage)		
fAHbrEEk	(fabric)		
nAHshAWnAHl	(national)		

"AW" .... as in "ball," "falter," "shawl," etc.

The Russians retain this "AW" sound but they pronounce it with their lips more pursed than do the Americans.

"EE" .... as in "he," "treat," "people," etc.

This long "e" is changed to short "i" in the Russian, as in "khi" h*e*). When it appears at the beginning of a word, it may add a consonantal "y" to it, as in "*y*ist-THAWr" (Easter).

DRILL WORDS

bi	(be)	kAWfi	(coffee)
bin	(bean)	sin	(scene)
flyi	(flee)	nyis	(niece)
pip'l	(people)		
bilyif	(believe)		
yitTH	(eat)		

NOTE: In the above list, the word "coffee" is pronounced as "kAWfi," with a short "i" ending. Because the Russian word is "kAWf*EH*," some Russians use it in their American dialect.

NOTE: When long "e" is used initially, it is changed in the dialect to "EH," as in "EHkAW-nAWmEEstTH" (economist).

"EH" .... as in "bet," "said," "friend," etc.

This short "e" vowel sound is flattened into "A," as in "bAtTH" (bed). It may also be given the American "EH" sound for a lighter dialect.

DRILL WORDS

sAtTH	(set)		nyAk	(neck)
sAtTH	(said)		tTHAl	(tell)
sAl	(sell)		mAntTH	(meant)
	rAdTHyi	(ready)		
	bAn'	(bend)		
	vAri	(very)		

"I" .... as in "ice," "aisle," "guile," etc.

Long "i," in the Russian, is pronounced as it is in American. When broken down, this vowel sound becomes "AH-EE," both parts of which Americans stress equally. Russians, though, lay more emphasis on the "EE" part.

"i" .... as in "it," "women," "busy," etc.

In the Russian dialect, this short "i" sound is changed to long "e" (EE), as in "yEEtTH" (it). It will be observed that, initially, the "i" may receive the added consonantal "y."

DRILL WORDS

flyEEtTH	(flit)		nAWtTHyEEs	(notice)
mEElk	(milk)		dTHAntTHyEEs'	(dentist)
sEEns	(since)		mEEstTHEHk	(mistake)
	khEEs	(his)		
	dEEk	(dig)		
	AWfEEs	(office)		

"O" .... as in "on," "bond," "John," etc.

A broadening of this vowel sound in the Russian changes it to "AW," as in "AWn" (on). The lips should be more pursed than in the American.

DRILL WORDS

blAWk	(block)		bAWdTHyi	(body)
sAWtTH	(sod)		tchAWnyi	(Johnny)
bAWn'	(bond)		AWpAWn	(upon)
	khAWnyAs'	(honest)		
	kAWnstTHAHn'	(constant)		
	prAWpAHgAHndTHAH	(propaganda)		

"OH" .... as in "bone," "sew," "dough," etc.

The Russians shorten this long "o" into "AW," as in "bAWn" (bone).

DRILL WORDS

sAW	(sew)	sAWp	(soap)
nAW	(know)	gAWl'	(gold)
tTHAWl'	(told)	khAWm	(home)

mAWn (moan)
rAWdTHvwEH (roadway)
rAWstTH (roast)

"AW" . . . . as in "off," "cough," "bought," etc.

This vowel sound is pronounced as it is in American, but the lips should be more pursed.

"OO" . . . . as in "food," "do," "blue," etc.

The Russians shorten this long double "o" (OO) into the short double "o" (oo), as in "bloo" (blue).

DRILL WORDS

sootTH	(suit)	dTHootTHyi	(duty)
soop	(soup)	moovi	(movie)
moon	(moon)	soop	(soup)

sAHloon (saloon)
bootTHlAgAWr (bootlegger)
footTH (food)

"oo" . . . . as in "good," "wolf," "full," etc.

This short double "o" (oo) is changed to the long double "o" (OO) of "food" following the Russian custom of shortening our long vowels and lengthening our short vowels, as in "fOOl" (full).

DRILL WORDS

vwOOlf	(wolf)	khOOtTH	(hood)
kOOtTH	(could)	pOOtTH	(put)
vwOOtTH	(would)	gOOtTH	(good)

kArfOOl (careful)
lOOk (look)
stTHOOtTH (stood)

"yOO" . . . . as in "unit," "cube," "beauty," etc.

This vowel sound has an initial added "y" in American. The Russian dialect retains this "y" and substitutes the short double "o" (oo) for the long double "o" (OO), as in "kyoop" (cube).

DRILL WORDS

yoos	(use)	myootTH	(mute)
pyoo	(pew)	kyootTH	(cute)
fyoo	(few)	stTHyoopEEtTH	(stupid)

yoonyEEfAWrm (uniform)
byootTHEEfOOl (beautiful)
yoonItTHAtTH (united)

NOTE: Some Russians retain the Russian pronunciation for American words similar to their own, as "moozyik" (music) and "koop" (cube). This is not suggested as it will make for too thick a dialect.

"U" .... as in "up," "love," "does," etc.

The short "u" in Russian is changed to "AW," as in "AWp" (up). A variation substitutes the "oo" of "good," as in "kloop" (club) and "ploos" (plus). These two examples are from the Russian language as are "front" and "serious" in the following drill words. There is no "U" sound, as we know it, in the Russian language so that, when learning American, Russians give it either the "oo" of their own language or "AW." The "AW" is preferred although "oo" is also acceptable.

DRILL WORDS

bAWk	(bug)	trAWk	(truck)
sEErEE-AWs	(serious)	mAWs'	(must)
frAWntTH	(front)	sAWpAWr	(supper)
pAWblyEEsh	(publish)		
khAWzbAHn'	(husband)		
sAWspEEshOOs	(suspicious)		

"ER" .... as in "curb," "earn," "fir," etc.

All the "er," "ur," "ir" and "or" combinations, pronounced as "ER" in the American, are changed to "AWr" in the Russian, as in "fAWr" (fir).

DRILL WORDS

gAWrl	(girl)	tchAWrtch	(church)
nAWrs	(nurse)	dTHAWrtTHyi	(dirty)
lAWrn	(learn)	vwAWrk	(work)
tTHAWrstTHyi	(thirsty)		
tTHAWrsdTHEH	(Thursday)		
dTHyEEstTHAWrp	(disturb)		

"OW" .... as in "out," "cow," "house," etc.

This diphthong, pronounced "AH-OO" in American, is cut down in the Russian to "AH:," the (:) sign indicating that it is to be elongated, as in "AH:tTH" (out).

DRILL WORDS

mAH:tTH	(mouth)	lAH:tTH	(loud)
dTHAH:tTH	(doubt)	khAH:s	(house)
kAH:	(cow)	khAH:	(how)
mAH:ntTHAHn	(mountain)		
tTHAH:sAHntTHs	(thousands)		
klAH:dTHyi	(cloudy)		

"OI" .... as in "oil," "boy," "noise," etc.

This diphthong, pronounced as "AW-EE" in American, retains the initial "AW" sound but substitutes a short "i" for the long "e" (EE) in the second part, as in "AWil" (oil).

DRILL WORDS

bAWi	(boy)	bAWil	(boil)
tTHAWi	(toy)	vAWis	(voice)
nAWis	(noise)	AHnAWi	(annoy)

AntchAWi (enjoy)
gAWitTHAWr (goiter)
AmbrAWidTHAWr (embroider)

WORD EXERCISES

Pronounce the following words in the Russian dialect using the material learned from the preceding vowel changes:

1. soviet
2. philosophy
3. plan
4. capitalism
5. propaganda
6. front
7. communism
8. worker
9. future
10. state farm
11. valuta
12. taskmaster
13. people
14. commissar
15. value
16. bolshevik
17. toiling
18. general staff
19. thousand
20. divorce

When the above words have been pronounced, refer to the list on the following page for corrections. Check the mistakes, correct them and repeat the corrections until they have been memorized.

1. sAWvEE-AtTH
2. fEElAWsAWfi
3. plAHn
4. kAHpEEtTHAHlyEEzm
5. prAWpAHgAHndTHAH
6. frAWntTH
7. kAWmoonEEzm
8. vwAWrkAWr
9. fyootchOOR
10. stTHEHtTHfOrm
11. vAHlootTHAH
12. tTHAHskmAHstTHAWr
13. pip'l
14. kAWmEEsAHr
15. vAHlyoo
16. bAWlshUHvEEk
17. tTHAWilEEnk
18. tchAnAWrAHlstAHf
19. tTHAH:sAHntTH
20. dTHEEvAWrs

CONSONANT CHANGES

B—The consonant "b" is sounded as in American. But, at the end of words, it is changed to "p," as in "krEEp" (crib). If, however, a word ends with "b" and the next word is related in sense and begins with a voiced consonant ("b," "v," "d," "z," or "g"), the final "b" is not changed, as in "krAHb dTHEEnAWr (crab dinner), where the "b" is retained before the voiced consonant "d"; and in "krEEp fAl" (crib fell) where the "b" is changed to "p" before the unvoiced consonant "f." Other unvoiced consonants which affect final "b" are "p," "t," "s," "sh," and "k."

C—For the soft sound of "C," see "S." For the hard sound, see "K."

D—The Russians dentalize this consonant. Instead of sounding it with the tip of the tongue placed against the teeth at the front part of the roof of the mouth, as in American, they place the tip of the tongue immediately behind the cutting edge of the upper front teeth. This thickens the "d" sound into "dTH," as in "*d*THIm" (*d*ime), and "lAH*d*THAWr" (la*dd*er).

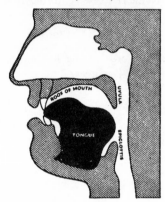

The tongue tip, pressed against the backs of the front teeth, introduces into the "d" sound the additional "TH," creating the sound, "dTH." The American "d" is produced by touching the gum ridge of the upper front teeth with the tongue tip.

Final "d" (dTH) is changed to "t" (tTH) if the next word is related in sense and begins with a voiceless consonant ("p," "f," "t," "s," "sh," or "k"), as in "bAH*tTH* sAWn" (ba*d* son).

When final "d" (dTH) belongs to the last word in a sentence or a sense group, it also changes to "t" (tTH).

When, at the end of a word, "d" is preceded by another consonant, especially "n," it may be dropped, as in "vwEEn'" (win*d*), "bAWn'" (bon*d*) and "bAWl'" (bal*d*).

F—The sound of "F" remains the same in Russian as in American. Words spelled with "f" but pronounced as "v," as in the American "Ov" (of), may retain the "f" sound, as in the Russian dialect "AWf" (of). For the "v" sound of "f" see "V."

If final "f" precedes a word that is related to it in sense and begins with a voiced consonant ("b," "d," "z," or "g"), it changes to "v," as in "stTHAH*v* *d*THy-EErAktTHAWr" (sta*ff* *d*irector), where the "f" is changed; or as in "stTHAH*f* *pr*AWblAm" (sta*ff* *p*roblem), where the "f" is retained before another voiceless consonant.

G—Russians pronounce hard "g" as Americans do unless it is final. At the end of a word, "g" changes to "k," as in "bAH*k*" (ba*g*), unless the next word is related in sense and begins with a voiced consonant ("b," "v," "d," "z," or "g"), as in "stTHAH*g* *d*THyEEnAWr" (sta*g* *d*inner), where the "g" is not changed; or in stTHAH*k* *p*AHrtTHyi" (sta*g* *p*arty), where "g" becomes "k" before a voiceless consonant. For the soft sound of "G," see "J."

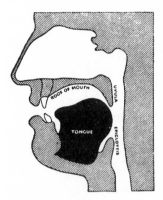

The back of the tongue is raised to touch the uvula at the end of the soft palate. When a stream of breath is brought up past this conjuncture, it is roughened and voiced, producing the Russian gargled "kh" sound. Neither the tongue nor the uvula vibrates when this sound is produced.

H—The pronunciation of this consonant is one of the most characteristic of the consonant changes. Since there is no "h" sound in Russian it is treated with the same gargled "kh" that is in the Scotch word "loch," which is achieved by setting the back of the tongue against the soft palate in position to sound "k" but sounding "h" instead and by bringing up the breath past the tongue without vibrating against the soft palate. The effect is a gargled, guttural "kh," like the "ch" in the German word "ach." It has been designated as "kh" phonetically, as in "*kh*AH:s" (*h*ouse) and "Anyi*kh*AH:" (any*h*ow). If the "kh" combination cannot be mastered, a strong "h" may be used. "k" should never be substituted. (See illustration).

J—The Russians substitute "tch" for this consonant, initially, medially and finally, as in "*tch*AWr*tch*" (*George*) and "lAW*tch*" (lo*dge*).

Occasionally, when an American word is similar to a Russian word, it retains the Russian hard "g," instead of the "j" sound of soft "g," as in "rilyEEgEE-AWs" (religious).

K—This "k" sound is pronounced the same as in American unless it is final and precedes a related word that begins with a voiced consonant ("b," "d," "z," or "g"), in which case it is changed to "g," as in "bAH*g* dTHAWr" (bac*k* *d*oor), where the "k" is changed; or as in "tTHyEE*k* soop" (thic*k* soup), where it remains unchanged.

L—The Russian "l" is always sounded as a dark "l." Americans use this dark "l" when it is final, or when it is followed by a consonant, as in "fOOl" (fool) and "bild" (build). The clear "l" heard in the American words "liv" (live) and "fEHlOH" (fellow), is not found in the Russian dialect. In this dark "l," the back part of the tongue is raised toward the soft palate of the roof of the mouth. Since this dark "l" adds considerable color to a Russian dialect its use should be cultivated. American words such as "pEEp'l" (people) and "trUb'l" (trouble) can be used to practice this dark "l." See "The Added Consonantal 'Y'" for an additional change to the Russian "l."

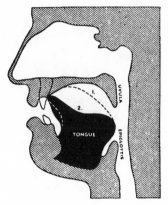

The black area indicates the position of the tongue when a clear American "l" is produced. The center part of the tongue is depressed into a trough instead of being raised in the position of the Russian "l," indicated by the dotted line.

M—Pronounced as in American.

N—Pronounced as in American except before the vowel sounds "EE," "i," "EH" and "A." See "The Added Consonantal 'Y'."

P—This consonant is pronounced as it is in American unless it is final and the following word is related and begins with a voiced consonant ("b," "d," "z," or "g") in which case the "p" is changed to "b," as in "grEH*b dTH*yEEsh" (gra*p*e *d*ish), where the "p" is changed; or as in "soo*p st*THEHn" (sou*p s*tain), where it is unchanged.

Q—Instead of sounding "q" as "kw," as in American, the Russians pronounce it as "kvw," as in "*kvw*EEk" (*q*uick) and "*kvw*in" (*q*ueen). See "W."

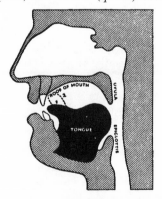

The black area indicates the position of the tongue as it begins trilling the Russian "r." The dotted line shows the tongue curling upward to touch the forward part of the roof of the mouth. An extended series of this rapid interchange of positions causes the trilled Russian "r."

R—The Russian "r," like the Scottish burred "r," is pronounced with a deep roll of the tongue as the tip vibrates against the juncture of the upper front teeth and the roof of the mouth. It must always be fully and strongly sounded—rolled—because it is an important dialect characteristic.

S—The consonant "s" is always hissed vigorously and for a longer duration than the American "s." A great many Russians sometimes change it to "ts" as in "*ts*EE-gOr" (*c*igar), "*ts*ikrAtTH" (*s*ecret), and "prAW*ts*AntTH" (percent).

Final "s" changes to "z" if the next word is related and begins with a voiced consonant ("b," "d," "z," or "g"), as in "gAHz *b*AWrnAWr" (ga*s b*urner), where the "s" is changed, or as in "gAH*s* *p*lyEHtTH" (ga*s p*late), where it is not.

T—The Russians dentalize the consonant "t." Instead of pronouncing it with the tip of the tongue placed against the forward part of the roof of the mouth, as in American, they place it immediately behind the cutting edges of the upper front teeth. This thickens the "t" sound so that it is pronounced with the voiced "TH," as in "*t*THyi" (*t*ea), "lA*t*THAWr" (le*tt*er) and "bEE*t*TH" (bi*t*).

The consonant "t" is sometimes dropped medially, as in "tTHAWr'i" (thir*t*y), "poor'i" (pre*tt*y) and "tsvwAn'yi" (twen*t*y).

Like "s," the consonant "t" is sometimes changed to "ts," as in "*ts*vwAn'yi" (*t*wenty) and "*ts*vwIs" (*t*wice). When "t" is used at the end of a word and is preceded by another consonant, it is usually dropped, as in "kAHn'" (can'*t*), "kAp'" (kep*t*), and "mAWs'" (mus*t*).

Final "t" (tTH) should be changed to "d" (dTH) if the next word is related and begins with a voiced consonant ("b," "d," "z," or "g"), as in "lA*d*TH gAW" (le*t* go).

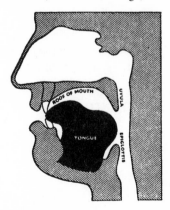

The tongue tip, pressed against the backs of the front teeth, introduces into the "t" sound the additional "TH," creating the sound, "tTH." The American "t" is produced by touching the gum ridge of the upper front teeth with the tongue tip.

V—Most Russians pronounce the consonant "v" as Americans do. Some of them, however, become confused because the "v" looks so much like the "w," which is extremely difficult for them. They therefore pronounce "v" as "vw." The "w" should never be completely clear. Although this "vw" sound may be used, the plain "v" is preferred.

Final "v" changes to "f" unless the following word is related and begins with a voiced consonant ("b," "v," "d," "z," or "g"), as in "lI*v* dAWk" (live dog), where the "v" is retained and "lI*f p*AWpi" (live puppy) where the "v" is changed to "f."

W—The consonant "w" is very difficult for most Russians. They might have lived and worked in America many years but they will never pronounce "w" as Americans do. They treat "w" either as "v," as in "*v*AWrk" (*w*ork) or—and this is more common—they add a light "w" sound after the "v," as in "*vw*AWrk" (*w*ork). To pronounce this "vw" sound, you should set your mouth in position for "w" but pronounce "v" instead. The lower lip must not touch the cutting edge of the upper front teeth.

X—Pronounced as in American.

Y—When "y" is used initially, it is sometimes treated as "j" by those Russians who do not substitute "tch" for "j," as in "*j*AHnkis" (*Y*ankees) and "*j*AlAW" (*y*ellow). The American pronunciation, though, is preferred in most cases.

Z—The consonant "z" sound is used initially and medially only when the spelling indicates it, as in "lyEH*z*i" (la*z*y). When the "z" sound is spelled as "s," it is always given a very sibilant "s" sound, as in "khAH*s* (ha*s*) "yEE*s*" (i*s*), and "gAW*s*" (goe*s*).

Final "z" is changed to "s" unless the following word is related in sense and begins with a voiced consonant ("b," "v," "d," "z," or "g"), as in snyi*s* pAH:dTHEHr" (snee*z*e powder).

SH—Ordinarily "sh" is pronounced as it is in American. Sometimes American words that are similar to Russian words retain their Russian sounds, as in "nAHt-sEE-AWnAHl" (national), with the sound "ts" instead of "sh."

TH—The voiced "th" of "the" is dentalized and pronounced as "dTH" (See "D" and "T"), as in "*dTH*yi" (*th*e), "bEH*dTH*" (ba*th*e) and "fO*dTH*AWr" (fa*th*er).

th—The unvoiced "th" of "thin" is also dentalized and sounded as "tTH," as in "*tTH*yEEn" (*th*in), "bAH*tTH*" (ba*th*) and "*tTH*EEnk" (*th*ink).

TCH—Pronounced as in American.

ZH—The "zh" consonant sound of "z" in "azure" is often treated as "sh" in the Russian dialect, as in "vEE*sh*AWn" (vi*s*ion), "AH*sh*OOr" (a*z*ure), "lA*sh*OOr" (lei*s*ure) and "trA*sh*OOr" (trea*s*ure).

NK—Words with an "nk" in them retain the sound of both consonants. That is, in American, "bank" would be pronounced as "bAng-k," the "n" not receiving its normal pronunciation. But in the Russian dialect the "n" is retained so that "bank" is pronounced as "bAHnk," with the "n" receiving the full treatment of "n."

ER—Final "er" may be pronounced as "AWr" or "EHr," as in "fOdTH*AWr*" (father) or "fOdTH*EHr*" (fath*er*). Medial "er" is sometimes reversed, as in "prAWt-sAntTH" (per cent).

WORD EXERCISES

Pronounce the following words in the Russian dialect using the material learned from the preceding Consonant Changes:

1.	uniform	11.	bathing beach
2.	big drive	12.	guardhouse
3.	German	13.	cab driver
4.	quality	14.	whiplash
5.	bad time	15.	logbook
6.	world wide	16.	has been
7.	knows	17.	black boots
8.	Jap soldier	18.	twice
9.	half-baked	19.	stop them
10.	thick soles	20.	staff sergeant

When the above words have been pronounced, refer to the list below for corrections. Check the mistakes, correct them and repeat the corrections until they have been memorized.

1.	yoonyEEfAWrm	11.	bEHdTHyEEng bitch
2.	bEEg drIf	12.	gOrtTH khAH:s
3.	tchAWrmAHn	13.	kAHb dTHrIvwAWr
4.	kvwAHlyEEtTHyi	14.	vwEEp lAHsh
5.	bAH' tIm	15.	lAWg bOOk
6.	vwAWrl'vwIt	16.	khAHz bEEn
7.	nAWs	17.	blAHg bootTHs
8.	tchAHp sAWltchAWr	18.	tTHvwIs
9.	khAHv bEHkt	19.	stTHAWb dTHAm
10.	tTHyEEk sAWls	20.	stTHAHf sOrtchAHntTH

GRAMMAR CHANGES

The most characteristic change in the Russian's use of English grammar comes with his dropping of the articles "a," "an" and "the." There are no articles in the Russian language and this absence is carried over into the dialect.

"vwi khEHf pAWblyEEsh bOOk."   "yoo vwAWn' tsEEgOr?"
(We have publish book.)   (You want cigar?)
(We have published a book.)   (You want a cigar?)

"yoo tTHEHk AWrAHntch."
(You take orange.)
(You take *an* orange.)

Similarly, the dialect omits "am," "is" and "are" because they have no counterpart in Russian, as in:

"I nAWtTH sAW gOOtTH filyEEnk."
(I not so good feeling.)
(I *am* not feeling so well.)

"khi bAs' mAHn EEn yoonyAWn."
(He best man in union.)
(He *is* the best man in the union.)

"dTHEH nAWtTH khAWm."
(They not home.)
(They *are* not home.)

The absence of prepositions in the original language accounts for their absence from the dialect.

When, however, a Russian emigre becomes conscious of this lack he, like the Cockney who adds "h's," uses prepositions where they don't belong—and often uses incorrect ones.

"I gAW tchAWrtch sAWndTHEH."
(I go church Sunday.)
(I go *to* church on Sunday.)

"dTHAHtTH kIn' svwEEmEEn' sootTH"
(that kind swimming suit)
(that kind *of* swimming suit)

"I bAWtTH yEEtTH bI drAWkstTHAWr."
(I bought it *by* drugstore.)
(I bought it *at* the drugstore.)

"fAWr vwI yoo nAWtTH AHnsAWr?"
(*For* why you not answer?)
(Why didn't you answer?)

The Russian, like most foreigners, prefers to use the present tense of a verb to the past participle, as in:

"khi vwAWn' AWl kIn's tTHyEEnks."
(He *want* all kinds things.)
(He *wanted* all sorts of things.)

"I vwAWs plAntTHyi skAr."
(I was plenty *scare.*)
(I was quite scared.)

"vwi bEEn yAHsk."
(We been *ask.*)
(We have been *asked.*)

The omission of "have" in the last example illustrates another omission habit in the dialect. Rather than use "have," the Russian usually resorts to "was" in forming the present perfect, regardless of number, as in:

"vwi vwAWs vwAWkEEnk EEn pOrk."
(We *was* walking in park.)
(We *have been* walking in the park.)

"dTHEH vwAWs tTHAWkEEng 'bAH: yoo."
(They *was* talking about you.)
(They *have been* talking about you.)

"I vwAWs vwAri lAWnsAWm."
(I *was* very lonesome.)
(I *have been* very lonesome.)

For the use of "have," "has" or "had," to express possession or lack of possession, the Russian uses only "got," as in:

"dTHEH gAWtTH nAW mAWnyi."
(They *got* no money.)
(They *have* no money.)

"khi gAWtTH lAWtTHs tTHrAWbOOl."
(He *got* lots trouble.)
(He *has* a lot of trouble.)

"dTHEH gAWtTH nAWbAWdTHyi dTHEH shAHl khAlp."
(They *got* nobody they shall help.)
(They *have* no one to help.)

The use of "shall" in the last example sentence is illustrative of its substitution for "to," as in:

"khi tTHrI khi shAHl svwEEm."
(He try he *shall* swim.)
(He tried *to* swim.)

"shi vwAWn' shi shAHl bI EEtTH."
(She want she *shall* buy it.)
(She wanted *to* buy it.)

The Russians split the auxiliary and the principal verb form with the adverb instead of using the adverb after the principal verb, as in:

"dTHEH vwAWz gOOtTH filyEEnk."
(They was good *feeling.*)
(They were feeling *fine.*)

"khi vwAWs fAHs' vwAWkEEnk."
(He was *fast* walking.)
(He was walking *fast*.)

"yoo vwAWs lAWdTHz dTHrEEnkEEnk."
(You was *lots* drinking.)
(You were drinking a *lot*.)

Many verbal auxiliaries are omitted in the dialect, especially forms of "do," which forms are not found in Russian interrogative or negative sentences, as in:

"khAH: yoo fil?"
(How you feel?)
(How *do* you feel?)

"vwAr yoo si dTHAHtTH?"
(Where you see that?)
(Where *did* you see that?)

"I nAWdTH gAWEEng dTHAr."
(I not going there.)
(I *am* not going there.)

The adverb "there" is dropped by a great many Russians, as in:

"vwAWs sEHlAWr yEEn bAWtTH."
(Was sailor in boat.)
(*There* was a sailor in the boat.)

"vwAWs mAnyi pip'l yEEn lyEHk."
(Was many people in lake.)
(*There* were many people in the lake.)

"yEEs AWnlyi vwAWn vwEH."
(Is only one way.)
(*There* is only one way.)

The subject is often preceded by other parts of the sentence which, in American, usually follow the subject, as in:

"sAW kAWms yEEn AWl kIn'z dTHAWks."
(So, comes in all kinds dogs.)
(So, all sorts of dogs came in.)

"yEEn stTHAWr dTHEH bI glAHs."
(In store, they buy glass.)
(They bought a glass in the store.)

"dTHAr tTHoo fAlAWs vwAWs."
(There, two fellows was.)
(Two fellows were there.)

A substitution of "what" for "that" and "who" is also common among the Russians, as in:

"dTHyEEs khAH:s vwAWtTH vwAWs tTHoo rAn."
(This house *what* was to rent.)
(This is the house *that* was for rent.)

"dTHyEEs vwAWs vwEEmAHns vwAWtTH yoo vwAWn."
(This was womens *what* you want.)
(This is the woman *whom* you want.)

"dTHyi bAWi vwAWtTH lAHf, khi vwAWs yEEdTHyEEAWtTH."
(The boy *what* laugh, he was idiot.)
(The boy *who* laughed was an idiot.)

SENTENCE EXERCISES

Pronounce the following sentences in the Russian dialect making the necessary changes in grammar learned from the preceding section:

1. The enemy was quite scared.
2. We have been making social gains.
3. They have a new system of working.
4. We are not going to give up the fight.
5. A lot of women were running fast.
6. Was there a man in the plane?
7. The man who shirks is a traitor.
8. We tried to take the last trench.
9. You can find the map in the drawer.
10. I have been working at the tractor plant.

After each sentence, refer to the following versions for the correct changes. Make the corrections and pronounce the sentence again using the correct words. Do this with every sentence.

1. AnAHmi vwAWs plAntTHyi skAr.
2. vwi vwAWs mEHkEEnk sAWshAHl gEHns.
3. dTHyEH gAWtTH noo sEEstTHAHm AWf vwAWrkEEnk.
4. vwi nAWdTH gEEv AWp fIt.
5. lAWtTHs voomAHn vwAWs rAWnyEEnk fAHs'.
6. vwAWs mAHn yEEn plEHn?
7. mAHn vwAWtTH shAWrk yEEs tTHrEHtTHAWr.
8. vwi tTHrI vwi shAHl tTHyEHk lAHs' tTHrAntch.
9. yEEn drAWr yoo fIn' mAHp.
10. I vwAWrg bI tTHrAHktTHAWr plAHntTH.

RUSSIAN LANGUAGE CARRYOVERS

goodbye	*do svidan ya*	dAW svEEd*THAH*nyUH
excuse me	*izvinite*	izvi*n*EE*t*THEH
thank you	*spasibo*	spUH*sEE*bAW
yes	*da*	dTHAH
no	*net*	nyEHtTH
how do you do	*kak vy pozhivayete*	kAHk vEE
		pAWzhivA*HyEHt*THEH
I beg your pardon	*prostite*	prAW*stTHEEt*THEH
it doesn't matter	*nichevo*	nitchEH*vAW*

RUSSIAN MONOLOG

(*Adapted from a character in the authors' dramas written for "Your Dream Has Come True" on the NBC network.*)

Oh! I very good fellow! why? because I Cossack. I very big Cossack. Yah! I captain of Royal Cossack Guard in Moscow—in old country. Oh! I got fifty—hundred—five hundred Cossack they was under me. I be big mans. And womens, they love me lots. Nastia Alexanderovna—she big ballet dancer in Czar ballet—Countess Irina Balushkovna, she love me. All womens they love me. And men? Ach! they be 'fraid from me. They hating me. Why? because I big Cossack. I ride big horse. Drink lots vodka. Oh! I very big mans. Was fellow hate me lots. I shoot him. Is only way. In war, they be 'fraid from me, too. Why? because I big Cossack. They hope I die soon. But I be good feeling. Why? Because I big Cossack. Was general in army, was sailor in navy—all try kill Ivan Michaelovitch—is me. You think so they kill me? No! I kill all first. Why? Because I big Cossack. I wear fine uniform. Gots lots money. Gots lots girls. Why? Because I best soldier in Cossacks. I have go lots places, I have . . . what? what I doing now? Oh, now I gots good job. I wear nice uniform. I give lots orders for people. I still big chief—big Cossack. Yah! I be doorman for Petrushka Russian Tea-Room!

PHONETIC REPRESENTATION

(*The bold-face syllables are to be emphasized*)

"**AW!** Iv**Ar**i g**OO**. .tTH   **fa**   v **wI**?   **kAW**
.l**AW**!   bik**AW**s I   s**AH**k."

I vAri **bEEk** kAWsAHk. **yAH!** I **kAH**ptTHAHn AWf **rAW**iyAHl **kAW**sAHk **g**Ort-THs yEEn **mAW**skvAH—yEEn **AWl'** kAWntTHri. **AW!** I gAWtTH **fEEf**tTHyi—**kh**AWndTHAWrtTH—**fIf** khAWndTHAWrtTH **kAW**sAHk dTHEH **AW**nd-THAWr mi. I bi **bEEg mAH**ns. AHn' **vv**EEmAHns, dTHEH lAWf mi **lAW**tTHs. **n**AHstTHyAH AHlyEHksAHndTHAW**rAW**vnyAH—shi **bEEg bAH**lyEH dTHAHnsAWr yEEn tsAHr bAHlyEH—kAH:ntTHAs yEE**rEE**nyAH bAHly-ooshk**AW**vnyAH, **shi** lAWf mi. **AW**l vwEEmAHns, dTHEH **lAW**f mi. AHn' **mAn? AHkh!** dTHEH bi **'frEH**tTH frAWm mi. dTHEH **khEH**tTHyEEng mi. **vwI?** bikAWs I **bEEk kAW**sAHk. I rIdTH **bEEk kh**AWrs. dTHrEEnk **lAW**tTHs v**AW**dTHkAH. **AW!** I v**Ari bEEg mAH**ns. vwAWs fAlAW kh**EH**tTH mi **lAW**t-THs. I **shoo**tTH kh**EE**m. yEEs **AW**nlyi **vwEH.** yEEn v**wAW**r dTHEH bi **frEH**tTH frAWm mi, tTHoo. **vwI?** bikAWs I **bEEk kAW**sAHk. dTHEH kh**AW**p I **dTHI** soon. b**AW**tTH I bi **gOO**tTH fil**yEE**nk. **vwI?** bikAWs I **bEEk kAW**sAHk. vwAWs tchAnAW**rAH**l yEEn **O**rmi, vwAWs s**EH**lAWr yEEn **n**yEH**vi—AW**l tTHrI **kEE**l yiv**AH**n mEEkhAHlyAWv**EE**tch—yEEs **mi.** yoo tTHyEEnk sAW dTHEH **kEE**l mi? **nAW!** I **kEEl AW**l f**AW**rs'. **vwI?** bikAWs I **bEEk kAW**sAHk. I vw**Ar fIn** yoony-EEf**AW**rm. g**AW**tTHs **lAW**tTHs **mAW**nyi. g**AW**tTHs **lAW**tTHs **gAW**rls. **vwI?** bikAWs I **bAs' sAW**ltch**AW**r yEEn **kAW**sAHks. I khAHv g**AW lAW**tTHs **pl**yEHsEHs, I khAHf .... **vwAW**tTH? vwAWtTH I dTHoo**EE**ng **nAH:? AW! nAH:** I g**AW**tTHs **gOO**tTH **tchAW**p. I vwAr **nIs** yoon**yEE**fAWrm. I g**EE**v **lAW**t-THs **AW**rdTHAWrs f**AW**r pip'l. I st**TH**y**EE**l **bEEk** tchif—**bEEk kAW**sAHk. **yAH!** I bi **dTHAW**rmAHn f**AW**r p**yEH**tTH**roo**shkAH **rAW**sh'n **tTH**yiroom!

CHAPTER SEVENTEEN

Middle European Dialects

THE LITHUANIAN DIALECT

Because Lithuanian is of the Slavic group of languages, and because Lithuania was once a part of the Russian Empire, there are many similarities between it and Russian. Much of the material given in the "Russian" chapter can, therefore, apply to the Lithuanian.

VOWEL CHANGES

SOUND	WORD	CHANGE	DIALECT
AY	take	EH	tEHk
UH	sofa	AH	sAWvwAH
AH	father	O	vwOdAWr
A:	ask	EH	EHsk
A	bat	EH	bEHt
AW	ball	O	bOl
EE	he	i	hi
EH	bet	EH	bEHt
I	nice	AHi	nAHis
i	sit	EE	sEEt
O	on	AW	AWn
OH	bone	AW	bAWn
AW	off	AW	AWvw
OO	food	oo	vwoot
oo	good	oo	goot
yOO	unit	oo	oonEEt
	unit	yoo	yoonEEt
	cute	yoo	kyoot

U	up	O	Op
ER	curb	AWr	kAWrb
	permit	EHr	pEHrmEEt
	circus	EEr	tsEErkOs
	work	AWr	vwAWrk
OW	house	OW	'OWs
OI	oil	AWi	AWil
le	noble	EHl	nAWbEHl
el	label	EHl	lEHbEHl
ial	social	yAHl	sAWshyAHl

CONSONANT CHANGES

These are the important consonant changes.

D—changed finally to "t," as in "vwrEHnt" (frien*d*).

F—changed initially to "vw," as in "vwrEHnk" (Frank); changed finally to "v," as in "EEv" (if) or to "vw," as in "EEvw" (if).

G—changed finally to "k," as in "hOnk" (hung).

H—often dropped initially and medially, as in "'AWtEHl" (hotel) and "On'EHpi" (unhappy).

J—changed to "tch," as in "*tchOtch*" *(judge)*.

S—changed initially to "sh" before another consonant, as in "*sh*tAWr" (*s*tore).

T—sometimes dropped medially, as in "pOr'i" (party).

V—sometimes changed to "vw," as in "vwEEktEEm" (victim).

W—changed to "vw," as in "v*w*AWs" (*w*as). Changed initially also to "m" in the word "mEEt" (with).

Z—changed to "s" when so spelled, as in "hEHs" (has).

TH—changed to "z," as in "zi" (the) or to "d," as in "di" (the).

th—changed to "t," as in "tEEnk" (think).

One of the most difficult consonant sounds for the Lithuanian is "F." In the dialect this sound may become "v" or "vw." The "vw" sound is made by setting the mouth in position for "w" and sounding "v." When, however, you sound "v," you must not allow the lower lip to touch the cutting edge of the upper front teeth. If produced correctly this "vw" sound will be similar to the "h" in the American word "h-wI" (why).

"H" is another sound which is not in the Lithuanian language. It is usually dropped in the dialect but, if used, it should be more forceful than in American.

When "i" is between a consonant and a vowel, it often changes to the consonantal "y," as in "n*y*is" (n*i*ece) and "v*y*AWlEEn" (v*i*olin).

THE JUGOSLAV DIALECT

The Jugoslav language is of the same group as the Russian. Much, therefore, of what was written about the Russian dialect can be applied also to the Yugoslav dialect.

VOWEL CHANGES

SOUND	WORD	CHANGE	DIALECT
AY	take	EH	tEHk
UH	alone	AH	AHlAWn
AH	father	O	fOdAHr
A:	ask	O	Os'
	ask	EH	EHs'
A	bad	EH	bEHt
AW	ball	AW	bAWl
EE	he	i	khi
EH	get	EH	gEHt
I	nice	AHi	nAHis
i	sit	i	sit
O	on	O	On
OH	bone	AW	bAWn
AW	off	AW	AWf
OO	food	oo	foot
oo	good	oo	goot
yOO	unit	yoo	yoonit
U	up	O	Op
ER	curb	oo	koorp
OW	out	AHoo	AHoot
OI	oil	AWi	AWil
le	rustle	'l	rOs'l
el	shovel	'l	tchOv'l
er	slipper	AHr	shlipAHr
ex	expensive	dropped	'spEHnzif

CONSONANT CHANGES

B—Sometimes changed to "p," as in "krEHp" (cra*b*) and "pAWi" (*b*oy).

D—dropped finally when following a consonant, as in "bEHn'" (bend), and changed to "t" medially, as in "nit'l" (nee*d*le).

G—dropped from "ing" endings, as in "livwin'room" (livin*g*room).

H—changed to "kh" initially, as in "*kh*AHooz (*h*ouse).

J—changed to "tch," as in "*tch*O*tch*" (*j*udge).

Q—changed to "kv," as in "*kv*ik" (*qu*ick).

R—dropped medially, as in "shtEH'z" (stai*r*s).

S—hard "s" initially, as in "*s*im" (*s*eem); often changed to "z" medially, as in "kO*z*'l" (ca*s*tle); changes to "sh" initially before another consonant, as in "*sh*lip" (*s*leep); changes to "z" finally, as in "khAHoo*z*" (hou*s*e).

T—dropped medially, as in "s'ri'kOr" (stree*t*car); dropped finally after a consonant, as in "fAWl'" (faul*t*); changed to "d" medially, as in "vAW*d*AHr" (wa*t*er).

V—changed to "f" finally, as in "li*f*" (li*v*e); sometimes changed to "vw" medially, as in "AW*vw*AHr" (o*v*er).

W—changed to "*v*" initially, as in "*v*EHs'" (*w*est) or changed to "vw," as in "*vw*EHs'" (*w*est); changed to "v" medially, as in "AH*v*EH" (a*w*ay) or to "vw," as in "AH*vw*EH" (a*w*ay).

Z—changed to "s," as in "khi*s*" (hi*z*).

TH—voiced "th" changed to "d," as in "*d*i" (*th*e).

th—unvoiced "th" changed to "t," as in "*t*ink" (*th*ink).

ZH—changed to "sh," as in "EH*sh*oo'" (a*z*ure).

SH—sometimes changed to "tch," as in "*tch*EHl" (*sh*all).

THE CZECH DIALECT

The Czech language is common to the Czechs, the Moravians, the Silesians and Slovaks. Therefore, the following changes will apply to the dialect of any of these groups.

VOWEL CHANGES

SOUND	WORD	CHANGE	DIALECT
AY	take	EHi	tEHik
UH	about	AY	AYbAH'
	sofa	UH	sAWfUH
AH	father	O	fOdEHr
A:	ask	AH	AHsk
A	bad	EH	bEHt
	bad, also	AH	bAHt
AW	ball	O	bOl
EE	he	i	hi
EH	get	A	gAt

I	ice	AHi	AHis
i	sit	EE	sEEt
O	on	AW	AWn
OH	bone	AW	bAWn
AW	off	AW	AWf
OO	food	OO	fOOt
oo	good	OO	gOOt
yOO	unit	OO	OOnEEt
U	up	AH	AHp
ER	up, also	oo	oop
	curb	OOr	kOOrb
	fir	ir	fir
ER	word	AWr	vwAWrt
	her	EHr	hEHr
OW	out	AH	AHt
OI	noise	AWi	nAWis

The stress in words of more than two syllables should usually be placed on the first syllable, as in "**kAW**ndEEshoon" (condition), "**Ag**zprAs" (express) and "**klAH**imAHtEEk" (climatic).

A great many Czechs have learned their English language from the British while others have been affected by the French. This accounts for a considerable diversity in many vowel and consonant changes. The voiced "th" of "the," for instance, would ordinarily be pronounced as "d," but a great many Czechs treat it with the French "z," as in "*z*is" (*th*ese). At the same time, they would pronounce the unvoiced "th" as "s," as in "*s*EEnk" (*th*ink), where it would usually be pronounced as "t," as in "*t*EEn" (*th*in).

Other important consonant changes are as follows:

D—sometimes dropped medially, as in "kOO'n't" (coul*d*n't); sometimes dropped finally when preceded by a consonant, as in "fAHn'" (foun*d*).

G—sometimes changed to "k," as in "pEE*k*" (pi*g*) and "*k*rAW" (*g*row).

J—changed to "tch," as in "*tch*AHtch" (*j*udge); sometimes changed to "dz," as in "*dz*AW" (*J*oe).

K—sometimes changed to "g," as in "tEEn*g*" (thin*k*).

Q—changed to "kv," as in "*kv*EEk" (*q*uick).

R—trilled more than usually and sometimes dropped after a vowel, as in "fO'ms" (fa*r*ms).

T—usually dropped finally, as in "AYbAH'" (abou*t*); sometimes changed to "r" medially as in "tir'i" (thir*t*y).

V—often changed to "vw," as in "ri*vw*AWlt" (re*v*olt).

W—changed to "vw," as in "AY*vw*EHi" (a*w*ay); sometimes changed to "v," as in "*v*As'" (*w*est).

X—changed to "gz," as in "A*gz*prAs" (e*x*press).

Z—changed to "s," as in "vAW*s*" (wa*s*) and "hEH*s*" (ha*s*).

The consonants "d," "t," and "n" are often followed by the consonantal "y" sound which is discussed at length in the Russian chapter.

THE FINNISH DIALECT

The Finnish dialect lengthens its vowel sounds considerably, especially its "a's." But the most important characteristic of the dialect is that many of its words must end with a vowel or an aspirate "uh," like the Italian. This is done because, in the Finnish language, as in the Italian, most of the words end with a vowel.

VOWEL CHANGES

SOUND	WORD	CHANGE	DIALECT
AY	take	EHi:	tEHi:'
UH	about	EH	EHpAH:tuh
AH	father	AH:	vwAH:deruh
A:	ask	AH:	AH:s'uh
A	bat	EH:	pEH:tuh
AW	ball	oo:	poo:luh
EE	he	i:	hi:
EH	bet	EH:	pEH:tuh
I	nice	AHi:	nAHi:suh
i	sit	i:	si:tuh
O	on	AH:	AH:nuh
OH	bone	AW:	pAW:nuh
AW	off	oo:	oo:vwuh
OO	food	oo:	vwoo:duh
oo	good	oo:	goo:duh
yOO	unit	yoo:	yoo:ni:tuh
U	up	AW:	AW:puh
ER	curb	AH:	kAH:'p
OW	out	AH:	AH:tuh
OI	boil	AWi	pAWiluh

Because two consonants never come together initially in the Finnish language, the Finns find it difficult to pronounce American words like "fly," "street" and "plain." They usually drop the first consonant, as in "'lAHi" (*f*ly), "'tri:tuh" (*s*treet) and "'lEHi:nuh" (*p*lain). This omission, although characteristic, must not be overdone.

The absence of an "f" sound in Finnish causes the Finns either to drop "f" completely, as in "AH:'tuh" (*after*) or to change it to "vw," as in "*vw*i:luh" (*feel*). See "W" in Russian chapter.

Like most foreigners, the Finns substitute "t" for the unvoiced "th" of "thin" and "d" for the voiced "TH" of "the." Because "th" and "TH" are very difficult for Finns to pronounce, these changes should be used occasionally, even for a light dialect.

The important consonant changes are:

B—changed to "p," as in "*p*AHi:" (*b*uy) and "mEHi*p*i:" (may*b*e).

J—changed to "dz," as in "*dz*AW:*dz*uh" (*ju*d*ge*).

Q—changed to "kuhvw," as in "*kuhvw*i:kuh" (*q*uick), the "uh" being an aspirate separating the two consonant sounds.

R—trilled.

W—changed to "vw," as in "*vw*EH:i:" (*w*ay) or to "v," as in "*v*oo:kuh" (*w*alk).

Z—changed to "s," as in "hAH:*s*uh" (ha*s*).

SH—changed to "s," as in "*s*oo:luh" (*sh*awl).

TCH—changed to "ts," as in "sEH:*ts*EHl" (sa*tch*el) and "ri:*ts*uh" (rea*ch*).

Because of the presence of so many aspirate "uh's" at the end and in the middle of words, the dialect has the effect of words being run together in a steady flow of sound with few inter-word pauses between. There are no articles or prepositions in the language or in the dialect, as in the Russian, from which many errors in grammar can be adopted. The stress in Finnish is on the first syllable.

THE HUNGARIAN DIALECT

The Hungarian language is not one of the Slavic group but is, instead, linked with the Finnish. This fact may account for some of the similarities in the American dialects of the Hungarian and the Finn.

VOWEL CHANGES

SOUND	WORD	CHANGE	DIALECT
AY	take	EHi	tEHik
UH	sofa	AH	sAWfAH
AH	father	AH	fAHdEHr
A:	ask	EH	EHsk
A	bat	EH	bEHt
AW	ball	AW	bAWl
EE	he	EE	hEE
EH	get	EH	gEHt

I	nice	AHi	nAHis
i	sit	i	sit
O	on	AW	AWn
	on, also	AH	AHn
OH	bone	AW	bAWn
AW	off	AW	AWf
	off, also	AH	AHf
OO	food	oo	food
	saloon	AW	sAHlAWn
oo	good	oo	good
yOO	unit	yoo	yoonit
U	up	AW	AWp
	trouble	oo	troob'l
	bucket	AH	bAHkEHt
ER	curb	AWr	kAWrb
OW	house	AH:	hAH:z
OI	boil	AHi	bAHil
y	baby	i	bEHibi

The substitution of "oo" for "U" in Hungarian is similar to the Finnish and shows their common root language. There is also an "oo" substitute of "AW," as in "boord" (board) which is another example.

CONSONANT CHANGES

L—sometimes dropped finally, as in "AW' mEHn" (old man).

R—always strongly trilled.

S—Sometimes changed to "z" medially, as in "bEHizmEHnt" (basement); sometimes changed to "z" finally, as in "hAH:z" (house).

T—sometimes changed to "d" medially, as in "pAHrdi" (party.)

W—changed to "v," as in "vAHi" (why) and "AHvEHi" (away); changed to "vw," as in "kvwik" (quick).

Note: For the pronunciation of "w" as "vw" see the material under "w" in the Russian "Consonant Changes."

Z—changed to "s" finally, as in "grAWs" (grows); retained medially, as in "lEHizEE" (lazy).

TH—changed to "d," as in "dEHt" (that).

th—changed to "t," as in "tink" (think).

There is a tendency to drop unaccented syllables and vowels, as in "AWp'rEHishAWn" (operation). Also there is running together of certain common phrases, as in "rAHidUHvEHi" (right away), "vAHtsUHmEHdEHr" (what's the matter), and "dAHtsAWrAHit" (that's all right).

There is one other similarity to the Finnish. The final consonants are aspirated quite heavily. This is done not so heavily or so often as in Finnish but it should be used sufficiently to establish the presence of the aspirate "uh."

CHAPTER EIGHTEEN

The Polish Dialect

THE POLISH LILT

The Poles, like the Russians, have a guttural language that keeps the pitch down in the lower registers. Usually, the keynote of the language language—and the dialect—starts about two or three notes lower than in ordinary American. In matter-of-fact conversation, except for a very gradual rising inflection, there is little variance in the pitch range—either rising or falling.

But under emotional stress, the rising inflection is, naturally, exaggerated, and reveals the speech pattern inherent in the dialect, as in:

“AHi nOt vwAWrk tAWrsdEHi!”
(I not work Thursday!)

The emphasis word of the sentence was “tAWrsdEHi” and it will be observed that it received glide-vowel treatment in the rising inflection of “AW” and in the falling inflection of “EH.” The vowel sounds in the other words were not glided. This habit of gliding on stressed vowels in stressed words evidences itself also in certain interjections common to the dialect. For example, the interjection, “boy,” when spoken alone, would read as follows:

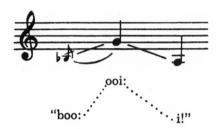

Here it can be seen that the rising and falling motif of the speech pattern is to be found in the single word as well as in the sentence. Even in the command form of sentence, this same pattern is noticed, as in:

"yoo gAW hAWm fAWr shtEHi!"
(you go home for stay!)
(You're going home to stay!)

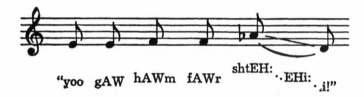

It can also be observed that, ordinarily, the sentence is composed of one beat, and that most of the sentence is spoken with a rising inflection, with the last word being used as a glide-vowel rise with a short glide-vowel fall. This is the pattern of the Polish speech and much of the dialect is spoken with it. Even the speech of the children, who do not speak the dialect, is tinged with this same use of the long rise and short fall and the final elongated glide-vowel, as in:

"You tore my coat Marie!"

EMPHASIS

The Polish language makes a point of emphasizing the next-to-the-last syllable in a word. When the dialect is spoken by an educated Pole, and his speech includes words of three or more syllables, he retains, to a great degree, the Polish tendency of emphasizing the next-to-the-last syllable, as in "AmfAH*s***AHi***s*UHd" (emphasized) in which the final syllable, "ed," is pronounced as "*s*UHd" instead of being almost assimilated, as in American.

The word emphasis in a sentence has been treated in the section on lilt. The words that are not important are treated with about the same emphasis as in American—very little—but the meaning word is given stress emphasis and tonal emphasis, the glide-vowels carrying the burden of the tonal emphasis. The stressed emphasis should be considerably heavier than that given stressed words in American.

The tempo of the dialect should ordinarily be slow and deliberate, especially in the emphasis words that have vowel-glides. The tempo should be accelerated only under the stress of emotion. Even then, however, the glide-vowels in the stressed word should be kept at their usual slow pace.

THE ADDED CONSONANTAL "Y" SOUND

Because his original language has the same Slavic roots as the Russian, the Pole is quite often given to the addition of the consonantal "y" sound to certain vowels when preceded by certain consonants. See "The Added Consonantal 'Y' Sound" in the Russian chapter for a more detailed discussion of this important element in the dialect. This "y" is not used so much as it is in Russian. In Polish, it seems to be added mostly to "n" when the "n" is followed by either short "i" or short "e," as in "mAW*nyi*" (mo*ney*) and "*nyEH*i*b*AWr" (*nei*ghbor). Sometimes it is added to "t," when the "t" is followed by a narrow vowel or even a wide vowel, as in "fOk-*ty*AWri" (fac*to*ry). At other times, it is added to "p" as in "*py*EHin" (*pai*n). "M" occasionally is followed by this consonantal "y" sound, as in "*myi*lk" (m*i*lk). But, in the dialect, it would be best to confine the added "y" only to "n" when it is followed by either a short "i" or a short "e" sound.

VOWEL CHANGES

"AY" . . . . as in "take," "break," "they," etc.

Shortened by the Pole, this long "a" vowel sound becomes "EHi," as in "t*EH*i*k" (t*a*ke). The "EH" is the same sound as in the American word "get," the "i" is the "i" of "it" and the two sounds are joined smoothly to make "EHi."

DRILL WORDS

pEHi	(pay)	AHvwEHi	(away)
pEHin'	(pain)	hEHi	(hey!)
shtEHi	(stay)	dEHi	(they)

bEHikUH'	(baker)
mEHikin'	(making)
OlvwEHis	(always)

NOTE: Refer to "Consonant Changes" for the pronunciation of the "vw" in the above examples.

"UH" .... as in "alone," "final," "sofa," etc.

This mute "a" is changed to "AH" by the Poles, as in "sAWfAH" (sofa). Sometimes, it is dropped initially, as in "'lAWn" (alone) and finally, as in "AHidi'" (idea).

DRILL WORDS

AHvwEHi	(away)	kAHnAri	(canary)
AHlAWn'	(along)	bAHnOnAH	(banana)
lAHpAl	(lapel)	AHfAWr'	(afford)
pAHrEHi'	(parade)		
sAHloot	(salute)		
sAHloon	(saloon)		

"AH" .... as in "father," "arm," "park," etc.

This broad "a" is shortened into the "O" of "rod," as in "pOk" (park).

DRILL WORDS

kOm	(calm)	shtO'v	(starve)
Oms	(alms)	kO'v	(carve)
fO'm	(farm)	O'mi	(army)
dO'lin'	(darling)		
spO'k'l	(sparkle)		
fOdUH'	(father)		

NOTE: The "r" after "O" is always dropped.

"A:" .... as in "ask," "draft," "laugh," etc.

This lengthened "a" also becomes the "O" of "rod" as in "drOf'" (draft). For the correct pronunciation of "f" see "F" in "Consonant Changes."

DRILL WORDS

pOt	(path)	lOs'	(last)
grOs	(grass)	fOs'	(fast)
lOf	(laugh)	pOs'	(past)
bOskit	(basket)		
sOmp'l	(sample)		
dOns	(dance)		

"A" .... as in "bad," "am," "narrow," etc.

This shortened "a" is also treated as "O," as in "bOd" (bad).

DRILL WORDS

Om	(am)	bOnk	(bank)
dOt	(that)	shtOb	(stab)
mOd	(mad)	bOg	(bag)

OksAp' (accept)
nOrAW (narrow)
fOm'li (family)

"AW" .... as in "ball," "falter," "shawl," etc.

The "O" of "rod" is given also to the broad "a," as in "bOl" (ball).

DRILL WORDS

Ol (all)
kOt (caught)
fOl (fall)

OlvwEHis (always)
sOl' (salt)
gOl (gall)

rAs'rOn' (restaurant)
syOl (shawl)
mOltid (malted)

"EE" .... as in "he," "treat," "people," etc.

The Poles shorten long "e" to short "i," as in "hi" (he).

DRILL WORDS

si (see)
bi (be)
syi (she)

shtrit (street)
sin (seen)
nyis (niece)

biliv (believe)
pyip'l (people)
ivnin' (evening)

Note: This long "e" sound is sometimes dropped at the end of a word in its "y" form, as in "Av'r" (every).

"EH" .... as in "bet," "said," "friend," etc.

This short "e" is changed to the "A" of "bad," as in "bAt" (bet).

DRILL WORDS

bAl' (belt)
sAl (sell)
hAd (head)

tAl (tell)
mAnyi (many)
bAn' (bend)

rAdi (ready)
vAr' (very)
frAn' (friend)

"I" .... as in "nice," "aisle," "guile," etc.

The shortening process affects the second part of this long "i" vowel sound (AH-EE) so that the vowel becomes "AHi," as in "nAHis" (nice).

DRILL WORDS

mAHi (my)
vwAHi (why)
bAHi (buy)

rAHi' (right)
fAHin' (find)
fAHi' (fight)

krAHi (cry)
pAWlAHi' (polite)
shtAHil (style)

"i" .... as in "sit," "women," "busy," etc.
This vowel sound is pronounced as in American.

"O" .... as in "on," "bond," "John," etc.
This vowel sound also is pronounced as in American.

"OH" .... as in "bone," "sew," "dough," etc.
This long "o" pronounced as "AW," as in "bAWn" (bone).

DRILL WORDS

sAW	(so)	hAWm	(home)
gAW	(go)	dAWn'	(don't)
nAW	(know)	tAWl'	(told)

fAlAW (fellow)
klAWs (clothes)
tAlAHfAWn (telephone)

"AW" .... as in "off," "cough," "bought," etc.
This vowel sound is pronounced as it is in American. But it should be given a full, rich "AW" treatment instead of the narrow pronunciation we give it.

"OO" .... as in "food," "do," "blue," etc.
The short double "o" (oo) of "good" is substituted for this long double "o" (OO), as in "doo" (do).

DRILL WORDS

bloo	(blue)	food	(food)
soop	(soup)	tchoon	(June)
noo	(knew)	soovwuh'	(sewer)

noospEHipuh' (newspaper)
bootlAguh' (bootlegger)
sAHloon (saloon)

"oo" .... as in "good," "wolf," "full," etc.
This vowel sound is pronounced as it is in American.

"yOO" .... as in "unit," "cube," "beauty," etc.
The Poles substitute the short double "o" (oo) of "good" for this long double "oo" and retain the initial "y," as in "kyoob" (cube).

DRILL WORDS

pyoo	(pew)	myoosik	(music)
fyoo	(few)	yoonAHi'	(unite)
kyoot	(cute)	kyoo'	(cure)

yoonyifAW'm   (uniform)
byoorifool   (beautiful)
fyoon'rAHl   (funeral)

"U" .... as in "up," "love," "does," etc.

This vowel sound is broadened in the Polish dialect into "AW" as in "lAWv" (love).

DRILL WORDS

AWp	(up)		trAWk	(truck)
bAWg	(bug)		mAWs'	(must)
shlAWg	(slug)		frAWn'	(front)
	hAWsbAHn'	(husband)		
	sAWpuh'	(supper)		
	dAWs	(does)		

"ER" .... as in "curb," "earn," "fir," etc.

In all its combinations—"ir," "er," "ur" and "or"—this vowel sound is changed to "AW," as in "fAWr" (fur).

DRILL WORDS

vwAWrk	(work)		dAWr'i	(dirty)
vwAWrt	(worth)		gAWrl	(girl)
nAWrs	(nurse)		kAWrb	(curb)
	tAWr'i	(thirty)		
	sAWrt'n	(certain)		
	tAWrsdEHi	(Thursday)		

The "er" endings, are, however, usually slurred into "uh," as in "fOduh" (father).

"OW" .... as in "out," "cow," "house," etc.

The Poles shorten this diphthong vowel sound from "AH-OO" to an elongated "AH:," as in "hAH:s" (house), the (:) sign indicating the elongation.

DRILL WORDS

nAH:	(now)		mAH:t	(mouth)
kAH:	(cow)		AHbAH:'	(about)
lAH:d	(loud)		mAH:s	(mouse)
	mAH:nt'n	(mountain)		
	tAH:sAHn'	(thousand)		
	AH:'sAHi'	(outside)		

"OI" .... as in "oil," "boy," "noise," etc.

The two parts of the diphthong "OI" (AW-EE), are changed and shortened to "oo-i," as in "noois" (noise).

DRILL WORDS

booi	(boy)		voois	(voice)
tchooi	(joy)		Antchooi	(enjoy)
ooil	(oil)		tooi	(toy)

gooituh	(goiter)
shpooil	(spoil)
pooin'	(point)

SUFFIXES

EN	listen	AWn	as in	lisAWn
OR	sailor	AWr	as in	sEHilAWr
LE	noble	'l	as in	nAWb'l
EL	label	'l	as in	lEHib'l
ON	nation	AWn	as in	nEHishAWn

WORD EXERCISES

Pronounce the following words in the Polish dialect making the necessary changes learned from the preceding Vowel Section:

1.	noise	11.	asking
2.	payday	12.	farmer
3.	jaw	13.	about
4.	yellow	14.	always
5.	worker	15.	steel mill
6.	Joe	16.	money
7.	trust	17.	goodbye
8.	house	18.	church-pew
9.	man	19.	potatoes
10.	street	20.	boss

When the above words have been pronounced, refer to the list below for the proper pronunciation. Check the mistakes and correct them, repeating the correction until it has been learned.

1.	noois	11.	hOskin'
2.	pEHidEHi	12.	fO'muh
3.	tchAW	13.	'bAH:'
4.	yAlAW	14.	OlvwEHs
5.	vwAWrkuh	15.	shtilmil
6.	tchAW	16.	mAWnyi
7.	trAWs'	17.	gootbAHi
8.	hAH:s	18.	tchAWrtchpyoo
9.	mOn	19.	pAWdEHidAWs
10.	shtrit	20.	bAWs

CONSONANT CHANGES

B—Pronounced as it is in American.

C—In both its hard and soft forms, this consonant may be treated as it is in American. Since, however, "c" in the Polish language represents a "ts" sound, many Poles often carry this "ts" into their American speech, as in "*ts*An'" (*c*ent).

D—Initially and medially, the consonant "d" is pronounced as it is in American.
Finally, "d" is dropped when it is preceded by any consonant but "r," as in "sOn'" (san*d*) and "tAH:sAHn'" (thousan*d*). Final "d" may be changed to "t" if it is preceded by a vowel sound, as in "goot" (good).

F—There is no clear "f" sound in the Polish language. Consequently, a great many Poles cannot sound it as in American and they seem to treat it as "p," as in "*pi*pti *p*AHi" (*f*ifty *f*ive). Actually, it is not a clear "p" sound but is an "f" sound pronounced through lips that are pursed to pronounce "w." Shape the lips for "w" and sound "f" instead, and an approximation of the Polish "f" will result. This sound may be achieved by pronouncing it like the "h" in the correct pronunciation of the American word "h-wI" (why). The lips must be kept tense.

G—The hard form of "g" is sometimes treated finally as "k" but, usually, it receives the same "g" pronunciation as in American, initially and medially. Finally, "g" is quite often dropped, especially from the "ing" endings, as in "vwAWrkin'" (workin*g*) and "rAWn'" (wron*g*). The soft form of "g" is discussed under "j."

H—Ordinarily, this consonant is pronounced as it is in American. Sometimes, however, it is added to words beginning with a vowel, as in "*h*Ol" (all) and "*h*AH:r" (hour).

J—The Poles substitute "tch" for the consonant "j" in all its forms, as in "*tch*Ob" (*j*ob), "gO*tch*'t" (ga*dg*et) and "*tch*AW*tch*" (*ju*d*ge*).

K—Ordinarily, this consonant is pronounced as it is in American. Sometimes, however, when preceded by a consonant other than "r" it is dropped finally, as in "Os'" (as*k*).

L—The American "l" is also used in the Polish dialect but is occasionally dropped, as in "O'rAHi'" (a*ll* righ*t*).

M—Pronounced as it is in American.

N—Initially and finally, the consonant "n" is pronounced as it is in American. But medially, and only when it is followed by a short "i" or short "e" vowel sound, it is quite often changed to "ny," with the added "y," as in "mAW*ny*i" (mo*ne*y).

P—Pronounced as it is in American.

Q—The American pronunciation of "kw" given to "q" is changed to "kv," in the

Polish, as in "*kv*ik" (*q*uick) and "*kv*in" (*q*ueen). It may also be changed to "kvw," as in "kv*w*ik" (*q*uick). See "*V*" in this section.

R—The Poles roll or trill their "r's" a bit longer than in American.

When preceded by an "O" sound, "r" is usually dropped, as in "pO'k" (pa*r*k), "kO'v" (ca*r*ve) and "fO'm" (fa*r*m).

S—When "s" is followed by a consonant and comes at the beginning of a word, it may be changed to "sh," as in "*sh*tAWr" (*s*tore) and "*sh*lip" (*s*leep). Medially and finally it is usually pronounced as in American.

T—Initially, "t" is pronounced as it is in American.

Medially, however, it is sometimes changed to "d," as in "kO*d*'n" (co*tt*on). Medially, also, it is sometimes changed to "r" as in "mO*r*uh" (ma*tt*er) and "bA*r*uh" (be*tt*er).

It is also sometimes changed to "r" finally, especially when it is followed by a word beginning with a vowel, as in "shAW*r*AWp" (shu*t* up) and "gA*r*AH:*r*AWhi:" (ge*t* ou*t* of here). It is also frequently dropped when preceded by a consonant other than "r," as in "frOn'" (fron*t*) and "fAl'" (fel*t*). It is quite often dropped finally when it is preceded by a vowel, as in "rAHi'" (righ*t*) and "gO'" (go*t*) and "lEHi'" (la*t*e).

V—The Polish dialect sometimes treats "v" as "vw." A "v" pronunciation may also be used if the "vw" cannot be approximated, as in "vAWt" (vote), "lAWv" (love) and "moovin'" (moving). For the "vw" sound, the lower lip should *almost* touch the bottom of the upper front teeth and "w" should be sounded.

W—The consonant "w" is also pronounced as "vw" but a clean "v" substitute may be used, as in "*v*AWrl'" (*w*orld), "Ol*v*EHis" (al*w*ays), and "*v*imin" (*w*omen). The "vw" is preferred.

X—This consonant is pronounced as it is in American in all its forms. For a heavier dialect "X" may be limited to only the "ks" sound.

Y—Pronounced as it is in American.

Z—When spelled as "z," the consonant "z" sound is pronounced as in American. But when spelled as an "s," it is pronounced as "s," as in "hO*s*" (ha*s*) and "grAW*s*" (grow*s*).

TCH—Pronounced as it is in American.

SH—Sometimes this "sh" consonant sound is pronounced as "sy," as in "*sy*oos" (*sh*oes).

Even when it is pronounced as "sh," a "y" is often added to it, as in "*shy*AW" (*sh*ow).

When this "sh" sound is spelled as "ch," as in "Chicago," it is pronounced as "tch," as in "*tch*ikOgAW" (*Ch*icago).

TH—The voiced "th" of "the" is usually changed to "d," as in "*di*" (*the*) and "*dOt*" (*that*).

th—Unvoiced "th," as in "think," is usually changed to "t," as in "*tink*" (*think*) and "bO*t*" (ba*th*).

ZH—This sound of the "s" in "vision" is pronounced as "sh" in the Polish dialect, as in "vi*sh*AWn" (vi*s*ion) and "lA*sh*oor" (lei*s*ure).

WORD EXERCISES

Pronounce the following words in the Polish dialect using the material learned from the preceding Consonant Section:

1.	parkway	11.	cigarette
2.	uniform	12.	voter
3.	George	13.	wicked
4.	always	14.	chamois
5.	strong	15.	rouge
6.	thinking	16.	get out
7.	bitter	17.	puzzle
8.	quick	18.	excuse
9.	themselves	19.	all right
10.	shoe store	20.	safe

When the above words have been pronounced, refer to the list below for the proper pronunciation. Check the mistakes and correct them, repeating the correction until it has been learned.

1.	pO'kvwEHi	11.	tsigAHrAt
2.	yoonyifAWrm	12.	vwAWduh'
3.	tchAW'tch	13.	vwikit
4.	hOlvwEHis	14.	tchOmi
5.	shtrAWn'	15.	roosh
6.	tinkin'	16.	gArAH:d
7.	biruh'	17.	pAWz'l
8.	kvik	18.	Akskyoos
9.	dAmsAlfs	19.	hO'rAHi'
10.	syooshtAW'	20.	sEHif (see "F")

GRAMMAR CHANGES

The most significant of all the errors in grammar of the Polish dialect is the incessant use of the verb "be" in place of the other forms of the verb, "to be," as in:

"AHi nOt bi hir."
(I not *be* here.)
(I *am* not here.)

"AHi vwOn' yoo bi goot."
(I want you *be* good.)
(I want you *to be* good.)

"AHi bi skAr lAHik Anyitin'."
(I *be* scare like anything.)
(I *was* as scared as anything.)

"yoo bi kAWl' hir?"
(You *be* cold here?)
(*Are* you cold here?)

"vwi bi si mAnyi tinks."
(We *be* see many things.)
(We *saw* many things.)

The omission of the pronoun, "it," is quite common in the Polish dialect, as in:

"mEHibi AHi Antchooi."
(Maybe I enjoy.)
(Maybe I will enjoy *it*.)

In the above sentence, the omission of the auxiliary verb, "will," illustrates another typical error in the dialect, as in:

"AHi gAW hAWm nAks' vwik."
(I go home next week.)
(I *will* go home next week.)

"hi nOt vwAWrk tAWrsdEHi."
(He not work Thursday.)
(He *will* not work Thursday.)

The dropping of the articles "a," "an" and "the" is observed by the Poles, as in:

"yoo bi bAHi book nAH:?"
(You be buy book now?)
(You will buy *a* book now?)

"dEHi bi si syAW nAks' tAHim."
(They be see show next time.)
(They will see *the* show next time.)

The substitution of "don't," for "doesn't," is quite common, as in:

"syi dAWn' gOt too vwAWrk."
(She *don't* got to work.)
(She *doesn't* have to work.)

The substitution of "got" for "have" is a major grammatical change in the dialect, as in:

"AHi gOt plAnti gAWrls."
(I *got* plenty girls.)
(I *have* many girls.)

The substitution of "for" for "to" is also characteristic, as in:

"hi vwOn' fAWr bilAWnk too klAWb."
(He want for belong to club.)
(He wanted *to* belong to the club.)

"yoo lAHik gAW hAWm fAWr shtEHi?"
(You like go home *for* stay?)
(Would you like to go home *to* stay?)

The above sentence illustrates another error—the dropping of the auxiliary verb, as in:

"yoo lAHik si mAHi hAH:s?"
(You like see my house?)
(*Would* you like *to* see my house?)

The substitution of "by" for "at" is another distinctive grammatical change, as in:

"yoo vwAWrk bAHi mAHi shtAWr?"
(You work *by* my store?)
(Do you work *at* my store?)

"dEHi liv bAHi hAWl mOnz hAH:s"
(They live *by* old man's house.)
(They live *at* the old man's house.)

"AHi bOt it bAHi drAWkshtAWr."
(I bought it *by* drugstore.)
(I bought it *at* the drugstore.)

"lAHik bAHi AWduh plEHis."
(like *by* other place.)
(as it was *at* the other place.)

The substitution of "like" for "as," in the above sentence, is another common error in grammar, as in:

"AHi bi doo it lAHik OlvwEHis."
(I be do it *like* always.)
(I shall do it *as* I always do.)

"it bi nOt sAW goot lAHik dOt."
(It be not so good *like* that.)
(It is not as good *as* all that.)

The Poles are also susceptible to the misuse of "leave" for "let," as in:

<table>
<tr><td>"liv it bi!"</td><td>"syi nOt liv mi doo it."</td></tr>
<tr><td>(Leave it be!)</td><td>(She not leave me do it.)</td></tr>
<tr><td>(Let it be!)</td><td>(She won't let me do it.)</td></tr>
</table>

The negative, in Polish, is often stated with the all-embracing "no," as in:

<table>
<tr><td>"nAW gOt tchAris."</td><td>"nAW mEHik lOts mAWnyi."</td></tr>
<tr><td>(No got cherries.)</td><td>(No make lots money.)</td></tr>
<tr><td>(I haven't any cherries.)</td><td>(I don't make much money.)</td></tr>
</table>

"nAW gOr'm tchOb."

(*No* got'm job.)

(I *haven't* got a job.)

In the last example sentence, the verb "got" was lengthened into "got'm." This method of pronouncing verbs is typical, as in:

<table>
<tr><td>"poor'm in bOks."</td><td>"mEHik'm goot vwAWrk."</td></tr>
<tr><td>(Put'm in box.)</td><td>(Make'm good work.)</td></tr>
<tr><td>(Put it in the box.)</td><td>(Put good work into it.)</td></tr>
</table>

"fiks'm Awp goot."

(*Fix'm* up good.)

(Fix it up well.)

It can be seen that the added "m" replaces an unspoken "it."

The double negative is another trap for the Poles, as it is for most foreigners, as in:

<table>
<tr><td>"yoo nAW doo dOt nAW mAWr."</td><td>"AHi nAW gOt nAW mAWnyi."</td></tr>
<tr><td>(You *no* do that *no* more.)</td><td>(I *no* got *no* money.)</td></tr>
<tr><td>(*Don't* you do that *any* more.)</td><td>(I *haven't any* money.)</td></tr>
</table>

The present tense of verbs is preferred to the past when the past tense is required, as in:

"dEHi vwOn' fAWr trAHi slAWks."

(They *want* for try slugs.)

(They *wanted* to try slugs.)

<table>
<tr><td>"AHi bi it lOs' nAHi."</td><td>"hi shtil frAWm shtOsh."</td></tr>
<tr><td>(I be *eat* last night.)</td><td>(He *steal* from Stash.)</td></tr>
<tr><td>(I *ate* last night.)</td><td>(He *stole* it from Stanley.)</td></tr>
</table>

The heavy Polish dialect incorrectly adds an "s" to many of its verbs, as in:

<table>
<tr><td>"AHi gOts nAWt'n."</td><td>"dEHi vwOns vwoomAHns."</td></tr>
<tr><td>(I got*s* nothing.)</td><td>(They want*s* woman*s*.)</td></tr>
<tr><td>(I have nothing.)</td><td>(They want the woman.)</td></tr>
</table>

The adverb "there" is almost always dropped in the dialect, as in:

"is nAW yoos."   "is too kAHin' pyip'l."

(Is no use.)   (Is two kind people.)

(*There* is no use.)   (*There* are two kinds of people.)

The last example also illustrates another common error: the confusion in number agreement between the subject and the verb, as in:

"dEHi vwOs too tAHir."   "hi tEHik it AHvwEHi."

(They *was* too tire.)   (He *take* it away.)

(They *were* too tired.)   (He *takes* it away.)

When a Pole improves his vocabulary so that he can use the more complex verb forms, he still errs frequently in his verbs, as in:

"yoo shoot vwOs dAr."

(You *should was* there.)

(You *should have* been there.)

SENTENCE EXERCISES

Pronounce the following sentences in the Polish dialect making the necessary changes in grammar learned from the preceding section:

1. Will you take the job right away?
2. I haven't any time to look for it.
3. Do you let him go outside?
4. We should have been there already.
5. There are four sandwiches in your box.
6. We haven't any room for as many as that.
7. I will go to visit her now in the hospital.
8. We will go to the show right away.
9. I don't care to know what he wanted.
10. They were always driving as fast as anything.

After each sentence, refer to the following versions for the correct changes. Make the corrections and pronounce the sentence correctly. Do this with every sentence.

1. yoo bi tEHik tchAWp rAHidAHvwEHi?
2. AHi nAW gAWruhm tAHim look fAWr it.
3. yoo bi livw him gAW AH:'sAHi'?
4. vwi syoot vwOs dAr hAW'rAdyi.
5. is fAWr sOnvwitch in bAWks.
6. vwi nAW gAWruhm room fAWr sAW mAnyi lAHik dOt.
7. AHi gAW fAWr vwisit hAWr nAH: in hAW spitAHl.
8. vwi gAW bAHi syAW rAHidAHvwEHi.
9. AHi nAW kAr nAW wOri wOn'.
10. dEHi bi hOlvwEHis drAHivw sAW fOs' lAHik hAnitin'.

COMMON EXPRESSIONS

There are a number of expressions—interjections and phrases—that are thrown into the Polish dialect for no particular reason other than habit or popularity. The word most frequently used is the word "you," which is used like the American word "Golly," as in:

"vwOs AHi skAr, yoo!"
(Was I scare, you!)
(Was I scared, you!)

"look, yoo, vwOt hi dAWn."
(Look, you, what he done.)
(Look, you, what he's done.)

"yoo! ril shtAWf!"
(You! real stuff!)

The phrase, "by Joe!," is used quite often and may have been adapted from the British, "by Jove!," because it is used in the same way, as in:

"bAHi tchAW! yoo bi vwAWrk hOd!"
(By Joe! you be work hard!)
(By Joe! you work hard!)

Another common interjection is the word "boy" and sometimes, "boy-o-boy!" used to express such emotions as surprise or amazement, as in:

"booiAWbooi! is hOt!"
(Boy-o-boy! is hot!)
(Boy-o-boy! it's hot!)

Word combinations that have been run together also become common expressions, as in:

"shAWrAWp yoo!"
(Shut up, you!)

"gArAH:rOhi!"
(Get out of here!)

Agreement is always signified with an emphatic "yAH!" (yes), as in:

"yAH! AHi gAW hAWm kvwik!"
(Yes! I go home quick!)
(Yes! I shall go home right away!)

POLISH LANGUAGE CARRYOVERS

hello	*dziendobry*	jEHn**dAW**bri
goodbye	*do widzenia*	dOH vid**zEHn**yAH
excuse me	*przepraszam*	pzh**EH**prAH**shAH**m
thank you	*dziekuje*	jEH**kooy**EH
yes	*tak*	tAHk
no	*nie*	nyEH

POLISH MONOLOG

"A LETTER FROM THE FRONT"
(An original monolog for radio presentation)

ANNOUNCER: Somewhere at the front, in a dugout entrance, a Polish peasant soldier approaches an American newspaper correspondent. He looks warily about. Then, hollering over the thunder of the shells, he says:

SOUND: *Background of cannon, minnie whines, etc.*

SOLDIER: 'scuse, please! you be American writer, no? I be got big favor you be do for me. Come by dugout and we talk so nobody they hear . . .(*laughing cajolingly*) . . .come on! you no be scare from Steve Kuloc. I be talk American just so like you. Is because I live in America long time. I be work by steelmill by Pittsburgh, U.S.A. Oh! come on! you be good fellow. You listen please! I be want for you should take letter back home for my Anna when you be leave front soon. She be so happy that you do so. Oh! I be write her lots letter, yah! but you know . . .what you call him . . . censor fellow . . . what he be do with letter. All I write he be push out with pencil. I want for tell my Anna all so she no be make lots worry. So I think maybe you be good fellow you take this letter for my Anna, no? I be write so . . . Dear Anna . . . she always be like I say that . . . I write: please no be worry for Steve. I be O.K. I be eat lots food, I be strong, I be healthy. Here by front is lots cold. But I got good uniform, got lots good place for sleep. Is lots shooting, Anna, but no be scare. I be come home soon when war be over. I no be sore by nobody—nobody they be sore on Steve. Yesterday we be catch prisoner. You be surprize what kind fellow he be, Anna—just so like me. I make talk with him. He say me he be got wife and kids back home by farm too. Now he be glad he be catch prisoner—he be fight no more. Soon, war be done and I be go home by farm by you and by little Katie. By Joe! is be lots work by farm I bet you! First I kiss you lots. Then I kiss little Katie lots. Then I go out for milk cow. I no kiss cow. Then I be go fix'm up house plenty good. I bet you no be fix'm up hole by roof yet. I be fix'm up hole. Then I be go out by barn fix'm up plow—make ready for Spring when I put'm seed in ground and . . . Anna . . . maybe, next year, we be got lots more kids and . . .

SOUND: (*Loud whine of minnie followed by close explosion*)

SOLDIER: (*Groaning after a long pause*) . . . Anna . . . I be think . . . maybe . . . next year no be come . . . Steve . . . he no be . . . back home . . . by . . . farm . . . no . . . more . . .

PHONETIC REPRESENTATION
Syllables in bold face are to be accented.

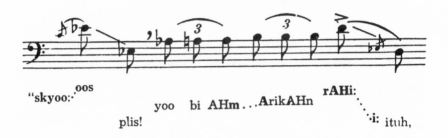

"skyoo:·^oos

plis!   yoo   bi **AHm**...**ArikAHn**

rAHi:

·i: itᴜh,

nAW? AHi bi gOt **bik fEH**ivAWr yoo bi doo fAWr mi. kAWm bAHi **dAWkAH:'**
On' vwi tOk sAW **nAW**bOdyi dEHi **hir** ... **kAWm On!** yoo nAW bi shkAr frAWm
shtiv **kool**Ok. AHi bi tOk AHmArikAHn **tchAWs'** sAW lAHik **yoo**. is bikOs AHi
liv in AHmArikAH **lAW**nk **tAH**im. AHi bi vwAWrk bAHi **shtil**mil bAHi **pi'**s-
bAWrk, **yoo**AsEHi. **AW! kAWm On!** yoo bi goot **fAl**AW. yoo **lis**AWn **plis!** AHi bi
vwOn' fAWr yoo shoot tEHik **lAdAWr** bOk **hAWm** fAWr mAHi **On**AH vwAn yoo
bi liv **frAW**n' soon. syi bi sAW **hO**pi dOt yoo **doo** sAW. **AW!** AHi bi rAHi' hAWr
lOts lAdAWr, **yAH!** bAWt yoo nAW ... vwOt yoo kOl him ... **sAn**sAWr **fAl**AW ...
vwOt **hi** bi doo vwit **lAdAWr**. Ol AHi rAHi' hi bi poosh **AH:'** vwit **pAn**sil. AHi
vwOn' fAWr tAl mAHi **On**AH Ol sAW syi **nAW** bi mEHik lOts **vwAW**ri. sAW AHi
tink mEHibi yoo bi goot **fAl**AW yoo tEHik dis **lAdAWr** fAWr mAHi **On**AH, **nAW?**
AHi bi rAHi' **sAW** ... dir **On**AH ... syi OlvwEHis bi **lAH**ik AHi sEHi dOt ... AHi
rAHi' : plis nAW bi **vwAW**ri fAWr **shtiv**. AHi bi **AWkEHi**. AHi bi it **lOts** foot, AHi
bi **shtrAW**nk, AHi bi **hAl**ti. **hir** bAHi **frAW**n' is lOts kAWl'. bAWt AHi gOt **goot**
yoonyifAWrm, gOt **lOts** goot **plEH**is fAWr **shlip**. is lOts **syoo**tin', **On**AH, bAWt
nAW bi **shkAr**. AHi bi kAWm **hAWm** soon vwAn vwOr bi **hAW**v'r. AHi nAW bi
sAWr bAHi **nAW**bOdyi—**nAW**bOdyi dEHi bi sAWr On **shtiv.** yAstuhdEHi vwi
bi kOtch **pris**'nAWr. yoo bi sAW'**prAH**is vwOt kAHin' **fAl**AW hi bi, **On**AH—
tchAWs' sAW lAHik **mi**. AHi mEHik **tOk** vwit him. hi sEHi mi **hi** bi gOt **vwAH**if
On' **kits** bOk hAWm bAHi fOm, **too**. nAH: hi bi **glOt** hi bi **kOtch pris**'nAWr—hi
bi **fAHi' nAW** mAWr. soon, vwOr bi **dAW**n On' AHi bi gAW hAWm bAHi **fOm**
bAHi **yoo** On' bAHi li'l **kEH**ityi. **bAHi tchAW!** is bi **lOts vwAW**rk bAHi fOm,
AHi **b**Atchoo! **fAW**rs' AHi kis yoo **lOts**. dAn AHi kis li'l **kEH**tyi lOts. dAn AHi
gAW **hAH:'** fAWr milk **kAH:**. AHi **nAW** kis **KAH:**. dAn AHi bi gAW fiks'm hAWp
hAH:s **plAn**tyi goot. AHi **b**Atchoo yoo **nAW** bi fiks'm hAWp **hAWl** bAHi **roof**
yAt. AHi bi fiks'm hAWp **hAWl**. dAn AHi bi gAW hAH: bAHi **bOn** fiks'm hAWp

plAH:—mEHik rAdyi fAWr **shprink** vwAn AHi pood'm **sit** in **grAH:n'** On' . . .
OnAH . . . mEHibi, nAks' yir, vwi bi gOt lOts mAWr **kits** On' . . . .

(*Sound effect of explosion*)

(*Groaning after a long pause*) . . . **On**AH . . . AHi bi tink . . . mEHibi . . . nAks' yir
nAW bi **kAWm** . . . shtiv . . . hi nAW bi . . . bOk hAWm . . . bAHi . . . fOm . . . nAW
. . . mAWr . . .

CHAPTER NINETEEN

The Greek Dialect

THE GREEK DIALECT

The Greeks should have more than a word for it. With eleven vowel sounds, fourteen diphthong sounds and twenty consonant sounds in their alphabet, they should have an entire lexicon of words for it—whatever "it" may be.

To a great extent, the Greek dialect is influenced, not only by the Greek language spoken in modern times, but also by classic Greek, compared to which modern Greek is only a *patois*. For one thing, the method of accenting words and syllables with tonal emphasis instead of stressed emphasis is a distinct throwback to classic Greek. Also, the dialect is affected by the Greek system of classifying the two types of breathing in speaking which have their effect on the lilt, tempo, and vowel and consonant changes in American. What may be called "rough-breathing" is reserved for the gutturals and aspirates, while "smooth-breathing" is used for the other classifications.

Four of the twenty consonants in the Greek language, for instance, are given a guttural palatal treatment—the gargled "kh"—"k," "g," "kh" and "h." These sounds, in the Greek-American dialect, also receive the gargled "kh." What is more, the Greeks cannot differentiate, in their own language, between their guttural and their velar consonants—"q," "g," "qh" and "gh"—which are consonant sounds made from the soft palate instead of from the roof of the mouth. Therefore, in the Greek-American dialect, the same confusion exists and in it, too, these sounds are sometimes given the gargled "kh."

Most of the vowel and consonant sounds are listed in order later in this chapter where they will be treated accordingly.

THE GREEK LILT

There are a few characteristics of the Greek lilt that can be used and copied, as tricks, to simulate the dialect. These have been adopted by such comedians as "Parkyakarkus" and George Givot and much of their success can be attributed to this lilt. One of the most effective tricks is to use the rising inflection in a vowel glide on the first word of a sentence, as in:

"khooAWrUHyoolAHikTHAHtTH?"
(How do you like that?)

The sentence on the preceding page was written with all the words thrown together because of the tendency in the dialect to pronounce idiomatic expressions as one word. Now, with the keynote of the first word spoken about three notes above that of the normal American, the Greek would sing out the sentence, as follows:

Observe that the first word, "khooAW" has a rising inflection on its vowel glide, "ooAW." Also notice that it carries with it the "r" substitute for the "d" in the following word "do." This is typical of the dialect lilt and makes for the rhythmic flow of the words. It also explains the reason for pronouncing the sentence as one word. Notice, also, that the sentence has three distinct beats: the first starting with "khooAW," the second starting with "yoo," and the third starting with "THAH."

The rhythmic flow, however, is not typical of the dialect as a whole. Because of the presence of aspirated gutturals, glottal stops, and a general lengthening of the vowel sounds, there is a tendency to treat the rhythm in fits and starts. This can be seen in the above sentence in which the second beat dropped down below the keynote after the first beat rose to the high note in the sentence. It would be even more readily observed in lengthier sentences.

The Greek pitch is normally higher than in American and it ranges more. The pitch range varies also because of the inherent habit of the Greeks to speak declamatorily, as though their speech were part of an oration. The tempo, too, is faster, which accounts for the Greek habit of running words together.

In Greek, where individual syllables and even single vowels are sung in rising and falling tones—as in the Cockney—the syllabic emphasis comes usually on the lowest note of the rising tone or the highest note of the falling tone—or on both. In the above quoted sentence, for example, it will be observed that the sentence was divided into three separate beats. The low note in the first beat was the "khoo" and it would receive the stressed emphasis. The low note in the second beat was "lAH" and it would receive the stressed emphasis of that beat. The third beat, however, was a falling beat and its *highest* note, on "THAH," would receive its stressed emphasis.

In the ancient classic Greek, word accent was achieved with tonal emphasis—a change in musical pitch—rather than with stressed accent—with an extra expulsion of breath. This tonal emphasis is still carried over, in a limited way, in modern Greek—hence, the juxtaposition of tonal emphasis and stressed emphasis. A general rule might state that the accented syllables in the Greek dialect are those that reach the high notes before the falling inflections and those that start on the low note in the rising inflections.

Insofar as syllabic emphasis is concerned, it would be wise to use the American system wherever possible. Short words ending with a consonant, which are given the aspirate "uh," would naturally neutralize the initial syllable accent, as in "bAHruh" (bar), in which the main emphasis would be placed on the initial syllable, "bAH," and the secondary emphasis on "ruh."

Combination words—especially those in which the first part ends with a consonant—have equal emphasis on the initial syllable in both parts of the word, as in "**kooAWluhmAHin**" (coal mine). Words ending in a heavily aspirated consonant usually reverse the emphasis, from the first syllable to the last syllable, as in "bAHsuhkAtTHuh" (basket) and "tTHikAtTHuh" (ticket). A general rule—not to be observed too inflexibly—might state that the emphasis should be placed on the initial syllable of a word when it is preceded by the aspirate "uh" of a word ending in a heavily aspirated consonant, as in "yooAWnguh m**AH**nuhkhoodTH" (young manhood).

It will be observed that an aspirate "uh" is often used to separate two consonant sounds. This aspirate "uh" must be very slight. It is a short puff of air usually heard after certain consonants. Pronounce "take" and it will be heard after the "k." This "uh" and not "UH" or "AH" is the aspirate. This "uh" between consonants will be indicated only occasionally but it should be used after "p," "t" and "k."

VOWEL CHANGES

"AY" .... as in "take," "break," "they," etc.

This long "a" vowel sound is flattened out by many Greeks into the short "e" (EH) sound of "bet," as in "tTHEHk" (take).

DRILL WORDS

lEHk	(lake)	tTHEHstTHi	(tasty)
fEHtTH	(fate)	mEHbi	(maybe)
mEHl	(mail)	khEHtTH	(hate)

sEHlooAWr   (sailor)
vEHkEHsooAWn   (vacation)
bEHsuhmAn'   (basement)

Note: For pronouncing the final syllable in such words as "sEHlooAWr" (sailor) in the above list, refer to the discussion of the vowel sound "O."

"UH" .... as in "alone," "final," "sofa," etc.

This mute "a" is changed to "AH" in the dialect, as in: "sooAWfAH" (sofa).

DRILL WORDS

AHbooAWv	(above)	sAHlootTH	(salute)
AHlooAWn	(alone)	pAHrEHdTH	(parade)
AHplAHi	(apply)	sAHloon	(saloon)
AHgooAW	(ago)		
mAHlisooAWs	(malicious)		
lAHpAl	(lapel)		

"AH" .... as in "father," "arm," "park," etc.

The same "AH" as in American is given to this vowel sound.

"A:" .... as in "ask," "draft," "laugh," etc.

This lengthened short "a" is pronounced in Greek as "AH," as in "AHsk" (ask).

DRILL WORDS

grAHs	(grass)	glAHns	(glance)
tTHAHsk	(task)	bAHskAtTH	(basket)
pAHs	(pass)	sAHmpooAWl	(sample)
lAHf	(laugh)		
mAHstTHooAWr	(master)		
pAHstTHyooAWr	(pasture)		

"A" .... as in "bad," "am," "narrow," etc.

This short "a" is also pronounced as "AH," as in "bAHdTH" (bad).

DRILL WORDS

sAHk	(sack)	nAHrooAW	(narrow)
pAHdTH	(pad)	mAHgnAtTH	(magnet)
sAHp	(sap)	lAHdTHooAWr	(ladder)
sAHli	(Sally)		
bAHlAHns	(balance)		
kAHpitTHAHl	(capital)		

"AW" .... as in "ball," "falter," "shawl," etc.

This "a" is shortened into "O" (in "rod") but, before it, the Greeks sound the short "oo" of "good," as in "booOl" (ball). (See "O.")

DRILL WORDS

ooOl	(all)	ooOdTHiAns	(audience)
kooOl	(call)	kooOtTH	(caught)
looOn	(lawn)	sooOs	(sauce)

                        sooOl   (shawl)
             looOndTHri   (laundry)
              bikooOs   (because)

"EE" .... as in "he," "treat," "people," etc.

The Greek shortening process changes this long "e" to short "i," as in "khi" (he).

DRILL WORDS

bi	(be)	ooidTH	(weed)
si	(she)	ooin	(wean)
mi	(me)	si	(see)

risitTH	(receipt)
rooAWsbif	(roastbeef)
ibvnin'	(evening)

"EH" .... as in "bet," "said," "friend," etc.

The short "a" of "bat" is substituted for this short "e," as in "bAtTH" (bet).

DRILL WORDS

sAl	(sell)	yAlooAW	(yellow)
ooAl	(well)	mAni	(many)
gAtTH	(get)	sooAl	(swell)

frAn'	(friend)
khAlth	(health)
ooAlth	(wealth)

"I" .... as in "ice," "aisle," "guile," etc.

Just as long "e" (EE) is shortened to short "i," in the dialect, the long "e" (EE) portion of long "I" (AH-EE), is changed to short "i" so that long "i" becomes "AHi," as in "AHis" (ice).

DRILL WORDS

nAHis	(nice)	pooAWlAHitTH	(polite)
bAHi	(buy)	rAHitTH	(right)
tTHrAHi	(try)	mAHisAlf	(myself)

bAHisikooAWl	(bicycle)
mAHinooAWr	(minor)
dTHibvAHin	(divine)

"i" .... as in "it," "women," "busy," etc.

The Greeks retain this short "i." Sometimes, though, it is given an elongation into "ii" but it can stand singly.

"O" .... as in "on," "bond," "John," etc.

It is with the pronunciation of all the "o's" that the Greek dialect achieves its most distinctive characteristic. The three "o's"—in "on," in "bone," and in "off"—

all receive the same treatment. In all of them, the "o" is changed to "AW." But the Greeks enrich this "AW" with a shortened "oo" sound, as in "good," so that the "o" becomes "ooAW," "ooAWn" (on), "booAWn" (bone) and "ooAWf" (off). It must be remembered that the initial "oo" sound is of very short duration—only barely suggested and almost an initial aspirate "uh"—but it should be present, nevertheless. Use the example word, "cosmopopolos" pronounced phonetically as:

"kooAWsmooAWpooAWpooAWlooAWs"

The application of this important addition to the Greek dialect should aid considerably in achieving authenticity. See the consonant "W" for additional information.

NOTE: For a lighter dialect, this "oo" sound may be dropped from a great many of the words. But a few of them sprinkled in can color the dialect with the desired rounded quality. This applies to *all* the vowel sounds enriched with the initial "oo." Remember, when this initial "oo" is used before "AW" it should be suggested very faintly.

DRILL WORDS

tTHooAWm	(Tom)	zhooAWni	(Johnny)
gooAWtTH	(got)	spooAWtTH	(spot)
khooAWtTH	(hot)	booAWndTH	(bond)
nooAWbooAWdTHi	(nobody)		
kooAWnAK'	(connect)		
khooAWtTHkEHk	(hotcake)		

"OH" .... as in "bone," "sew," "dough," etc.

As was explained in the preceding vowel sound, this long "o" also receives the initial "oo" before its "AW" substitution, as in "booAWn" (bone).

DRILL WORDS

gooAW	(go)	pooAWs'	(post)
sooAW	(so)	gooAWs'	(ghost)
stTHooAWn	(stone)	rooAWdTH	(road)
dTHooAWn'	(don't)		
klooAWTHs	(clothes)		
fAlooAW	(fellow)		

"AW" .... as in "off," "cough," "bought," etc.

This "o," too, receives the initial "oo" before its substituted "AW" sound, as in "ooAWf" (off).

DRILL WORDS

kooAWs'	(cost)	klooAWth	(cloth)
sooAwf'	(soft)	kooAWrn	(corn)
gooAWn	(gone)	stTHooAWr	(store)

fooAWrtTHi (forty)
skooAWrbooAWrdTH (scoreboard)
kooAWrs (course)

"OO" .... as in "food," "do," "blue," etc.

The double "o" (OO) of "food" is changed to the double "o" (oo) of "good," as in "foodTH" (food).

DRILL WORDS

dTHoo	(do)		tsoo	(chew)
khoo	(who)		noo	(knew)
sootTH	(suit)		zhoon	(June)
	moobvis	(movies)		
	stTHoop	(stoop)		
	bloo	(blue)		

"oo" .... as in "good," "wolf," "full," etc.

This vowel sound is pronounced as it is in American.

"yOO" .... as in "unit," "cube," "beauty," etc.

The change of long double "o" (OO) to short double "o" (oo) also affects this long "u" so that it becomes "yoo," as in "yoonitTH" (unit).

DRILL WORDS

kyootTH	(cute)		byoorooAW	(bureau)
kyoo	(cue)		byoogooAWl	(bugle)
myootTH	(mute)		ribyook	(rebuke)
	myoosik	(music)		
	byoorifool	(beautiful)		
	fyoozhitTHibv	(fugitive)		

"U" .... as in "up," "love," "does," etc.

The dialect substitutes "AW" for this short "u." But this "AW" sound also receives an initial "oo" sound before it, as in "ooAWp" (up).

DRILL WORDS

dTHooAWn	(done)		kooAWm	(come)
khooAWtTH	(hut)		frooAWn'	(front)
kooAWtTH	(cut)		dTHooAWs	(does)
	sooAWmthin'	(something)		
	looAWbvli	(lovely)		
	khooAWmbooAWg	(humbug)		

"ER" .... as in "curb," "earn," "fir," etc.

This short "u" is changed to "AW" in the dialect and it also takes the initial "oo," as in "koo-AWrbv" (curb).

DRILL WORDS

khooAWr	(her)	ooAWrth	(worth)
fooAWr	(fur)	looAWrn	(learn)
gooAWrl	(girl)	fooAWr	(fir)

kooAWrTH'n   (curtain)
dTHistTHooAWrb   (disturb)
khAHmbooAWrgooAWr   (hamburger)

"OW" .... as in "out," "cow," "house," etc.

This diphthong, pronounced "AH-OO" in American, is changed to "AW" in the Greek, with the initial "oo" before it, as in "ooAWtTH" (out). See "O."

DRILL WORDS

nooAW	(now)	mooAWs	(mouse)
khooAW	(how)	dTHooAWn	(down)
kooAW	(cow)	flooAWr	(flour)

dTHooAWntTHooAWn   (downtown)
flooAWrpooAWtTH   (flowerpot)
prooAWdTH   (proud)

"OI" .... as in "oil," "boy," "noise," etc.

This diphthong, pronounced as "AW-EE" in American, is changed to "ooOI" in the Greek with the initial "oo" sound before it, as in "ooOIl" (oil).

DRILL WORDS

booOI	(boy)	spooOIl	(spoil)
sooOIl	(soil)	tTHooOI	(toy)
zhooOIn	(join)	nooOIs	(noise)

gooOItTHooAWr   (goiter)
sooOIbin   (soybean)
tTHooOIl   (toil)

Many Greeks, however, do not use this slight "oo" sound; so, it may be dropped.

"OUS" ... "OR" ... "ER" ... "ION" ... "LE" ... "EL" ENDINGS

Words ending with any of the above combinations are treated as "ooAW," as in "fEHmooAWs" (famous), "sEHlooAWr" (sailor), "fAHitTHooAWr" (fighter), "bvEHkEHsyooAWn" (vacation), "byoogooAWl" (bugle), and "khAHpooAWl" (apple).

"ION" ENDING

This ending may also be treated with the Franch nasal sound, as "yAWn̦." The "n̦" signifies that the "n" is silent and that the preceding vowel is nasalized, as in "stTHEHsyAWn̦" (station).

WORD EXERCISES

Pronounce the following words in the Greek dialect using the material learned from the preceding section on Vowel Changes:

1.	fruit store	11.	enjoy
2.	doughnuts	12.	something
3.	hospital	13.	moving picture
4.	girl-friend	14.	pineapple
5.	laughter	15.	ambitious
6.	downstairs	16.	healthy
7.	few	17.	potato sack
8.	application	18.	hothouse
9.	tasty	19.	mailman
10.	applesauce	20.	pudding

After pronouncing the above words, refer to the following list for the correct pronunciations. Check the mistakes made in the vowels, repeat the corrections and memorize.

1.	frootTHstTHooAWr	11.	AnzhooOI
2.	dTHooAWnooAWtTHs	12.	sooAWmthin'
3.	khooAWspitTHAHl	13.	moobvin'pitsooAWr
4.	gooAWrlfrAn'	14.	pAHinAHpooAWl
5.	lAHftTHooAWr	15.	AHmbisyooAWs
6.	dTHooAWnstTHArs	16.	khAltTHi
7.	fyoo	17.	pAWtTHEHrAWsAHk
8.	AHplikEHsyooAWn	18.	khooAWtTHkhooAWs
9.	tTHEHstTHi	19.	mEHlmAHn
10.	AHpooAWlsooOs	20.	poodTHin'

CONSONANT CHANGES

B—Ordinarily, the consonant "b" is treated as it is in American. But some Greeks sound it as "bv," as in "kooAWr*bv*" (cur*b*). This "bv" sound is achieved by keeping the lips slightly open while pronouncing "b."

C—The soft sound of "c" is always pronounced as "s." For the hard sound, see "K."

D—This consonant receives a number of changes in the Greek dialect, perhaps because it is not in the Greek alphabet. The most important change is that it is commonly dentalized, with the tip of the tongue placed immediately under the cutting edge of the upper front teeth instead of in the forward part of the roof of the mouth, as in American. This gives it a "dTH" pronunciation, as in "fid*TH*ooAWl" (fi*dd*le).

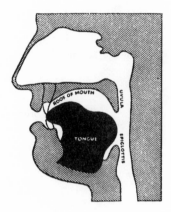

The tongue tip, pressed against the backs of the front teeth, introduces into the "d" sound the additional "TH," creating the sound, "dTH." The American "d" is produced by touching the gum ridge of the upper front teeth with the tongue tip.

For clarity's sake or for a lighter dialect it is suggested that this treatment be confined to the middle of a word only, although, if the treatment can be expertly handled, it can be used initially, medially, or finally, as it is designated in this chapter.

Medially, "d" is often changed to "r," especially in word sequences that are run together, as in "'i*r*ooAWnooAW." (He *d*on't know.) It accounts for radio-comedian Parkyakarkus' pronunciation of "khooAW*r*UHyoolAHikTHAHtTH?" (How do you like that?)

It is nearly always dropped at the end of a word when it is preceded by another consonant, as in "frAn'" (frien*d*), "stooAHr'" (stewar*d*) and "booAWn'" (bon*d*).

F—Ordinarily pronounced as it is in American. Sometimes, though, it is dropped medially, when it is followed by a consonant, as in "fi'tTHi" (fi*f*ty).

G—Hard "g" is pronounced as it is in American. In the ending, "ing," it is almost always dropped, as in "pAHrkin'" (parkin*g*). Sometimes it is sounded as the gargled "kh," as in "Ani*kh*mAH" (enigma). For the soft sound of "g," see "J."

H—It is with the consonant "h" that the Greek dialect receives most of its guttural "rough-breathing" quality. Sometimes, it is dropped initially, as in "'ooAWt-THAl" (*h*otel), "'i" (*h*e) and "'ooAWm" (*h*ome). But usually, when it is used initially and medially, it is treated as the gargled "kh" (as in the Scotch "loch") which has been described in detail in the chapter on the Russian dialect. The sound is pronounced then, as in "*kh*AHpi" (*h*appy), "*kh*ooAWtTHAl" (*h*otel), and "rAdTH*kh*ooAWtTH" (red*h*ot).

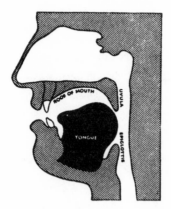

The back of the tongue is raised to touch the uvula at the end of the soft palate. When the breath is brought up past this conjuncture, it is roughened and voiced, producing the Greek "kh" sound. Neither the tongue nor the uvula vibrates when this sound is produced.

Sometimes, the Greeks add an "h" to words beginning with a vowel, like the Cockney, in which the "h" is also given the gargled "kh," as in "*kh*ooOlbvEHs" (always) and "*kh*AHmpooAWl" (apple).

J—Because there is no "j" sound in the Greek language, the dialect treats it as "zh," as in "*zh*ooAW*zh*" (*j*ud*g*e) and "*zh*ooAW*zh*" (*G*eor*g*e). Note the exact pronunciation for the two words. Other examples are "khAHbi*zh*" (cabba*g*e) and "grEH*zh*'ooAWl" (*g*ra*d*ual). In the word "gradual" the (') sign indicated that the "u" was dropped. This was done because of the initial "oo" sound preceding the "AW" sound of "al."

In a variation, "dz" is substituted for "j," as in "*dz*ooAWmp" (*j*ump).

K—This is another sound that contributes to the guttural quality of the Greek dialect. Like the "h," it may be given the gargled "kh" pronunciation when it is in an American word of Greek origin and spelled "ch," as in "*kh*rooAWmooAW" (*ch*romo) and "tTHA*kh*nik" (te*ch*nique). This gargled "kh" is also substituted for the "k" sound when it precedes "AW," and "AH," as in "*kh*AHndTHi" (candy) and "*kh*ooAWm" (comb).

In a variation, hard "g" is substituted for "k," as in "tTHAHn*g*" (tan*k*) and "bAHn*g*bvAtTH" (ban*q*uet) where the "k" sound is derived from the "kw" of "q."

For a light dialect the normal "k" can be used throughout.

L—The consonant "l" is pronounced quite fully in the Greek dialect where it receives a very slight aspirate "uh" after its pronunciation, as in "booOl*uh*" (ball) and "fooOl*uh*tTHooAWr" (falter). This aspirate will not be indicated in this chapter but its use should be remembered.

M—Usually pronounced as it is in American.

Sometimes, though, it is added, medially, as in "khAH*m*pooAWl" (apple) and "stTHrooAW*mb*Ari" (strawberry). This addition, if used, should come before "p" or "b" only.

N and **P**—Pronounced as in American.

Q—In American, "q" is pronounced as "kw." But a great many Greeks change the "w" to "bv." It is pronounced as in "*kbvik*" (quick), "*kbvin*" (queen), and "*kbvooOlitTHi*" (quality). This change, though, applies only when "q" is used at the beginning of a word.

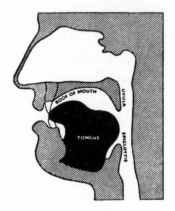

The tongue tip, pressed against the backs of the front teeth, introduces into the "t" sound the additional "TH," creating the sound, "tTH." The American "t" is produced by touching the gum ridge of the upper front teeth with the tongue tip.

When "q" is used medially, after a consonant, it changes from "kw" to "gbv," as in "bAHn*gbv*AtTH" (banquet) and "zhooAWn*gbv*il" (jonquil).

For a light dialect, use the normal "k" sound throughout.

R—Although the Greek dialect uses gutturals, it does not thicken its "r," as does the German. Instead, the "r" is rolled with the tip of the tongue.

S—The consonant "s" sound is always hissed in the dialect.

T—Like the consonant "d," the consonant "t" is dentalized because it is produced with the tip of the tongue placed directly under the cutting edges of the upper front teeth instead of up in the forward part of the roof of the mouth, as in American. The resultant sound is "tTH," as in "*tTHA*Him" (time), "fAHi*tTH*ooAWr" (fighter) and "mAH*tTH*" (mat). (See illustration, page 000).

A great many Greeks substitute an "r" for medial "t." This change is an important dialect variation and should be used wherever possible, as in "bA*roo*AWr" (better), "ooO*roo*AWmooAWbil" (automobile), "sooAW*roo*AWp!" (shut up!), "si-*ri*mooAWp" (sit him up), "kooAW*ri*rooAW'" (cut it out), and "ooOsUHmAH-*roo*AW'?" (what's the matter?)

Medially, the consonant "t" is dropped very often, as in "tTHbvAn'i" (twenty), "tTHooAWr'i" (thir*ty*) and "dTHooAWr'i" (dir*ty*), which may also be used instead of the change of "t" to "r."

V—The Greeks thicken the consonant "v" so that it is pronounced as "bv," as in "*bv*Ari" (*v*ery), "looAW*bv*in'" (lo*v*ing), and "looAW*bv*" (lo*v*e). The lips should be almost in position for "b," that is, slightly parted, and "v" should be pronounced without touching the upper teeth with the lower lip. Many Greeks are able to pronounce "v" as in American, so that for a lighter dialect the American "v" may be used.

W—A slight "oo" (as in "good") sound usually precedes "w" in the Greek dialect, as in "*oow*AHi" (*w*hy), "AH*oow*EH" (a*w*ay), and "*oow*An" (*w*hen). In this chapter the "w" is dropped when preceded by "oo." The resulting sound remains the same. The consonant "w" may also be pronounced as "bv," as in "*bv*ooOk" (*w*alk), "AH-*bv*EH" (a*w*ay), and "*bv*in" (*w*in). This change may be used sometimes as a character variance. For the pronunciation of "bv" see "*V*" above.

X—The Greeks substitute "gs" for the "gz" sound of "x," as in "AHn*gs*AHitTHi" (an*x*iety).

When the "x" is pronounced "ks," as in "flax," the "k" is sometimes treated as a gargled "kh" and the "s" is retained, as in "flAH*khs*" (fla*x*).

Y—The consonantal sound of "y" is pronounced as in American.

Z—When this consonant sound has a natural "z" spelling, it is pronounced as "z," as in "krEH*z*i" (cra*z*y). But when it is spelled as "s" but sounded as "z," it retains its "s" treatment—the Greek hiss—as in "'i*ss*" (hi*s*), "pri*ss*ooAWn" (pri*s*on), and "blooAW*ss*" (blow*s*).

SH—The substitution of a sibilant "s" for the "sh" sound is another characteristic change in the Greek dialect. Since there is no "sh" sound in the original Greek, the common tendency is to treat the "sh" words as "ss," as in "*ss*ooAWbv" (*sh*ove), "fAH*ss*ooAWn" (fa*sh*ion), and "kAH*ss*" (ca*sh*).

TH—The same as in American, as in "*TH*i" (*th*e).

th—Pronounced as in American but with considerably more forcefulness, as in "*th*in" (*th*in).

TCH—Because this sound is not in the Greek language, the Greeks have difficulty with it. They simply cut it down to a sibilant "ts," as in "looAWn*ts*" (lun*ch*), "*ts*oos" (*ch*oose), and "ooO*ts*mAHn" (wa*tch*man).

ZH—The Greeks favor the sibilant "s" and so, in this "zh" sound of "z," they substitute "sy," as in "AH*sy*ooAWr" (azure), "lEH*sy*ooAWr" (lei*s*ure), and "si*sy*ooAWr" (sei*z*ure).

WORD EXERCISES

Pronounce the following words in the Greek dialect using the material learned
from the preceding section on Consonant Changes:

1.	cabbage-soup	11.	thirty-five
2.	quantity	12.	bandstand
3.	thinking	13.	steam heat
4.	veal-stew	14.	banquet
5.	bottle	15.	ice cream
6.	these	16.	valuable
7.	cashier	17.	watchmaker
8.	water	18.	frozen
9.	middle-class	19.	get it on
10.	shut him up	20.	fifty cents

After pronouncing the above words, refer to the following list for the correct
pronunciation. Check the mistakes in the consonants, repeat the corrections and
memorize.

1.	khAHbvAHzhsoop	12.	bAHn'stTHAHn'
2.	kbvAHntTHitTHi	13.	stTHimkhitTH or
3.	thi:nkin' (see under "th")		stTHim'itTH
4.	bvilstTHoo	14.	bAHngbyAtTH
5.	booAWtTHooAWl	15.	khAHiskrim
6.	THis	16.	bvAHlyooAHbooAWl
7.	kAHssir	17.	ooOtsmEHkooAWr
8.	ooOtTHooAWr	18.	frooAWssooAWn
9.	midTHooAWlklAHs	19.	gArirooAWn
10.	ssooAWrimooAWp	20.	fi'tTHisAn's
11.	thooAWr'ifAHibv		

GRAMMAR CHANGES

Like most foreigners, the Greeks find their greatest hurdle, in English grammar,
in the use of the verb. For instance, they will use the simple past tense as the past
participle in perfect tenses, as in:

"is brooAWk."
(Is *broke.*)
(It is *broken.*)

They also substitute the present tense of a verb for the past, as in:

"khi gooAW tTHoo sooAW."
(He *go* to show.)
(He *went* to a show.)

"AHi si khim in khooAWs."
(I *see* him in house.)
(I *saw* him in the house.)

There is also a tendency to leave out the verb or auxiliary entirely, as in:

"ooi ooAWf THi rooAWdTH."
(We off the road.)
(We *are* off the road.)

"khooAW ooAWl' yoo?"
(How old you?)
(How old *are* you?)

"ooAWtTH yoo dTHoo khir?"
(What you *do* here?)
(What *are* you *doing* here?)

"ooAWtTH yoo sEH?"
(What you say?)
(What *do* you say?)

When the adverb "there" is indicated in the beginning of a sentence, it is dropped, as in:

"ooAWs sEHlooAWr."
(Was sailor.)
(*There* was a sailor.)

"ooAWs bvAri big ooin."
(Was very big wind.)
(*There* was a strong wind.)

"is nAHis zhooAWb ooiTH khim."
(Is nice job with him.)
(*There* is a nice job for him.)

There is also a noticeable omission of the subject from sentences, particularly when the subject is a pronoun, as in:

"is goodTH fAHitTHooAWr, nooAW?"
(Is good fighter, no?)
(*He* is a good fighter, isn't he?)

"ooAWs booAWs' ooOl tTHoo pisis."
(Was bust all to pieces.)
(*It* was all smashed to pieces.)

"nooAW itTH ooOl dTHEH."
(No eat all day.)
(*I* did not eat all day.)

The last example also illustrates another common error in the dialect: the substitution of "no" for "not," as in:

"AHi nooAW khAHbv tTHAHim."
(I *no* have time.)
(I did *not* have time.)

"si nooAW brin' mooAWts."
(She *no* bring much.)
(She did not bring much.)

The double negative is also a favorite of the Greeks, as in:

"yoo nooAW dTHoo nooAWthin'."
(You *no* do *nothing*.)
(You *don't* do *nothing*.)

"khirooAWnooAW nooAWthin'."
(He *don't* know *nothing*.)
(He *doesn't* know *anything*.)

There are a number of other omissions in the Greek dialect which add to the flavor, as in the dropping of "that."

"nooAW yoo gooAW, khoo tTHEHk kAr?"
(Now you go, who take care?)
(Now *that* you're going, who'll take care?)

The dropping of the connectives, "and" and "or" is also common, particularly in the numerals, as in:

"AHi khAHsk 'im fooAWr fAHibv tTHAHim."
(I ask him four five time.)
(I asked him four *or* five times.)

"khi tTHAl mi khooAWnrEH' fi'tTHi tTHAHim."
(He tell me hundred fifty time.)
(He told me a hundred *and* fifty times.)

The omission of the article "a" in the above sentence is another common error, as in:

"nooAW gooAWtTH ooAHif."
(No got wife.)
(I haven't got *a* wife.)

"khi tTHEHk khooAWrAHnzh."
(He take orange.)
(He took *an* orange.)

"The" is also left out in the dialect, as in:

"yoo gooAW AHn' zhooAWb is tTHook."
(You go and job is took.)
(You go and *the* job is taken.)

"tTHEHk bAHnAHnAHs AHbvEH."
(Take bananas away.)
(Take *the* bananas away.)

The word "the," however, is added to the numerals when it is unnessary, as in:

"AHi gooAW tTHoo THi fooAWrtTHin stTHritTH."
(I go to *the* fourteen street.)
(I am going to Fourteenth Street.)

The last example also illustrates another error common to the dialect: the substitution of the noun form of a numeral instead of the adjective form, as in:

"khir is tTHooAntTHi fAHibv stTHritTH."
(Here is *twenty-five* street.)
(Here is *Twenty-fifth* Street.)

There is a tendency in the Greek dialect to add "um" to its verbs. This may have been a result of a heavily aspirated final consonant that degenerated into "uhm," as in "mEHkhuhm" (make-um) and "siuhm" (see-um). Whatever the reason, the "um" is often used as follows:

"AHi nooAW bAHiyuhm rooAWs'bif."
(I no *buy-um* roast beef.)
(I didn't *buy* roast beef.)

"khi mEHkuhm khooAWr mAHdTH."
(He *make-um* her mad.)
(He *made* her mad.)

"AHi siyuhm ooOl UH tTHAHim in stTHooAWr."
(I *see-um* all the time in store.)
(I *saw* it all the time in the store.)

The substitution of "like" for "as," is also noticed in the dialect, as in:

"lAHik in ooAWl' tTHAHim."
(*like* in old time)
(*as* it was in the old times)

"khi ooAWk lAHik khi sik."
(He walk *like* he sick.)
(He walked *as* though he were sick.)

SENTENCE EXERCISES

Pronounce the following sentences in the Greek dialect using the material learned from the preceding section on Grammar Changes:

1. There was a girl there who didn't dance.
2. I asked him why he took the oranges away.
3. He told me to cut it out or he would break it.
4. I haven't got a banana in the store.
5. Did you see him going to the police-station?
6. We are on the last page of the book.
7. I went to see three or four times.
8. You talk as though I won't pay the bill.
9. He has made a mistake in the check.
10. How will you know there is nothing in the ice-box?

After pronouncing the above sentences, refer to the following sentences for the correct treatment. Check the mistakes, repeat the corrections and memorize.

1. ooOss gooAWrl THAr khoo nooAWtTH dTHAHns.
2. I ooAHs' khim ooAHi khi tTHEHk khooAWrAHnzhiss AHbvEH.
3. khi tTHAl mi kooAWrirooAW' ooAWr khi bvrEHk itTH.
4. nooAW gooAWtTH bvAHnAHnAH in stTHooAWr.
5. yoo si khim gooAW tTHoo pooAWlis stTHEHsyooAWn?
6. ooi in lAHs' pEHzh ooAWbv book.
7. AHi gooAW si thri fooAWr tTHAHim.
8. yoo tTHooOk lAHik AHi nooAW pEH bvil.
9. khi mEHkuhm mistTHEHk in tsAk.
10. khooAW yoo nooAW iss nooAWthin' in AHisbvooAWks?

GREEK LANGUAGE CARRYOVERS

hello	*kalimera*	kAHli*m*EHrAH
goodbye	*kikreteh*	*khi*khrEHtTHEH
excuse me	*sinkoriteh*	sinkhooAW*rit*THEH
thank you	*ef kawristaw*	EHfkhooAWr*ist*THooAW
yes	*neh*	nEH
no	*awki*	*ooAW*khi
how do you do?	*ti kaneteh*	tTHi *kAHn*EHtTHEH

GREEK MONOLOG

THE DEAF CHEF

(*Adapted from a character in the authors' series of dramas written for "This Is Life" on the Mutual Network.*)

(*Nick Voutsas stands outside his little restaurant and discusses the chef problem with his friend, Nick Patras, and tells him of one, Nick Popolous, who applied for a job.*)

Was fellow, Nick Popolous, he come my place look for job. "I good chef," he say me "make-um good hamburger—all kinds lunch for highclass bill-of-fare." Was greenhorn, you know—no speak so good English like me. So I say him, "You hire," and I put him in kitchen. I stand by showcase wait for customer. Comes in fellow he want beefstew. "Beefstew," I holler for chef he should make. Then I go get beefstew for customer. Chef, he got stewed prunes. "Hey, you! what's the matter?" I say, "I holler for beefstew." He scratch head. "I don't know," he say, "I think you holler for stewed prunes." So I get beefstew, go back to customer. Comes in next another fellow. "Hotcakes," say he want. "Hotcakes!" I holler for chef he should make. So I go back to kitchen for hotcakes. What I find? Hotcakes? No! Beefsteak? Yeh! "What's the matter with you?" I holler, "You don't know I order hotcakes? You make beefsteak. You no understand English good?" He say, "What?" "What's the matter?" I holler, "You no hear good maybe, no?" He say again, "What?" Is plenty enough for me. "Get out of here!" I holler, "get out of my place before I throw you out!" How do you like that? Deaf chef!

PHONETIC TRANSCRIPTION

Syllables in bold face are to be accented.

"ooAWS fA looAWr_nik poo AW. pooAW looAWS, khi kooAWm"

mAHi plEHs **look** fooAWr **zhoo**AWb. "AHi goodTH **sAf**," khi sEH mi, "**mEHk**uhm **good**TH khAHm**boo**AWrgoo AWr—ooOl kAHin's **loo**AWnts fooAWr khAHiklAHs bilooAW**fAr**." ooAWs **gri**'khooAWrn, yoo nooAW— nooAW spik sooAW goodTH khinglis lAHik **mi**. sooAW AHi sEH khim, "yoo **khAH**ir," AHn' AHi poorim in **kits**ooAWn. **AHi** stTHAHn' bAHi sooAWkEHs ooEHtTH fooAWr **koo**AWstTHooAWmooAWr. kooAWms in **fA**looAWr khi ooAWn' bifst**THoo**. "bifst**THoo**," AHi khooAWlooAWr fooAWr sAf khi soodTH mEHk. THAn AHi gooAW **gAt**TH bifstTHoo fooAWr kooAWstTHooAW- mooAWr. sAf, khi gooAWtTH stTHoo**proo**ns. "**khEH**, yoo! ooAWs- AH**mAH**rooAW?" AHi sEH, "AHi khooAWlooAWr fooAWr bifst**THoo**!" khi skrAHts khAdTH. "AHirooAW**nooAW**," khi sEH, "AHi think yoo khoo- AWlooAWr fooAWr stTHoo**proo**ns." sooAW AHi **gAt**TH bifst**THoo**, gooAW bAHk tTHoo **koo**AWstTHooAWmooAWr. kooAWms in nAks' '**noo**AWTHooAWr **fA**looAWr. "**khoo**AWtTH **kEH**ks," sEH khi ooAWn.' "**khoo**AWtTH **kEH**ks!" AHi khooAWlooAWr fooAWr sAf khi soodTH mEHk. sooAW AHi gooAW bEHk tTHoo **kits**ooAWn fooAWr khooAWtTH **kEH**ks. **ooAW**rAHif**AH**in? kh**oo**AWtTH **kEH**ks? **noo**AW! bifst**THEH**k? **yA**! "ooAWsAH**mAH**rooAW yoo?"

AHi khooAWlooAWr, "yoorooAWnooAW AHi khooAWrdooAWr khooAWtTH kEHks? yoo mEHkuhm bifstTHEHk. yoonooAW'stTHAHn' khinglis goodTH?" khi sEH, "ooAWtTH?" "ooAWsAHmAHrooAW?" AHi khooAWlooAWr, "yoo nooAW khir goodTH mEHbi nooAW?" khi sEH AHgAn, "ooAWtTH?" is plAnt-THi 'nooAWf fooAWr mi. "gArooAWdTHuhkhir!" AHi khooAWlooAWr, "gAr-rooAWdTHuh mAHi plEHs bifooAWr AHi throoAW yoo khooAWtTH!" khooAWrUHyool-AHikTHAHtTH? dTHAf sAf!

CHAPTER TWENTY

The Yiddish Dialect

THE YIDDISH LILT

As in the Irish, the Cockney, and the Swedish, the Yiddish lilt is one of the most important factors in the dialect. With the substitution of a few vowels and consonants, the use of a few variations in syntax, and the lilt, a Yiddish dialect can be portrayed quite successfully.

A graphic representation of the lilt, particularly in question form, can be observed in the following sentence:

> "sAW EEf yoo dEEd'n' kEH, sAW vAHi bi mEHt?"
> (So if you didn't care, so why be mad?)

The sentence would sing as follows, with the keynote placed about three notes above that in American:

Here is another speech pattern, in a sentence, that is given disparagingly:

> "look hoos tUk'n'!"
> (Look who's talking!)

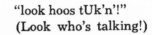

"look hoos tUk'n'!"
(Look who's talking!)

Although not shown here, the glide in the word "tUk'n" (talking), was achieved, not on the vowel sound "U," as it would be in most dialects, but on the consonant "k" which blends into a glottal stop followed by the nasalized "n." This nasalization is typical of the dialect, especially in the assimilation of the participial "ing" ending to the nasalized "n."

The effects of this sing-song can be seen in the varied meaning-changes given to the same sentence, as in:

"hi dAWn' kEH."
(He don't care.)

DECLARATIVE

INTERROGATIVE

EXCLAMATORY

The pitch of Yiddish speech is much higher than in American and the falsetto is reached many times, especially under the stress of emotion. That is why the Yiddish dialect should have a wide pitch range which, at times, reaches almost incredible, squeaking peaks. But it seldom descends to the lower registers. This wide pitch range accounts also for the nasality in the speech which occurs when the high notes are produced in falsetto through the nose, instead of from the throat and chest. The emotional coloring does not, however, speed up the tempo of the speech, as might be expected. On the whole, Yiddish is delivered at a slower pace than American—the vowel glides contribute to the slow pace—and it quickens its pace only under *severe* emotional stress.

In general it is best, when simulating the Yiddish lilt, to sound the keynote of the sentence about three or four notes above the American and sing the first few syllables on the same note. Then, on the stressed keynote word, make a sudden rising inflection on the vowel or sometimes on the consonant and make either a rising or falling inflection on the balance of the syllable. This will endow your dialect with the Yiddish lilt. But remember that the word meaning which affects the lilt and is changed by a combination of stressed and tonal emphasis, can change the speech pattern.

EMPHASIS

Syllabic emphasis, in Yiddish, varies little from the American. There are a number of words in which the emphasis changes erroneously but, on the whole, the same syllabic attack prevails. The emphasis, however, is, like the American, more tonal (musical) than stressed (breathed). This accounts for the singing out of such interjections as "AH hAAAAAH!" (a-hah!) and "sOOOOOH?" (so?), the latter being used in surprised indignation, and "yEHHHHH?" (yeh?) which is used when waiting for additional information.

The tonal emphasis is used also in emphasizing the words in a sentence. It ordinarily follows the rising glide inflection and the high point of emphasis is usually reached at the peak of the glide. Generally, in Yiddish, the elements of a sentence are accented in the following order: verb, adjective, adverb, and noun. A change of meaning would, of course, affect this rule which should not be applied inflexibly. For instance, where the inverted German form is used, as in "iz hir AH stU':?" (Is here a store?), the noun would be most heavily stressed, then "hir," then "iz" and "AH" would be least emphasized, as in:

The emphasis is also affected by another speech habit in the Yiddish dialect. Vowel sounds unaccented in American are often dropped from between consonants, as in "bUt'l" (bottle), "voom'n" (woman), "nid'l" (needle), "lEEd'l" (little), "mis'ls" (measles) and "'lAf'n" (eleven). This telescoping is done not only in single words but in phrases that are characteristically run together, as in "U:l'f'sAH'n" (all of a sudden), "bUd'fAlt" (board of health) and "vUts'mE-HdEH?" (what's the matter?). Here, the weakly stressed syllables are dropped and what remains is a sequence of heavily stressed vowel sounds.

VOWEL CHANGES

"AY" .... as in "take," "break," "they," etc.

This long "a" vowel sound, in Yiddish, is shortened and flattened into "EHi," as in "tEHik" (take).

DRILL WORDS

pEHi	(pay)	pEHin'	(paint)
stEHi	(stay)	hEHi	(hey!)
lEHik	(lake)	vEHi	(weigh)

mEHibi	(maybe)
wEHikEHish'n	(vacation)
EHiUHnpi	(A & P)

"UH" .... as in "about," "final," "sofa," etc.

This mute "a" is broadened into "AH," as in "fAHinAHl" (fin*a*l). Initially, however, it is often dropped, as in "'sAWshiEHit" (*a*ssociate) and "gAW 'hAt" (go *a*head).

DRILL WORDS

sAWfAH	(sofa)	kAHnAri	(canary)
AHvEHi	(away)	lAHpAl	(lapel)
AHgAW	(ago)	pAHnEHnAH	(banana)

pAHrEHit	(parade)
AHmAHng	(among)
AHbAH:	(about)

"AH" .... as in "father," "arm," "park," etc.

The Yiddish dialect shortens this "a" from "AH" to the "O" of "rod," as in "fOdEH" (father). Before "r," which is not sounded, the "O" is elongated, as in "fO:" (far).

DRILL WORDS

stO:	(star)	gO:d'n	(garden)
pOm	(palm)	stO:f	(starve)
O:mi	(army)	spO:k'l	(sparkle)

dO:link	(darling)
bO:bEH'	(barber)
mO:tch	(march)

"A:" .... as in "ask," "draft," "laugh," etc.

This lengthened "a" is changed to "EH," as in "EHsk" (ask).

DRILL WORDS

lEHf	(laugh)	glEHns	(glance)
lEHs'	(last)	nEHsti	(nasty)
pEHs'	(past)	pEHt	(path)

bEHsk't	(basket)
mEHstEH'	(master)
dEHns	(dance)

"A" .... as in "bad," "am," "narrow," etc.

This "a" is also pronounced "EH," as in "EHm" (am).

DRILL WORDS

fEHk'	(fact)	vEHlyoo	(value)
fEHt	(fad)	rEHtEEsh	(radish)
sEHm	(Sam)	hEHpi	(happy)

'mEHj'n	(imagine)
bEHgitch	(baggage)
mEHdEH	(matter)

"AW" .... as in "ball," "falter," "shawl," etc.

The shortened "U" of "up" is substituted for this broad "a," as in "bU:l" (ball). The sign (:) indicates that the sound is elongated. A variant is "AW."

DRILL WORDS

U:l	(all)	U:lvEHis	(always)
hU:l	(hall)	vU:l	(wall)
kU:t	(caught)	shU:l	(shawl)

nU:ti	(naughty)
dU:dEH'	(daughter)
kvU:dEH'	(quarter)

"EE" .... as in "he," "treat," "people," etc.

This long "e" vowel sound is changed to short "i" in the Yiddish, as in "hi" (he).

DRILL WORDS

bi	(be)	krim	(cream)
fli	(flea)	sin	(scene)
shi	(she)	nis	(niece)

stim'it	(steam heat)
kU:fi	(coffee)
grin'U:'n	(greenhorn)

"EH" .... as in "bet," "said," "friend," etc.

The short "e" of this vowel sound is changed to "A," as in "bAt" (bet).

DRILL WORDS

gAt	(get)	tAl	(tell)	rAdi	(ready)
mAt	(met)	mAn	(men)	bAnt	(bend)
sAl	(sell)	vAt	(wet)	wAri	(very)

"I" .... as in "ice," "aisle," "guile," etc.

In American, this vowel sound is pronounced as "AH-EE" but, in Yiddish, the "EE" part is changed to short "i," as in "AHis" (ice).

DRILL WORDS

nAHis	(nice)	rAHit	(right)
fAHin	(fine)	bAHi	(buy)
mAHi	(my)	fAHin'	(find)

pAWlAHit	(polite)
tchAHinAHvEH:'	(chinawear)
AHidi	(idea)

"i" .... as in "it," "women," "busy," etc.

The substitution of long "e" (EE) for short "i," as in "EEt" (it), is typical of Yiddish as it is of most dialects.

DRILL WORDS

mEElk	(milk)	nAWtEEs	(notice)	lEEs'n	(listen)
vEEt	(with)	dAntEEs'	(dentist)	U:fEEsEH	(officer)
bEEzi	(busy)	mEEstEHk	(mistake)	sEEgO:	(cigar)

"O" .... as in "on," "bond," "John," etc.

This short "o" is changed to the short "u" (U) of "up" as in "Un" (on). A variant substitutes "AW," as in "bAWn'" (bond) but the former is preferred.

DRILL WORDS

hUt	(hot)	bUn'	(bond)
nUt	(not)	AHpUn	(upon)
bUdi	(body)	tchUn	(John)

kUnwinyAns	(convenience)
spUtEEnk	(spotting)
kUntEEnyoo	(continue)

"OH" .... as in "bone," "sew," "dough," etc.

The Yiddish dialect shortens this long "o" into "AW," as in "bAWn" (bone).

DRILL WORDS

gAW	(go)	nAWtEEs	(notice)
sAW	(sew)	dAWn'	(don't)
nAW	(no)	fAlAW	(fellow)

klAWdEEnk	(clothing)
gAWld'n	(golden)
UtAWmAWbil	(automobile)

"AW".... as in "off," "cough," "bought," etc.

The preferred treatment of this "o" is "U," as in the American word "up," but a variation is the "AW" sound. The former, however, is preferred.

DRILL WORDS

U:f	(off)	klU:t	(cloth)
kU:f	(cough)	hU:ti	(haughty)
bU:t	(bought)	kU:s'	(cost)

vU:dEH'	(water)
U:f'n	(often)
krU:l	(crawl)

"OO"....as in "food," "do," "blue," etc.

Yiddish reverses this long double "o" from "OO" to the short double "o" (oo) of "good," as in "doo" (do).

DRILL WORDS

soop	(soup)	skool	(school)
dooti	(duty)	soor	(sewer)
moovi	(movie)	soot	(suit)

sAHloon	(saloon)
bootlAgEH	(bootlegger)
soow'ni:	(souvenir)

"oo"....as in "good," "wolf," "full," etc.

The American pronunciation of short double "o" (oo) is retained in Yiddish. Sometimes, however, it is changed to "OO."

"yOO"....as in "unit," "cube," "beauty," etc.

Because, in the Yiddish, long double "o" (OO) is changed to short double "o" (oo), this vowel sound changes its long double "o" (OO) to "oo" and retains the initial consonantal "y" sound, as in "kyoob" (cube).

This "u" is sometimes dropped in Yiddish, as in "grEHj'EHt" (graduate) and "grEHj'l" (gradual).

DRILL WORDS

yoo	(you)	Akskyoos	(excuse)
fyoo	(few)	myoozEEk	(music)
yooz	(use)	kyoot	(cute)

yoonEEfU:'m	(uniform)
byoodEEfool	(beautiful)
yoonAHidit	(united)

"U"....as in "up," "love," "does," etc.

This short "u" is changed to "AH," in Yiddish, as in "AHp" (up). Another pronunciation is "AW" but the "AH" is preferred.

DRILL WORDS

bAHk	(bug)	slAHk	(slug)
nAHt	(nut)	sAHpEH'	(supper)
trAHk	(truck)	mAHs'	(must)

hAHzbAHn'	(husband)
sAHspEEshoos	(suspicious)
bAHdEH'	(butter)

"ER". . . .as in "curb," "earn," "fir," etc.

The preferred substitution for this "u" in Yiddish is "UH" (this is the sound of "a" in the American pronunciation of "alone"), as in "fUHr" (fur). But a common substitute, especially in New York, changes "ER" to "OI," as in "kOIb" (curb). In the phrase "per cent," when used in Yiddish, the "ER" sound is sometimes reversed so the phrase becomes "prUH tsAn," the "s" sound in "cent" also changing to "ts." Another example of this syllabic reversal comes with the word "jewelry" pronounced as "tchoolUHri." In the word "aspirin," the "ER" sound retains the "r" only and drops the vowel, as in "EHsp'rEEn" (aspirin). The word "grocery," too, drops the "ER," as in "grAWs'ri."

DRILL WORDS

gUH'l	(girl)	lUH'n	(learn)
nUH's	(nurse)	dUH'di	(dirty)
vUH't	(worth)	kUH'lz	(curls)

dEEskUHritch	(discourage)
tUHzdEHi	(Thursday)
tUHdi	(thirty)

"OW". . . .as in "out," "cow," "house," etc.

In Yiddish this diphthong is shortened into "AH:," the (:) sign indicating that it is to be drawn out, as in "kAH:" (cow).

DRILL WORDS

AH:t	(out)	lAH:t	(loud)
mAH:t	(mouth)	hAH:s	(house)
dAH:t	(doubt)	hAH:	(how)

mAH:nt'nz	(mountains)
tAH:zUHnz	(thousands)
klAH:di	(cloudy)

"OI". . . .as in "oil," "boy," "noise," etc.

This diphthong sound is pronounced in Yiddish as it is in American.

WORD EXERCISES

Pronounce the following words in the Yiddish dialect using the material learned from the preceding section on Vowel Changes:

1.	watermelon	11.	starving
2.	schoolroom	12.	about
3.	listen	13.	radish
4.	half past	14.	living room
5.	painter	15.	baloney
6.	darling	16.	steam boiler
7.	many	17.	butter dish
8.	excuse	18.	cigarette
9.	worthwhile	19.	clothing store
10.	hot dog	20.	fish market

After pronouncing these words, refer to the following list for the correct pronunciation. Check the mistakes made in the vowels, repeat the corrections and memorize.

1.	vUdEHmEHlAWn	11.	stO:vEEnk
2.	skoolroom	12.	'bAH:'
3.	lEEs'n	13.	rEHtEEsh or rEHdEEtch
4.	hEHfpEHs'	14.	lEEvEEnkroom
5.	pEHintnEH'	15.	bAHlAWni
6.	dO:'lEEnk	16.	stimbOIlEH:'
7.	mAni	17.	bAHdEH:'dEEsh
8.	Akskyoos	18.	tsEEgAHrAt
9.	vUHrtvAHil	19.	klU:dEEnkstU:'
10.	hU'dUk	20.	fEEshmO:'kAt

SUFFIXES

"ed"	... "it," as in vU:ntit (wanted).
"er"	... "EH," as in "bAHdEH (butter).
or	... "UH," as in bAHdUH (butter).
"en"	... "UH," as in lEEsUHn (listen).
"or"	... "UH," as in tEHilUH (tailor).
"ance"	... "ingz," as in EEnshooringz (insurance).

CONSONANT CHANGES

B—Ordinarily, this consonant is treated as it is in American. But sometimes, especially by people who have recently arrived from Europe, "b" is sounded as "p," as in "kEH*p*" (ca*b*). However, the habit is retained for some time and even those who seldom make the "p" substitution pronounce "*b*anana" as "*p*AHnEHnAH."

C—Soft "c," sounded as "s," is usually pronounced as it is in American. Sometimes, however, and especially by Russian Jews, a "ts" treatment is given, as in "prUH *ts*An'" (per *c*ent) and "tsEEgAH" (*c*igar).

For the hard sound of "c," see "k."

D—Initially, the consonant "d" is pronounced as in American. But, medially, it is most always changed to "t," as in "rEH*t*EEsh" (ra*d*sh). There are a number of people, though, who retain the "d" in some words and substitute "t" in others.

When "d" comes at the end of a word and is preceded by another consonant, it may be dropped, as in "sEHn'" (san*d*) and "kAHin'" (kin*d*). But when it is preceded by a vowel, it usually changes to "t," as in "bEH*t*" (ba*d*) and "sA*t*" (sai*d*). Final "d" is sometimes pronounced as "d" in some words and as "t" in others by the same people.

The "d" is also added sometimes, medially, as in "fin*d*ish't" (finished).

F—Pronounced as in American.

G—The hard form of the consonant "g" is an outstanding element in the dialect and is greatly affected by the mother tongue of the speaker. The German-Yiddish sound "g" as "gk," as in "rEH*gk*it" (rag*g*ed). The Russian-Yiddish treat it as "k," as in "A*k*plEHnt" (eg*g*plant). Others treat it in various ways. Ordinarily, it would be best to pronounce "g" normally when it comes at the beginning of a word, as in "*g*AW" (*g*o). Medially and finally, "g" can be pronounced as "k," as in "bEH*k*itch" (ba*g*gage) and "nEH*k*" (na*g*).

When hard "g" is used finally in the ending, "ing," it is pronounced as "k," as in "svEEmEEn*k*" (swimming) and it is sometimes dropped, as in the telescoped phrase "bAHit'n'yooEEnpisis" (biting you in pieces).

Soft "g," pronounced as "j," will be found under "J."

H—Generally, the consonant "h" is pronounced as it is in American. But a great many Russian Jews treat it as the gargled "kh," as in "*kh*AHt*kh*AH:s" (*h*ot*h*ouse).

The English Jews and many others usually add an "h," like the Cockney, to words beginning with a vowel, as in "hAWni" (only), "hEHp'l" (apple) and "hAHnyUHn" (onion).

J—This consonant is pronounced as "tch" in Yiddish as in "*tch*AH*tch*" (ju*dge*), "mEHi*tch*EH" (ma*j*or), "*tch*Ali" (*j*elly), "bEHnti*tch*" (banda*ge*) and "vEHi*tch*is" (wa*ge*s).

The Lithuanian-Yiddish dialect treats this "j" sound as "ts," as in "*ts*Ali" (*j*elly) and "*ts*AH*ts*" (ju*dge*).

K—Ordinarily, the consonant "k" is pronounced as it is in American But a number of people give it the German-Yiddish substitution of "gk," as in "*gk*Ul" (call), "nEH*gk*EH" (na*gg*er) and "bEH*gk*" (ba*ck*).

The Russian-Yiddish dialect sounds initial "k" as hard "g," as in "*g*U:s't" (corset), "*g*lU:k" (dock) and "*g*lAWks" (cloaks). The American treatment is preferred for a lighter dialect. The others can be used for character variations.

L—The consonant "l" is pronounced as it is in American. But it is dropped sometimes, especially in a telescoped phrase, as in "U:'rAHi'" (a*ll* right) and in "U:'rAdi" (a*l*ready).

M—Pronounced as in American.

N—In most cases, the consonant "n" is pronounced as it is in American. But the Russian-Yiddish dialect would add the Russian consonantal "y" (as the "ni" in "onion"), as in "tvAn*yi*" (twenty) and "n*yi*d'l" (needle). For a more detailed discussion of this "y" addition, see "N" "The Added Consonantal 'Y'" in the chapter on the Russian dialect.

An unusual treatment adds an "n" in "Ar'nplEHinz" (airplanes), "pEHint*n*EH" (painter) and "fOdEHrEEnlU:*n*" (father-in-law).

NG—This combination, as in "si*ng*er," is another characteristic variant in the Yiddish dialect. In American it would be sounded as nasalized "n" followed by an unvoiced "g." But in Yiddish the "n" is nasalized only slightly and the "g" is sounded very hard so that the result would have the same "ng" sound as in the American pronunciation of "finger," where the "n" is weakly nasalized and the "g" is hit hard.

P—Pronounced as in American.

Q—The American pronunciation of "q" is "kw," as in "quick" but, in the Yiddish, it becomes "kv" because of the substitution of "v" for "w," as in "k*v*in" (*q*ueen) and "k*v*UdEH" (*q*uarter). A variant is "kf."

R—When "r" comes at the beginning of a word, it is pronounced according to the mother tongue of the speaker. The German-Yiddish dialect speaker would pronounce it gutturally (See "R" in "Consonant Changes" in the German dialect). The Russian-Yiddish dialect speaker would give it only a slight roll with the tip of the tongue. Another variation adds an aspirate "uh," as in "*uhr*EEb'n" (*r*ibbon). Ordinarily, however, it would be best to pronounce it as in American.

Medially, "r" is never pronounced in Yiddish when it is one of the "ar," "er," "or," "ur" or "ir" combinations and is followed by another consonant, as in "pO:k" (pa*r*k), "pUHs'n" (pe*r*son), "dUHdi" (di*r*ty), "fU:di" (fo*r*ty) and "bUHn" (bu*r*n).

When "r" is followed by a vowel, it is always pronounced, as in "wA*r*i" (ve*r*y) and "b*r*EEnk" (b*r*ing).

New Yorkers drop the "r" sometimes, as in "Av'itEEnk" (eve*r*ything) and "Av'i" (eve*r*y).

Final "r" is never sounded, as in "fO:" (fa*r*), "bU:" (bo*r*e), "ni:" (nea*r*) and "hi:" (he*r*e). But the vowel sound that precedes it is elongated and the elongation is noted phonetically in this chapter with the (:) sign.

When "r" follows long "i" it is changed to "UH" as in "fAHi*UH*" (fire).

S—The Yiddish "s" is always hissed, more so than in American.

A variation substitutes a "z" for the "s" in such words as "yoo*z*" (u*s*e), as in "what's the use?" and "*z*oop" (*s*oup). A Russian-Yiddish variation, noted already under hard "c," substitutes "ts," as in "mAdEE*ts*EEn" (medi*c*ine), "U:fEE*ts*EH" (officer) and "*ts*EHn-vEEtch" (*s*andwich).

T—The Yiddish dialect treats the consonant "t," at the beginning of a word, as it is in American.

But, medially, "t" is changed to "d," as in "bA*d*EH" (be*tt*er), "sEH*d*EEsfAHi" (sa*t*isfy) and "sA*d*'l" (se*tt*le). Sometimes, medial "t" is changed to "r," as in "sEH*r*EEsfAHi" (sa*t*isfy), "poo*r*i" (pre*tt*y) and "byoo*r*EEfool" (beau*t*iful). When "t" is used between two consonants, it is sometimes dropped, unless the three-consonant combination occurs at the beginning of a word, as in "strEEk'li" (stric*t*ly) and "'zEHk'li" (exac*t*ly).

Final "t" is almost always dropped when it is preceded by another consonant, as in "dAWn'" (don'*t*) "fEHk" (fac*t*) and "pAHin'" (pin*t*).

Sometimes, final "t" is dropped when it is preceded by a vowel sound, as in "mAHi' bi" (migh*t* be) and "sEE' dAHn" (si*t* down). This is particularly true when the following word begins with a "d" or a "t."

Final "t" is sometimes changed to "r" when it is followed by a word beginning with a vowel and is in a telescoped phrase, as in "shAH*r*AHp" (shu*t* up).

Although it is a practice common mostly to the Russian-Yiddish dialect, a number of people substitute "ts" for initial "t" when it is followed by a "w," as in "*ts*vAHis" (*tw*ice), "*ts*vAnyi" (*tw*enty) and "*ts*vAlf" (*tw*elve).

V—Ordinarily, "v" is sounded initially as it is in American. The Russian-Yiddish version, though, changes it to "vw," as in "v*w*EHlyoo" (*v*alue) and "v*w*Ari" (*v*ery). This is also done medially and finally by the Russian Jew, as in "'lA*vw*'n" (ele*v*en) and "lAH*vw*" (lo*v*e). This "vw" sound is achieved by setting the mouth in position for "w" and then pronouncing "v" instead. Be careful that the lower lip is not touching the cutting edge of the upper front teeth. The American "w" or "v" may also be used.

Medially, most Yiddish speaking people substitute an "f" for "v"—the German influence—as in "sA*f*'n" (se*v*en), "lEE*f* EEnk" (li*v*ing), and "hEH*f* EEnk" (ha*v*ing).

When "v" is used at the end of a word, it usually is changed to "f," as in "lAH*f*" (lo*v*e), "U:*f*" (o*f*) and "bilEE*f*" (belie*v*e). An unusual change substitutes "m" for medial "v," as in "sA*m*ni" (se*v*enty).

W—The consonant "w" is usually changed to "v" in the Yiddish dialect, as in "*v*EEt" (*w*ith), "AH*v*EHi" (a*w*ay) and "*v*i" (*w*e).

X—The consonant "x" is pronounced as it is in American. But when "ex" is used initially in a word, it is often dropped, as in "'zEHm'n" (*ex*amine), "'zEHkli" (*ex*actly) and "'spAk'" (*ex*pect).

Y—The consonant "y" is pronounced as it is in American. But a rare variation treats it as a hard "g," as in "*g*AlAW" (*y*ellow) and "*g*AstUHdEHi" (*y*esterday).

Z—Generally, the "z" sound is pronounced as in American except that it is overemphasized, as in "gAW*zz*" (goe*s*), "hEH*zz*" (ha*s*) and "pAH*zz*'l" (pu*zz*le).

The Russian and Austrian-Yiddish versions, however, usually substitute a sibilant "s" for all the "z" sounds, as in "hEH*s*" (ha*s*), "EE*s*" (i*s*) and "fEE*s*'l" (fi*zz*le).

SH—This consonant sound is usually pronounced as it is in American. But in the Lithuanian-Yiddish dialect—referred to as "lEEtvAHk" (Litvak) in Yiddish—it is one of the most important dialect changes. For there it becomes a sibilant "s," as in "sU:l" (*shawl*), "fEHs's'n" (*fashion*) and "fEEs" (*fish*). In rare cases, this "sh" sound is changed to "tch," as in "rEHdi*tch*" (radi*sh*).

TCH—This sound is ordinarily pronounced as it is in American. But in the Lithuanian-Yiddish dialect, "tch" becomes "ts," as in "*ts*UH*ts*" (*church*), "bEHt-slEH" (*bachelor*) and "mAH*ts*" (*much*).

An odd syllabic reversal involving "tch" occurs in the pronunciation of "hEHntchUHkif" (handkerchief).

TH—The voiced "th," in the Yiddish dialect, is always changed to "d," as in "*d*i" (*the*), "bEHi*d*" (ba*the*) and "fA*d*EH" (fea*ther*).

th—Unvoiced "th," in the Yiddish dialect, is always changed to "t," as in "*t*EEn" (*thin*), "kEHt'r'n" (Ca*the*rine) and "rEH*t*" (wra*th*).

ZH—This "zh" sound given to the "s" in "vision," is pronounced as "sh" in Yiddish, as in "vEE*sh*'n" (vi*s*ion), "lA*sh*'r" (lei*s*ure) and "roo*sh*" (rou*ge*).

WORD EXERCISES

Pronounce the following words in the Yiddish dialect using the material learned from the preceding section on Consonant Changes:

1.	grape-jelly	11.	sandwiches
2.	seventy-five	12.	dog biscuit
3.	satisfaction	13.	three
4.	forty-one	14.	medicine
5.	quick	15.	hosiery
6.	sandpaper	16.	evening
7.	these	17.	bigger
8.	everywhere	18.	newspaper
9.	expect	19.	get up
10.	bringing	20.	yardage

After pronouncing these words, refer to the following list for the correct pronunciation. Check the mistakes in the consonants, repeat the corrections and memorize.

1.	grEHiptchAli	11.	sEHn'vEEtchis
2.	sAvAHntifAHif	12.	dU:kbEEskEEt
3.	sEHrEEsfEHksh'n	13.	tri
4.	fU:'divAH:n	14.	mAdEEtsEEn
5.	kvEEk	15.	hAWshAHri
6.	sEHn'pEHipEH:'	16.	hif'nEEnk
7.	dizz	17.	bEEgkEH:'
8.	hAv'rivA:'	18.	noospEHipEH:'
9.	'spAk'	19.	gArAHp
10.	brEEngEEnk (sound the "g")	20.	yU:'dEEtch

GRAMMAR CHANGES

The grammar changes in the Yiddish dialect, as in other dialects, are due to confusion in the use of American idioms and verb forms. The errors represent not
only the peculiarities of the Yiddish language itself, but also those of all the na-
tionalities that contribute to its make up. The following examples are typical:

"dit yoo kEHim bAHi y'sAlf?"   "dEHi nUt sU: dAm."
(Did you *came* by yourself?)   (They not *saw* them.)
(Did you *come* by yourself?)   (They *didn't see* them.)

"dEEdn' yoo hEHt nAW tEEk't?"   "nOO? sAW vU:t dit hi sAt?"
(Didn't you *had* no ticket?)   (Nu? so what did he *said?*)
(Didn't you *have* a ticket?)   (Well? what did he *say?*)

Confusion between "lay" and "lie" is also present in the dialect, as in:

"lEHi dAH:n EEn di sEHn."
(*Lay* down in the sand.)
(Lie down in the sand.)

Another common confusion substitutes "stood" for "stayed" and accounts for
the title of a Broadway play based on this misuse. The sentence was:

"dEHi shoot hEHf stoot EEn bAt."
(They should have *stood* in bed.)
(They should have *stayed* in bed.)

"shi stoot EEn di stU: U:l dEHi."
(She *stood* in the store all day.)
(She *stayed* in the store all day.)

The substitution of "will" for "would" is common, as in:

"hAH: vEEl EEt look EEf AHi vAn' vEEt?"
(How *will* it look if I went with?)
(How *would* it look if I went along?)

"vEEl yoo doo EEt lAHik sAW?"
(*Will* you do it like so?)
(*Would* you do it this way?)

The omission of the verbal auxiliary is typical of the dialect, as in:

"hAH yoo nAW?"   "sAW, vUt hi sEHi?"
(How you know?)   (So, what he say?)
(How *do* you know?)   (So, what *did* he say?)

The addition of the verbal auxiliary where it is not required is noticeable, as in:

"dEEt di vUHk vUz dEEt?"
(*Did* the work *was did?*)
(Was the work completed?)

The inversion of subject and predicate is observed in the speech, as in:

"dAn rAHns AH: tri kits."
(Then runs out three kids.)
(Then three kids ran out.)

"vUz kAHmEEnk mAni kAHin'z pip'l."
(Was coming many kinds people.)
(Many kinds of people were coming.)

The preposition "of" is constantly being dropped in the dialect, as in:

"tri kAHin'z hAks vUz sAWl."
(Three kinds eggs was sold.)
(Three kinds *of* eggs were sold.)

In many cases, the pronoun is omitted from a sentence, as in:

"vEEl bi plAnti mU: trAHb'l."   "vUs AH nAHis pAH'di."
(Will be plenty more trouble.)   (Was a nice party.)
(*There* will be much more trouble.) (*It* was a nice party.)

The use of "might" for "maybe" or "perhaps" is to be found quite often in Yiddish speech, as in:

"mAHi' dEHi vEEl kAHm."   "mAHi' yoo sh'l doo dEEs, nAW?"
(Might they will come.)   (*Might* you shall do this, no?)
(Maybe they'll come.)   (Perhaps you will do this?)

The last sentence illustrates another error common to the dialect: the misuse of "shall" and "will." Both are interchanged, as in:

"yoo sh'l tEHik EEt hAWm."
(You *shall* take it home.)
(You *will* take it home.)

"There is" is often shortened to "is," as in:

"EEz AH bOI hi vU:n's AH bO:g'n."
(Is a boy he wants a bargain.)
(*There* is a boy who wants a bargain.)

On the other hand, a great many people add an extra "who," as in:

"hoo yoo tEEnk yoo AH:', hoo?"
(Who you think you are, *who?*)
(Who do you think you are?)

Like most foreigners, the Yiddish-speaking people are addicted to double negatives, as in:

"vi nAf'r hEHt nAW yoos fAW' hEEm."
(We *never* had *no* use for him.)
(We *never* had *any* use for him.)

"yoo EHin' gUt nAW AHidi' hAH: mAHtch."
(You *ain't* got *no* idea how much.)
(You *haven't any* idea how much.)

The interchange of "what" for "that" is another popular substitution, as in:

"dEHt EEz di stU: vUt yoo nit."
(That is the store *what* you need.)
(*That* is the store you need.)

"di bEHk vUt yoo vUn' EEz gU:n."
(The bag *what* you want is gone.)
(The bag *that* you want is gone.)

The substitution of "mine" for "my" is one of the most characteristic marks of the dialect, as in:

"mAHin! mAHin! hAH byoorEEfool!"
(*Mine! mine!* how beautiful!)
(*My! my!* how beautiful!)

"EEz mAHin kAWt rAdi yAt?"
(Is *mine* coat ready yet?)
(Is *my* coat ready yet?)

"hi vUz U:lvEHiz bAHi mAHin hAH:s."
(He was always by *mine* house.)
(He was always at *my* house.)

The above sentence demonstrates another error in the grammar; the substitution of "by" for "at," as in:

"AHi vUz bAHi di tAHntuh rAWkh'lz hAH:s."
(I was *by* the Aunt Rachel's house.)
(I was *at* Aunt Rachel's house.)

In sentences in which two verbs are used, the second being in its infinitive form, the dialect substitutes "shall," "should," etc., preceded by repetition of the personal pronoun, in place of "to," as in:

"dEHi vUn' dEHi sh'l hEHf U:l di nooz."
(They want *they shall* have all the news.)
(They want *to* have all the news.)

"vi tAWl' hEEm bAdUH hi sh'l liv EEt gAW."
(We told him better *he should* leave it go.)
(We told him it would be best *to* let it go.)

The foregoing sentence contains a number of typical errors. The substitution of "better" for "would be better," is very common, as in:

"bAduh hi sh'l nAW EEt."
(*Better* he shall know it.)
(*It would be better* if he knew it.)

The substitution of "leave" for "let" is another common error, as in:

"liv hEEm bi, yoo booli!"   "hi vood'n liv mi doo EEt."
(*Leave* him be, you bully!)   (He wouldn't *leave* me do it.)
(*Let* him alone, you bully!)   (He wouldn't *let* me do it.)

The substitution of "as" for "than" after the word "better," results in such sentences as:

"shi lAHik tchAW bAduh' EHz fEEl."
(She liked Joe better *as* Phil.)
(She liked Joe better *than* Phil.)

"AHi nAW yoo bAduh' EHz hEEm."
(I know you better *as* him.)
(I know you better *than* him.)

The pronoun "it" is often dropped, as in:

"vood'n bi bAduh' fU' yoo?"
(Wouldn't be better for you?)
(Wouldn't *it* be better for you?)

"vEEl bi bAduh' toodEHi EHz yAstUHdEHi."
(Will be better today as yesterday.)
(*It* will be better today than yesterday.)

There are a number of words thrown into the Yiddish dialect that are always used. Among them are "nAW?" (no?), "sAW" (so), "yA:" (yes) and "noo?" (nu) used instead of the questioning, "well?"; other examples include "vAl?" (well), "nAH:" (now), "lEEs'n" (listen), "yAt" (yet), and "EHn'" (and). Used in sentences, they would read:

"noo! sAW sEHi yAs U nAW!"
(*Well?* *so*, say yes or no!)

"sAW hi dEEd'n'vUs gU:n?"
(So he didn't was gone?)
(*So*, he wasn't gone?)

"hi gEEfs hEEm, yAt."
(He gives him, *yet*.)

"nAH:, yoo dEEdn' sEHi nAW, nAW?"
(*Now*, you didn't say no, *no*?)

"lEEs'n! EEz U:l fU di bAs."
(Listen! is all for the best.)
(*Listen*! it's all for the best.)

Another common habit in the Yiddish dialect is the duplication of certain words used in the same sentence and repeated for emphasis, as in:

"lEEs'n too hEEm, lEEs'n!"   "look hooz tUkEEnk, look!"
(Listen to him, *listen*!)   (Look who's talking, *look*!)

"hoo yoo tEEnk yoo O:, hoo?
(Who you think you are, who?)
(Who do you think you are, *who*?)

TYPICAL PHRASES

The color of a dialect is affected by the sentence structure and by certain typical phrases. Yiddish has a great many odd expressions that identify it. For example, an expression of contempt would be voiced by repeating a word immediately after it was spoken by another person and then adding a rhyming word beginning with "shm," as in:

"di pEEkshUH vUz bEHt."   "AH! bEHt-shmEHt!"
(The picture was bad.)   (Ah! bad-shmad!)

It does not matter what was spoken, noun, verb, or adjective, the word is simply repeated and then repeated again with a "shm" added, as in:

"AHi vUz gAWEEnk nAH:."   gAWEEnk-shmAWEEnk!"
(I was going now.)   (Going-shmowing!)

Other typical expressions are:

"shiz mEHikEEnk vEEt di fEEngUH."
(She's making with the finger.)
(She's beckoning to you.)

"mEHik lAHik EHn EHktUH."
(Make like an actor.)

"dEEjUH AvUH!"
(Didja ever!)

"yoo shoot Akskyooz mi."
(You should excuse me.)

"AH fAHin hAWdUHyUHdoo."
(A fine how do you do).

"AH nAHis kAHp'l dU:lUHz."
(A nice couple dollars.)

"AHp too dEHi"
(up to date)

"yoo shoot lEEf sAW lAWnk."
(You should live so long.)

"AHi nit EEt lAHik AHi nit AH hAWl EEn mAHin hAt."
(I need it like I need a hole in mine head.)

"AH hAHndUHt prUHtsAn' vool"
(a hundred per cent wool)

"troo lAHik AnitEEnk"
(true like anything)

"voot bi AH shEHim fU di nEHibUHz"
(would be a shame for the neighbors)

"plEHin tU:k"
(plain talk)

"iv'n bAHi mAHin vUHst AnAmi EEt shood'n hEHp'n."
(Even by mine worst enemy it shouldn't happen.)

"shAHrAHp vEEt di frAsh tUk!"
(Shut up with the fresh talk!)

"lAmi AksplEHin yoo."
(Lemme explain you.)
(Let me explain to you.)

"hi pUzEEtEEfli gUt rAHi'"
(he positively got right)

"AH hAWl bAHntch pip'l"
(a whole bunch people)

"di fAHinAs' fUHm di fAHin!"
(the finest from the fine!)

SENTENCE EXERCISES

Pronounce the following sentences in the Yiddish dialect using the material
learned from the preceding sections on Grammar Changes and Typical Phrases:

1. Why did you stay in the doorway and beckon to me?
2. Let me explain why I was at her house.
3. Pretend you're a dog, Shirley, so they will laugh, no?
4. It would be better if you told the truth.
5. Well? don't you have any fashionable fur-coats, no?
6. Did he say that a lot of people were at the place?
7. So. Perhaps you'll pay more next time.
8. Do you think that I'll lie in bed a whole week.
9. Good grief! Did you come alone in this kind of weather?
10. So! No kidding! Now tell me! What did he say?

After pronouncing the above sentences, refer to the following sentences for the
correct treatment. Check the mistakes, repeat the corrections and memorize.

1. vAHi dEEt yoo stoot EEn di dU:'vEHi EHn' mEHik vEEt di
    fEEngEH:'?
2. lif mi 'splEHin yoo vAHi AHi vUs bAHi hUH:' hAH:s.
3. mEHik lAHik AH dAWk, shOIli, dEHi sh'l lEHf, nAW?
4. bArEH:' yoo sh'l tUk plEHin tUk.
5. noo? dEEd'n' yoo hEHt nAW AHp too dEHi fUH:'kAWts, nAW?
6. dEEt hi sAt AH hAWl bAHntch pip'l vUs bAHi di plEHis?
7. sAW. mAHit yoo sh'l pEHi AH nAHis kAHp'l dU:lUHs nAks'
    tAHim.
8. yoo shoot lEEf sAW lUnk AHi sh'l lEHi EEn bAt AH hAWl vik.
9. mAHin! mAHin! dEEt yoo kEHim AHlAWn EEn dEEs kAHin
    vAdEH:'?
10. sAW! plEHin tU:k! tAl mi UlrAdi! vUt dEEt hi sAt?

YIDDISH MONOLOG

"IN THE PARK"

*(Adapted from the authors' radio drama, "The Seventy-Five Pound Baby," in the
CBS "Campbell's Short Short Stories.")*

*(Mrs. Al Gordon stands at the window and stares out into the street. Suddenly,
she hears the thin wail of an ailing baby coming from the areaway and she turns to
her husband, to say:)*

Listen, Al! Mrs. Feigen's baby got the colic again. What's the matter with that
woman? Babies she should have! They don't cry unless something is wrong with
the mama, believe me! By this time, you think she already knew how she shall
take care from a baby. Seven, already, she's got. And we don't got none. If I was
stronger, maybe, huh? And you always wanted a son real bad, no? But, thanks

God, we been so happy like anything. Better I shall not get sentimental or I'll be crying yet. Come by the window, Al. Outside, already, is Spring. A whole bunch people is in the park with baby carriages and dogs. Give a look by that puppy, Al. Make like a dog, Al. Make a whistle he shall come over here. Only a little whistle, Al, on account he's only a little dog. Look! he didn't hear. Might be we should get a dog, Al, huh? Mine! mine! is a beautiful day. Give a look across the street, Al, at the little girl. Didn't we saw her someplace before, no? Someplace. . . .and the little boy, also—with the red hair, I mean. I am positive I saw him also. The way he looks when he gives with the smile. Don't laugh from me, Al! Twenty-five years, already, we been married. And all the time we live across from the park. And, always, I think like I know all the kids. Every year is by me the same thing. Is a fine how-do-you-do, no? But is true like anything. Always, I think I. . .Al! you want I shall tell you something! You know why I think I know all these kids now? Is because we was living by the park for twenty-five years. And, now, we was seeing the children of the children we first saw twenty-five years ago!

PHONETIC REPRESENTATION

(Syllables in bold-face are to be accented.)

gUt di **kU:lEEk** AHgAn. vU:ts di **mEHdEH** vEEt dEHt voom'n? **bEHi**bis shi shoot hEHf! dEHi **dAWn' krAHi** AHnlAs' **sAHm**tEEnk EEs rU:nk vEEt di **mAH**mAH, bi**lif** mi! bAHi **dEEs** tAHim, yoo tEEnk shi UlrAdi noo **hAH:** shi sh'l tEHik **kEH** frUm AH bEHibi. **sA:f'**n, UlrAdi, shiz gUt. **EHn'** vi dAWn' gUt **NAHn.** EEf AHi vUz **strU:**nkUH, mEHibi, **nAW?** EHn' yoo U:lvEHiz vU:n'UHt AH **sAHn ril** bEHt, **nAW?** bAH', **tEHnks gU:t,** vi bEEn sAW hEHpi lAHik AnitEEnk. bAdEH AHi sh'l nUt gAt sAntEE**mAnt'l** U AHil bi **krAHi**EEnk yAt. kAHm bAHi di **vEEn**dAW, EHl. **AH:**tsAHi', UlrAdi, EEz **sprEEnk.** AH **hAWl** bAHntch pip'l EEz EEn di pO:k vEEt **bEHi**bikEHrEEtch'z EHn' **dU:ks.** gEEf AH look bAHi dEHt **pAH**pi, EHl. **mEHik** lAHik AH **dU:k,** EHl. **mEHik** AH vEEs'l hi sh'l kAHm **AW**v'r hi'. AWnli AH **lEEd'**l vEEs'l, EHl, Un AHkAH:n' hiz AWn'i AH **lEEd'l** dU:k. **look!** hi dEEdn' **hi'.** mAHi:' bi **vi** shoot gAt AH dU:k, EHl, **hAH? mAHin! mAHin!** EEz AH **byoor**EEfool dEHi! gEEf AH look AHkrUs di **strit,** EHl, EHt di lEEd'l **gUHl. dEE**dn' vi sU hUH sAHmplEHis bifU:, **nAW?** sAHmplEHis ...

EHn' di' lEEd'l bOI, **U:lsAW**—vEEt di rAt **hA**, AHi min. AHi EHm **pU:zEEtEEf** AHi sU hEEm **U:ls**AW. di vEHi hi looks vAn hi gEEfs vEEt di **smAHil. dAWn' lEHf** frUm mi, EHl! **tvAn'ifAHif yi:z**, UlrAdi, vi bEEn mEHrit. EHn' **U:l** di **tAHim** vi lEEf AHkr**U**s frUm di **pO:k**. EHn' **U:lvEHiz**, AHi tEEnk lAHik AHi nAW **U:l** di kEEts. **Avri** yir EEz bAHi mi di **sEHim tEEnk**. EEz AH **fAHin** hAH:dUHyUHdoo, **nAW**? bAHt EEz **troo** lAHik **An**itEEnk. **U:lvEHiz**, AHi **tEEnk** AHi . . . **EHl**! yoo vU:n' AHi sh'l **tAl** yoo sAHmtEEnk! yoo nAW vAHi AHi tEEnk AHi nAW U:l diz kEEts nAH:? EEz bik**U:**z vi vUz **lEEfEEnk** bAHi di **pO:k** fU **tvAn**'ifAHif yi:z. EHn, **nAH:**, vi vUz siEEnk di **tchEEl'r'n** U:f di tchEEl'r'n vi **fUHs'** sAW **tvAn**'ifAHif yi:z AHg**AW**!